D0075784

Business and Politics in America from the Age of Jackson to the Civil War

Contributions in Economics and Economic History

No. 1 American Financing of World War I
Charles Gilbert

No. 2 The Depression of the Nineties: An Economic History
Charles Hoffmann

No. 3 Paternalism and Protest: Southern Cotton Mill Workers and Organized Labor, 1875–1905
Melton Alonza McLaurin

No. 4 Business and Politics in America from the Age of Jackson to the Civil War: The Career Biography of W. W. Corcoran
Henry Cohen

No. 5 Business Depressions and Financial Panics: Collected Essays in American Business and Economic History
Samuel Rezneck

No. 6 Towards an Integrated Society: Reflections on Planning, Social Policy and Rural Institutions in India
Tarlok Singh

Business and Politics in America from the Age of Jackson to the Civil War

The Career Biography of W. W. Corcoran

HENRY COHEN

Contributions in
Economics and Economic History, Number 4

Greenwood Publishing Corporation
Westport, Connecticut

Library of Congress Catalog Card Number: 79-98708
SBN: 8371-3300-9

Greenwood Publishing Corporation
51 Riverside Avenue, Westport, Connecticut 06880

Printed in the United States of America

To Paul Wallace Gates

Thus economic causes play a part in governing the growth of population as a whole as well as the supply of labour in any particular grade. But their influence is largely indirect; and is exerted by way of the ethical, social and domestic habits of life. For these habits are themselves influenced by economic causes deeply, though slowly, and in ways some of which are difficult to trace, and impossible to predict.

ALFRED MARSHALL
Principles of Economics

Contents

Illustrations

Preface

This study of the varied career of W. W. Corcoran leads to conclusions that have serious implications for enduring problems of American society. Largely forgotten by history, Corcoran was one of the outstanding financiers who invaded the power vacuum left by the demise of the Bank of the United States. For the better part of a decade in the 1840s and 1850s, he was the chief intermediary between Wall Street and Washington. As time went on he scattered his investments, the most notable of which was closely linked to the conflicts among railroad empire-builders who anticipated the coming interstate systems. Corcoran also assisted in forming the alliances that brought James Buchanan to the White House in 1856. Important in his own right and as a member of potent interlocking groups, Corcoran is representative of centrifugal forces that created the context of approaching civil war. His career exemplifies a classic American problem: the explosive growth and fragmentation of power.

Corcoran's career divides logically, if imperfectly, into two parts, to which the two parts of this book correspond. At first he was chiefly a financier, a member of groups whose efforts tended toward maintaining some cohesion in the American political economy. In the second period, his myriad investments became largely speculative, scattered, and unwittingly divisive. But the distinction is not sharp. The themes of the second half of his career could already be found in the first half, and his role changed unevenly in different spheres over a period of years. Therefore, this study follows the interaction between Corcoran, the groups to which he was related or opposed, and their context; the immediate focus shifts according to the dictates of the situation under examination. Finally, while I was not primarily interested in personal biography, I have not neglected it but have allowed it to emerge as fully as existing materials permit, for in his mingling of gusto, taste, exaggeration, modesty, and bravado, he seems a representative American of his time.

This is an inductive study; its conclusions did not exist as hypothesis when, almost casually, I began my investigations. I hope that the book will contribute to an understanding of the historical process that is organic and three-dimensional; and that the vital themes, inductively discerned, will be clear and convincing by the concluding Chapter 13, to which the reader who may wish further preface is invited to turn.

Corcoran was first mentioned to the author by Paul Gates, whose support helped make possible completion of the study. Others too have given valuable help. I am grateful to Roland T. Carr, vice-president of the Riggs National Bank of Washington, which made available the ledgers of its antecedent institutions. The Social Science Research Council financed more than a year of research and writing. Aid was also received from a Volker Fund grant administered by New York University, Cornell University, Ohio State University, and Long Beach State College. At the latter institution, Hiden T. Cox, Darwin Mayfield, and the political science department assisted by extending hospitality to a scholar in exile. Scores of librarians and secretaries at the institutions mentioned above and in the bibliography were most helpful. Two gracious readers, Irwin Unger and Frank Gatell, made especially thorough and useful criticisms of the first four chapters.

A word of deep appreciation is due the chief protagonist at the beginning of a work that is sometimes critical of him: with responsibility and foresight, Corcoran preserved his papers for the future enlightenment of the public whose business was his.

Part I

Corcoran & Riggs, Government Bankers

1

The Founding, 1836–1841

The Origins of Corcoran's Career

At his birth in 1798 William Wilson Corcoran had a few modest advantages. His father, Thomas, had risen in position from shoemaker to moderately prosperous merchant, real estate dealer, and politician in Georgetown. A Democrat, Thomas was appointed justice of the peace by President Jefferson and later held office for many years as mayor, member of the local Jackson campaign committee in 1828, and postmaster of Georgetown until his death in 1830. A more valuable asset to his son, however, was Thomas' friendship with Elisha Riggs, a merchant from a prominent and successful family.

Drawn by the excitement and promise of business, William Corcoran left school at seventeen to become a clerk in the dry goods store owned by his older brothers. By 1820 he had become a senior partner in "W. W. Corcoran & Co., Auctioneers and Commission Merchants," but after a promising beginning the company went bankrupt in the Panic of 1823. Thereafter Corcoran managed his aging father's affairs and began to learn the world of banking. As was common practice among bank directors at the time, Thomas had easy access to loans at the Union Bank and, apparently, at the Bank of Columbia, where Elisha Riggs' brother Romulus was on the board. Thomas took full advantage of his position and borrowed freely to buy and improve Washington real estate. As part of his apprenticeship in finance, Corcoran was manager for his father and a number of absentee landlords, including another Riggs brother, George W., of Baltimore. He also became a clerk in the Bank of Columbia, and when the bank failed in 1828 its assets were assigned to the Bank of the United States. His early clerkship and family ties served him in good stead as Corcoran became the real estate and suspended debts manager for the Washington branch of the bank until it closed in 1836.

Corcoran was socially active and popular. He was a Mason and a colonel of the militia. His library was that of a moderately—if haphazardly—well-read man; the shelves held Greek and Roman writers in translation, Addison, Boswells *Johnson,* Burns, Scott, and more or less well-known contemporaries. There were some travel books and history but little about economics—Ricardo's *Political Economy and Taxation,* some of Hume's *Essays,* and a volume of Hamilton's letters seem to have been the extent of his collection in the field. A religious miscellany, doubtless reflecting his wife's interest, made up the rest.

Culminating a romance complicated by differences of age and status, Corcoran's marriage was a minor local sensation. In 1883(at the age of thirty-five, he fell in love with Louise Morris, the thirteen-year-old daughter of Navy Commodore Charles Morris. Her parents were scandalized; although this was an era of early marriages, the twenty-year age difference was completely unacceptable to them. They considered Corcoran a fortune hunter; he in turn suspected their motives were "interest and ambition." Her father "seems to have persuaded you that I am really an *old* man," Corcoran chided Louise. "I am not the beggar they would fain persuade you." The affair continued through three harrowing years of forced separations, secret meetings, and furtive correspondence.

Louise, sometimes surprisingly mature and perceptive, was given to a melancholy deepened by the grinding emotional pressures. Corcoran all the while proclaimed his ardor in formal, high-flown rhetoric. Each was a child of a sentimental age.

In December 1835 the couple eloped. Mortified, Louise's parents would have nothing to do with Corcoran. Her father refused to see either of the couple, while Mrs. Morris maintained a hurt, sad posture. Throughout the first year of the marriage, Corcoran remained conciliatory. Finally, after the birth of a grandchild in September 1836, the Morrises and Corcorans were reconciled.

Although the couple were happy with each other, Louise's health and morale gradually deteriorated. Two more children were born, but only the last survived past infancy. Corcoran's preoccupation with business and frequent absences undoubtedly contributed to his young wife's despondency. She tried to moderate his materialism with religion, but Corcoran was unable to interest himself in it seriously. He must prosper for his family's sake, he insisted: "I have thro' life set too little value upon money." Louise died in 1841 at the age of twenty-one. Corcoran never remarried.

It is, then, a rather general impression that may be drawn of the man at the beginning of his rise: energetic and ambitious, capable of being at once headstrong, calculating, and sentimental. His business ability was respected by the once-preeminent financier, Nicholas Biddle. He was proud—proud enough to leave among his papers the dunning letters of a tailor from the days of his bankruptcy; and he seems to have fought a duel about 1829. Corcoran was fairly well known in the still small Georgetown community, having entrée to politicians and, of special importance, to the merchant, Elisha Riggs.[1]

In 1836 the federal charter of the Bank of the United States expired; its renewal had been prevented by a coalition that had gathered behind President Andrew Jackson. This left a vacuum of services, profits, and power to be fought for by

Corcoran and others in the years to follow. The Bank had been the chief fiscal agent of the government. It held and transferred government funds, supported public long- and short-term credit, managed interest payments and redemption, and performed other, minor services such as making pension payments. It provided a mechanism for safe credit expansion (despite charter limitations) by making loans against bonds as collateral. It was almost the only dealer in domestic exchange and the leader in foreign exchange. The Bank performed key functions for the economy as a whole, furnishing much of its currency and regulating the volume of the rest, holding the major specie reserves, and correctively influencing the business cycle through the expansion and contraction of credit.[2]

The Jacksonian assault upon the Bank was motivated by a chiefly agrarian hard money doctrine and by a distrust of concentrated economic power, of which the Bank was an early flowering. A smaller and contradictory Jacksonian element consisted of businessmen who wanted to free themselves of institutional control. Some of the latter recognized that the Bank performed vital functions and attacked it in the hope of supplanting it. Hostile politicians sought to transfer part of its power to the federal or state governments.

Astute bankers profited from the resulting confusion. Corcoran was among those financiers who did well when the Bank came under attack. He sought the patronage of the Jacksonian administration and its major allies on Wall Street, basing his claims on his contacts in Washington and Elisha Riggs' in New York. After the possibilities had been proven, the firm of Corcoran & Riggs was founded in 1840. Its considerable initial success was further enhanced when it was appointed a federal depository, giving it the status of a government institution. Thereafter, Corcoran and his allies sporadically collaborated with the Treasury, undertaking with short-lived success some of the burdens of regulating credit and of other functions formerly carried out by the Bank of the United States.[3]

But all this lay in the future. Meanwhile, as another young

banker, Jay Cooke, later remarked, "It was a grand time for brokers and private banking."[4]

Government Business and the Riggs Connection

The expiration of the federal charter of the Bank of the United States and the closing of its Washington branch in 1836 compelled Corcoran to search for new opportunities. After an abortive real estate speculation with Elisha Riggs,[5] he became a note broker in Georgetown. This was an age when gold and silver were money, when paper normally could serve as such only on the assumption that it was convertible into the precious metals. There was as yet no national paper currency and banks issued their own. During this period the Bank of the United States, with its overshadowing size, specie reserves, and federal resources, had circulated much of the country's reliable paper money. The Bank also restrained the currency issues of the state-chartered banks by returning their notes and demanding redemption in specie or in its own notes. With the severance of the federal connection and the closing of its branches in 1836, the Bank's former powers were sharply reduced. State (that is, state-chartered) banks filled the vacuum, increasing in number and expanding their issues of paper money. Brokers such as Corcoran bought these notes for resale or redemption, much as foreign exchange dealers trade in national currencies and gold. He also fulfilled such other functions as exchange dealer, collections agent, and stock broker, and may also have lent money and discounted notes on a small scale.[6]

The Panic of 1837 facilitated Corcoran's progress. The preceding years had seen an overexpansion of transatlantic commerce with a corresponding boom in American land sales, cotton growing, consumer goods, and internal improvements. The boom led to heavy deficits in the balance of trade, which were covered by British short-term credits and purchases of American securities. Alarmed in turn by a loss of specie, the

Bank of England slowed down the overheated Atlantic economy by raising the discount rate and contracting credit—especially American credit. In May 1837 American banks generally had to cease paying out specie to creditors and clients.[7]

The turmoil brought fiscal difficulties to the federal government. The years of prosperity had yielded high revenues from customs duties and public land sales. Most of a large revenue surplus, which had piled up in the Treasury, was distributed among the states between 1836 and 1837. Then collapsing trade slashed receipts from tariffs while the Specie Circular of 1836, which required payment in coin for purchases of public lands, cut land sales. These events left the Treasury with heavy deficits to cover. Despite its conservative fiscal ideals, the Van Buren administration was forced to resort to the issue of Treasury notes. Under the Act of October 12, 1837, the maximum interest rate was set at 6 percent and the minimum denomination at $50. The notes could not be sold by the Treasury at less than par. They were redeemable after one year but later legislation permitted their reissue.[8]

The notes were welcomed by the business community, which used them as a means of payment at a time when, in the absence of a national money system, suspension of specie, hoarding of specie, and contraction of credit left few means of making remittances beyond the immediate locality. The great demand was for New York funds: even in a city as near as Washington, bank checks payable in New York were avidly taken at a 1½ percent premium. Specie could be obtained only at 5¼ percent, while the Baltimore banks, for example, were paying 6 percent. (For more distant points, the rates were much higher.) There were fluctuations, of course, but these quotations were typical. Yet the administration, which was committed to an essentially "hard money" (specie) system and opposed to a large-scale use of credit and paper money, would issue notes only as fast as they were needed to pay public creditors, and in amounts less than the hard-pressed business community wished. As the competition was intense for relatively small Treasury note issues, an able agent in Washington was a valuable contact for a businessman. Appropriately, in November 1837, Corcoran moved his office from Georgetown to a location across the street from the Treasury. Serving as broker for Elisha Riggs in New York, he bought notes in a thin but steady stream, usually at the rate of several thousand dollars a week.[9]

Corcoran already was favored by administration patronage, especially by Postmaster General Amos Kendall and Secretary of the Treasury Levi Woodbury. The Treasury, collecting payments for sales of public lands, accumulated surpluses in the West while its largest expenditures were in the Northeast. For the Post Office Department, the situation was exactly the reverse: its receipts were greatest in the East while it had to ship funds West. Some of these transfers could easily have been handled within the government with large savings. Instead, they were turned over to the Bank of the United States before it lost its federal agency, and afterward to various banks and brokers. For example, Kendall once offered Corcoran large specie surpluses in New York, Philadelphia, and Boston at par for western funds that Corcoran had just bought from the Treasury, yielding the young banker an immediate 4 to 4½ percent profit. Although the profits on government transfers were usually smaller, the turnover was rapid.[10]

In nongovernmental business, too, Corcoran was joined by politicians and their business allies. Former Treasury agent Reuben Whitney and Jackson's old friend, William B. Lewis, advised Corcoran on exchange dealings, the latter with reference to his home state of Tennessee. An expert on banks there, Lewis seems to have been an agent for at least one of them or was a dealer or speculator on his own account. J. F. H. Claiborne, a Congressman from Mississippi and agent of the Rodney Bank there, advised Corcoran and borrowed almost $10,000 from him to join in one operation.[11]

As Corcoran gained experience and demonstrated his financial acumen, his relationship with Riggs expanded to include handling securities operations on joint account. In this field, too, political contacts were valuable. The War and Navy

Departments administered pension funds, and the former managed Indian trust funds derived from sales of lands ceded to the United States. After the federal debt was liquidated in 1835 the money was invested in state and local government bonds. These trusts sometimes sold securities from their portfolios but usually functioned as buyers.[12] In a typical transaction with a trust as buyer, Corcoran acted as the Washington broker for a recklessly speculative (if not unscrupulous) investment and real estate bank—the North American Trust and Banking Co.—which was the creation of entrepreneurs linked to the "Regency" political machine of New York State. As agent for the bank, Corcoran sold $500,000 of Arkansas 6 percent Real Estate Bank bonds to Secretary Woodbury for the portfolio of the newly endowed Smithsonian Institution. The stamp of federal confidence helped the North American Bank to use almost $2 million of Arkansas-issued or -endorsed bonds as collateral for loans from unwise Englishmen, although the state was still an almost empty frontier. To effect the sale to the Smithsonian against the competition of other state bonds Corcoran had negotiated a price of 99¾₀ percent, although state law barred sale below face value. Within a year the state was unable to pay interest and soon after repudiated the entire debt, an outcome that proved highly embarrassing to Corcoran.[13]

Thus, Corcoran's government connections were useful in a number of fields: exchange, public finance, and trading in securities. Federal finance, however, was where his main chance lay, and with it came an involvement in the wider conflicts of Jacksonian finance.

George Newbold and the "Bank War"

Corcoran played a revealing if minor role in the war that culminated in the collapse of the Bank of the United States. In the financial markets, the key anti-Bank centers were Wall Street and the Treasury. Corcoran was active, personally and through Elisha Riggs, at both points, and used his success with one to enhance his position with the other.

Wall Street's leading financier at this time was George Newbold, president of the Bank of America. The board of directors of the institution included many of New York's business elite, among them Elisha Riggs. The bank's power was indicated by its liquidity: from the time of the first available figures in the 1820s until the middle 1850's, it consistently maintained one of the largest, and much of the time the largest, specie reserves in the country. Its reserve ratio of specie to current liabilities (bank notes outstanding plus deposits) was also consistently among the highest, usually over 30 percent. First among his equals, Newbold's authority was enhanced by the intimate collaboration and similar policies of John J. Palmer, president of another major bank, the Merchants.

As the acknowledged leader on Wall Street, Newbold sought to wrest national preeminence from Philadelphia. In 1833, when Jackson and his advisers were reaching the decision to withdraw the federal deposits from the Bank of the United States, the government first had to line up substitute depositories. As the nation's major metropolis and rival of Philadelphia for the status of financial capital, New York seemed likely to cooperate. Yet the respect for and fear of the Bank of the United States and the prestige of the Bank of America were such that Wall Street institutions—including those controlled by Democrats—hesitated to accept federal deposits until Newbold led the way.[14]

Impressed by his bank's resources, conservative liquidity policy, and leadership, Treasury Secretary Roger Taney invited Newbold to coordinate the new depository system. Newbold, however, preferred to remain at his base of power, New York. Nevertheless, for years he was the most influential adviser to the Treasury. He performed various services for the Jacksonians, including making loans to politicians and to favored Democratic or depository banks in difficulty—always on adequate security. Reciprocally, the large federal deposits helped the Bank of America to maintain a powerful creditor position toward its sister institutions and, either directly or through them, to expand its loans, profits, and influence.[15]

The severest test of the "pet bank" (as Treasury depositories were called) system came with the depression of 1837 when most of the nation's banks suspended specie payments. Against the resistance of the Bank of the United States of Pennsylvania (where the former federal institution had obtained a state charter), Wall Street led an early resumption of payments in 1838. The Bank followed suit but remained extremely vulnerable because of its immense cotton and securities operations and credit extensions that were designed to bolster the economy of the South and West. In London, where the Bank was deeply in debt, the money market tightened ominously in 1839. A long industrial boom had just ended on the Continent, reducing the demand for British exports, while crop shortages raised British food imports. To halt the drain of specie the Bank of England raised its interest rates and curtailed credit, thus ending the heavy purchases of American cotton and securities. The Bank of the United States, faced with heavy London debts, tried to meet the emergency by the sale of notes to New York. Its intent was twofold: to raise specie for shipment to England, and as its second suspension of specie payments loomed inevitable, to force New York's banks to suspend payments by draining them of specie.[16]

Against this onslaught Treasury Secretary Levi Woodbury and Newbold fought as allies. True, there were no longer any federal surpluses that might be deposited in allied banks, but federal debts could serve the same purpose; Treasury notes, authorized to finance budget deficits, also did service as a weapon in the "Bank War." To help maintain the market and build ramparts against the Bank's raid on the New York money market, Woodbury gave Newbold exclusive management of the note issues of 1839. Notes were issued (as distinct from sold) to the Bank of America. They were left on deposit there until they were disposed of or paid out to public creditors; the proceeds of the note sales, left on deposit, would bolster the America's reserves. Newbold's bank could then lend out the money (as well as collect commissions on note sales). Funds could be shifted from surplus to deficit points among the Treasury and the depositories, thus helping repel raids from Chestnut Street. (The New York State Democratic administration at Albany, itself an important source of the dynamism of the Jacksonian campaigns, also aided the New York banks against Philadelphia by issuing canal bonds to them for sale in advance of need, leaving the deposits with them to help support convertibility.)[17]

The most trying period was the spring and summer of 1839, but by September the New York banks were secure. During the worst battles of the Bank War Corcoran, by then the Washington correspondent for the Bank of America, was able to purchase blocks of as much as $200,000 of notes for investors. As his first operations in federal debt financing, these transactions were large enough by the standards of the day to give him his first significant, if modest, prestige. Newbold, whom Corcoran particularly courted, acknowledged as much.[18]

The Founding of Corcoran & Riggs

Most of the Washington banks suspended by October 1839. For Corcoran this meant enlarged opportunities: he was able to increase his share of government business in exchange and securities. He had been contemplating a move to New York City where the prospects seemed better; but his tie with Riggs assured him that he would have the necessary New York backing in any case, and by remaining in Washington he could fully exploit his government connections.

With little capital, Corcoran depended on Riggs' endorsement to enable him to borrow whenever an operation required more than a few thousand dollars. This was not given automatically: Elisha kept tight control over his buoyant junior, sometimes refusing a line of credit and cautiously examining each proposal. Although Corcoran almost always won his point, the irksome delays caused opportunities to be missed. But since there was no prospect of a suitable alternative to the highly respected Riggs, whose very cautiousness was an asset in Wall Street, Corcoran seized the chance to make the tie both more intimate and more permanent.

He proposed a partnership to Riggs' son, George W., Jr., who had recently returned from a London apprenticeship with the eminent George Peabody. Young Riggs deferred to his father, who preferred that he take over in New York, saying, "It would be to my interest to act as he wishes." Elisha, however, was won over. Corcoran was worth $40,000, he wrote, and had put a "good Capital" into his "brokerage"; moreover, he has "the friendship of the government offices at Washington which is very desirable at this time of the deranged currency of the country."

The "good capital" was a mere $2,500, which young Riggs matched. Although the partners deposited their personal funds, these never exceeded $20,000 before 1847. It was Elisha's financial support that allowed the young firm to assume more ambitious undertakings. On April 15, 1840, almost three months before the resumption of specie payments by the District banks, the "Exchange Bank of Corcoran & Riggs" opened in Washington. Corcoran was recognized de facto as the senior policy-making partner and consistently managed the house's "outside" business; his partner, although always consulted, apparently was in charge of internal operations.[19]

In a city where the incorporated banks had almost all been allies of the Bank of the United States, the Jacksonian administration warmly welcomed the new, non-note-issuing specie-paying partnership run by fellow Democrats. Secretary Woodbury made this welcome tangible by allowing the firm to meet or undercut lower bids for Treasury notes. In one instance, when Corcoran offered interest of 5⅔ percent for half of a $1 million issue, Woodbury informed him of a lower bid of 5⅖ percent.[20] Corcoran & Riggs matched this in a new bid that Woodbury accepted. Of course, this cooperation produced feelings of bad faith among other bidders towards the government (assuming they were not rigging their bids, as sometimes happened); however, it was advantageous to the Treasury since it assured the government the lowest attainable interest cost. In the longer run, Woodbury's subversion of the existing competitive structure strengthened competition by encouraging the growth of another financial power.[21]

The partners, through Elisha, sold most or all their notes to New York banks for investment. The elder Riggs further rewarded the partners with the exclusive management of an additional $500,000 to enable them to maintain the price of the notes. These sales were handled as secretly as possible, for if word were to leak out the hostility of competitors (and perhaps of institutions paying the higher prices) would make the continuation of the arrangement impossible. It was ended, in fact, a few months later when issues grew too large for continued secrecy.

Corcoran & Riggs quickly established itself as a leader in federal finance. Of more than $7.1 million of notes issued under the Act of March 31, 1840, the young firm contracted over $1.25 million (in addition to which Elisha took over several hundred thousand dollars in his own name). Despite their limited resources, the partners managed to support a large volume: by paying for $50,000 worth of notes at a time, they were able to use the proceeds from the sale of one installment to pay for the next. However, the most important contractor of Treasury notes remained their New York correspondent, the Bank of America. In fact, the partners received chiefly (perhaps solely) the flotations in which Newbold was not interested. At such times they could be useful to Woodbury without being objectionable to the powerful Bank of America.[22]

Various government business was the major source of profit for the young firm. Treasury notes must have yielded over $5,000 in 1840 before sharpened competition cut the firm's operations. The first detailed profit and loss statement extant, covering the first six months of 1841, reveals other governmental sources of profit.[23] Total net earnings were $12,000. Of over $15,000 gross, $8,200 was made on exchange dealings which were transacted chiefly from the government. (The exchange profit derived from $21,500 of premiums received, less $13,300 of premium paid. Profit margins on this part of the business declined as business revival and improving communications narrowed the range of fluctuation.) The relatively small interest account, with $2,500 earned and $800 paid, reflects Corcoran & Riggs' conservatism and the depressed securities market. Second in importance as a source of profit in this period were state and city bonds which produced about $4,000, much of it from transactions with federal trust funds. Commissions and interest, which yielded $1,800 and $1,700 respectively, were largely earned on Treasury notes or trust fund business.

For most of the depression year of 1841–1842 fragmentary figures indicate net profits of only $3,500, including a claim against the Indian Department that netted $3,600. Corcoran & Riggs continued to sell state bonds to Woodbury from the Smithsonian, the Secretary again disclosing competitive offers to the firm. His patronage was of some importance in this period of stagnant bond sales.[24]

The firm was often slightly overdrawn with Elisha Riggs but carefully maintained a credit balance with the Bank of America. The expense account indicates Corcoran's role: he traveled to Baltimore and New York often, sometimes leaving Washington three times in a month, but George Riggs almost never left the city. The same holds true for visits to the executive departments and legislators.

The day-to-day flow of business that was routinely registered in the ledgers defines the firm's Wall Street alignments. Its borrowings, totaling over $360,000 during the first half of 1841, were almost entirely from Elisha Riggs, the Bank of America, and the latter's intimate ally, the Merchants Bank. The volume of business—chiefly exchange—with the America was over $1.5 million; with Elisha Riggs, $175,000. There was a large secondary business with Baltimore where the Riggs family was also well established, but this was to decline in importance.[25] Dealings with Philadelphia were negligible since the chartered banks of Washington, which had also been forced to suspend, were that city's allies. These patterns were to endure throughout the firm's lifetime.

2

The Whig Moment and the Tyler Transition, 1841–1844

Shifting Treasury Alliances Under Ewing and Forward

In 1841, in the midst of a severe depression, a Whig administration took office with a portfolio of important bills and the votes to pass them in Congress. Included on the agenda were a loan to cover the anticipated budget deficit; repeal of the Independent Treasury Act of 1840, which had established government offices in place of the state banks as depositories for Treasury funds; and chartering of a new national institution along the lines of the earlier Bank of the United States. Unfortunately, the death of President Harrison after one month in office put the states-rights advocate and erstwhile Democrat, John Tyler, in the White House. Nevertheless, the Whigs in Congress and Secretary of the Treasury Thomas Ewing pressed forward with the original Whig program. Simultaneously, Ewing moved to align the Treasury with loyal Whig financiers on mutually advantageous terms. He turned particularly to the Bank of Commerce, organized in 1838 by an imposing group of Whigs and rapidly becoming New York's largest financial institution.

The prime occasion for cooperation was provided by the

federal budget deficit. On July 21, 1841, Congress authorized a $12 million three-year loan at a maximum interest rate of 6 percent. Over one-third of the loan was needed during 1841, and Ewing turned to John A. Stevens, president of the Commerce, asking for a 5 percent interest rate. The financial community generally refused even to compromise at 5½ percent, but the Commerce acepted 5 percent to the extent of $1 million. Others, mostly from New York and Boston, joined in when Stevens conveyed assurances that heavy government balances would be maintained, and Ewing was able to dispose of $3 million. The quid pro quo for Stevens was appointment of the Commerce as federal depository in New York, the Independent Treasury Act meanwhile having been repealed.[1] (In the first year of operation in 1839 the Commerce had sought this appointment from the Van Buren administration but was rebuffed on the pretext that it was only an "association" under the Free Banking Act of 1838, not an incorporated bank as required by federal law.[2])

The Secretary had not intended to isolate the Treasury from other powerful factions of the business community. Although the Bank of America was unwelcome because of its leading role in the opposition, an effort was made to detach Newbold's ally, the Merchants Bank, with the offer of Treasury deposits. But before appointing the Merchants a depository, Ewing insisted on collateral security for federal deposits. Personal bonds of the directors were acceptable to the Secretary as collateral, but directors were usually reluctant to assume unlimited individual responsibility for each other and their banks. The alternative was to deposit United States bonds, which would assure the government of a continuing demand for them. Although Stevens had accepted the terms, John J. Palmer of the Merchants Bank testily refused to deposit collateral on the grounds that his bank's resources and liquidity were adequate security. He also may have been reluctant to pay for United States bonds on Ewing's terms, since to commit himself at that time to the government securities market would have meant abandoning established friendships and alliances.[3]

With the Bank of America frozen out, Corcoran & Riggs

considered transferring their New York account from the America, evidently to the Commerce. On Elisha's advice they decided not to, since Newbold's bank had always treated them well. They were not to regret this decision, for within weeks the situation altered radically.[4]

On September 9, 1841, Tyler vetoed the last major effort for a federally chartered national bank. This brought an immediate split with the Whig party, the entire cabinet resigning (except Secretary of State Daniel Webster, who remained for foreign policy reasons). On September 13, Walter Forward of Pittsburgh was appointed to the Treasury. He found it low on funds, even the 5½ percent notes selling very slowly. Political difficulties compounded those of the depression: financiers who had kept aloof remained estranged from government dealings, while those who had supported Ewing would do no more. Forward abandoned Ewing's rate and offered 6 percent instead.[5]

In effect, Forward began to turn toward the prominent public financiers of previous Democratic administrations; the increase in the interest rate did not please Ewing's allies, who had just bought heavily at the lower rate. Yet, bankers to the former Democratic administrations remained aloof because of the short three-year maturity of the bonds. Only $2.5 million was raised. To cover worsening deficits Forward resorted to short-term 6 percent notes with somewhat greater success—the Bank of America buying heavily for itself and others. Still, deficits piled up, and in April 1842 Congress authorized a $17 million twenty-year loan at 6 percent. The terms were more attractive but the money market was at its tightest as the depression reached bottom. Only $1.7 million was sold at 97½; lower bids were rejected.[6]

After being cast out by the congressional Whigs, Tyler ran the gauntlet between the two major parties, seeking to draw support from each. This effort was paralleled by Secretary Forward: his agents negotiated separately with the America and the Commerce, secretly promising favoritism to each. However, the officers of the two banks compared notes on his opportunistic tactics and then broke off negotiations. Unable to borrow anywhere at long term, the Secretary again fell back upon notes to the extent of $9 million par value in 1842. These were attractive enough to bring Newbold back into the market: he took $1 million for sale to investors. A skillful diplomat, Newbold volunteered advice and services to the inexperienced Secretary. On his suggestion, Forward stopped paying notes to public creditors—they tended to be sold immediately instead of being held for income, thus depressing the market. Newbold volunteered up to $40,000 for redemption of expiring notes, the appropriation for which was delayed in a hostile Congress. The Secretary then promised to issue equivalent notes to the Bank of America. By August 1842 the Bank of America was the sole depository in New York City.[7] The monopoly, however, lasted only six months. Heavy borrowing was in prospect for the new year, far beyond the ability of any single Wall Street faction. In January of 1843 Forward appointed the Bank of Commerce an official federal depository, and in August he did the same for the Merchants. Palmer now willingly deposited the required $250,000 collateral.[8]

Alliance with Newbold

The alliance with the Bank of America marked the acceptance of Corcoran & Riggs as a peer of the business community. Curiously, the very episode that painfully exposed his previously inferior status helped Corcoran surmount it. In January 1843, the Treasury offered the reviving money market a $4.9 million loan. Corcoran, who was in New York at the time, went to the Bank of America to make the required advance deposit against a $300,000 bid. He was stunned when the imperious Newbold refused to receive the deposit and chastised him as a speculator, coolly adding that he would neither subscribe himself nor advise "friends or others" to do so. Newbold wrongly believed Corcoran had not planned to subscribe until learning from him that John Ward, a leading private banker and ally, would bid for all that remained of the loan. Shaken and mystified, Corcoran vainly asked Secretary Forward to reserve $300,000 for him. At the same time he sought to learn the disposition of $600,000 of the loan not publicly accounted for.

By then Newbold knew that his suspicions of Corcoran were unfounded, but it was too late to reverse his refusal since the loan had been entirely allocated.[9] In fact Newbold had still greater cause for chagrin. A month after the close of the bidding A. W. Marks, son-in-law of Secretary Forward, returned to the capital from New York in the company of cashier Richard Smith of the Bank of the Metropolis, the largest bank in Washington. Immediately, $500,000 of bonds was issued to Smith as the agent for a group of unnamed parties. Sleuthing at the Treasury, Corcoran learned "a good part of it [the $500,000 of bonds] *belongs to the Bank of America.*" To complete the context, the Metropolis was the Treasury depository in Washington. If, as is probable, Corcoran hoped to usurp its position, the collaboration of Smith and Newbold must have doubled his dismay.

Although the embarrassed Newbold evidently wished he would drop the subject, Corcoran repeatedly appealed to his sense of justice, both directly and via Elisha Riggs. Newbold "seems to forget that Mr. Ward bought a speculation as well as ourselves," he pointed out in a letter to Elisha. "You know that we ordered the purchase before we dreamed of Ward's coming on, and what is singular [is] that George [Riggs] . . . proposed to go in for a large sum. This letter [was] commented on by both of us, in consequence of his being opposed to everything like speculation." Corcoran next appealed to President Tyler, and at last he was successful. The wrangle was finally settled when the firm received a commitment for the first $300,000 of notes soon to be issued by the Treasury. In the end the tenacious and straightforward defense of his interests, combined with proper respect toward his seniors, brought Corcoran a sizable gain in goodwill.[10]

Corcoran's hopes for the leading role in the next important Treasury flotation were forestalled, but he did gain his first direct and major participation with Newbold and other strong allies. The loan was $7 million at 5 percent for ten years. John

Ward & Co., the current leader in federal finance, organized a list of bidders for the whole loan. Newbold's portion was to be $2 million; Corcoran & Riggs accepted a 20 percent share of that. Other participants included August Belmont, the United States agent of the Rothschilds, 20 percent; William H. Aspinwall, an outstanding merchant in the Latin American trade, 25 percent; and Newbold and another director of the Bank of America, 5 percent each. Ward's bid of 101.01 took all but $500,000 of the $7 million loan.[11]

Corcoran & Riggs began selling at 105 and up, confident of a further rise. Instead, the new loan declined to 102 and moved very slowly, although other government bonds and the market in general were going up. Corcoran explained that there was widespread suspicion of a rigged market. The tactics of the partners gave partial credibility to this suspicion: Elisha and the Washington house had entered dummy bids totaling $1.4 million at just under Ward's winning figure to excite demand and publicize the young firm. The trick was obvious if not blatant. Corcoran was content to hold when the market turned dull, since the firm borrowed at 4 percent at Palmer's Merchants Bank and at 3½ percent in Baltimore to pay for the bonds which yielded almost 5 percent. However, George Riggs shared his father's conservatism rather than his partner's ebullience. (Also the relationship with the Treasury was uncertain since the cooperative John C. Spencer, who succeeded Forward, was about to end his brief stay in the Cabinet.) The bonds, therefore, were slowly liquidated at a small profit.[12]

Thus, at the beginning of a long economic upswing, Corcoran & Riggs gained full acceptance in one of the financial community's most powerful factions. At the highest levels of government, too, Corcoran had entrée. But these developments were only well begun; the next two years would see them brought to completion.

3

At the Centers of American Finance, 1844–1847

The Completion of the Tyler Transition

Despite growing acceptance in centers of finance, Corcoran & Riggs' success was incomplete. The firm, still small, was not a federal depository; it coveted the greater financial power that Treasury deposits could provide. Exchange and securities transactions with the government were only occasional. Treasury business, done routinely through Washington's chartered commercial banks, tended to cement the latter's relationships with depository banks elsewhere. Despite its advantageous ending, the episode of the disputed notes of 1843 posed an ominous implication:[1] regardless of the existing correspondent relationship with the firm, the powerful Bank of America might yet prefer the Bank of the Metropolis as its major Washington ally. The biggest of the city's banks, the Metropolis had the juiciest plum—the general account of the Treasury. Other accounts (such as those of the Speaker of the House, secretary of the Senate, Postmaster General and others) were kept with the Bank of Washington and the Bank of the Potomac. These institutions, guided by Whigs and old allies of the Bank of the United States, had been government depositories since their appointment by Secretary Ewing in 1841.[2] In addition, Secretary Forward's bipartisan patronage policies in Wall Street had been reflected in his appointment of the Patriotic Bank, the Washington correspondent of the Merchants Bank of New York, as a government agency.

However, the chartered banks of Washington were politically vulnerable. Their very existence had long been under Jacksonian attack. Hard money advocates charged them with inflationary note issues, and their congressional charters were the targets for rhetorical salvos against monopoly and special privilege. The goal of the most zealous and partisan Jacksonians was to deny the Washington banks' recharter, thus presumably forcing them to liquidate. But reality imposed one major restraint: the District of Columbia did, after all, need banking facilities. Compromise charter extensions were made for brief periods—the latest came at the beginning of Tyler's administration for the three years ending on July 4, 1844.

During Tyler's administration the political situation of the chartered banks deteriorated. First came the Whig repudiation of the President in the fall of 1841 over the national bank issue. In 1842 the Whig party renounced the Compromise Tariff of 1833, which Tyler had helped to carry, and enacted a protective measure. The President, faced with the alternative of leaving the government without revenue, capitulated and signed the bill, but gave up efforts to conciliate the Whigs. By 1843 he had veered back toward the Democrats, even dreaming of the presidential nomination. His campaign was abortive, but careful wooing by the Democrats in 1844 confirmed his rapprochement with the party. Meanwhile, in the 1842 election the Democrats had made a strong comeback, regaining control of the House of Representatives.[3]

Furthermore, there now existed a bank with sufficient prestige, connections, and access to financial resources to provide the Jacksonians an acceptable alternative to the old District banks as agency for the government. As a private unincorporated bank, Corcoran & Riggs was invulnerable to charges of special privilege by legislative charter, nor could it be attacked by hard money believers since it did not issue notes. But probably the decisive factor favoring the firm's appointment as federal fiscal agent was Corcoran's spreading political influence. Although he and his partner were Democrats, the firm shared the good will of both parties by helping to support their national organs. Publishers Joseph Gales and W. W. Seaton of the Whig Washington *National Intelligencer,* Francis P. Blair and John C. Rives of the Democratic Washington *Globe,* and Thomas Ritchie and John P. Heiss of the *Globe*'s successor, the *Union,* all borrowed in four- and sometimes five-figure amounts.[4]

In his dealings with politicians Corcoran adhered to strict business principles. Collateral was almost always required and the few exceptions seldom extended to renewal of loans. "You need be under no apprehension of our dealings with Members of Congress or politicians," Corcoran wrote to the more cautious (and perhaps more scrupulous) Elisha Riggs. "We have even less confidence in their promises than you." In exceptional circumstances Corcoran would resort to bribery, but as a rule he expected to be repaid, even when he received important services from the borrower. Most politicians who persisted in regarding a loan as a "loan" ultimately found themselves haled into court, although in some cases leniency was granted in the form of indefinite extensions, and some debts were eventually forgiven. It should be noted that most loans to politicians had no noticeable political consequences, but many of these transactions brought a valuable dividend of good will, and some a very tangible quid pro quo.

If any one of Corcoran's many political friends can be singled out as crucial, it was Senator Robert J. Walker of Mississippi. There seem to have been no direct transactions between them (nor would there be until after Walker's term as Secretary of the Treasury late in the decade), but Walker's financial and political affairs involved him deeply with other Mississippi politicians who were co-speculators wth Corcoran. Ex-Congressmen William Gwin and J. F. H. Claiborne were instrumental in bringing Walker and the banker together.[5]

The speculation originated in 1843 to exploit the removal of the Choctaw Indians westward from their Mississippi homeland to make room for land-hungry whites. The Indians were compensated with scrip representing title to over 1.8 million acres, the sale of which was supposed to remunerate them. The speculators, organized as the Choctaw Company, tried to monopolize the scrip by purchasing it in the open market and receiving it in payment for provisions sold to the deported Choctaws at exorbitant prices. For at least six years the company's influence helped prevent purchases of the former Choctaw lands by any means other than exchange for scrip. Walker, although apparently not directly involved in the Choctaw Company, tried to protect it from competition by introducing a bill in the Senate to prohibit speculators from taking large tracts of public land at the expense of actual settlers. Speculators holding large nearby tracts might retard settlement which the company wanted to encourage to increase demand and raise land prices. Of course Walker's bill also had a broad political appeal, synthesizing as it did both a special and a general interest. But despite elaborate efforts, the speculation yielded little profit, and Corcoran & Riggs transferred its interest when it became a political liability. Thus begun, however, the relationship with Walker soon paid off in more important ways.[6]

A shrewd politician, Walker was one of the key figures of the decade. The son of a prominent western Pennsylvania lawyer and judge, he began his political career in Pittsburgh. He married into the influential Bache and Dallas families, then moved to the frontier state of Mississippi where he eventually won election to the Senate as a Jacksonian Democrat. Following the schism between Tyler and the Whigs, Walker became a major advisor to and spokesman for the administration. Making especially clever use of the Texas annexation issue, he was of central importance in reconciling Tyler with the Democrats, frustrating Martin Van Buren's presidential ambitions, and nominating and electing James K. Polk in 1844. Behind the scenes he contributed to Corcoran & Riggs' rapid rise in ensuing months. The firm began to profit from the skirmishes of these campaigns as electoral politics influenced the country's financial programs.[7]

After the Democratic victory in the 1842 elections, Congress renewed the charters of the banks of the District of Columbia for ten years, but the bill also included tight restrictions designed to compel the banks to liquidate. Ten years was a long time, however, perhaps long enough for a later Congress and President to enact new laws. Tyler, whose constitutional scruples had led him to oppose Jackson's withdrawal of federal deposits from the Bank of the United States in 1833, would not order a similar withdrawal. Feeling secure, the Whig banks announced their intention to apply for new charters while continuing to operate under the common law as private partnerships. They implied a threat of their own—to finance sympathetic politicians in the hard-fought electoral campaign of 1844. But Corcoran confidently expected to gain at the expense of the chartered banks. "We do not think that their determination to go on in violation of law will aid them in their applications," he commented. What was needed was some action that would serve as a warning to the banks and a curb on their resources—but such action had to be limited enough for the scrupulous Tyler to allow. The solution was the appointment of Corcoran & Riggs as a Treasury depository in August 1844.

There were conditions attached. Collateral was required for deposits. The firm was required to pay out deposits in specie or in bank notes convertible in the vicinity and to render all other services the Bank of the United States had performed or which might legally have been required of it. Weekly returns to the Treasury were to be made and the books were to be open for government inspection at all times with the sole exception of the current accounts of individuals.[8] In solving the problem of raising collateral security, the firm had the assistance not only of its customary allies but also of the government. Only federal securities had been acceptable, but a week after the appointment Treasury Secretary George Bibb agreed to receive state bonds that were selling above par.[9] In addition, the Treasury transferred $100,000 of its bonds to the firm's name in exchange for a like credit on its books. Elisha Riggs lent the firm at least $175,000 of his investment portfolio of bonds, much of which remained on loan for years.[10] The Bank of America and the Merchants lent hundreds of thousands of dollars for short periods to finance bond purchases until the government deposits could provide Corcoran & Riggs with the means of repayment.

These manipulations provided an agreeable opportunity to chastise Whig banks. Corcoran bought $241,000 of United States bonds from the Merchants and the Mechanics Banks in New York, paying for them with a $250,000 Treasury draft on the Commerce. The cashier of the Commerce tried to beat his rivals to the purchase of available securities in an attempt to force them to pay a higher price, but this was a futile exercise. The Metropolis in Washington also lost part of its federal deposits. Corcoran & Riggs' progress was clearly at the expense of leading Whig banks.

Thus, as a result of basically political factors, Corcoran & Riggs became a leading government depository in Washington. Its deposits for the rest of 1844 were $1 million or more; the Metropolis held about $750,000 and other Washington banks much smaller amounts. Also, Corcoran & Riggs was awarded much of the government's profitable domestic exchange business; the Metropolis received little or none. The firm was careful of appearances, generally pledging the largest collateral of any bank in the country although its government deposits were sometimes smaller than those of Wall Street institutions. However, the market value of collateral securities was usually exceeded by the deposits. For example, by the end of September collateral was stabilized for some months at about $840,000 while Treasury deposits exceeded $1 million, with one peak of $1.4 million. The largest excess of Treasury deposits over collateral was about $600,000 for several months late in 1844, two-thirds of which was to repurchase government bonds. The excess was usually 20 to 30 percent. Collateral was usually built up at scattered, brief intervals, chiefly when public reports on the condition of the Treasury were required by Congress. From London George Peabody expressed his envy: he would have been delighted to have such sums interest-free.[11]

After November 1844 Corcoran prepared the way for further

gains by his usefulness to President-elect James K. Polk. He assisted in the replacement of Blair and Rives by Ritchie and Heiss as editor-publishers of the Democratic *Globe*. Blair, a devoted partisan of Van Buren, had bitterly opposed the rapprochement of Tyler with the expansionist wing of the Democrats. After Polk's nomination the *Globe* had remained conspicuously reluctant in its support of his presidential campaign. When Blair's erstwhile friend and Jacksonian colleague, Amos Kendall, attempted to supplant him and Rives as government printers, Blair counterattacked by exposing Kendall's role in the Choctaw Company and editorially castigating the selection of Kendall's co-speculator, Corcoran & Riggs, as government depository. Any further articles in the *Globe,* Corcoran predicted, would have a different flavor.

His forecast was quickly borne out. To help reconcile the warring factions of his party, Polk negotiated the sale of the *Globe,* rebaptised the *Union,* to Ritchie and Heiss. Corcoran extended the new owners a credit that reached $14,000. Ostensibly in Corcoran's own name, the loan actually was taken from the Treasury deposits and was repaid simultaneously with the final withdrawal of those same government funds years later. Since Corcoran & Riggs was performing the same service for important Whigs, the firm never feared a partisan attack.[12]

The chain of intrigue against Corcoran's rivals stretched still further. In December 1844 the House of Representatives appointed a special committee to investigate the District banks' response to the act requiring their liquidation. Corcoran worked closely with the committee chairman, Edmund Burke, a New Hampshire protégé of Levi Woodbury.[13] Burke cajoled the officers of the Bank of the Metropolis into believing that they had plenty of time to answer the committee's questionnaire. Then, without warning, the committee released a report charging them with "contumacy" for not replying and denouncing all the chartered banks for continuing to operate against Congress' enacted policy of dissolution. The report cited the below-par market price of their stocks as evidence of misfortune or mismanagement and a reason for requiring them to close; on the other hand, if the banks were making money they should close to give others a chance to profit instead of monopolizing the benefits of congressional charters.[14]

Decades later an exchange of letters took place between old friends who had been out of touch with each other for many years. Burke wrote Corcoran that when he was a member of Congress fighting the "rotten district Bks. I was Chairman of the Comee. appointed to investigate their affairs and did something toward the defeating of the renewal of their Charters. In that combat I received valuable information and aid from Mr. C." But his estimate of the banker was not based merely on that, Burke went on, for the banker was already a generous philanthropist. Corcoran was deeply gratified: "[Burke's praises] of *my character* are greatly valued, because I know that sincerity is one of the prominent traits of *your own*."[15]

By the last months of Tyler's presidency the handwriting on the walls of the District banks required no translation.[16] The groundwork had been laid for Corcoran's capture of a monopoly of government banking at the Capital.

Walker and the Polk Administration

The dying Andrew Jackson, kept informed by Blair, warned President-elect Polk against Walker as a "perfect bankrupt" compromised by the "fraudulent" Choctaw claims. Nevertheless, Polk chose him as his Secretary of the Treasury, and in June 1845 Walker made Corcoran & Riggs sole Washington depository of the Treasury.[17] Successful in its intrigues, the firm was sensitive to public and business opinion. Care was taken to maintain a high proportion of collateral to deposits "as in the beginning it will not do for us to ask too much of the Secretary." When spare cash was used to trade or contract public securities it was done with utmost secrecy through Elisha Riggs; sometimes even Palmer and Newbold were kept in the dark, despite their increasingly intimate alliance. Elisha urged lending on securities, amply margined, in preference to purchasing: "I have been asked by several how you come on with the stocks you hold, bought with the money of the Government. Seeing the effect, I have always said you had but little stock on your own account, but had the stock of others which you render on. You cannot be too careful in this." The partners themselves wanted the reputation of sound, conservative commercial bankers rather than that of brokers—"brokers" at that time connoted speculative and sharp practice.[18]

Corcoran assiduously practiced personal diplomacy, taking pains to ingratiate himself with Polk and his entourage in various ways. He became the investment advisor to the President (and served in that same capacity for Calhoun and other important politicians). He secured introductions to New York bankers for Polk's nephew-in-law, Isaac Barnett, a Memphis lawyer seeking clients in the North. The firm lent money to and wrote letters of recommendation for the Chief Executive's brother, Congressman William H. Polk (against whom legal action for recovery eventually became necessary). When the President, heedful of the Catholic vote, attended St. Matthew's Roman Catholic church one Sunday, Corcoran accompanied him. Already Washington's leading host, Corcoran even shared in the enjoyable but time-consuming chore of helping refurnish the White House.

While these approaches doubtless helped, Walker added a negative rationale for further shifts of business to favored banks by maintaining that they would weaken some Whig institutions and warn others against opposing reenactment of the Independent Treasury. The President's account and the Speaker's account for the House of Representatives were transferred to the firm from the Bank of the Metropolis, and that of the Senate from the Bank of Washington. Only a scattering of small deposits remained with the other District banks.[19] Corcoran & Riggs profited in still other ways from government patronage. In December 1844 Secretary Bibb commissioned the firm to buy up $400,000 of United States 5 percent bonds on the open market. The purchases were made but the bonds were not redeemed until June 1845; meanwhile the firm retained ownership and collected over $10,000 in interest, leaving the bonds with the Treasury as collateral for government deposits.[20] Secretary Walker also channeled his department's foreign transactions through Corcoran & Riggs and their London friend and correspondent, George Peabody, then the leading European dealer in American securities. Until the end of 1841 the firm's correspondence with Peabody was handled via Elisha Riggs; foreign exchange transactions followed that route until 1843, when a direct relationship was established. The number and size of these transactions were trivial but Peabody, reminded of Corcoran's intimacy with the administration, charged the low rate of ¼ percent for accepting drafts and charged nothing for collecting bills to cover. Peabody paid the firm's commissions since the government could not be charged. Corcoran tried to persuade the State and Navy Departments to appoint Peabody their overseas agent in place of Baring Brothers & Co. This time Corcoran failed because the House of Baring (along with the Rothschilds) had the greatest prestige and most far-reaching connections among international financiers. The Barings had held the Navy account even under Democratic Presidents, although it was considered a Whig bank because of its American agent, Thomas W. Ward, and because it represented British holders of state bonds defaulted by Democratic administrations. Minister to London Louis McLane and Navy Secretary George Bancroft firmly resisted the party pressures that were added to Corcoran's on Peabody's behalf.[21]

Domestic exchange patronage was much more important to the firm than foreign. Even when not chosen to transfer funds, it often learned in advance of moves planned by the Treasury. For instance, in September 1845 Walker ordered large transfers to New Orleans, the major base for possible military moves toward Mexico. Corcoran took advantage of the inside news to speculate profitably. He was almost afraid, he wrote, to offer New Orleans exchange in the New York market, for the banks would charge the firm with "speculating on them."[22]

By the end of 1845 Corcoran & Riggs was, in effect, part of the institutional structure of the federal government, the relationship having become continuous and routine. An intimate of the administration and of rival politicians as well as an important member of the business community, Corcoran served as an intermediary among these groups. During the Oregon crisis he channeled communications between British and American statesmen and their business constituents. Late in December 1845 he conveyed the assurances of the administration and of leading Senate spokesmen of both parties to the British minister that an offer of the 49th parallel boundary—with Britain retaining Vancouver Island and navigation of the Columbia River for some years—would be accepted. This settlement had already been proposed through the American minister in London. By having Corcoran transmit it through George Peabody to British business leaders, important influence could be exerted upon Her Majesty's government. Similarly, leading British businessmen warned their American counterparts of the need for a quick settlement in view of the threatened defeat of the Aberdeen ministry over the Irish Coercion Bill. These warnings were relayed by Palmer in New York to the statesmen at Washington via Corcoran.

If businessmen were not particularly frightened by the possibility of war with Mexico, they were nevertheless apprehensive and hoped for a peaceful settlement. The administration used Corcoran to reassure them. In December 1845 he denied a report that John Slidell, special envoy to Mexico, was sent to obtain California. In fact, that region was one of Slidell's objectives, although perhaps secondary; Polk's course was ambiguous and permits varied interpretations. In any case Corcoran's letters, with one exception, reflect Wall Street's peaceful hopes. It is impossible to say whether the financier was a conscious or unconscious instrument of calculated administration ambiguity in Mexican policy; he had certainly been an instrument of candor in Anglo-American diplomacy.[23]

Banker to the Independent Treasury

To the disappointment of its beneficiaries, the depository system came under administration attack. Hard money Democrats, whose attitudes found systematic expression in the writings of William Gouge, wanted the maximum separation of government from the banks, with the former retaining custody of its funds. Cooperation, they believed, should be ad hoc and occasional, not institutional and customary. Although for tactical reasons the Jacksonians had allied themselves with state bank interests until the defeat of the Bank of the United States, they had asserted their independence with the enactment of the Independent Treasury in 1840. After less than a year it was repealed by the Whigs. A stalemate then followed when Tyler, a states-rights conservative who was trying to erect a political platform between the two major parties, vetoed the establishment of both a powerful national bank and the Independent Treasury; meanwhile, Congress stymied his proposal for a fiscal agency dealing in exchange and short-term discounts where states permitted. For want of an acceptable alternative, the "pet" system was restored.[24]

With Polk in the White House, Corcoran thought he had good reason to be confident that there would be no sub-Treasury (as the Independent Treasury was also known)—in 1835 Polk, then chairman of the House Ways and Means Committee, had opposed it. Corcoran failed to understand that Polk's earlier stand had been inspired by political tactics, not financial policy. Although the new administration moved slowly at first, by the spring of 1846 Corcoran regretfully informed his friends that the sub-Treasury would be enacted after settlement of the Oregon dispute. As the Mexican crisis turned into war, Corcoran, with Wall Street support, worked to delay and later suspend operation of the new system for the duration. Various arguments were used: withdrawal of specie from banks to federal vaults would deprive business of the means to pay customs duties, which were receivable in specie, thus forcing reductions of imports and, in turn, reducing customs revenues. (Some protectionists allegedly supported the new system for this very reason.) Moreover, banks could be seriously hampered in financing war loans.[25]

But despite his dislike for the sub-Treasury, Corcoran was as loyal to friendly politicians as to businessmen, a fact that was fully appreciated by both factions. On the administration's behalf he attempted to reassure the financial community, insisting that the new system would do no serious harm. When the New York banks contracted credit in mid-April, 1846, ostensibly to prepare for the government withdrawals but probably to exert pressure against the change, Corcoran bluntly told Palmer that there was no reason to contract, for withdrawals would be made gradually. Credit was eased and an incipient panic promptly subsided. Wall Street fears of a business downturn did not materialize and the administration was conciliatory. "It will give the Treasury Department and officers of the Government more trouble than anyone else and all seem embarrassed about carrying it out," Corcoran wrote in August after the Independent Treasury Act was signed. "The Secretary is however disposed to be very lenient with the Banks, and will extend to them all the indulgence in his power." Wall Street acquiesced and made the best of the new system.[26]

In one respect Corcoran was disappointed. He was mistaken in expecting deposits to be replenished until the end of the year; this would have left him larger resources to contract wartime Treasury note issues. Still, the federal funds were drawn out gradually, as promised, and Corcoran & Riggs was favored for its services. On June 1, 1846, the firm held $500,000 of deposits; in comparison, five New York City banks each had $700,000 to $1 million. Corcoran's firm still held $500,000 in early September but by the 26th of the month the deposits had declined to $300,000; by then each of the four leading New York depositories had been reduced to under $350,000. Corcoran & Riggs still had $300,000 on December 14 and $170,000 in April 1847. It was almost the last bank to lose its Treasury deposits.[27]

Whereas the Act of 1846 ended the regular use of Treasury funds for private purposes, Corcoran & Riggs retained the accounts of other federal agencies. These deposits did not approach the size of the Treasury's general funds but they had an important compensating advantage—no collateral was required. The House Speaker's account, replenished quarterly, held from $10,000 to $100,000; the balance of the Commissioner of Indian Affairs was usually over five figures; and other government agencies maintained modest deposits. Also rewarding to Corcoran & Riggs were Treasury appointments to pay semiannual interest on outstanding loans. Corcoran would gladly have dispensed with this before the Mexican War because, other than earning goodwill, the labor and expense were not justified by the small deposits ($18,000 of a national total of $266,000 in January 1845 for the loans of 1841 through 1843). However, a larger share of the patronage was later allotted by Walker: $138,000 for payments due July 1, 1846; and the great war loans brought sharp increases in semiannual deposits to $280,000 for January 1849, $410,000 a year later, and over $500,000 per installment thereafter. These amounts, which totaled 20 to 25 percent of the government's interest bill, made the job worthwhile. Corcoran & Riggs continued to enjoy this patronage under the Whig administrations of Zachary Taylor and Millard Fillmore, even when all other interest payments on federal loans had been taken over by Treasury branches. In fact the Whigs under Fillmore added an agency to redeem interest-bearing Mexican War bounty-land scrip, for which $240,000 was deposited. It was not until June 1850, when there was tension with the Taylor administration, that the firm was required to return to the Treasury some $62,500 left over from interest installments dating back to 1846.

These government agencies were advantageous in a number of ways. Deposits were made before the due dates until when the money was lent on call. (To reciprocate, the agent might occasionally advance funds without charge when appropriations were late or government money was not at the right place.) Invariably, portions of each interest installment were not called for promptly, and in some cases not at all. Of the $138,000 for the July 1, 1846, payment, $12,000 was still in the firm's vault on November 13, 1848, and $6,000 remained on account in February 1849. Similar fractions accumulated of the much larger later installments. By 1850 the firm probably held more than $100,000 from five years' unclaimed interest, in addition to much larger sums available semiannually for periods covering from several days to several months. After the beginning of Walker's tenure as Secretary, the special deposits for interest on loans, which often exceeded $100,000, required no collateral.

Besides holding deposits, Corcoran & Riggs also served profitably in other ways. While Secretaries Bibb (1844–1845), Walker (1845–1849) and Thomas Corwin (1850–1853) were in office, the firm managed half or more of the federal debt retirement. Large sums were involved from 1848 on: the public debt greatly expanded during the Mexican War, as did debt reduction after the war (a result of rising commerce and tariff revenues). From 1848 to 1853 redemptions by the firm probably exceeded $4 million. Commissions were ¼ percent, money was available for call loans, and there was an advantage in the ability to judge market conditions.[28]

Government funds were particularly helpful to a bank with as little initial capital as Corcoran & Riggs. The partners had invested $2,500 apiece and each maintained personal balances of perhaps $10,000. Profits before the Mexican War did not add significantly to these sums, and deposits of private individuals and businesses were small, never approaching $100,000. The Treasury provided the working capital to support the firm's rapid growth.

Still, the catalog of advantages from government business is not complete. The firm managed a large share of the heavy wartime exchange transactions, ironically earning commissions under the Independent Treasury that had not been charged under the depository system.[29] Some bankers are known to have profiteered outrageously on transfers paid for months in advance of performance, using the money for call loans in the interim. "Our government, unsustained as it is by Banks and Capitalists, is the worst of financiers," wrote prominent banker Samuel Ward. Newbold had earlier warned that the sub-Treasury "under existing [wartime] circumstances is *Ridiculous* as well as *Mischievous* and *Suicidal*." Corcoran & Riggs also profited, but apparently not to the extremes one writer calls "customary." In fact, Corcoran wrote Newbold that his one regret was "that I was silly enough to agree to terms so favorable to the U. States. Now I suppose it will be trumpeted in the street that I offered a large amount considerably below the market rate. . . . You know my motives." Perhaps Corcoran's relative self-restraint helps explain. Walker's favoritism toward him.[30]

Thus, Corcoran & Riggs gained almost as much from federal patronage under the Independent Treasury as before. Uniquely, the firm retained significant deposits that enabled it to increase its loans more rapidly than its borrowing. The first half of 1841 yielded an income on interest accounts of less than $1,700; in the same period of 1845 (the next year for which figures survive and the first to benefit substantially from Treasury deposits) net earnings on interest were $5,200. For the full year of 1845 the net on interest was $3,000; in 1846, $10,800.[31] The gains rose to $18,000 in 1847 under the sub-Treasury system owing to the retention of funds of other agencies and to various special deposits that were established to service or redeem the growing public debt. Exchange operations, the other major component of profits before the war loans, also originated largely from federal business: surviving figures show a net of $13,400 on this account in 1846.

Probably federal patronage directly accounted for more—perhaps much more—than half of the net income in 1845 and 1846, but the usefulness of the deposits as working capital may have been more important than the direct profits. The profits were still small: each partner drew $17,000 and $13,800 in the two years. They were able only to double their personal deposits, to about $20,000 each. For other banks of the old depository system, chiefly incorporated commercial banks that were well capitalized and had large business clienteles, federal patronage was minor although worth contending for. For Corcoran & Riggs, a firm small in resources but highly ambitious, federal support was vital until the Mexican War successes secured the firm's financial foundations.[32]

4

Financing the Mexican War

The Lines Form

During the diplomatic crises of 1845 and 1846, Corcoran reflected Wall Street's wish for peace; yet he was noticeably less fearful of war with Mexico than with Britain. In case of a conflict with Mexico, he predicted, "Our field for making money will be greatly enlarged." Still, optimist though he was, Corcoran could hardly have foreseen the dominant personal role he would play in war finance.

War loans up to $10 million were authorized by Act of Congress in July 1846. Secretary Walker began issuing notes at a purely nominal interest rate of 1/10 percent. Though this was gradually raised to 5 2/5 percent, less than $2 million was disposed of in two months; the financial community thought the rate of interest too low and disapproved of Walker's decision not to replenish balances in the depositories. By the end of September only $4 million remained in the Treasury. As a result of these difficulties the Secretary temporarily relaxed his nonreplenishment policy. Concessions on the interest rate also seemed advisable, and President Polk approved a loan at 6 percent for twelve months.

Walker immediately attempted a personal coup, melodramatically departing for a secret rendezvous at Princeton, New Jersey, to negotiate a loan of $3 to $4 million. There he met George Newbold and Newbold's former colleague in the Bank of America, Cornelius Lawrence, who held the politically important post of collector of the port of New York. The Secretary offered 5 percent; the bankers demanded 6 percent. He was willing to compromise; they were not. After two futile weeks in Princeton and New York Walker finally left, angrily predicting success at Philadelphia—but he failed there too. Returning to Washington, he proposed to issue 5⅖ percent notes (which conveniently equaled $.01½ per day per $100) to public creditors. However, Secretary of State James Buchanan, probably receiving Wall Street's opinions via Elisha Riggs and Corcoran, objected that such notes would promptly be returned in payment of dues to the Treasury. The chagrined Walker finally yielded and decided on a $5 million ten-year loan at 6 percent.[1]

Despite these concessions Newbold, whose predictions were apt to be as sombre as those of Corcoran were sunny, doubted the loan would be taken at par. His pessimism (and that of others) resulted partly from a dislike of Walker's general policies and his conduct of the loan negotiations. The Secretary "has not acted like a good patient man in the whole of this negotiation," chided Riggs. Corcoran judged from bids received that the loan would be fully subscribed, although he could not be certain: "But for the strong hostility to it [the loan, broadly understood to include the preliminaries], the amount offered would be four times the amount wanted." In the end the loan was oversubscribed, a fact which one financier attributed almost wholly to political supporters of the administration.

Corcoran & Riggs bid successfully for $300,000 for which they lacked funds despite liquidation of other holdings. Corcoran, supported by Elisha and possibly by other Wall Street bankers, persuaded Walker to relax sub-Treasury policy by accepting certified checks in payment instead of specie. Anxious to regain business support, the Secretary made another, more important concession: he promised to use the sub-Treasury to aid the money market, a pledge he was to redeem amply.[2]

Despite Walker's compliance the partners were anxious to liquidate, offering to sell their whole allotment to John Ward below the market price. Ward, the leading contractor of federal loans since the beginning of the decade, had taken a large share, but he would not commit himself until he heard from Boston. Capitalism combined interestingly with Puritanism there: the Boston people were hostile to government loans, George Riggs reported, and broker Edward Whitehouse described some bank directors as refusing to lend on collateral of United States bonds in support of an "unrighteous war." Nevertheless, Ward finally took $200,000 at par; that is, without profit to the firm. Elisha encouraged the sale to make the firm "easy" before the next loan, which was expected soon.

George Riggs was elated: not only was he more cautious than his prudent father, but he disagreed completely with his partner over the policy of heavy involvement in war loans. He did not want to speculate with borrowed money or mix investment with commercial banking:

> Our situation here induces many people to put confidence in us such as would not be placed if it were known that we speculated largely. I think it wrong for persons who do a banking or collecting business to operate in stocks unless possessed of money to carry on such operations without taking from the regular business.

But his partner made policy.[3]

Corcoran soon learned that the Secretary would ask Congress for new authority to borrow $23 million. The firm stepped up its sales, the government buying its last $120,000 of United States securities for trust funds. The Smithsonian Institute had already taken $240,000 on Corcoran's initiative before the $5 million loan. Keeping these securities off the open market helped support the price, of course.[4]

Meanwhile, through Corcoran, Walker solicited Wall Street

advice. Mounting government expenditures and the futility of his earlier posture had made him more pliable. He proposed a bill giving him the option of short- or long-term debt and gave approval to the convertibility of Treasury notes into 6 percent twenty-year bonds, a proviso judged to be worth 2 to 3 percent. Future Treasury surpluses were earmarked for buying up outstanding bonds, but an amendment by Representative Preston King, an old antibank radical of New York, prohibited purchases above par. No provision was made for calling the loan. In this form the bill passed. On February 9, 1847, Walker announced $18 million of Treasury notes, bids receivable until April 10. In the interim he contracted for about $4 million under the new act, along with over $1 million under earlier law.[5]

Walker administered the loan to strengthen his support in Congress. He set aside well over $100,000 in 6 percent notes for purchase by members at par. At least thirty senators and representatives of both parties bought for themselves, friends, and constituents. Corcoran & Riggs handled many of the transactions, apparently advancing funds for some. Among the more important congressional buyers were George Ashmun, John A. Dix, Charles J. Ingersoll, Jacob Thompson, and William W. Woodworth.[6]

Besides the goodwill it engendered, favoritism in public finance lent itself to concrete political purposes. Allotment of $300,000 of Treasury notes to Representative Woodworth (Dem., N.Y.), a banker, may have involved Corcoran in the politics of slavery. Early in 1848 John L. O'Sullivan, editor and publisher of the *New York Democratic Review,* learned that many congressmen believed Woodworth obtained the notes at par on May 31, 1847, without having bid for them first. Since the market price had risen to 105 this would have been, in effect, a bribe of $15,000. The purpose allegedly was to convert him from supporter to opponent of the Wilmot Proviso. O'Sullivan's inquiries at the Treasury were answered by letters ostensibly showing that Woodworth's early bid had been mislaid, found after the notes were awarded, and granted on grounds of justice by reissue of notes returned to the Treasury for duties. This explanation cannot be disproved, but neither is it convincing. Woodworth paid Corcoran nearly $10,000 in interest on the latter's personal account over the next few years: clearly the Washington banker was financing his operations in federal securities. Corcoran also seems to have obtained Newbold's relinquishment of 5⅖ percent notes in exchange for 6 percent notes, helping Walker furnish $271,000 worth of the former to Congressman Washington Hunt (Whig, N.Y.), an influential financier.[7]

While the political paths were being smoothed, the infighting on Wall Street grew rougher. Before bids were closed for the major loan of 1847, Corcoran & Riggs joined Matthew Morgan & Co. to contract $2.4 million of 6 percent Treasury notes. Corcoran, his partner, and William B. Astor each took $100,000 on personal account, with $50,000 each to Elisha Riggs, George Newbold, John J. Palmer, and David Thompson, cashier of the Bank of America, Riggs' share being kept secret as long as possible because of growing jealousy and fear of the Riggs clan. Morgan's allies included the Bank of Commerce, which absorbed $300,000, and groups of financiers connected with it and with the rapidly growing Bank of the State of New York.

The free-wheeling Morgan was New York agent of the important Canal & Banking Company of New Orleans and worked closely with the Bank of the State of New York.[8] His cooperation with Corcoran's group was short-lived; even before the operation was concluded, this ruthless competitor attacked his momentary allies, unsuccessfully demanding that they pay in specie, although Morgan himself had deposited certified checks.

Corcoran made the mistake of agreeing to Morgan's management of the operation until April 1 while he and his allies kept out of the market. Under their agreement the two groups took $500,000 each, the rest remaining on joint account. The Morgan group sold off its own and the joint account notes at about a 2 percent premium. Morgan even had to be prodded into properly crediting the joint account instead of that of his allies. When he turned in his accounts near the end of March his group was clear; Corcoran's had not begun to sell. With the deadline approaching for the $18 million loan, the Morgan faction and John Ward joined in bearing the market, selling heavily from their portfolios to cut their rivals' profits and lower the price of the new flotation. When Corcoran and his friends finally liquidated their notes the average profit was barely 1 percent. With the new loan looming he still had on hand over $1 million in 6 percent notes previously contracted for his personal account. So far the partners had gained more in experience than in money.[9]

The Loan of 1847

The new loan provided the chance to cash in on experience. Elisha Riggs reported from Wall Street that he, Ward, Newbold, Palmer, and others had agreed that a united list of subscribers should be presented by a New Yorker, probably Ward. These men were slow to comprehend that Morgan was challenging for leadership; only belatedly did they learn of a list being formed at the State Bank. Ward then began negotiations with Morgan. The latter would not be an acceptable spokesman, Elisha commented, but it would be well to know what he was up to. Meanwhile, ostensibly on behalf of Wall Street, Riggs delegated Corcoran and Ward to sound out the Secretary of the Treasury: would Walker permit payment in installments?

At first Elisha agreed to the partners' bidding for $200,000 to $300,000 on their personal accounts. Then he reconsidered, asserting that there was too much talk of the partners' large interest in the last loan. Neither should do anything to implicate the firm: "If he [Corcoran] takes steps unusual with sound public opinion you injure your own credit." He reiterated that, in effect, the firm should limit its operations to some presumed reasonable factor of its capital and should, both from ethics and expediency, seek its advantage as a junior associate of Wall Street. The partners should work their way up through the ranks, not try to vault into leadership.[10]

In the presence of breathtaking possibilities Corcoran was not about to undergo paroxysms of modesty. He looked forward to a fifty-fifty division of the entire loan with Ward. The situation was suddenly scrambled, however, when that worthy went over to Morgan. They decided to bid 100.05 percent for two-thirds ($6 million each) and offered Corcoran & Riggs the remaining third. It was a take-it-or-leave-it proposition. They did not believe Corcoran & Riggs independently would be able to manage more than $1 million or $2 million, let alone a far greater sum.

Corcoran paused to analyze the situation. The market was firm, with 6 percent Treasury notes at a premium of 1½ and the 1856 and 1867 bonds at 102¼ and 103 respectively. There were heavy orders for the forthcoming notes from institutions and individuals, and he was aware that very large bids would be submitted by Winslow & Perkins of New York and Samuel Henshaw of Boston. Corcoran also knew that Newbold and Palmer deeply distrusted and resented Morgan. The Bank of America was on Ward's list for $600,000, but if the New Yorker's bid was unsuccessful Newbold (and others) would gladly buy elsewhere.

Corcoran & Riggs offered a ⅛ percent premium for the entire loan. Walker awarded all other equal or higher bids the full amount sought. These totaled $3.3 million, of which half was Elisha's at 100.15. Of that $1.65 million, half was for Corcoran & Riggs, $525,000 for Elisha himself, and the rest was divided equally among members of the Riggs family. In lieu of a commission Elisha returned the interest the partners had paid him for the loan of Missouri bonds for depository purposes. This arrangement was not according to his first understanding, Elisha later commented, but by then he was deferring to Corcoran. The firm itself held the extraordinary sum of $14.7 million.[11]

Response to the news varied. According to Elisha, frustrated competitors charged that Secretary Walker was personally involved with him and Corcoran & Riggs. "I am not in a desirable situation and think more than I like to speak," Elisha said, asking that his connection with the firm's bid be kept secret. He was doubly sensitive to the accusations because he shared the widespread belief that Corcoran had violated financial ethics with his "speculative" bid. Having had no inkling of his intention (conceivably, neither did Corcoran himself until the moment he acted), Elisha objected: "I have been made the dupe or catspaw by Mr. C. and I feel very sore under it. I like fair open dealings." But Corcoran curtly dismissed his complaints, merely labeling them "extraordinary."[12]

Whig newspapers published attacks, probably receiving ammunition from disappointed Whig financiers. The most damaging comments charged, perhaps with some grounds, that Walker had assured Corcoran that money would be received in installments while other firms were left in some doubt. Only near the deadline did the administration organ at Washington indicate that installments would probably be taken. But those (such as Morgan) who inquired directly of the Secretary were informed in ample time that $3 million per month was the expected maximum requirement and quite possibly less would be needed, although no guarantees could be made. Corcoran might have been given more definite assurances; on the other hand, the point remains that he knew essentially what his rivals would do while they completely underestimated him. One competitor, Richard Winslow, joined those he could not beat. He disavowed the charges against Corcoran in a letter to the editor of the *Journal of Commerce,* whose consequent strong support ended the controversy. Winslow & Perkins was appointed one of the New York brokers for the loan.[13]

It was a coup, but the job was only begun. Newbold, who effused congratulations "with all my heart," subscribed for $500,000 for the Bank of America and more for himself. Corcoran took a large amount for his personal account and Morgan and Ward took $500,000 each at 1¼ percent. The firm began offering slowly to the public at 104 and up. Large blocks were sold to institutions, which were granted small price concessions. Subcontracts and sales to institutions and investors at up to 107 enabled the firm to pay for the first $4 million of notes with little borrowing. Sales were halted in anticipation of victory and peace in Mexico and a rising market.[14]

Instead the war dragged on, demand dwindled, and prices slipped below par in January 1848. Corcoran & Riggs had to borrow up to $1 million for much of the last half of 1847 while interest rates, initially 4 percent, rose to 6 percent. These loans, chiefly from the usual friends, helped the firm ride out the bear raids of Morgan and his allies with little difficulty.[15]

Fortunately the Treasury's monthly needs were usually below the 10 to 15 percent initially forecast. Walker was sometimes cooperative: he agreed to postpone several installments to enable the firm to await an easier money market and lower interest rates. On the other hand, when the sub-Treasury was overflowing, he refused to accept deposits until the accumulation had been reduced. This sometimes occurred when money was abundant at as low as 4 percent and the contractors would have preferred depositing to gain the difference between the preferential rate and the 6 percent borne by the Treasury notes.[16]

Deposits in sub-Treasuries at distant points made possible some lucrative exchange and interest operations resulting from the loan. To illustrate: Elisha's nephew, Lawrason Riggs of Riggs & Levering, was St. Louis agent with instructions to deposit in the sub-Treasury, on account of the loan, whenever he could get a premium for checks on New York. He then sent Elisha a draft on Corcoran & Riggs at the Bank of America in favor either of Elisha or a purchaser requiring exchange in New York or he drew on Elisha and simultaneously notified the firm, which deposited to Elisha's credit to meet the draft. If the premium on exchange was 2 to 3½ percent, as Jay Cooke later recalled, it contributed about $8,000 of profits on the $275,000 Lawrason deposited for the loan of 1847. The purchaser of exchange paid for the deposit, from which date the notes drew interest at 6 percent. In addition, interest on call loans was earned during the ten days or more the drafts took to reach the East. (Similarly, the following year $580,000 was deposited in St. Louis and a smaller amount at Jeffersonville, Indiana, against the loan of 1848. There were smaller deposits at the major Gulf ports of New Orleans and Mobile, although the bulk of deposits was almost entirely in the Northeast.)

When the last of the loan of 1847 was finally worked off in February 1848, Corcoran & Riggs recorded a profit of over $250,000, dwarfing the earnings of all its preceding years.[17]

The Loan of 1848 in Domestic and International Finance

By the fall of 1847 it was understood that the government would borrow heavily again. It seemed possible that Mexico, despite her unending defeats, would attempt to wage guerrilla warfare indefinitely. Moreover, Walker schemed for a long occupation to make possible annexation of the whole country. Although he calculated this might require twenty years, the Secretary thought one year would suffice to make the occupation financially self-sustaining. Even without the deficit expected under this scheme, an unbalanced federal budget was in prospect. It was doubtful whether American investors could support another great increase in the national debt. It was logical, therefore, to turn to Baring Brothers' American agent, Thomas Ward of Boston. Moreover, senior partner Thomas Baring had considerable influence with the British government, an important point because Walker's Mexican plans had implications for Anglo-American diplomacy. Bankrupt Mexico had defaulted on debts to British investors of $60 million; legally, if the United States annexed the country she would annex the debts as well. The prospect of the debts becoming collectable made Her Majesty's government, otherwise unfriendly to American expansion, more receptive. Walker's proposal "to pay the whole debt of Mexico" interested the Barings, for the British creditors composed an important part of their financial constituency. Negotiations ended, however, because of widespread American hostility to the absorption of all Mexico.[18]

The Secretary had already decided that a $23 million loan would be needed for the fiscal year 1848–1849, and a bill to authorize this was introduced in Congress. The estimate was not changed despite the remarkable revelation that Walker had understated government receipts by $6 to $7 million, allegedly due to a clerical error. Wonders will never cease, the puzzled Newbold commented, and even more wonderful—the error remained undiscovered for two months. He asked whether the disclosure would mean a corresponding reduction in Walker's request. It would not, he was informed, and Newbold wrote that he still could not understand the figures. Palmer said he had noticed the error but thought the full amount would be needed anyway. Later it became obvious that the lower estimate was much more accurate, and would have been even without a peace treaty. Ward had described Walker as "bold, ardent . . . reckless to an extent." He was notably so, even in an age whose style encouraged such attributes. Given his expansionist philosophy and his belief it could make him President, it seems clear that Walker contrived the "error" to be financially prepared should his Mexican hopes yet prove realizable.[19]

Financiers generally thought the government would have to give terms at least as favorable as the previous loan, but Walker would have no more of fundable notes. They had begun returning to the Treasury in payment of duties at the time prices declined late in 1847, and the several options made finances uncertain. The administration and Congress did make one important concession, authorizing the Secretary to use unappropriated surpluses to support the market by purchasing bonds at least at par. The Act of March 31, 1848, authorized a twenty-year 6 percent loan, but the signing of a peace treaty with Mexico, ending hopes of annexation, led to reduction of the planned loan to $16 million.[20]

The previous war loans had been absorbed almost wholly within the United States. In Britain, purchases of American securities had practically ceased because of the Mexican War and an internal railway boom that ended with the financial crisis of 1847. Interest in American investments revived as conditions in Britain improved and peace in Mexico drew near. In the spring of 1848 revolutions in Europe brought flights of capital seeking secure investments such as the United States government bonds.

The improved outlook came at a time when the American market was nearly saturated. In the fall of 1847 Corcoran & Riggs had tried without success to borrow in England against Treasury notes. Yet the prospective return of foreign capital to the American market received a somewhat ambiguous welcome on Wall Street, for it also promised increased competition. Most closely watched was the august House of Rothschild. August Belmont, its American agent, was a Democrat, and his position appeared to grow stronger when Walker awarded him the transfer of the first $3 million installment due Mexico under the peace treaty. Baring Brothers, which had sought this patronage, considered joining the Rothschilds in the forthcoming loan.[21]

Events showed Corcoran that, close as they were, Walker might yet act independently. In February 1848 the Secretary offered a $5 million loan. Corcoran & Riggs, with a minority position of 40 percent, joined N. M. Rothschild & Sons of London in a bid of 101.26 which apparently captured all but $750,000. Only then did they learn that the Secretary had privately disposed of almost $2 million a month earlier, leaving the two houses with $2.35 million. Corcoran & Riggs still had much of its share on hand as attention focused on the $16 million loan.[22]

With the attitudes of overseas financiers more important than in recent years, Corcoran was encouraged to compete for the loan by his friend George Peabody. However, other European principals were less sanguine than were the American agents. Belmont, who viewed the loan not only as an end in itself but also as a means of entrée for future government business, was unable to persuade the Rothschilds to enter the competition. Thomas Ward was somewhat more successful, although he surprised the Barings with an excess of optimism: he thought the loan could be easily absorbed at home. There was little demand in Europe, the Barings skeptically replied, but by the end of May they cautiously prepared a bid of $1 million. Ward then moved to minimize competition. He estimated there was only $2 million to $3 million of floating capital available for investment in the United States; therefore the loan would be speculative and prospective subscribers should unite in a "fair but low" bid. Although the Rothschilds declined to join, they ordered Belmont to cooperate in holding down prices by staying out of the market until after the bidding. Ward then turned to Corcoran & Riggs, tacitly acknowledging its domestic leadership in federal finance. "I am not good at dealing with men who mislead," Ward noted ambiguously, "but I hear well of Corcoran and that he is man of property."[23]

Corcoran, preparing to repeat his earlier stroke, first had to face internal disagreement. His partner had had to be dragged into success the year before; under the less favorable conditions of early 1848 reluctance turned into resistance. The differences between the partners broadened, and eventually George Riggs quit the firm. In his place Corcoran accepted young Elisha Riggs, Jr., recently graduated from Heidelberg with honors, as partner with a 25 percent interest. He then turned to reach a speedy agreement with Ward, from whom he accepted the largest single subscription, $1.25 million. Another $1.4 million was taken directly for foreign account, including most of the Barings' $1 million and $750,000 in the name of Peabody but actually on joint account with Corcoran & Riggs and Elisha Riggs. By the June 17 bidding deadline, Corcoran claimed—probably with much exaggeration—that his list totaled over $10 million and that he had rejected $1.3 million more that same day.

From reports by Secretary Walker and Wall Street friends, Corcoran knew that competition was heavy despite the absence of the great rival coalitions of 1847. He estimated that a bid of 102½ would leave as much as $6 million to $7 million in other hands, some of them weak. He offered 103.02 and, after allowance of all equal or higher bids, was awarded $14,050,550.[24]

Corcoran was elated, but in reality the situation was not very favorable. He had sold much of his 1847 Treasury notes at 103 in an attempt to hold down a rising market and discourage higher bids and had been perhaps too successful: practically all his subscribers stipulated prices below 103, with only the Baring group prepared for a higher bid. About half the original orders were canceled because of the greater premium, assuming Corcoran's claim of $10 million of subscriptions was not exaggerated (as in fact it appears to have been). The amount actually taken probably fell short of $5 million. Nevertheless, sales began well at 104 and up. One genuine cause for satisfaction was the active participation of the Barings and Peabody, which marked a notable step toward the recovery of American credit less than a decade after the last depression had caused a wave of state bond default and repudiation.

Corcoran anticipated a gradual, steady rise. Earlier, remembering the depression years after 1837, he had agreed with conservative counsel that selling opportunities should be seized even at narrow margins. Now he quickly adapted to the changed atmosphere of prosperity and from 1847 on saw that his main chance lay in speculating on a bull market. It soon became clear that Walker would not require the loan as early as expected when the original stipulation of five monthly installments had been advertised. Using the funds from his subscribers for the first installments, Corcoran withdrew from the market early in July. "We will not sell a dollar of our portion of the loan for some months to come. The Govert. having plenty of funds from others who are anxious to pay at once."[25]

The result was not as expected, however. Demand was quickly filled by Corcoran's subscribers and his own sales began to lag. There was intense competition for investment funds from the increasingly prosperous private sectors of the economy. As Baring Brothers feared, money grew tight in America and the price of the bonds dropped below 103.[26] Nor was relief found readily in Europe—demand from the Continent was mild. Corcoran's allies had to support the market when bonds were sent over by American subscribers and again when the Rothschilds unloaded their inventory.[27]

As money tightened, Corcoran concluded that the only hope lay in boldly confronting Britain's financial leaders. He enlisted the cooperation of the administration: on the pretexts that the Mexican treaty required the United States to pay several million dollars of Mexico's debts and that Congress had raised army pay, Walker formally requested a $5 million advance against the loan. The need for such an advance was fictitious, for installments were being postponed (and were to be drawn out even longer). The real goal of the banker and the Secretary was a swift, massive infusion of foreign capital to relieve the American money market. To bestow official authority on Corcoran, Walker appointed him agent of the Treasury Department to negotiate the sale of up to $5 million of the loan overseas.[28]

Corcoran's mission elicited a very mixed response in the House of Baring. Its agent, Ward, supported Corcoran, finding him free of petty, irritating personality traits and praising his "quiet and straight course, with *labor* and *intelligence* . . . comprehensive mind . . . growing. . . ." The Bostonian thought Corcoran might be the first-rate American correspondent the Barings had been looking for. "I give him a good deal of confidence," he continued. "So far as now appears, I should like to have him gradually connected with you."[29]

The Barings, however, tried to discourage Corcoran's coming. Personally, they bore a grudge against him for having tried to deprive them of the federal accounts in favor of Peabody.[30] In general they held a somewhat jaundiced view of the American character—perhaps excepting New Englanders, some of whom were taken into the partnership. They considered Corcoran and Peabody, among others, "boasters" who always overstated their wealth and hid their losses. The Barings may have known of Corcoran's reputation for occasional sharp practice, finding too much of the broker in him. It may offset these judgments to quote a later American minister, John Bigelow, who found Thomas Baring "a mean fussy looking man who looks as if he had been accustomed all his life to ignoble pursuits." Ward, a gentler and broader personality, tried to bridge the rifts between his employers and their American cousins. His favorable comments outweighed his criticisms of Corcoran as a "loose & incomplete" administrator "overrun with business & society & politics."[31]

But these were secondary reasons for the Barings' coolness; financial conditions were more to the point. In France the Revolution of 1848 had cut off income from investments while the investments themselves, which otherwise might have been disposed of to take advantage of higher yields on United States bonds, remained unsalable. At the same time, the crushing of the radicals dulled the impulse toward capital flights. Elsewhere in Europe revolution was being put down and capital was hesitant. In Britain, poor crops foreshadowed large food imports while the depressed securities and heavy short-term credit demands of British railways drew off available capital. As for American securities, many investors preferred those of New York, Ohio, and Massachusetts.

Thus cataloging their reasons, the Barings remained gloomy and reiterated that it would be futile for Corcoran to approach them. They had always thought $16 million was too large a flotation for the United States market, they wrote, adding drily, "The American mode of making a large loan by throwing a large amount into weak hands makes an interest dangerous for European houses. . . . There is some mystery in the connection of the government & Mr. Corcoran which we cannot altogether understand." But while they emphasized the shadows in this mixed picture, Corcoran could only dwell on the brighter aspects. He traveled to Boston to enlist on his behalf a Whig spokesman, ex-Governor John Davis of Massachusetts, who would be welcomed by the Barings for having recently helped negotiate resumption of payments on the largely

British-held defaulted bonds of Illinois. Armed with supporting letters from Ward, ex-Minister to London Abbott Lawrence, and the Secretary of the Treasury, Corcoran and Davis arrived in England at the end of August.[32]

Corcoran's persistence was not the mere flight of an optimist's temperament; he understood there were impressive arguments in his favor. Baring Brothers, with a heavy inventory of various American securities issues, undoubtedly would be hurt by continued price weakness. More important, the British were capable of a broader view of their interests. They interpreted the financial situation much as the Americans did: the London money market had been easing, but severe contraction in the American market could undermine the entire Atlantic economy. For at least the second time since the 1830s the desire to maintain a high level of trade would motivate a large loan to America. Finally, the government at Washington had pointedly and publicly made the mission its own. Failure and a resulting curtailment of American economic expansion might have undesirable political and diplomatic consequences, whereas success would deepen the Anglo-American rapprochement. Although subordinate to factors more explicitly economic, this important consideration was not neglected by British financiers.[33]

Corcoran, abroad for the first time, was guided through the details of the negotiations by his old friend Peabody. He offered to sell the Britons $3 million, interest from September 15 to be paid for in sixty-day bills at the fixed exchange rate of four shillings and sixpence per dollar. Corcoran & Riggs was to draw no more than one-third per month from October through December without prior approval, but would be allowed 5 percent from the time interest commenced on the bonds until maturity of the bills. By arrangement with Secretary Walker, interest on the bonds was allowed from the contract date. So that the United States market "may be made fully to feel the effect of my sales to you," Corcoran would sell no more than $1 million per month during the last quarter of the year.[34]

The deal was finally concluded after three weeks of negotiations in London and Paris. Baring Brothers took $750,000 for itself and Hottinguer & Cie. of Paris, which was consulted along with the Rothschilds and presumably other French banks.[35] Peabody, whose share was secretly on joint account with Corcoran & Riggs, James Morrison, and Overend, Gurney & Co. each took $500,000. Denison & Co. and Samuel Jones Loyd joined soon after for $500,000 and $250,000 respectively. The total was $3 million and the price was 93¾ payable in England, with Corcoran & Riggs assuming the burden of exchange. At the going exchange rate, there would be a loss of a little less than 1 percent to the firm, and the rate was still declining, but this was unimportant compared to the results achieved; Corcoran had been prepared for worse. The Europeans received options on an additional $1 million at the contract price, prorated.

Corcoran was happy despite the rather stiff terms. If a failure of the negotiations might have had unpleasant repercussions for the British, it would certainly have left his firm in an impossible predicament. Audacious, shrewd, and lucky, he had gone beyond his depth, and a swimmer in trouble does not spurn a raft just because he cannot have a boat. Of course the profits on what remained promised to compensate more than adequately for what had been surrendered. An added gain was the promising alliance that had been initiated with the Barings. (Corcoran's defense of his earlier course with regard to the government accounts soothed that sore point.) After the loan agreement the two houses formed an alliance for the transfer of the indemnity due Mexico under the peace treaty. Corcoran realized that the whole range of contacts made among British and French financiers might prove useful.[36]

In America the general action was relief and praise. However, the market promised to remain weak until the flow of funds from England increased. The market became bearish and at the same time the Riggses lost their nerve. The inexperienced Elisha, Jr., guided by his timid father, took advantage of Corcoran's absence and hedged with heavy sales. Elisha unloaded $414,000 for his own account, of which he actually owned only $250,000; the rest was sold short. Sales by Elisha, Jr., for the firm were apparently well over $1 million and may have approached $2 million. Lacking the insight and confidence of the senior partner, the Riggses had been bearing the market against themselves.[37]

Upon his return from England Corcoran resumed control and began aggressively supporting the market. The Europeans continued to operate smoothly. The Rothschilds sold their $100,000 of federal securities to the Barings, whose sales were chiefly in France. The Hopes, Widow Borski, and Ketwich & Voomberg plied the Dutch market, Peabody centered on his German outlets and Overend, Gurney sold heavily in Britain. The price rose gradually, reaching the American equivalent of 107 at year's end. As Corcoran had hoped, his British allies held sales down to allow the American price to catch up. "You are all indebted to Baring and myself," Peabody rejoiced, "who have been continually advancing the price & exciting the market which has induced parties to send orders to New York to buy without limit." Corcoran prided himself that, after many years, United States bonds at last ranked with the best municipals in the investment market.[38]

Large sales of sterling were troublesome. The firm had never entered the international exchange market, being located off the mainstream which ran through the Atlantic commercial ports. Its small sales had been made chiefly through Riggs relations and Baring agents and correspondents. The exchange operation was harrassed by the most powerful American dealer, Brown Brothers & Co., with whom Corcoran finally came to terms in order to relieve himself of the burden. By mid-December they had taken at least £350,000, paying 8 percent and selling at 9¾. Corcoran continued to sell small amounts elsewhere at higher rates, until the Browns learned of it. Jealous of their market domination, they demanded and obtained a monopoly of the sales. (The Browns gave a small part of the business to William Pickersgill, a member by marriage of the Riggs clan.)[39]

The need for cooperation between Corcoran and the Treasury continued to grow for, although the London contract provided vital immediate relief, it did not prevent recurring tightness in the American money market. A major day-to-day problem was the piling up and sterilizing of specie in the sub-Treasury as booming commerce caused tariff collections to rise. Under the circumstances the Treasury's continued sale of bonds was perverse. To alleviate the problem Walker and his Whig successor, William B. Meredith, repeatedly postponed receipt of remaining loan installments. In addition, as early as November 1848, the Treasury went into the market to buy back $500,000 of its outstanding obligations. With $5 million of the last loan still to be received at 103.02 the government found itself in the absurd position of paying 3 percent more for redemptions on the open market, and continued to buy at still higher prices before receiving the last installment from Corcoran & Riggs.[40]

Other means were devised to shift money from the Treasury back into the economy. Sometimes these expedients had a dubious quality: in one instance Walker made a large interest-free loan to the Morgans (Matthew and his son William R.) and their allies by buying $800,000 of Treasury notes from them for specie and selling them back at the same price on credit (except for a 2 percent deposit). The Morgan group continued to draw interest on the notes, which remained in the Treasury pending full payment, while they profitably eased the money market by lending the funds on call. Taking the notes off the market and replacing them with gold also helped to keep up the price of United States loans. Corcoran appointed Matthew Morgan broker for the firm's projected market-support purchases of up to $300,000, which were ended at $250,000 when the money market eased and prices responded favorably. However, Morgan, his appetite whetted, began dumping his notes, forcing the price down. Corcoran, target of the bears, hastily made his peace with Morgan by arranging renewal of the $800,000 loan. Order was thus restored.[41]

Early in 1849 Secretary Walker, nearing the end of his

term with a newly elected Whig administration about to take office, halted operations to reduce Treasury surpluses on the pretext of leaving his successor a free hand. Mid-February found almost half the specie in New York locked up in the sub-Treasury, causing a contraction of business and a dip in the stock market. Politically sensitive, the canny Secretary calculated his tactics to drive the inexperienced incoming Secretary, William Meredith, to continue his measures, thus protecting himself against potential partisan attack. He was largely successful: although suspicious of his inheritance, the new Secretary nevertheless maintained a continuity of agents and policies when he took office in March.

Ironically, one of Walker's measures directly benefiting Corcoran & Riggs later served to protect the rival Whig party from partisan attack. In February 1849 he advanced $1 million to the firm on account of the first installment of the indemnity to Mexico. Instead of cash, however, Walker turned over Treasury notes which were credited to the government at par, although they were selling on the open market at 108. Later, in 1850, when Democrats charged Whig Secretary of State Daniel Webster with corruption and favoritism toward his close friend, Corcoran, Democratic Chairman Thomas H. Bayly of the House Ways and Means Committee helped stifle the onslaught by baring his own party's identical vulnerability. Democratic critics immediately quieted down.[42]

If some of the victorious Whigs distrusted Corcoran, many assured him of their support and did what they could to stimulate demand for government securities. In critically important New York State, these undertakings were carried out by such leaders as Vice-President-elect Millard Fillmore and his elected successor as state comptroller, Washington Hunt, along with William Marcy at the head of conservative Democrats. For some years influential financiers had been lobbying for a bill, an amendment to the Free Banking Act of 1838, to add federal bonds to those of the state as acceptable collateral for state banknote issues. Rufus H. King of the State Bank of Albany and Dudley Selden of the Bank of the State of New

York, both interested in federal securities, were among the original lobbyists in 1847. The reciprocal effects of such a bill would be to facilitate a needed expansion of the money supply and to encourage long-term investment in the federal debt. Despite opposition from hard-money adherents and from bankers who feared that increased competition would result, the bill was enacted in 1849 and the price of government bonds promptly rose.[43]

Aided, then, by government action on many fronts to alleviate monetary tightness, federal credit firmed and Corcoran & Riggs profited in proportion. In the spring of 1849, when the bonds of 1848 climbed above 115, the firm felt confident enough to enter the market as a buyer. It continued to trade profitably and, although the price leveled off, maintained an inventory of well over $1 million of government securities which were used as collateral to borrow at interest rates lower than they bore. The borrowed money, in turn, financed a rising volume of investment banking, especially in railroad and state bonds. Corcoran explained these considerations to more conservative European financiers who criticized his "tenacity" in holding federal securities. His policy was determined partly by expectations of inflation incited by the mounting flow of recently discovered California gold. But he also grasped the renewed vigor of the American appetite for capital and the fresh willingness of Europeans to try to satisfy that appetite by absorbing American securities.

Liquidation was not begun until December 1849. Prices remained on a plateau of about 116 to 120. The only sales as low as 114 were made in February 1850 when the crisis over slavery seemed to be growing critical. When Daniel Webster made his famous Seventh of March speech in favor of compromise, Corcoran expressed his gratitude by tearing up $7,000 of the orator's overdue notes and sending him a check for an additional $1,000. Besides being a generous and sincere gesture of support for moderation, the gift represented an accurate estimate of the value of the speech in sparking a recovery of prices to earlier levels. Still, even after passage of the Compromise of 1850, continuing controversy over the Fugitive Slave Act spurred Corcoran's determination to liquidate federal securities. At least $1.25 million were sold by the firm in 1850, as well as much or all of Corcoran's personal holdings.[44]

Mexican War finance and government patronage made Corcoran a man of wealth. His half of the firm's profit was $43,000 on July 1, 1847, and $138,000 three months later, and he made well over $100,000 on Treasury notes on his personal account. These were the last substantial divisions of profit before constitution of the second Corcoran & Riggs partnership on July 1, 1848. In 1849, Corcoran's three-quarter share of the earnings yielded $130,000; in 1850, $120,000. He also made about $140,000 from the 1848 bonds on his personal account. By contrast, in 1851, after the liquidation of the loan of 1848 had been completed, the senior partner's share declined to $84,000 and the following year to $71,000. This decline reflects the contraction of government activity in the money markets. That the government business was still valuable in peacetime and prosperity is indicated by the drop in Corcoran's dividend to $43,000 in 1853, the first year after the severance of relations by the Treasury.[45]

5

The Mexican Indemnity: A Chapter in Finance, Diplomacy, and Politics

We do not do business exclusively for gain. I am of Sydney Smith's opinion that "there is something else in the world besides the almighty dollar."
—Baring Brothers to William H. Aspinwall[1]

To the casual observer, the transfer of the Mexican indemnity might appear to have been routine. It consisted of the down payment and four annual installments of $3 million each (plus 6 percent annual interest on the balance outstanding) owed by the United States under the Treaty of Guadalupe Hidalgo for the territory taken in the Mexican War. Yet, circumstance and the rules of the game entangled this operation in a complex of conflicts: the competition of businessmen, great and small; the self-interest of creditors and debtors; the ambitions and plights of nations; and the rivalries of politicians.[2]

Mexican Debts and Beckoning Profits

Mexico, weak and fragmented before the war with America, was in even greater difficulties afterward. There were chronic, enormous budget deficits and, more serious, a huge burden of debts incurred in foreign and domestic flotations. The British debt alone, represented by the Committee of Mexican Bondholders, exceeded 50 million pesos, and large sums were owed to citizens of France and Spain. Obligations of domestic origin totaled 40 million pesos or more, much of which was held by foreign residents. Payments on the national debt had been defaulted at the beginning of the war, and foreign governments pressed for their resumption. Interior creditors also exerted heavy pressure. Yet, revenues were scarcely half the operating expenses of the government, estimated at 16 million pesos for the fiscal years 1849 and 1850. The government tried to borrow for current needs at 1 percent per month, without success.[3]

Thus, not only did the indemnity transfer seem attractive as an exchange operation, but loans of the money in advance of stipulated payment dates promised to earn substantial interest. In the fall of 1848 Corcoran, in London for his loan negotiation, held preliminary discussions with Baring Brothers; two months later they agreed to bid for the transfer as equal partners. The Barings' influential Mexican correspondent, Manning & Mackintosh (who were soon to fail, however), was given a 20 percent interest. Corcoran was in charge of matters in Washington.[4] The anticipated profits aroused competition. Foremost were the Rothschilds whose agent in Mexico, Lionel Davidson, had furnished exchange for American forces there and who, with agent August Belmont in New York, had handled part of the 1848 treaty down payment without profit to gain favor for future installment transfers. Their quarrel smoothed over, Belmont made cordial overtures to Corcoran for an alliance. But the greatest harassment was destined to come from a smaller house, Hargous Brothers: Louis and Peter, American citizens and merchant bankers of Mexico City and New York.[5]

The Goal of Interocean Transit

Hargous Brothers enjoyed support because it had obtained from the hard-pressed Manning & Mackintosh an interest in the Garay grant, a concession of land and right-of-way across the Tehuantepec Isthmus for a road, canal, or railway linking the Atlantic and Pacific Oceans. The Hargouses were to have a 10 percent commission on the sale of the grant, or an equivalent participation if the Manning & Mackintosh group formed a company to develop the concession. The purpose of the Hargous' serving as front men was "to Americanize" the project. By enlisting American capital, a plank road might be built quickly to draw California traffic that had been using the Panama route. Federal engineering and even financial assistance would be sought for a railroad. Most important, the United States would be asked to seek a treaty with Mexico giving rights of intervention, without which there seemed no hope of attracting investors in view of the country's chronic instability. Minister to Mexico Nathan Clifford proposed that Hargous Brothers manage the indemnity transfers and use them as a lever to compel acceptance of a treaty.

But there were rival ambitions. A steamer service from New Orleans to Vera Cruz was projected by New Orleans interests and southern imperialists such as Senators David Yulee and Henry S. Foote. Powerful New Yorkers promoted a Panama route, and westerners, led by Senator Thomas Hart Benton of Missouri, wanted a transcontinental railroad. The major achievement of these groups was to frustrate each other.[6]

Polk's Conciliatory Policy Aborted

Rivals for the indemnity transfer had to reckon with Treasury Secretary Walker's continued favoritism toward Corcoran & Riggs as government bankers. Just as Walker was ready to accept the firm's proposal of a 3 percent premium for the 1849 installment, Hargous Brothers bid 4 percent. Other higher bids were reportedly forthcoming. Walker warned Corcoran, whose prompt offer of 4½ percent was immediately accepted. The figure, although higher than planned, was expected to yield a handsome profit.[7]

Installments were payable each May 30 in Mexico's capital in her silver coin. The logical technique was to accumulate silver there by selling foreign exchange, especially the prime international money, sterling (bills on London), to any in Mexico who wished to transfer funds abroad. (Similarly, the dollars that were the source of the indemnity payment would be converted into sterling exchange or otherwise credited to the English contractors.) Thus the expensive carrying, insurance, and interest costs of shipping coin to Mexico would be avoided. Patience and skill were essential, for the primitive Mexican money market could absorb only limited offerings without forcing the exchange rate below profitable levels. Pending payment date, accumulated funds could be advanced to the needy government at handsome interest rates. This meant, however, that unless Walker could be persuaded to advance Treasury funds before the payment date, the contractors might have to remove large sums from their ordinary business, a move Corcoran & Riggs could ill afford.[8]

The administration was inclined to cooperate in the interest of its Mexican policy. Once his territorial goals were achieved by the Treaty of Guadalupe Hidalgo, Polk had inaugurated a rapprochement. The President hoped to frustate "the machinations of foreign governments injurious to the United States" and persuade Mexico to reduce its "absurd and unreasonable tariff." He wished to support the Herrera regime, which was liberal in domestic politics and gave priority in foreign policy to friendly relations with the United States. Threatened by a conservative military rebellion and distracted by Indian warfare, the Mexican government asked for American troops—transported, maintained, and paid out of the indemnity—to help restore internal security. This plea was regretfully refused, although some surplus military equipment was sold to Mexico. The Mexican government managed to suppress the rebellion, but severely strained finances led to a request for advances out of the indemnity. President Polk declined, although "deeply impressed" by Clifford's supporting letter, on the grounds that agreement would necessitate a new treaty which a hostile Congress would refuse to ratify. However he kept open the possibility of reconsideration and eventually made plans to ask Congress to authorize advances.[9]

Before this decision could be implemented, leaders of the opposition Whigs in Congress learned of the existence of a "protocol" to the peace treaty and mounted a partisan attack. As signed, the treaty had given Mexico negotiable certificates of indemnity with the option of having the entire outstanding amount paid at any time after two years. Fearing the money might be used to resume the conflict, the Senate deleted these provisions before ratifying. Their financial predicament caused the Mexicans to resist the alteration; therefore, the American commissioners agreed to the protocol. It stated, among other things, that the treaty amendments were not intended to limit Mexico's right to convey the $12 million (plus interest) remaining due. In February 1849 the Whigs charged the protocol had unconstitutionally altered the treaty without the consent of the Senate. The administration defended itself by asserting that the protocol did not change the treaty—in other words, the protocol was meaningless. The Mexicans, unable to do anything about it, could only object in a prolonged correspondence.[10]

In view of congressional hostility Polk gave up his plan to speed payments. Walker, by this time a lame duck, had been negotiating with Corcoran for the 1850 installment but declined to commit his successor. Sensitive to partisan criticism, he limited advances to $1 million in order to leave the Treasury with a large surplus. The outgoing Secretary attached an ambiguous condition which reflected conflicting motives: on the one hand he wanted to assist Mexico; on the other he feared being charged with making a bad bargain. In a confidential instruction he limited the rate the contractors could charge Mexico on funds advanced by the United States to the treaty rate of 6 percent, with any excess to be turned over to the Treasury. Thus the contractors had no incentive to charge a higher rate, yet any failure to earn more would be their responsibility. But another way was found to sweeten the bargain: the $1 million was paid Corcoran & Riggs in 1847 Treasury notes at par. The profits were considerable, for the notes were selling on the open market at 107 or more.[11]

The Taylor Administration and the First Installment

The new administration was hardly enthusiastic about having Corcoran & Riggs as a government banker; at the same time Corcoran suspected that friends of President Taylor were angling for the indemnity. Samuel Jaudon, former lieutenant of Nicholas Biddle, sought the agency with the aid of Daniel Webster and his "Ministers of Finance" (as Thomas Ward termed them), Richard M. Blatchford and Edward Curtis. Curtis was a director of the Bank of Commerce and had acted as an intermediary between the high Whig element on Wall Street and Secretary Walker; Blatchford was a close friend, business agent, and ex-law partner of William Seward.

Corcoran feared that Taylor's friend, Baylie Peyton, would be appointed minister to Mexico and assist a rival transfer syndicate. Peyton had been prominent in New Orleans as a politician, lawyer, and businessman. He was believed to be connected with the Hargouses, whose chief support for their isthmian scheme came from New Orleans and who thought they had the advantage. But, as intended, Corcoran's contract with Walker and the steps already taken doomed any competing ambitions.[12]

The contractors sought additional advances from Walker's successor, Philadelphian William Meredith, but he was wary of Corcoran. The latter apealed to Newbold to apply pressure. "He is evidently a timid man and such is his character in Phil.," Corcoran wrote. "I think a remonstration [*sic*] from your city by letter and through the newspapers would wake him up." Such influential Whig friends in Boston and New York as merchant Abbott Lawrence and publisher James Watson Webb obligingly wrote the new secretary citing tight money and the accumulation of specie in the sub-Treasury. The inexperienced Meredith, groping for a policy, procrastinated until the end of April when the Treasury surplus became positively embarrassing. He then agreed to a $1 million advance request and offered an additional $670,000.

Baring Brothers did not welcome the advances made at Washington. Indeed, the Britons were startled to learn of the size of Corcoran's borrowing from the Treasury and feared it was excessive for current conditions, which found money in plentiful supply. Corcoran had been trying to hypothecate or sell $500,000 to $1 million of his United States bonds. The Barings believed, perhaps unfairly, that he wanted the advances so that, lacking profitable alternatives, they would agree to accept his bonds as collateral for loans. The Barings were resentful but could only acquiesce and lend him the money. Meanwhile, in Mexico, $800,000 had been profitably advanced to the government and another $1 million had been promised in January by Manning & Mackintosh. This was the Barings' share of a loan of $2.3 million by a consortium of bankers, much of it spent to put down another insurrection. The loan to the impecunious government was secured by the indemnity, the collateral remaining under the control of the contractors.[13]

But the Barings' special indemnity agent in Mexico, Francis deP. Falconnet, ran into difficulties. Exchange made available by the flow of trade was limited and capital was fleeing the chaotic country. Most important, perhaps, the California gold discoveries caused a sharp fall in sterling exchange rates. Britain was on the gold standard; Mexico was on the silver standard. From an initial 43¼ d. per dollar (or peso) the rate rose to 46½ by the time Falconnet completed the operation early in June. Unable to raise $3.72 million in exchange, he was fortunate to be able to borrow $20,000 at 1 percent per month from other lenders to the government, who were induced to comply with his needs by the fact that he controlled the collateral for their loans, the indemnity.[14]

As an exchange operation it had not been worth the trouble, Falconnet concluded, but interest on advances to the government compensated fully. The profits were £36,000, about 4½ percent. The loans to Mexico had been made at 1 percent per month, but the United States was not credited with the excess beyond ½ percent as Walker's contract had stipulated. Ward told Meredith, quite falsely, that Treasury funds had not been received in time to advance them to Mexico. The profits were sizeable, although not much more than Baring Brothers thought justified to cover the risks (which Falconnet, however, considered slight) and leave a fair profit. Moreover, Falconnet had been disadvantaged by a late start because the appropriation had been delayed in Congress. Since the bill as finally enacted included the appropriation for 1850, the agent for the next installment would have ample time to accumulate exchange in Mexico. Utilizing the power of Baring Brothers, Falconnet could dominate the market and give advances to the government at rates just below those of its usual creditors, but still higher than any other available investment.[15]

The Barings' sole reservations concerned their Washington ally. Corcoran does not understand business, they repeatedly complained. The American considered himself a peer of the Barings; they did not. "Corcoran should be kept in order, and must learn to follow orders strictly," wrote Baring partner Joshua Bates. Moreover, Bates learned during a visit to Washington that his ally was distrusted by the Taylor administration: "in every instance [cabinet members] would talk with me more freely when Corcoran was away. Mr. Corcoran's being on the other side in politics may operate against him but I judge his good-natured disposition and willingness to take trouble to oblige will in time give him the same sort of standing with the present administration that he had with the late one." But care was taken not to mention his name in dealings with the government. In September 1849, when Corcoran visited England, Bates decided he was under control, reasoning that the alliance had become important enough to prevent his going into opposition. Moreover, Corcoran, although "loose and not very clever . . . desires to be respectable and to connect himself with respectable people." For his part Corcoran suspected the cool and hesitant Barings of reneging on their understanding and contemplated collaboration with the Rothschilds. Thus marred by mutual suspicion, the Corcoran-Baring alliance came close to dissolution.[16]

Clayton Muddles Toward a New Policy

Neither Meredith nor the new Secretary of State, John M. Clayton, wanted the responsibility of picking among the contestants for coming installments.[17] Clayton expressed a quaint distaste for dealing with "speculators" and "brokers," and both politicians seemed to be trying to avoid the "odium of a bargain with Bankers." Furthermore, Clayton preferred a proposal made by the Mexican government: payment by drafts at New York or Washington, with a 5½ percent premium to the United States and 6 percent interest on advances, in contrast to which the Baring group would only offer a 2½ percent premium. Mexico could recoup most or all of the charges by the profits on the transfer while saving part of the heavy interest extracted by local capitalists. The Secretary also hoped the plan would smooth the path to a Tehuantepec treaty, which he had given the highest priority in relations between the two countries. Unfortunately, the beleaguered Mexican government was unable to obtain prompt legislative approval of the new arrangement. Still, Clayton tried to keep the road open. At the end of 1849 he transferred responsibility for the next installment to the newly appointed minister to Mexico, ex-governor of Kentucky Robert P. Letcher, with full discretion to negotiate drafts and to use this power to promote a Tehuantepec agreement.[18]

When the new minister departed for Mexico, Corcoran, under the illusion that the field was still open for the 1850 payment, arranged for John Parrott, an American consul traveling with Letcher, to act as his agent in return for a small interest. En route Letcher assured Parrott that if he, as representative of an American house, offered terms equal "in every respect" to those offered by a foreign house, "as at present advised," the American house would "most decidedly" be preferred. Governor Letcher was famous in his day as a comedian-politician, and Parrott, a born straight man, sent the letter to his private employer as proof that he had the inside track.[19]

By the time Letcher arrived in Mexico the situation was changed: the legislature had authorized an advance by draft on Washington for part of the 1850 installment. The government had already borrowed $1.54 million from the powerful Jecker, Torre & Co., which forwarded drafts to its New York correspondent, Howland & Aspinwall, for collection at the United States Treasury. Predictably, the major Mexican houses united behind Jecker, Torre to impose harsh terms on Letcher, offering a low premium of 1 percent for the remaining $2 million. This offer was not entirely due to ruthlessness: perhaps $3 million of coin was fleeing the country and the imminent failure of the prominent Manning & Mackintosh caused a near panic. Increasingly nervous, Letcher lowered his terms from 5 to 4 percent.

The minister worked closely with Hargous, partly because he had some influence and partly in hopes of promoting the Tehuantepec project. Letcher gladly accepted the offer by Rothschild agent Lionel Davidson of a 3½ percent premium plus 6 percent interest on advances. Hargous received a ½ percent finder's fee from the Mexican government, in accordance with the usual practice there. In view of market conditions and the hostility of the Jecker group, Davidson and his associates were taking serious risks. Corcoran & Riggs, who had a ⅖ option with the Rothschild group through August Belmont, thought the risks too great and declined to participate. The terms had been made extraordinarily favorable in hopes of gaining preference for the last two installments, for which 4 percent was offered with the added inducement that the same rate would be applied to the current transfer. It is doubtful that the Rothschild group broke even on the 1850 installment; it was estimated they lost £15,000 while Jecker, Torre made double that working against them.

Ironically, had Letcher held out a day or two longer he might have been able to implement Clayton's understanding with the Mexican minister, for the bitterly factionalized legislature be-

The Corcoran House, Lafayette Square, Washington, D.C. James Renwick, Architect. The center building was erected in 1819. In 1849, the new front, additional story, and gallery on the west wing were added. In 1850, the east wing, comprising the dining room and library, was added. Courtesy David E. Finley, Washington, D.C.

W. W. Corcoran, early in his career. Engraving from a portrait by Charles Martin, 1852. Courtesy Boston Public Library.

latedly authorized the government to accept payment in bills on Washington at 5½ percent. Letcher had succeeded in making funds immediately available to Mexico at a relatively low charge, but lost 2 percent on the premium. Moreover, he failed to advance his Tehuantepec diplomacy. In the end he would not threaten to withhold the indemnity to promote the isthmian project, although he termed it "the only possible card that can be played with effect," unless Clayton gave his specific "order or approbation." Letcher would not take responsibility for making threats that were so flagrant a violation of the peace treaty. Instead of the expected pat on the back Letcher received a reprimand from his friend, the Secretary, although Clayton's hesitant and vague instructions were partly responsible for the disappointment.[20]

Debts, Development, and Bribery

The Barings reconsidered their position for the 1851 installment and joined with Jecker, Torre and their American correspondents, Howland & Aspinwall. The latter, wealthy old hands in Latin American trade, were close to Secretary Meredith and, as Whigs, seemed more appropriate as Washington agents than the distrusted Corcoran. The Mexican house, replacing the now defunct Manning & Mackintosh, was a still more important source of strength. Juan B. Jecker, the managing partner, had risen steadily in power and riches. His firm's estimated resources of $800,000 were kept highly liquid, in contrast to residents with comparable wealth who invested heavily in land, mines, and occasionally even in manufacturing. In addition, the firm was backed by Gregorio Mier y Teran, a relative of the Spanish silent partner, Torre; he was believed to be the richest man in the country, worth $2 million to $3 million and enjoying commensurate political power. The house was rated the strongest in the country and Jecker was acknowledged to be preeminent in ability. The Barings considered dropping Corcoran & Riggs but William Aspinwall, active in Washington and a past director of the Bank of America, advised against it. Ward agreed and his principals conceded that Corcoran & Riggs should be included, if only to keep it from joining Belmont. The preliminary division of interest reflected these judgments: Jecker, Torre was to be offered one-quarter and Howland & Aspinwall one-eighth, later raised to one-quarter; Corcoran & Riggs was allowed only one-eighth.[21]

Belmont also renewed his efforts, volunteering to coordinate them with Letcher's for a Tehuantepec treaty. He promised Letcher entire control of advances, giving him "a most powerful political influence in the affairs of Mexico which in the present distracted state of that country is of the utmost importance. The arrangement we propose would put a similar negotiation of the Mexican authorities as the one with Jecker, Torre & Co. for 1½ millions and by which they became quite independent of the American Minister's paying or withholding the installment, quite out of the question." But Clayton warded off all proposals on the pretext that he could not negotiate until Congress passed the appropriation.[22]

In fact, Clayton was already committed to a proposition by a group including the Democratic editor-politician, Duff Green; his son Ben E. Green, Clayton's protégé and like his father an ex-diplomat in Mexico; and Isaac Domingo Marks, a merchant of Mexico and New Orleans. The Greens, experienced Mexican claims lawyers, also sought a Mexican concession for a railroad along the Gila Valley in the later Gadsden Purchase tract. They naturally asked Clayton's support for this as an American interest, and naturally they suggested use of indemnity advances as a lever. When Marks first approached the Greens he thought he could get a 25 percent premium for the indemnity transfer through his intimacy with the new Mexican President, Mariano Arista. This extravagant figure was later modified. As finally worked out, Mexico was to accept drafts on Washington in payment of the rest of the indemnity. The United States would receive a 4½ percent premium, plus the usual 6 percent interest on advances, out of the 8 percent commission the agents were to receive from Mexico. Duff Green recited the inevitable arguments that, in addition to the higher premium and the interest, the plan would increase American influence while strengthening a friendly regime and sparing it harsh charges for loans in Mexico.[23]

Such loans really were a prime means by which the Mexican treasury was bled. In a memorandum on the principal houses of Mexico, Baring agent Francis Falconnet characterized various of them as having "made on several occasions advances to the Government which have given him great profits," "made their fortune in transactions with the Government," "has no mercy for the Government in money transactions and he knows the value of every man in power," and so on. Two-thirds of the native and many of the foreign houses were so portrayed. Falconnet considered the level of ethics virtually depraved: "But what is morality in Mexico? in that respect none are to be trusted—cheating is cleverness, they call it 'viveza.' " One exceptional Mexican businessman stands out oddly: "Has the reputation of being a very honest man . . . he has constantly refused to make advances to the Government."[24] Edmond J. Forstall, a New Orleans banker representing interests hostile to Marks and the Greens, conceded that Mexico would gain considerably by their proposal, even if the premium were 10 percent through not having to borrow at an expected 2 percent per month. Nonetheless, the planned 3½ percent commission (with perhaps added interest on advances) would have yielded a large, if not exorbitant, profit of $100,000 per installment.

Marks, who had conceived the scheme, was to take charge in Mexico and the Greens at Washington, each group sharing equally. But well-placed allies were needed. The Greens signed R. W. Latham, a Washington banker who could provide financing; William A. Bradley, Whig party wheelhorse and postmaster of Washington; and Democrat Bernhart Henn, a minor Polk appointee who was soon to become Congressman from Iowa. They in turn enlisted "sundry important men," important enough to make success appear certain and to be worth a 1 percent commission. Perhaps this explains Clayton's spleen when the mails brought belated word of Letcher's contract for the 1850 installment. But arrangements were expedited for 1851–1852.

In Mexico the major political ally was Manuel Payno y Flores. A young moderate liberal and the son of an important politician, he was about to become minister of finance under Herrera and his successor, Mariano Arista. Probably Payno was involved at the inception of the scheme; in fact, the prospective spoils may have helped him gain the ministry. He was to have one-third of the commission, doubtless to be shared with others. The Hargouses, too, were involved. Payno wholeheartedly favored their Tehuantepec program, which was an integral part of his plans to stimulate economic development by collaboration with foreign capital.[25]

Tehuantepec had been the major external question complicating the indemnity transfer, but another cross-current roiled the waters: the conflicting claims on the Mexican public debt. Payno was a member of the Junta del Credito Publico, an official body including important legislators, creditors, and financiers attempting to resuscitate public revenues and refund the debt. He planned to use indemnity advances to pay part of the debt and meet current deficits while finances were comprehensively reorganized. At the same time he hoped to attract support from powerful creditor groups.

Having concluded his deal with Marks, in July 1850 Payno officially asked for Washington's prepayment of the balance of the indemnity. Clayton had already verbally agreed with the Mexican minister to accede to this request.[26]

"The God-like Daniel," the Golden Calf, and the Use of Power

Suddenly the situation was transformed—President Taylor was dead. Millard Fillmore succeeded him, and on July 22, 1850, Daniel Webster replaced Clayton at the State Department. Webster had intimate ties to the Barings, having long been retained as their counsel. They were also among the contributors who had raised hundreds of thousands of dollars for him during several decades, including $40,000 just solicited. Corcoran was, of course, persona grata for his gift of $8,000 after Webster's Seventh of March oration that year. Now a one-twelfth interest was set aside by the Baring consortium for Samuel Jaudon, who had been seeking the indemnity agency with Webster's support. Since there is not the faintest scrap of evidence that Jaudon did anything whatever, one may draw one's own conclusion as to what or whom the money was for. The contract was so much divided that no one would make a great profit, Joshua Bates complained, but he must have realized that this was one reason for the coalition's success.[27]

The new Secretary acted quickly to secure the agency for his friends. Conveniently, Belmont had only renewed his offer to Clayton verbally; Webster deemed it to have lapsed. Clayton also failed to inform him of the verbal agreement with Mexico, enabling the Secretary to pretend ignorance of her wishes—although actually he knew of them at least ten days earlier. The premium agreed on with the Baring group was 3½ percent, below the rival offers. The Treasury was to make interest-free advances to the contractors: on this point Webster feigned disapproval, but only until the appropriations bill had safely passed both houses of Congress. No restrictions were placed upon advances to Mexico. Corcoran managed the negotiation with Webster, and in the reapportionment his firm and Howland & Aspinwall emerged with 4/18 each and the Barings 10/18 of what remained of the profits after prior deductions of 7/32 for Jecker, Torre and 1/12 for Jaudon.[28]

The next battle took place in the House of Representatives. The floor manager there for the appropriations bill was Corcoran's friend, Thomas Bayly, a mover in the just-concluded intersectional Compromise of 1850. Prudence dictated that money be requested only for the 1851 installment. Critics who cited Belmont's higher bid were countered with the assertion that it had expired. Other members who pleaded Mexico's wishes, including Louisiana supporters of the Tehuantepec scheme, were told that she had made no official request concerning the method of payment. Bayly, himself a Democrat, deterred partisan attacks against the Whig administration by revealing Walker's 1849 bonus to the contractors through advances in Treasury notes at par when their market value was 108. Consistency required criticism of both Democrat Walker and Whig Webster, or neither; the members all consistently criticized neither.

Various more or less specious arguments were used in the administration's defense. Payment in the United States would not be to the letter of the treaty, it was argued. (A year later A. P. Edgerton [Dem., O.] pointed out that the advances already made were substantially identical in method to those Mexico requested.) Bayly asserted that if the government were overthrown a new regime might claim payment again: "We know what sort of people these Mexicans are; and we know what sort of faith they keep. They are constantly revolutionizing their Government. By a pronunciamento a President is made and by a pronunciamento a President is removed." Objections from the floor forced him to withdraw his contemptuous references to "these Mexicans": "Why the shortest way is to take it all back; I suppose everyone understood my remark to be jocular." Bayly even moralized that it would be improper to "shave our own paper" by charging Mexico a premium in a direct negotiation. Presumably it was proper to do so indirectly.

The most vocal opposition came from a remnant of radical Jacksonians whose criticisms, even when pertinent and telling, were vitiated by emotional outbursts against bankers as a class. One such critic, David Cartter of Ohio, was more effective than most: "Messrs. Corcoran & Riggs, of this city, are men of high respectability, of that there is no question. The Chairman of the Committee of Ways and Means [Bayly] is unwilling to shave Mexico: but he is quite willing to shave these bankers. Shave bankers! Shave Corcoran & Riggs! Why, sir, they live by shaving." Underlining the dollar gains to the Treasury by direct payments to the minister at Washington, Cartter continued that Mexico, "a sister Republic, who we know needs aid and assistance," should have the advantage of the operation instead of the "voracious bankers. . . . I had supposed that the time had gone by when it was necessary to encourage banks and bankers," he continued innocently; "I had supposed that General Jackson had given the finishing blow to the system." But the appropriation passed by a 128 to 36 vote.

In the Senate, Daniel Dickinson of New York led the floor fight. Pierre Soulé of Louisiana opposed him on behalf of the Greens and Hargouses, but his amendments were defeated 34 to 11 and the appropriation passed. Corcoran earned the praises of Thomas Ward and Edward Curtis for his lobbying. "I had so many and such unscrupulous adversaries that I had to keep myself in constant communication with members," he wrote, perhaps exaggerating somewhat. "It has however been handsomely done and at *not much cost* considering what we had to do."[29]

Meanwhile, during the summer and autumn of 1850, Payno's debt-refunding schemes labored through the Mexican Congress. The liberals' claim of a national majority was apparently borne out by the fall elections. But the conservatives controlled the Senate, which held, in Forstall's words, the wealth and talent of the nation, and divisions among the liberals weakened their effectiveness in the Chamber of Deputies. Moreover, there were sharp conflicts of interest among the Mexican creditors as well as with and among the foreign. Thus, legislative approval of Payno's plan for drafts on the American Treasury was delayed until after the change of administration in Washington, when it was too late.

During 1850 the necessary laws were finally enacted: on October 14 the British debt, with arrears of interest, was reduced to 51 million pesos at 3 percent; on November 30 the internal debts were consolidated in a single fund estimated—in fact underestimated—at 32½ million pesos at the same rate. The (British) Committee of Mexican Bondholders was to receive $2.5 million and the domestic creditors $2.36 million in two installments from the remaining indemnity payments. The government was to pay 6 percent interest until treaty payment dates. After debt payments $1.68 million would be retained for current expenditures while revenue reforms went forward.[30]

However, by October the government had been forced to borrow $700,000, and the recognition spread rapidly that funds would not be available to both maintain the government and carry out the new agreements. Some leeway was gained through a modification of the Act of November 30: interior creditors would keep only half the agreed sums, the rest remaining on loan to the Treasury as a current liability. Payments of certain other interior debts, which had been proceeding piecemeal, were suspended. Even these measures were inadequate and the government was unable to stem disintegration. Race wars and Indian conflicts raged in Yucatan and the North. The army had been weakened in efforts to ease budgetary strains, its pay was in arrears and mutinies erupted sporadically. The civil service was also unpaid and corruption was rampant. Tariff increases for fiscal and protective purposes proved self-defeating by curtailing open trade, while smuggling thrived. Much of the government's declining revenue was in receivership to foreign creditors. From the conclusion of peace to the end of 1850 creditors had been paid $16.5 million, most of which fled the country. Government leaders began to show signs of desperation.[31]

Payno, clinging to his program, took a leaf from the Yankee book by coupling indemnity advances with Tehuantepec. An isthmian transit treaty was signed, but it did not include the rights of intervention demanded by the Americans. No Mexican government, Letcher insisted, could make such a surrender of sovereignty and survive. At the same time, Payno tried to appeal past the intransigent Webster to his American cabinet counterpart, Secretary of the Treasury Thomas Corwin. He pleaded for Washington's acceptance of Mexican drafts for indemnity prepayments; simultaneously, he suggested that explicit intervention rights in Tehuantepec would be superfluous since "the U.S. may by the law of nations have its naval forces in the waters of the port of Tehuantepec." Payno missed the point. What Webster wanted was the open and acknowledged right, by treaty, to use force on any necessary occasion by executive decision. He did not want a continuous and costly commitment, nor did he want any future intervention subjected to the uncertainties of the need for congressional authorization. In any case Payno's approach to Corwin was ill-advised; he had already agreed to support Webster's course. Appeals were addressed to Fillmore but, not a strong President in any case, he accepted the determination of his powerful cabinet members. The indemnity remained in Webster's hands and he would make no concessions.[32]

The contractors were finally able to proceed with the 1851 installment. Edmond J. Forstall, their new agent in Mexico, began making money—and enemies. Brilliant, aggressive, rather egotistical, he wanted to do good and do well; in case of conflict the latter would take priority. Some of the erstwhile lenders offered to join him in advances to the government, threatening to force his rate below ½ percent per month if he refused. Forstall called the bluff. None would risk advancing against the indemnity without the collateral afforded by its control, which he alone possessed. With the same weapon Forstall also forced his rivals to discount with him their earlier advances of $450,000.

The Louisianan also broke custom and antagonized politicians by slashing the fee for the government's broker. In financial transactions Mexico had always employed an intermediary to whom the businessman paid a commission, usually ½ per cent but sometimes as much as 1½ percent. This was a lucrative morsel of patronage. It was also an anachronistic device for saving face (although useful, given Hispanic sensitivity, since the broker did the necessary bargaining and yielding). Perhaps Clayton would have valued such a custom, but Forstall considered it nonsense. He thought himself generous in permitting the message carrier a ⅛ percent commission as a gesture to native mores. Doubtless among Forstall's pleasures was the fact that the brokers included José and Antonio Suarez, friends and allies of the troublesome Hargous Brothers, Payno, Arista, and other antagonists. Payno, mortified, interceded uselessly.[33]

From the first it had been understood that interest on advances to Mexico would be the most lucrative source of profit.

With money relatively easy, Forstall commenced advances at 1¼ percent per month, compared to the earlier 2 percent for the first $200,000 and 1½ percent for the next $500,000. He congratulated himself for hastening to the presidential palace to offer loans at the time a military uprising flared: all other financiers had refused to make offers until it was certain the government would survive. He flattered himself that his rate was the lowest on record. It was, but only by ¼ percent, and that differential soon disappeared when he raised the rate to 1½ percent per month. At this point competition reappeared: Payno, his personal resentment whetting his desire to favor collaborators and compatriots, managed to find security for loans of $400,000 at 1⅜ percent to 1½ percent. Thereafter, he again had to borrow from Forstall at 1½ percent per month, with one $50,000 loan at 1⅝ percent. Altogether, $200,000 in interest was cleared by the Baring group from advances of $2.337 million from December 14, 1850 to the end of the following May. The overall profit of about 4 percent on the 1851 installment met Baring Brothers' standards for such operations; but Falconnet, Forstall told them, "has been opposed all along to my rates of interest as altogether out of place with your habitual liberality in matters of money."[34]

Demoralization and Success

In the winter of 1850–1851 Payno had to face the consequences of his miscalculations. Misled and frustrated by administrative chaos and incompetence, political opposition, his own over-optimism, and a ravaging cholera epidemic, he underestimated the interior debt by 20 percent and overestimated revenues. Unable to stabilize the government while satisfying all creditors, he belatedly had to devise some order of priorities. Payno chose to favor domestic creditors to strenghten his political base and in hopes of keeping some of the money in the country. He did not wish to alienate overseas investors (although he resented their demands as tainted with fraud and usury), but a reflux of funds from Europe was hardly to be expected; difficult though it would be to bring about, there was greater hope for repatriation or emergence from hiding of native and resident capital. Finally, Payno sought to draw American investment, with the Tehuantepec scheme intended as the first inducement.

Despite his proffered assurances, foreign creditors doubted whether Payno would or could consummate their agreement. Under the original plan resident and external creditors were to share in each of the last two indemnity installments; this was changed in order to pay the interior creditors immediately and hold off the British until 1852. The advances negotiated with Forstall were entirely for the interior creditors. More ominously, Payno brought about passage of a law enabling the government to unilaterally abrogate contracts it considered onerous.[35]

Meanwhile, the desperate government pleaded for American aid going far beyond indemnity advances. President Arista, Payno, and other liberals asked for United States support as a counterweight to the European powers. (Their conservative opponents viewed the Yankees as the ideological and historical enemy.) Arista was later quoted as seeing no hope for his country except in an inevitable American annexation. He made no effort to bring this about while president, probably because it would have meant political suicide—unless his response later in 1851 to Webster's threat of force over Tehuantepec should be read as a kind of invitation:

> Your government is strong; ours is weak. You have the power to take the whole or any portion of our territory you may think fit; we have not the [ability] to resist. We have done all we could do to satisfy your country and to gratify you personally. We can do no more.[36]

However, through Forstall, Arista did ask for a commitment of a scope not to be undertaken by American foreign policy for at least a generation. In November 1850, before being sworn in as President, he sent Webster a long analysis of Mexico's plight. Strongly emphasizing race as a cause of discord, Arista went beyond Herrera's earlier requests for aid, suggesting joint military action under United States command to train Mexican troops and control smuggling and Indian warfare. Mexico would bear the costs, presumably out of indemnity funds. Arista begged for a treaty of "peace, union and fraternity . . . a family Compact between the two Republics, the eldest and most powerful giving to the youngest countenance and dignity with other nations and aiding through its ministers and otherwise in its work of reorganization and regeneration." Not least among possible objections to this plan, the prospect of interceding with European creditor powers on behalf of what he considered the impossible Mexicans must have astonished Webster. There is no indication of either response to or comment upon this despairing plea.[37]

With futile persistence drafts for the entire indemnity were again sent to Washington early in 1851. Letcher, quite cynical about the policies he was called upon to execute, supported Payno's efforts, even attempting to bypass Webster, but was rebuffed when he sought an audience with President Fillmore while home on leave. Congress was approached again when the appropriation for the last installment came due in February 1851, but few there (or in the press) would risk speaking on the arcana of finance—and most of those who did were obviously not knowledgeable. This time the assault on the administration was led by abolitionists and Free-Soilers at war with Webster for his role in the Compromise of 1850. Most notable was the exposé by Charles Allen of Massachusetts of the $44,000 gift to Webster the previous summer. The uproar forced postponement of the last appropriation until the next session of Congress a year later, when it easily passed after a rehearsal of the earlier debates.[38] Meanwhile in Mexico Forstall counterattacked where Payno had left himself vulnerable, exposing his deal with Marks and Green and the miscalculations of his financial programs. The discredited Payno was driven from office by March 1851. He was charged with, among other things, having advised his successor to disregard the October 14 law; instead, the internal debt settlement was suspended.[39]

Fearful that the penurious debtor might yet renounce the October 14 law, the British bondholders bent their efforts toward obtaining direct payment by the United States of the money Mexico had pledged from the indemnity. As early as 1847, the Committee of Mexican Bondholders, supported by British diplomats and the Barings, had asked Washington for such a diversion of money from the forthcoming indemnity. The Polk administration had refused to intervene.[40] The approach was repeated to Clayton in 1849, but he stalled the British while working with Green and Payno.

Webster was much more cooperative. Clayton had instructed Letcher that if part of the indemnity were used to pay creditors of other countries, equal treatment would be expected for Americans. But when the American minister accordingly protested with representatives of other powers against the law favoring British creditors, Webster instructed him to cease in tacit cooperation with the British.[41]

The Secretary of State deferred any written commitments for the last indemnity installment until the last appropriation was passed. His reputation for Anglophilia had long been a political liability among American redcoat-baiters. In addition, the earlier congressional debates revealed an undercurrent of sympathy for enabling Mexico to use the indemnity internally; if an understanding with the bondholders became known Congress might explicitly require direct payment of the last installment to Mexico. Preparations for the transfer were therefore suspended pending final congressional action.[42]

First, however, the Barings had to deal with the unexpected reluctance of their financial allies to cooperate with the bondholders. The Americans argued that advances to Mexico would be much more profitable. Besides, they had little sympathy for the bondholders, whose conduct was so arrogant that even the Barings acknowledged they were prickly to deal with. But the most comprehensive critique came from Forstall. He believed Mexico had blundered suicidally in committing indemnity funds to creditors before establishing financial stability. For this he blamed foreign financiers and governments as well as incompetent Mexican statesmanship. Forstall argued that neither of the two refunding laws could have passed alone and that the logrolling among conflicting interests allowed and magnified the blunder. Moreover, he continued, the endless strife among creditors was a major cause of public disorder, while meeting their demands would prove so costly as to be incompatible with the very existence of any government. Here Forstall spoke from self-interest: his employers might suffer if a collapse of the existing regime left no successor to borrow, receive, and assure the security of money in his hands. Even short of this eventuality, the creditors' intrigues to prevent the government from using indemnity funds for current needs obstructed his profitable advances. Forstall believed the contractors had no obligation, moral or otherwise, to the creditors and advocated the course of maximum profit. Corcoran and Howland & Aspinwall shared his outlook. When Marks, Green, and the Mexican minister, with Letcher's support, sought an accommodation with the contractors by offering a 6 percent premium (out of their 8 percent commission), they proposed to accept.[43]

The Barings were taken aback. Deeming themselves upholders of sacred rights of property and contract, they animadverted upon their American colleagues' unseemly readiness to betray principles for immediate profit. It was a matter of honor, they insisted; the house would not participate in any action inimical to European creditors. The threat of dissociation was unnecessary: even before it was heard across the Atlantic, Baring Brothers, as preeminent partner in the alliance, was deferred to.[44]

Because of the late start in accumulating exchange caused by the appropriations delay, the contractors insisted on better terms from the United States government. Early in February 1852 Webster and Corwin agreed to pay a flat 3 percent commission, but Fillmore, who was sensitive to Webster's competition for the presidential nomination, rejected the proposal. When no other willing financiers could be found, the bumbling

President offered the Baring group a joint account. This seemed likely to yield the contractors larger profits than were promised by their own proposal. After further haggling, the contractors accepted, reserving a ½ percent fee plus any commissions to be paid by the bondholders. After deducting these commissions and the shares of Jaudon and Jecker, Torre, the remaining profits were to be divided evenly between the Anglo-American contractors and the government. In the end the gains exceeded £60,000, or 10 percent, of which £13,600 went into the United States Treasury. This was easily the most profitable of the installments.[45]

In the spring of 1851 Forstall had made a conditional contract with the bondholder's agent, Falconnet, to discount Mexico's $2.5 million receipt for 5 percent, but in London the committee indignantly rejected this as exorbitant. Finally the Barings, cultivating this strong and vocal investor group, agreed to receive, insure, transport, and distribute the $2.5 million plus $280,000 interest on the funded debt for a purely nominal 1 percent. Webster helped by officially recognizing the validity of the receipt given the bondholders, thus avoiding the risk of routing payment through Mexican hands.

Demoralization ramified from these intrigues. Forstall privately considered the agreement with the London bondholders' committee inimical to Mexican interests as well as to his employers', but when similar criticisms were directed at him by Marks, Green, and others he complained indignantly that he had protected Mexico from her own bad faith by compelling her to be true to her refunding agreement, thus reducing interest charges by $1 million per year. For these services Mexico did not pay the contractors one cent, he concluded—with three utterly humorless exclamation points punctuating his letter.[46]

Arista's progressive demoralization kept pace with his country's. Ignoring widespread protest, President Arista accepted $31,000 out of bribes totaling $60,000 to waive $200,000 of specie export duties on behalf of the bondholders. The bribe was arranged by Falconnet and the powerful Mexican businessman and landholder, Manuel Escandon. The faithful

Falconnet—"poor Falconnet," as a Baring letter put it—served time in a Mexico City jail for his work. The committee, which had refused to use bribery, disavowed its agent's acts. Although the other creditor powers strenuously objected, Letcher fulfilled Webster's pro-British policies by extending American diplomatic protection to the convoy carrying the specie to the coast.

Of the $400,000 remaining of the last installment, $330,000 was a receipt held by a Howland & Aspinwall correspondent, Iturbe, erstwhile opponent of the contractors in Mexico. It had been pledged to Mexican holders of interior debts. When they requested payment at Washington, Webster refused on the grounds that Mexico failed to accede to his Tehuantepec demands. Forstall then purchased the receipts at discounts as high as 16 percent and the money was paid to the contractors in America under a relaxation of treaty terms which Webster had heretofore inflexibly refused the Mexican government. This, with perfect congruity, completed the payment of the indemnity under the peace treaty of 1848.[47]

Conclusions

The Mexican government, distracted by foreign and domestic creditors while engulfed in social turmoil, lacked the revenues to simultaneously satisfy the claimants and maintain itself. A country united and astutely led might have been able to surmount these awful dilemmas—Mexico was neither. The violent antagonisms of liberals and conservatives, clericals and anticlericals were multiplied and exacerbated by shifting alliances of predatory financiers and politicians. In such conditions administrative incompetence and corruption proved irremediable. These pervasive and debilitating weaknesses almost mitigate the conduct even of those who helped perpetuate them.

Yet there was a real if short-lived beginning of reform. Swollen military and bureaucratic payrolls were reduced, bringing a better balance of revenues and expenditures. In the last half of 1850 there seemed a chance to halt the deterioration; if time could have been bought by substantial support the government might have had a chance to survive and stabilize. Given the overwhelming disintegrative forces the possibility was slight, but it was worth encouraging. The liberals in power turned toward the North, counting upon the indemnity and hoping for Yankee investment and management skills, diplomatic support, and military assistance to secure domestic peace. Viewed as a whole these pleas added up to the kind of overseas commitment that the United States never actually undertook until the end of the century.

The American response varied revealingly through three administrations. Polk favored the liberal and friendly Herrera regime against internal enemies and potential European influence. He (rather than Walker, perhaps) tried to limit the interest charge on advances to Mexico and refused cooperation to her foreign creditors. More important, he was the only American statesman to plan concrete assistance: revision of the treaty to pay the whole indemnity immediately. Unfortunately the United States was itself in an era of division and strife, and domestic politics interfered with foreign policy.

The Whig Clayton also viewed Mexico with sympathy and Britain as an antagonist. He completely mistrusted Corcoran, a Democrat and the intimate of Whig factional rivals, and showed signs of the agrarian's suspicion of bankers as a group. Unfortunately, Clayton was not very strong or able. His was the deviousness of an insecure man and perhaps of a man of troubled conscience. He invariably chose the least direct approach to his goals, with unhappy results. His blundering enabled Webster to alter policy immediately after President Taylor's death. Yet, despite Clayton's shortcomings, it was perhaps Mexico's misfortune that she failed to complete her indemnity plans while he was in office: at least he was cooperative.

Webster always gave highest priority to close relations with Britain, the paramount global military and economic power; for weak and fragmented Mexico he had only scorn.[48] Moreover, so long as his personal interests were taken care of he was the proud spokesman of eminent businessmen. He therefore gladly collaborated with Corcoran and his British allies, asking no particular quid pro quo other than a bribe. Webster's diplomacy went to grotesque extremes: unnecessary concessions to Britain and overweaning demands upon Mexico. Of the latter he required a substantial surrender of sovereignty while arrogantly refusing even the slightest consideration. He threatened to, but would not and could not, use force. He only blustered and bluffed, repeating his bluffs even after they were called. This was conduct—it could hardly be called statesmanship—of an extremely low order.

Letcher had written that only division among its enemies permitted the Arista regime to survive. To that may be added the indemnity money; once this was gone rebellions became uncontrollable. Already forced to call on conservative ministers more or less hostile to the United States, the government was finished by January 1853. Mexico continued through her long era of chaos. The loss of power and threat of oblivion after the fall of Arista was a painful lesson to Mexican liberals, who finally learned to cooperate under Juarez. (The creditors, many of whose names appear and reappear in important conflicts, continued to play an important role. Unfortunately the historiography of Mexico in this era is still primitive.)[49]

It need hardly be added that, with few exceptions, instances of broader responsibility on the part of businessmen and politicos were hopelessly subordinated to the quest for profit and the prerogatives of property.

6

The End of the Firm's Governmental Role

Dismissal

Fully appreciating the value of government patronage in money and prestige, rival financiers welcomed the 1848 Whig election victory with hopes of supplanting Corcoran & Riggs and their allies. A group of Philadelphians headed by E. W. Clark & Co. backed Corcoran & Riggs' correspondent, the young Washington firm of Chubb & Schenk, and there were reports of growing opposition from New York. The incumbents marshalled their forces for an aggressive defense. George Newbold assembled notables of the New York business community; twenty-three important firms and individuals joined him in a letter to Corcoran & Riggs for use against its detractors: "Your Mr. Corcoran has unquestionably done more, much more than any other private individual to sustain the Credit of the Government." Thomas Ward penned a supporting letter, which he prudently withheld until he sounded out the new Secretary. There was influential political support from the sectionalist Whig leader, Robert Toombs of Georgia, who wrote Secretary of War George Crawford that Corcoran was "one of our own people [i.e., a Southerner] & . . . an early and steadfast friend of 'Old Zack'."[1]

Although the new administration felt somewhat uncomfortable with Corcoran as bedfellow, it hesitated to risk the antagonism of a powerful business faction and the inconvenience of changing established routines. Moreover, although Secretary of State Clayton and Treasury Secretary Meredith were hostile, Corcoran was allied with powerful administration and southern Whigs in claims matters. In 1850 the firm was threatened with the withdrawal of certain government deposits when Corcoran was suspected of sabotaging administration policies on slavery and in Mexican relations, but this danger disappeared with the death of President Taylor. Under President Fillmore, Corcoran's position again became strong.[2]

The end of Corcoran & Riggs' privileged position came in 1853 when Franklin Pierce became President. Pierce's reign was as strong in administrative integrity as it was weak in political strength and skill. Upon taking office Secretary of the Treasury James Guthrie, one of the most determined of the reformers, withdrew the firm's government deposits of $493,000. He also terminated open-market redemptions to eliminate favoritism, adopting a policy of redemptions directly from the public by advertisement at stated prices. Corcoran & Riggs was not to suffer alone: all private agencies which transferred public funds, paid interest, and so on, were discontinued, returning $2.227 million to government vaults.[3] Corcoran tried to dissuade Guthrie from instituting these reforms, pointing to Treasury surpluses and tight money as arguments for "pet" banking and open-market purchases.[4] Ex-Secretary Walker vigorously agreed with Corcoran and urged Newbold, Cornelius Lawrence, and others to join in support.[5] Secretary of State William Marcy, however, gave only a weak semblance of aid. He did not care to risk disharmony in the new administration, especially when all signs pointed to the futility of opposing the change. Lawrence, taking the cue, diluted his support. Corcoran's goals were not important enough for his old confreres to press against a determined Secretary. Thus his career as government banker came to an end. After years of controversy and partial reform, the Independent Treasury was at last to be fully instituted.[6]

Risk Avoided, Opportunity Lost

Until the war loans were liquidated, Corcoran & Riggs declined major operations in other fields, but afterwards sought employment for their multiplied resources. Washington, a political capital with little commerce and industry, was an empty arena when government finance diminished. The great new fields were railroad finance and a growing volume of state, county, and municipal bonds, largely in aid of railroads. But the risks, too, were great and Corcoran, having made his fortune, grew more cautious. The firm had begun to deal heavily in railroad securities before the lucrative interruption of war, after which it again made good progress. But Corcoran wanted to avoid large risks, so he let pass the chance for leadership.[7]

The opportunity was presented by Robert J. Walker, who wanted to revive the successful personal collaboration of his years at the Treasury. He was offered the presidency of the Illinois Central Railroad, for which the first major federal land grant had just been enacted during the Compromise of 1850. If Corcoran, he wrote, "could be induced to take a part [apparently $8 million] of the loan with the option for a certain *time to take the whole* at a rate to be fixed now you could realize a large profit." Walker promised to consult the banker about the "choice of the directors & *many other matters*."[8]

The senators from Illinois added their solicitations. Stephen A. Douglas had just made a strong impression as the chief driving force behind the great Compromise and was already mapping a road to the presidency. Corcoran, by this time a noted and experienced hand in Washington's subsurface politics, would be a valuable ally if his interest could be joined to those of Illinois and Douglas. The latter's Senate partner, James Shields, asked Corcoran to confer with them about the railroad and related matters: "Our hope is that you may be able to take hold of the affairs of the state of Illinois in such a way as to benefit the State at this time, and also be an advantage to yourself."[9] Corcoran was favorably inclined provided he was not too heavily committed to Illinois Central flotations. He approached Baring Brothers through their agent, Thomas Ward, but they were becoming increasingly cautious about American railroads. Furthermore, unhappy experience with earlier loans in Illinois left them extremely cool toward investments there. In the absence of large-scale British support Walker's proposal languished until the following summer.[10]

In July 1851 the former Secretary informed Corcoran that the Illinois Central had secretly contracted a loan of $15 million to $17 million at 7 percent. More than $4 million was pledged by eight New York and Boston financiers who controlled the road; $5 million to $7 million more (depending on the size of the loan) was reserved to Walker for disposal abroad. He planned to leave for England at the end of August, just three years after Corcoran's notable trip. Walker also hoped to repeat the earlier stroke in its broader aspect. While money was plentiful in Britain and France, the American market had been tight to the point of panic in July. "Success will produce *a great change in the money market here* by causing a reflux in specie," Walker predicted. He wanted Corcoran to participate in the negotiations in England. Corcoran was strongly tempted but finally refused: "The amount to be borrowed is too large. It would go better if the one half of the cost of the road was paid by the stockholders & the other borrowed."

Corcoran's misgivings were borne out. Walker made the attempt, visiting England equipped with a £500 letter of credit from Corcoran & Riggs. In London, George Peabody shepherded him on his rounds but, although the ex-Secretary was feted grandly for his role in the recent Anglo-American rapprochement, he did not achieve his aims. Alternative investments in America and Europe offered too much competition, and an Illinois Central flotation of 1851 could not interest

British financiers nearly so much as had the United States loan of 1848.[11]

The ex-Secretary typified the many enterprisers who, shifting easily back and forth between business and politics, were helpful to Corcoran. Another was James Knox Walker, nephew and confidant of President James K. Polk and friend of the banker since 1844. Corcoran helped him secure contacts and correspondents when he entered banking in Memphis. Active in selling Tennessee bonds as early as 1839, Walker may have helped Corcoran & Riggs negotiate $150,000 of a state-guaranteed $250,000 loan of the Nashville & Chattanooga Railroad in 1851.[12] The firm extended credit to him, and they joined in several Tennessee issues. Corcoran & Riggs participated in at least $1.579 million of flotations of Tennessee, Memphis, and the Nashville & Chattanooga Railroad from 1851 to 1853, of which its share was $875,000. This was a larger volume of business than the firm did with any other state.[13]

Corcoran & Riggs was somewhat unusual among important investment houses in the high proportion of its business derived from the South. As the only substantial house between Baltimore or Philadelphia and New Orleans (and the capital city), the firm was the natural first stop for businessmen and politicians heading for the northeastern securities markets to float their loans; their northern compeers gravitated directly toward the important financial centers. The reverse of the formula was also true: competition being much heavier toward the North, Corcoran & Riggs focused southward where its major rivals were relatively less knowledgeable and the business potential was smaller and less tempting. That Corcoran was a southerner predisposed the more sectionally conscious from those parts in his favor. By the same token, since the firm had a fair-sized southern retail clientele, it was sometimes a useful partner for New York houses. But despite the advantages to the South, assured marketing required northern allies, particularly a New York house, even with the Peabody connection in London as a sometime source of strength.

Some of these themes—the interconnections between state

and railroad finance and between business and political leadership, the sectional link to the South, the alliance with Wall Street, plus the occasionally dubious ethics—are illustrated in a representative operation in 1851. The New York house of Winslow, Lanier & Co. was rising rapidly toward a brief preeminence in the railway securities market.[14] The Wilmington & Manchester Railroad, which had the financial support of both North and South Carolina, asked for bids for $300,000 of bonds. Its president, perhaps over-anxious about the success of the offering, acceded to Corcoran's proposal to bid for $100,000 at a minimum of 90 if the company would allow a secret rebate cutting the price to 85. Winslow, Lanier handled the bidding in New York and took a half-interest; $5,000 was allotted to Edward S. Whelen & Co. of Philadelphia. Bids received totaled more than $500,000. Of the other $200,000 accepted, almost all was from citizens of the Carolinas at above 90 whereas most of the $200,000 rejected was from New York houses at 86 to 90.[15] The firm participated in North Carolina finance at least once more: in 1853 the firm proposed to take $100,000 of a state issue of $500,000. Fifty thousand dollars was allotted to Cammann, Whitehouse & Co. of New York to secure its management of the operation, and the remaining $350,000 was reserved for joint account with Elisha Riggs and Peabody: "Without *Mr. Peabody's* being interested we should prefer not embarking in a negotiation of that magnitude." When the latter declined, the firm decided to take half of a bid with Cammann, Whitehouse and George Riggs. In the end, Corcoran & Riggs contracted $100,000 and was attempting to place $75,000 of that through George Newbold, presumably with New York financial institutions. Corcoran continued to be consulted by North Carolina officials thereafter on matters of public finance.[16]

The most glaring instance of business chicanery in Corcoran's career occurred in 1846 when the firm agreed to join Cammann, Whitehouse and Elisha Riggs in a purchase of St. Louis bonds at 77½ to 80. Later the competition of L. Benoist, a prominent Mississippi Valley banker, indicated a bid of at least 85 would be necessary, but the bonds seemed certain to retail at a healthy advance. Corcoran secretly arranged to have Palmer bid in their behalf as "it would hurt us very much if it were known that we bought the stock at 85 and sold it at 95." He then wrote a phony letter to Elisha saying that it would take six months to sell at that price and he would therefore not bid more than 80: this letter was to be shown to Cammann, Whitehouse to induce them not to participate. Corcoran & Riggs then would join Elisha and Lawrason in a purchase, if necessary at 87 or higher.[17]

As a rule Corcoran tried to avoid entangling himself in the management of enterprises in which he invested, although he advised freely and lobbied in their behalf. In a few cases he became more active. He became a director of the Philadelphia, Wilmington & Baltimore Railroad but failed to influence its policies.[18] Attempting to restore a mismanaged road that he had helped finance, Corcoran was more successful in intervening in the Maysville & Lexington.[19] But his vigor, good connections, and increasing caution in liquidating investments at the earliest signs of insecurity did not altogether spare Corcoran the common fate of nineteenth-century railway investors; he had to absorb some very heavy losses.[20]

Local patriotism, perhaps more than profit, spurred Corcoran's interest in the Chesapeake & Ohio Canal. He claimed credit for a successful flotation of its bonds in 1847, and a year later touted those guaranteed by Virginia as the best below-par security in the country at 97½. The firm held $28,000 for investment, and Corcoran kept more for his own portfolio. Disappointment was reaped instead of gains, despite his sporadic efforts over the decades.[21]

Toward an Active Retirement

Enjoying life in variety, Corcoran had long held the ambition to be a gentleman of leisure and had considered retirement as early as 1850, when his fortune was secured. Despite the declining profits of the early 1850s, he remained in business. Undoubtedly the government role was his major motive: he relished the authority, the prestige, and above all the sense of being at the center of things. Then came the divorce of the Treasury from the banking system in 1853. At almost the same time both Elisha Riggs and his son Joseph died in New York, leaving the firm bereft of its most intimate correspondent. The other faithful Wall Street allies, George Newbold and John Palmer, were growing old. The decision matured quickly; Corcoran retired, effective April 1854.

George Peabody warned his friend that he would miss the active life, but he need not have worried. Corcoran was to find ways to occupy himself at the edges of power. At the same time, with an income approaching $100,000 a year, he was able to combine business and politics with other pleasures.[22] He was the Capital's outstanding host. His annual ball for the Congress and his weekly gourmet dinners were practically institutions, as well as a useful instrument of goodwill. When Jenny Lind, the famous singer (and shrewd businesswoman), appeared in Washington it was natural that he was chosen to entertain her, and so with other eminent visitors.[23]

Local affairs and charities, small as well as great, were to Corcoran the pleasures, prerogatives, and responsibilities of a gentleman. He served on committees of various institutions, although he declined local government office. He contributed $10,000 of securities to endow the Corcoran Charity Fund of Georgetown, which gave firewood and sometimes provisions to the poor in winter; when the bonds were defaulted they were duly replaced. He had a particular tenderness for genteel but poor widows, whom he assisted with small gifts and pensions. Dorothea Dix, the famous mental health reformer, received carte blanche to levy upon him, of which she took scarcely any advantage.

Although little given to religious belief he increased the number and later the scale of church donations, probably due to a mixture of motives: devotion to the memory of his pious wife, prestige, social control, and the wish to be remembered after death. He contributed to Catholic as well as Protestant churches. He gave hearty support, solicited by the belatedly temperate Henry Clay, to the antidrinking crusade of the famous Irish priest, Theobald Matthew.[24]

Corcoran's expanding art collection, which he generously opened to the public twice a week, brought him particular pleasure and favorable publicity—some, happily, when he was under political attack. Unfortunately, his taste was rudimentary and, perhaps for want of a better alternative, he relied upon haphazard acquaintances for purchases abroad. American diplomats regularly performed this service. Minister to Belgium Thomas G. Clemson, son-in-law of John Calhoun, sent a landscape and a copy of an Auchenback by Robbe and "an old picture of flowers by the celebrated French artist Battiste." In Europe people with money bought as an investment, Clemson solemnly instructed. Lewis Cass, Jr., chargé in Rome, offered his services. The unsuccessful liberal revolutionaries were fleeing Papal persecution, he wrote in 1850; consequently he could obtain for $4,000 treasures worth four times as much. Corcoran sent over $2,000 for some nondescript items.[25]

During his travels in Europe, Corcoran cultivated a friendship with Alexander von Humboldt. After the death of the famous explorer he was given the first offer of his complete collections, including 15,000 volumes, maps, charts, instruments, precious stones, and works of art, for $100,000. Neither the late baron's family nor Prussia had shown any interest in him during his lifetime, his executor, H. Baldwin Möllhausen, bitterly observed; hence the collections should be made available to the public regardless of wealth, in the country Humboldt loved and which loved him. Möllhausen, an explorer and illustrator, said he might be despised at home and lose his post as custodian of the Kaiser's libraries for allowing the collections to leave Prussia but he would prefer the Americans to have them nevertheless. The price was more than Corcoran, who had already undertaken his gallery, was willing to pay alone, but he made efforts to interest other American collectors and philanthropists. The Prussian minister, Baron

Gerolt, whose American investments Corcoran managed, lent his aid.[26]

Corcoran laudably devoted himself to the encouragement of American art. In 1850 he paid $2,500 for a copy by sculptor Hiram Powers of his *Greek Slave,* sending it on tour through the West. Corcoran's patronage was often solicited by artists, sometimes outrageously. He paid as much as $4,000 for a painting before the Civil War and occasionally made grants, for example $500 to William D. Washington to finance a trip to Italy. By 1853 his collection was estimated, doubtless with exaggeration, to have cost at least $30,000. In 1856 he was elected a director of the new Washington Art Association, formed to build a permanent gallery and library, and in 1860, at its first annual meeting, he was chosen president of the National Gallery and School of Arts. He worked to end the taxation of art and book collections "not held as a means of gain." In 1859 he began construction of the Corcoran Gallery of Art, a pioneer donation of its kind in America. Finally, Corcoran maintained an active interest in the plans for beautifying Washington of landscapist and architect Andrew J. Downing and of architect and engineer Robert Mills. He employed Downing and his rising associate, James Renwick, to design his residences and private gallery.

Applied science attracted Corcoran. He was president of the Washington Horticultural Society in 1857 and contributed to founding an agricultural school in Maryland. Another Washington institution he supported was the Naval Institute. Not given to curiosity for its own sake, he declined Cyrus Field's request to help finance an expedition to seek an open polar sea route, having no confidence one would be found or that it would be of any use if it were. He combined interests in art and geography in his friendships with explorers and illustrators Humboldt, Möllhausen, and Eastman Johnson. Corcoran was close to the budding scientific community in Washington, especially to physicist Joseph Henry.[27]

And then there was politics. . . .

7

Summation: The Fragmentation of American Finance

Corcoran & Riggs had begun in 1840 with little capital. Through the elder Riggs the firm became a satellite of Wall Street's most powerful faction led by George Newbold of the Bank of America. The connection was at first tenuous, becoming routine and permanent only after Corcoran's talents at political intrigue institutionalized the relationship with the Treasury as federal depository. Thereafter, in a real sense Corcoran & Riggs was the Washington extension of two Wall Street banks, the America and the Merchants; they usually furnished the firm with the necessary working capital (beyond what the government deposits provided). It was a symbiotic relationship: as Wall Street was the source, so Corcoran & Riggs was an outlet for loanable funds. After the Mexican War expanding trade reduced the amount of cash the New York commercial banks could spare to finance investment banking—but by then war profits had given the partners their first considerable capital.[1]

The Mexican War loans were the climax of Corcoran's career; his 1848 mission to England was its apex. For the first time since the disasters of 1837–1841, Corcoran dramatically enlisted British support for the American economy. In a wider context the successful negotiation was one more step in the long-evolving Anglo-American rapprochement, standing with such achievements as the West Indies Trade Agreement of 1830, the Webster-Ashburton (Baring) Treaty, the Oregon Settlement, and the corn law repeal and Walker Tariff of 1846.

The London negotiations were also part of the developing cooperation between the Treasury and the banking community. The Treasury repeatedly inserted its reserves into the market to relieve monetary stringency, chiefly by buying back its own debt. Government and business cooperated as equals: after his early effort to hold down the cost of borrowing, Secretary Walker tacitly acknowledged that he represented but one—and not always the strongest—of several powerful interests. It was easiest and safest to accommodate the bankers; if the price in money and self-respect seemed occasionally outrageous, it proved supportable. The system was improvised and primitive, but was made to function. Walker's cooperation was essential, and he legitimately shared the credit, although any creativity may be largely attributable to Corcoran and other businessmen.[2]

While government aid was called in to ease the money supply, the leading bankers relied on themselves when restraint was needed. In New York three major banks, the America, the Merchants, and the Commerce, maintained relatively high specie reserves, usually 30 to 40 percent of notes and deposits. The rest of the city banks generally kept only 15 to 30 percent. The three led in contracting loans when their skill and foresight warned of overexpansion. They received credit for preventing runaway booms several times in the early 1850s.[3]

Most treatises on this era of banking tend toward the view that "against their notes and deposits, the state banks kept relatively small specie reserves. This was true even in the more conservatively managed banks of the Atlantic Coast."[4] This is true *on the whole,* but averages can be misleading. It should be clear by now that the Merchants, the America, and the Commerce were significant exceptions to the rule. In fact, Newbold indicated a dualistic or hierarchical conception of the banking system: "It is well known to practical men" that the greater institutions could not expand notes and deposits in the same proportion as the small; that the larger were perhaps less profitable, but safer. His view of the major banks as regulators of the rest emerges clearly and consistently.[5]

Unfortunately, skill and foresight were sometimes wanting, particularly in the Panic and Depression of 1857 when contraction was administered belatedly and lethally. The profitability of numerous banks with low specie reserves and heavy discounts apparently convinced even many conservatives that it was safe to relax earlier standards. Indeed, as banks multiplied competition sharpened, with some growing large enough to crowd the ranks of the leaders. In turn the latter, if they were to retain their power, had to reduce reserve ratios at least to keep pace with their rivals' rapid growth. Ironically, the leaders' reputations for conservatism and control encouraged overexuberance throughout the New York–centered banking system, even when control had in fact been foregone.

Yet, Wall Street has been excessively criticized by contemporaries and historians for its low reserve ratios. There was a substantial measure of flexibility and success before the system was overtaxed—and the signals misread—in 1857. A far richer and more sophisticated economy has only recently learned to do better. Moreover, the conservative reserve ratios of the famous Louisiana Law of 1842 seem far from ideal to a world that must reconcile limited specie with vast potentialities and boundless ambition. In their rejection of rigidly defined limits in favor of pragmatic flexibility, if not always in their use of that flexibility, Newbold and his colleagues may have been more modern than their recent critics.

The overriding difficulty was not so much the erosion of preventive restraint. This was important, but reserve ratios had often been much lower than they were in June 1857 without disruptive effects, and the ratios actually improved during the summer. That the ablest men of the time failed to foresee severe strains should perhaps suggest that errors of economic forecasting were— or are—inevitable. The real problems were disunity and, partly as a consequence, fear and paralysis of constructive response. The specie drain of panic days was reversed almost immediately, but the reactions of powerful banks were pathological as they contracted credit to bolster reserves against feared runs and raids. From late fall on the reserve ratios of the important banks ranged amazingly upwards of 50 percent to a characteristic extreme of 100 percent for the Bank of America in March 1858! Even in the worst of the panic and depression the New York banks had the strength to behave more as a central reserve, loosening credit to maintain and revive sagging business activity. The three leaders and some of their rising confreres might easily have been more expansive without violating the law of self-preservation.[6]

During the panic Corcoran played a revealing though futile role, privately joining in criticism of the Wall Street powers and trying to infuse in them some of the confident flexibility of earlier days. In October 1857 he urged Newbold to maintain specie payments and halt the drastic curtailment. It was a crisis of confidence and credit, he argued; Wall Street could afford a moderate expansion, which would strengthen confidence and forestall runs. Expansion would also speed crop exports to Europe and bring specie in return, which with added receipts of California gold would quickly overcome the crisis. Resuming his old role as intermediary between the government and Wall Street, Corcoran transmitted the concurring views of Secretary of the Treasury Howell Cobb.

Unfortunately, the government could offer little but advice since its own reserves were negligibile. The budget surpluses of the previous eight years had been used to retire two-thirds of the national debt. Continuing surpluses were viewed as an embarrassment, and low-tariff adherents, in their final triumph, had just secured substantial rate reductions. Given shrinking public land sales and the sharp curtailment of imports with the onset of business depression, the Treasury would shortly be confronted with unaccustomed deficits. In the absence of government reserves that could be deposited in the banks, business would be left to its own resources.[7]

The pleas of Corcoran were echoed throughout the business

community, even in New York. All were equally irrelevant to Newbold and his fellows. In the existing anarchy the banks compulsively had to protect themselves against each other and against outlying regions. The Bank War was long over but bank wars were not: the menace of raids, as well as runs, was always present.

Business at large thought its interests had been ruthlessly sacrificed and a severe depression needlessly provoked. Criticism was bitter. "The banks unnecessarily sacrificed the merchants," charged Bankers Magazine. A widespread opinion was that a few of the old, strong banks had conspired to force weaker institutions to liquidate in order to inherit their business. And these critics were scarcely populists! But resignation prevailed, reflecting a sense of futility and the instinctive hierarchical social order of the business community. "O John A. Stevens, O George Newbold, how *could* you serve us so!" was the cry of corporation lawyer George Templeton Strong's heart.[8]

Thus did the coalition of bankers, who had helped destroy but could only partly replace the Bank of the United States, prove their ultimate limitations in an increasingly atomized financial structure.[9]

Part II

The Politics of Special Interests

8

A Businessman and Politicians

As the demands of federal finance receded after the Mexican War, Corcoran scattered his business attentions and dabbled increasingly in politics. Considering his once-central position in American finance, some of his later involvements seem frivolous. Their variety, however, suggests a kind of cross-section of political life in the chaotic years before the Civil War.

The Collins Line

One of Corcoran's most conspicuous roles throughout his career was as a lobbyist. The Collins Line, as the shipping company was informally called after its founder and leading spirit, stimulated one of his most vigorous campaigns. Corcoran & Riggs, along with some of the New York business elite, participated actively in the original financing of this heavily subsidized American effort to compete with the British for the North Atlantic passenger trade. The founder, Edward K. Collins, had begun his career with the firm of the brother of John Slidell, the erstwhile New Yorker who was a power in

Louisiana politics. Collins went on to become manager of shipping lines between New York and Mexico and of the first packet service between New York and New Orleans. In 1841 he began to lobby for a federal mail subsidy, claiming the cost to the government would be recompensed by the diversion of postal fees from Britain to the United States. A few years later Corcoran joined the campaign. In 1845, on his last day as President, John Tyler signed a bill authorizing the Postmaster General to negotiate mail contracts, giving preference to vessels convertible to warships. In 1847 and 1848, Collins' New York backers won from Congress and the Polk administration a ten-year contract for $385,000 of mail subsidies, with an advance of a year's pay to help complete four ships already under construction whose cost had been seriously underestimated. The line was christened the New York & Liverpool United States Mail Steamship Co. [1]

Patriotism reinforced the profit motive to stimulate enthusiasm. Of the initial $1.4 million of stock, James and Stewart Brown of Brown Brothers & Co. took $500,000, some of which was for Philadelphia and Boston investors. Their Liverpool house was to be the European agent of the line. E. K. Collins & Co. subscribed for $300,000 and became the American agent. William S. Wetmore, Matthew Morgan, and one Foster were among other large subscribers. Elisha Riggs, who had enlisted Corcoran & Riggs' interest, took $130,000, of which the firm absorbed $50,000, and Samuel Riggs and George Peabody took smaller amounts. Elisha joyfully looked forward to returns of at least 40 percent per year (later he raised even this estimate) with only minimal risk, since he and the Washington house had received certain unrevealed guarantees. From later events it appears they were either given the option of converting their stock into bonds of equal face value or they received both stock and bonds. They were thus assured access to the expected enormous profits; if these did not materialize, they would have priority on interest payments at 7 percent and return of principal as lenders rather than stockholders.[2]

Fast, luxurious, burdened incongruously by quasi-military features, the hybrid Collins liners were costly to build and operate. In 1851 the company sought an increase in its annual subsidy to $600,000 per year. Partisan, sectional, and intercity opposition was severe; but perhaps most important, competing carriers sabotaged each other in Congress. Nothing was accomplished, but the drive for subsidies was renewed in 1852.[3]

The Collins men mounted a powerful campaign. Editorial support was mobilized behind the leadership of the Democratic national organ, the Washington *Union*.[4] Petitions for the company were sent to friendly merchants all over the country to be signed by prominent members of their political and business communities and returned for use in Congress.[5] Wetmore came down from New York to direct the lobby, which included such noted professionals as J. Knox Walker, Edmund Burke, John T. Sullivan, Benjamin B. French, Francis J. Grund, and Adam Glossbrenner. The Browns sent down their own agent, Orsamus B. Matteson of Utica, New York, a corruptionist whose brief career in Congress was to end under a cloud a few years later. The total of bribes must have run into the tens of thousands of dollars.[6]

It was a merry battle. A number of naval officers, including Matthew Perry, were hostile or skeptical, but this was partly offset by the adherence of New Jersey Senator Commodore Robert Stockton, who was about to launch a highly successful business career. Wetmore relied on Corcoran to control the situation in the Senate, especially among crucial Democrats; William Gwin of California was the pilot there. Strenuous attempts were made to enlist the forces of Lewis Cass and Stephen Douglas in that presidential year; Cass was won over but Douglas allied himself with the enemy Ebony Line out of considerations of New York State politics. After a series of close votes on amendments to trim the benefits, the Senate passed the subsidy increase on May 28 by a vote of 27 to 19. The action was much more intense in the House where Corcoran's close friend, Thomas Bayly, was in command. The undercurrent was running strongly against the measure, Corcoran reported. A heavy salvo of bribes was fired. The bill finally made port by 89 to 87.

Corcoran's importance is suggested by the alignment of

some of the personnel. Only three southern Democrats voted for the bill: Sam Houston and Thomas J. Rusk of the Lone Star State, who were working closely with Corcoran on the Texas debt, and Pierre Soulé of Louisiana. In addition, Cave Johnson, who negotiated the first subsidies as Postmaster General under Polk, reported in a letter on the congressional ship-subsidy scramble that Bayly was working for Cass. Also cited was Ausburn Birdsall, ex-Congressman from New York and crony of Senator Daniel Dickinson, both of whom were involved with Corcoran in the Texas debt.[7]

The act raised the annual subsidy to $858,000 for the three years through the end of 1854. Early in 1853 Corcoran reported the company was earning 30 to 40 percent annually and profits for the previous year were about $600,000, although the facts were disguised in public reports to avoid exciting congressional opposition to the subsidy. Competition, however, was intensifying. Then, in 1854, one of the liners went down in a collision. Disputes broke out as jittery investors tried to pull away from the faltering company. Corcoran & Riggs and Elisha, among others, had been carrying some of the insurance (perhaps a minor consideration in their earlier decisions to invest). They wanted to make payment with bonds of the company at par but the Browns insisted on cash. There were four major groups of creditors: Brown Brothers, which had made large advances as well as investments; the agents, including Collins himself and Brown Brothers' Liverpool affiliate; the bondholders; and the government. The Browns evidently hoped to recover part of their advances from the insurance but Corcoran insisted the government and the bondholders had first claims. He must have been on sound legal ground, for in 1855 he compelled the Browns to buy out his bonds at par after Franklin Pierce vetoed extension of the extra subsidy of 1852.

The company's troubles continued to increase, especially after the disappearance of another ship at sea. Attempts to revive the larger subsidy of 1852 failed in Congress, where many erstwhile supporters switched to the opposition. By the end of 1858 the original subsidy was terminated, the company went bankrupt, and the remaining ships were put up for sale. Corcoran and the Riggses, thanks to the government subsidy, had recovered their original investment and received 7 percent upon it.[8]

Some Other Collaborations

Corcoran appears in another instance as investor-lobbyist, joining in a venture to manufacture guns designed by Edward Maynard. After lending perhaps $5,000 to the inventor he took partial payment by a conveyance of patent rights. Corcoran received over $33,000 from a government contract he helped negotiate with Secreary of War Jefferson Davis in 1854, and patents and contracts were also sought abroad. In 1856–1857 the Maynard Arms Co. was organized, with the inventor taking one-quarter of the 1,000 shares, Corcoran and George Riggs one-sixth each, and Elisha Riggs, Jr., one-twelfth. The rest was divided among the former Whig congressman from Maryland, William Cost Johnson, Joseph Bryan of Alabama (earlier a source of Indian claims business for Corcoran & Riggs), Associate Justice James N. Wayne of the Supreme Court, and others. At least one and perhaps several of the smaller shareholders were former officers whose War Department contacts were expected to prove useful. Ambitions were momentarily thwarted in the fall of 1857 when a board of officers at West Point reported unfavorably on Maynard's carbine. Corcoran complained to Secretary of War John B. Floyd and supported the inventor's memorandum of the board's alleged errors. He flattered Floyd outrageously. "As a sportsman," Corcoran wrote, the Secretary would be able to judge between the two opinions. "Having heard of your skill with firearms," he continued, Maynard wanted Floyd to test the gun personally. Changes suggested by the "sportsman" were adopted and an order placed.

By the end of 1860 Corcoran had invested $19,000 and held a one-third interest in the patent apart from his stock in the company. Although the firm was then inactive, in the spring of 1861 Corcoran was ready to invest enough additional capital to raise his ownership to 25 percent. Despite his pro-southern sympathies—or unable to conceive of the war that was erupting—he proposed to build a factory in the North. Maynard wanted to sell out and Corcoran was ready to meet his price of $40,000. As the war developed in earnest the negotiation was broken off but Corcoran apparently sold his interest at a profit soon afterward.[9]

Sometimes Corcoran hired himself out as a lobbyist. In 1857, for example, he managed the sale of 1,100 acres on Blythe Island, off the Georgia coast, to the government for a naval depot. He received 3 percent of the $130,000 paid, less fees for Senator Solomon Foot of Vermont and ex-Senator George Badger of North Carolina. The sellers were a group who controlled the Brunswick & Florida Railroad. Peabody had introduced Corcoran to Foot in 1853 when Foot was president of the newly organized railroad. Samuel Barlow, who worked with Corcoran in the elections of 1856, was also prominent in the company.[10]

Old patrons, out of office, found Corcoran ready to extend help. In 1845, "after the failure of all our efforts to raise a dollar in New York or Philadelphia," Amos Kendall induced Corcoran & Riggs to lend $1,000 for a telegraph line between those cities. Backed by the firm's prestige, Kendall quickly raised the remaining $14,000 required and the first successful commercial venture in the new technology, the Magnetic Telegraph Company, began operations. Corcoran served as trustee of the company until 1847, when the original loan apparently was repaid. In 1851 Corcoran joined Kendall in a purchase of over 2,000 acres in Illinois, lending him the $6,000 he needed against collateral of a farm near Washington valued at $100 per acre. A year later Kendall bought Corcoran's share of the Illinois land in exchange for 80 shares of Magnetic Telegraph stock. The banker bought 20 shares more for a total of $10,000 par value on which he drew regular 8 percent dividends. Kendall eventually made his fortune in the new industry; for Corcoran it was but another modest investment. The only time he took an active role in Magnetic Telegraph was in an unsuccessful attempt to help Kendall unite the rival interests of Atlantic cable promoter Cyrus W. Field.[11]

Corcoran made large investments in lands which brought him into varied contacts with politicians. The bulk of his absentee holdings in the South and West were acquired perhaps partly with the connivance of Treasury Secretary Walker. These were public lands which had been entered by speculators and were later repossessed for nonpayment. Solicitor of the Treasury Seth Barton was replaced in 1847 by Ranson H. Gillett, confidant of President Polk, as prelude to an auction of lands under circumstances favorable to Corcoran. He was awarded over 80,000 acres in eleven states for $22,000.[12] Half this acreage proved practically worthless but the rest, with later additions, yielded as much as $200,000 in profits over four decades.[13]

The advertisements for the lands were published in the Washington *Union* at intervals for a month beginning August 17; bids were receivable until October 25. This was the season when many who might have been interested were away on vacation. Corcoran, given his location and contacts, was doubtless well informed of the value of the lands, and he had large cash resources available to meet the required immediate payments. When the awards were made, higher bids for some tracts were rejected on grounds that his bid for all the lands in a county—or state, in the lucrative instance of Illinois—yielded a greater total return to the government. The quality of the lands was uneven: a Texas tract of more than 48,000 acres, one of three formerly held by Swartwout, proved a losing proposition. Most, however, were bargains. For example, 960 acres of rich land in Stark County, Illinois, bid in by the government at bankruptcy sales at $.50 per acre, were sold to Corcoran for $365. The price of government lands obtained by ordinary means was $1.25 per acre.[14] A number of politicians were partners or agents of Corcoran in land dealings; many more had friendly, routine business with him.[15]

Certain urban real estate operations also originated through political contacts. By 1851 Corcoran had obtained ten lots in what is today midtown Manhattan, possibly from former Congressman William Woodworth to settle earlier loans. That year he bought thirty-five lots in Stoddard's Addition to St. Louis from Thomas Ewing in payment of the latter's debts of more than $13,000. Corcoran owned valuable lots in downtown Washington and in Georgetown, including for a time the Dumbarton estate, as well as cheaper speculations in undeveloped areas of the city. As a gentleman farmer he operated 474 acres in four holdings on the city's frontier and was the largest landowner in the District of Columbia. Among his important holdings was property acquired from Joseph Gales, publisher of the Washington *National Intelligencer*.[16]

Corcoran continued to accommodate publishers, most conspicuously conservatives who favored the Compromise of 1850. Thomas Ritchie of the official Democratic newspaper, the Washington *Union,* was heavily in his debt. A moderate conservative who, like Corcoran, cooperated with Whigs in support of the compromise, he failed to satisfy rival Democratic factions and was forced to sell out in 1851. Corcoran managed the negotiations for him. Of Ritchie's two successors, Andrew Donelson made some effort to avoid any ties to Corcoran but Robert Armstrong worked closely with him. The *Union* never offended Corcoran and sometimes—notably in the case of the Collins Line—gave valuable support. Another publisher who benefitted from the banker's help was Albert T. Burnley, a Kentuckian, who founded the Washington *Daily Republic* in 1849 as a Whig opponent of the Taylor administration. A supporter of the compromise, he received at least $6,000 in loans from Corcoran and secretly, through Robert Toombs, was offered a contribution of $1,000 in an abortive effort to keep the paper alive. N. Beverly Tucker, elected Senate printer in an 1853 drive led by Jesse Bright, obtained a $1,000 loan and W. W. Seaton, of the Whig Washington *National Intelligencer,* at least $3,000.[17]

Thus, Corcoran's precuniary transactions with politicians

ran the gamut of bribes, joint interest, commissions, loans as political quid pro quo, and loans and agencies as routine business, with goals ranging from pro-southern intersectional compromise to narrow special interests to simple goodwill. Out of these affairs and others still to be dealt with, certain more enduring and important alliances began to emerge.

9

The Claims Business

Of all the arenas for political corruption before the Civil War, perhaps the most senseless was the system for deciding on claims against the government. Not all claims were specious in origin or advocacy, but many were. There was no regular judicial procedure: special legislation was usually required to deal with each individual case. Claims days were set aside on the congressional calendar and became occasions for logrolling and sales of services by lawmakers and lobbyists working singly or in teams. Special commissions, sometimes legislated into existence to deal with particular claims, also proved vulnerable to corruption. But most important were the extraordinary ramifications of intrinsically insignificant cases, for the highly political adjudicative process enabled and encouraged willing politicians to establish alliances that would be serviceable in much more important matters.

The size of the fees helps explain why Corcoran devoted so much energy to the business. For merely collecting and transmitting awards obtained by others, his usual charge was 10 percent, although a special relationship with the claimant sometimes brought it down to 5 percent. Claims that were certain of quick payment might be bought for a discount of about 10 percent. More often, advances would be made against them, an assignment of rights serving as collateral. There was a market: at the end of 1843, 12 percent per year was the going rate on "undoubtedly safe" claims. In more questionable cases, or when much remained to be done, Corcoran might take a part interest as compensation, perhaps making advances against the balance. It was not uncommon for agents to devour half or more of the receipts, although Corcoran seems never to have exacted such a price.[1]

His earliest dealings originated with Indian provisioning or removal contracts and treaties. These came under the jurisdiction of the Bureau of Indian Affairs in the War Department and of the Treasury, which audited and paid the claims. In both departments Corcoran's connections were useful. At least as early as 1839, Commissioner of Indian Affairs Thomas H. Crawford advised him of the merits of particular claims offered for sale, enabling Corcoran to choose those which were secure.[2]

One of the most important claims, the Chickasaw, coincided with the Choctaw speculation in bringing together the unforeseeably consequential alliances among Robert Walker, William Gwin, Corcoran and others.[3] The Chickasaw Indians had been removed from Mississippi in 1837 to make room for white settlers. Years later Gwin, their attorney for certain claims against the government, came upon a charge of $112,000 against proceeds of sale of their land which he believed should have been paid by the government. He contracted with the Chickasaws to press this claim for a half-interest, waiving further fees from other cases he was handling for the tribe. Corcoran advanced funds and, with J. Knox Walker, was cut in for a share. Robert Walker, during his last year as senator and later as Treasury Secretary, promoted Gwin's cause but was unable to have the money paid. Secretary of War Marcy said he would "rot in my grave" before passing the claim and President Polk reportedly ruled against it. The Indian Bureau had unswervingly resisted the raid and continued to do so during the Taylor administration.

The enmity of Jacob Thompson also strengthened the opposition: Governor A. G. Brown had named him Senator from Mississippi when Walker resigned to enter the cabinet but Walker, entrusted with delivery of the appointment, withheld it in a misbegotten attempt to have Gwin succeed him. Not only were Gwin's and Walker's influence in Mississippi largely destroyed (Gwin moved to California where he became a Senator); Thompson waged direct warfare by becoming counsel to the Chickasaws. He attacked Gwin on grounds of improper procedure, irregularities, and the size of his fees, which already totaled $33,000. Thompson was in a position to know where Gwin was vulnerable, for as congressman he had pressed his case. At one point a compromise seemed attainable if Gwin would accept a reduction of about $15,000, but against the advice of Corcoran and Knox Walker he refused and retaliated with charges of attempted extortion.[4]

Alone the Chickasaw suit would never have been successful, but in the years following the Mexican War claims were launched in waves until the dam finally broke. Ransom Gillett, who as Francis P. Blair put it "belongs to the green room," sketched the machinery. Claimants of upwards of $20 million, he asserted, had organized the most adroit manipulators in Washington, with slush funds contributed pro rata. The figure is immense for that era, but is not far fetched when one considers that actual payments under enactments and decisions dealt with in this chapter alone easily exceeded $5 million. The reappearance of certain individuals in various claims—and in steamer subsidies, Texas bonds, and other affairs—lends added support to Gillett's and Blair's observations. Allied, these interests could do much for themselves and also serve other purposes.[5]

Pierre Chouteau, a founder of the city of St. Louis and long a power in Missouri business and politics, arranged for Corcoran's cooperation in one major campaign. He was associated with George W. and W. G. Ewing, influential Indian and fur traders, and politician and attorney Richard W. Thompson of Indiana, in a claim growing out of advances to the

Menominee tribe in Wisconsin. The elder Chouteau had succeeded John Jacob Astor as head of the American Fur Co. He was a close friend of Senator Thomas Hart Benton and his protégé, Frank Blair, son of Francis P. Blair. Chouteau was also allied to Corcoran through his daughter's marriage to Elisha Riggs' son Lawrason, a St. Louis merchant and politician. In the early 1840s all these men had worked together to channel several hundred thousand dollars of St. Louis and Missouri bond flotations through Corcoran & Riggs and Elisha Riggs.[6] At Chouteau's behest the collaboration was reactivated to work on the Menominee claim. Benton was put on Corcoran's personal payroll as claims agent with remuneration that finally totaled $2,600. Also, he received from Corcoran & Riggs over $5,000 of loans which were permitted to go unpaid for years—until he broke with the pro-slavery wing of his party. Benton and Corcoran also joined in support of the Senator's son-in-law, John C. Fremont, another large claimant. But the Indiana—and national—political ramifications of the Menominee claims were the most important: the prize, which ultimately totaled $242,000 may have been crucial in swinging Indiana for Buchanan in the 1856 presidential election.[7]

The lineup of interested politicians was extended with the involvement of rival Ohio Whig factional leaders. Robert G. Corwin, brother of Fillmore's Secretary of the Treasury, helped promote the Chickasaw claim. The Corwins were inundated with claims. They held direct interests in at least a dozen, most notoriously that of George Gardiner. Robert Corwin was in an especially good position to win friends as a member of the Board of Commissioners to adjudicate Mexican claims. (His helpfully ambiguous situation was shared in every respect by another Indiana Whig, Caleb B. Smith.) Thomas Ewing, Secretary of the Interior under Taylor, found a path to an unwonted unity with the Corwins; all were receiving large loans and outright payments from Corcoran for help on claims. Samuel Vinton, important Ohio Whig congressman, was another confidant and debtor, and help was exchanged with Free-Soil Democrat Lewis D. Campbell of Cincinnati. Last but not the least useful was Elisha Whittlesey, Whig from the Western Reserve and Comptroller of the Treasury. His office shared direct responsibility in determining the validity of claims. A long-time civil servant, he was universally considered a model of administrative integrity and the watchdog of the Treasury. But he was an old and close friend of Corcoran and of Ohio Whig leaders; he knew, of course, that they were honorable men; the watchdog never barked.[8]

Another allied scheme broadened the informal coalition to include strategically placed members of the Taylor administration and an array of powerful Georgia Whigs. The Galphin claim, dating back to the Revolutionary War, was passed by Congress in 1848. The payment of $44,000 three-quarters of a century after the origin of the claim was perhaps defensible, but almost insignificant by comparison with the award of an additional $190,000 for interest in the spring of 1850. Chief counsel for the claimants was Secretary of War George Crawford of Georgia, who received half of the total. (One may wonder how it was further subdivided.) Secretary of the Treasury Meredith, who made the decision to pay the interest, based his approval on a favorable opinion by Attorney General Reverdy Johnson, ally of Corcoran and the Texas creditors. Allowance of the claim clearly was a major goal of Georgia's Whigs, who sent to Congress the most important southern delegation of their party. Among them Corcoran was on excellent terms with Howell Cobb, Alexander Stephens, and especially Robert Toombs, who exerted heavy pressure for the claim. It was scarcely accidental that Interior Secretary Ewing finally overrode the bitter opposition of the Commissioner of Indian Affairs, Orlando Brown, to the Chickasaw claim at the time the Galphin raid was concluded. Corcoran & Riggs was at last able to collect Gwin's fee of $56,000.[9]

Many claims arose for supplies or property lost during the Mexican War. By 1852 Congress created an officers' board under the War Department to evaluate them, but special bills requiring congressional action were still sometimes necessary. In 1855 Gwin sponsored an appropriation of more than

$18,000 for Peter A. Hargous, of which Corcoran deducted a 5 percent commission (probably shared with the Senator). From 1852 to 1856 Corcoran enjoyed good relations with Senate Claims Committee chairmen, especially John Pettit of Indiana and Richard Brodhead of Pennsylvania, in whose states his friends Jesse Bright and James Buchanan, respectively, were powerful leaders.[10]

A number of claims originating in California were referred by or pressed jointly with James King of William,[11] whose stormy career in finance and politics was cut short by an employee's embezzlement and his assassination. After a brief apprenticeship as clerk at Corcoran & Riggs he had migrated to San Francisco, where he became the firm's correspondent.[12] Their dealings included a special joint account for claims, of which King's interest was one-quarter. John C. Fremont was advanced $40,000 at 4 percent per month against collateral consisting of $154,000 of drafts in his favor given by George W. Barbour, Indian commissioner, for supplies furnished California Indians to prevent a threatened rebellion. When the Secretary of the Interior refused payment King filed suit for repayment against Fremont in order to gain priority over other creditors. Three years after the original advance the $40,000 debt plus interest was settled for $56,000 when Gwin and other Corcoran friends joined interested California members in securing passage of a special Act of Congress to pay the disputed draft.[13]

Surpassing them all in melodrama was the Gardiner case. This was one of dozens brought before the Commission on Mexican Claims, which was established by Act of Congress on the last day of the Polk administration. The Commission had $3.25 million to dispense in implementation of Articles 14 and 15 of the Treaty of Guadalupe Hidalgo, under which the United States assumed responsibility for that amount of unsettled claims by American citizens against Mexico. Corcoran was enticed by this largest single fund the claims business offered. The Act of March 3, 1849, he asserted, "but for our exertions would not have been passed."

George A. Gardiner sought $350,000 for a silver mine allegedly destroyed by the Mexicans during the war; with interest allowed at 5 percent the total reached $428,000. His agents and co-owners included Waddy Thompson, former minister to Mexico, who arranged for a 15 percent cut before Congress passed the Act of 1849; Edward Curtis, Webster's old friend; F. T. Lally, brought in by Curtis; and the Corwin brothers. Lally was the son-in-law of George Evans, former Whig Senator from Maine, friend of Corcoran—and a member of the Mexican Claims Commission. In February 1850, before the claim was approved, the Corwins offered Corcoran a 25 percent interest for only $28,000. Gardiner, he was told, had to return to Mexico for more evidence but was not free to leave the States without settling with creditors, which in turn he could not do before the award was made. Corcoran, who declined, later explained, "I had no suspicions of anything wrong in the case; but it was not my desire nor was it in character with my business of banker to be interested in claims before the board of commissioners."

This was laughable. The banker had purchased several Mexican claims in the spring of 1849 at about 25 to 30 percent of face value and stopped buying only because it appeared the valid ones would equal two or three times the fund, leaving a mere return of investment and interest by the time payments were made. This was Corcoran's reason for limiting himself to the role of agent. But by February 1850, when the Gardiner plum was laid before him, he may already have known that the awards made, with 5 percent interest, would total less than the fund. Probably, Corcoran was suspicious of the very attractiveness of the proposition, which had been rejected by others for just this reason. Undoubtedly the conspicuous size and interlocking of numerous claims reinforced his cautiousness.

Corcoran did oblige the Corwins, however. He lent them $18,750, and they bought the quarter-share themselves for $22,500. The note had four co-signers: L. D. Campbell, D. Bruin, Moses R. Corwin (another member of the clan), and Caleb B. Smith. The latter was one of the Mexican claims commissioners and, with Campbell and the Corwins, a Chickasaw speculator. (The third commissioner, Robert Treat Paine, does not appear to have had any conflicts of interest.) Later Thomas Corwin, wary because of the outcry during Crawford's term in the cabinet against his connection with the Galphin claim, sold his share in Mexican claims—eleven of them—on becoming Secretary of the Treasury, but brother Robert kept his.[14] When the $428,000 Gardiner award was finally paid in May 1851, Waddy Thompson collected $55,000, Curtis $25,000, and the Corwins $20,000 (in addition to Robert's equity). Corcoran collected and disbursed the money, smoothly resolving a dispute over division of the spoils.

All told, there were 198 awards made and 110 claims rejected by the Mexican Claims Commission. Including interest allowed at 5 percent from date of loss, the awards totaled over $3.208 million. The smallest payment was $160; the largest was $530,000 to Louis Hargous, who also collected one of $72,000. S. L. M. Barlow was his agent. Another claim in which the Corwins were interested, that of John H. Mears, paid $153,000 and proved as fraudulent as Gardiner's; indeed, the latter was one of its promoters. John and William S. Parrott collected $178,000 for two claims; Richard S. Coxe, trustee, $59,000 for the Union Land Co. and $64,000 for the Trinity Land Co.; and John Baldwin, $71,000. Lally was reportedly an agent for these men and for Hargous. Daniel Webster appeared before the Commission for the Parrotts and others before becoming Secretary of State. James Reed collected $45,000 for five claims, Pierre Chouteau, Jr., $85,000 for one, and John Belden, $106,000 for one. Elisha Riggs received a $13,000 award. Corcoran's purchase of the Williams & Lord claim from W. B. Hart yielded a gross of $15,000. He apparently shared in payments of $17,000 to James W. Zachary. Many awards were, of course, divided in ways that do not appear in the record.[15]

But the Gardiner affair was still very much alive. Rumors of fraud, already circulating in an undercurrent, soon came to the surface, and in July 1851 Gardiner was indicted for perjury and forgery of crucial documents. Corcoran, in an exposed position, rushed back to the capital to inform the President and the Secretary of the Treasury of the nearly $100,000 of securities he held for Gardiner's account and another $130,000 deposited with the New York Life & Trust Company. The government attached the securities while Corcoran canceled what remained of a $10,000 letter of credit, leaving Gardiner just enough to pay his way back from Paris. Corcoran's position was bolstered when Assistant Secretary Hodge praised him for violating the banker's customary secrecy about the account of a client. (The banker, however, furnished funds for Gardiner's defense—until the latter criticized his conduct.) Gardiner, playing his game with true desperation, fought to a hung jury in his first trial. Then, at the second trial, on hearing himself convicted and sentenced to ten years at hard labor, he committed suicide in the courtroom.

Gardiner was an engaging and audacious confidence man who gambled for respectability as well as fortune. His stylish manner—plus their self-interest—induced his associates to maintain faith in him even after the initial damaging exposures. Corcoran, for example, professed himself confident of his innocence because he had left behind almost $250,000 of securities when he went to Europe. The financier was in some measure sincere, but also somewhat disingenuous. An incisive journalist reported that the investigation which revealed the crime was initiated by a government clerk who recognized on first glance that the case was fraudulent on its face. Gardiner's supporters had been had chiefly because they were willing to be had. In their anxiety for a good thing, they accepted the superficially plausible as if it were the most convincing of evidence. Political and legal entrepreneurs were becoming accustomed to building high on small foundations. It was perhaps understandable that they failed to perceive an unusually insubstantial support under so impressive and conventional an edifice.[16]

After the scandals Corcoran practically ended involvement with individual claimants against the government; the risk of embarrassment was becoming excessive.[17] But the claims business had served him very well. The profits, modest for a man of his fortune, were the least of it. What was invaluable was the entrée provided among influential politicians. The Choctaw affair had helped bring about the intimacy with Walker that proved so fruitful in the Polk years, and later claims helped Corcoran develop his collaboration with important men of all factions, Whig and Democratic, during the Taylor and Fillmore administrations. Indeed, the interlocking of other claims with the Galphin may help account for Corcoran's survival as government banker to an administration as suspicious of him as Taylor's was.[18] The usefulness of claims as a cement for diverse political factions remained vital as late as 1856.[19]

And then there were group claims, so to speak, which were equally important.

10

Creditor Politics

The frustrations of creditors and the avarice of speculators did not roil the waters as violently in America as in luckless Mexico, but they caused turbulence enough. If the financial effects—in this rich and comparatively competent society—were merely a few dollars shifted from one place to another, the political effects could be unforeseen and important, particularly in the growth of lines of communication and cooperation.

The Texas Debt

In 1850 Corcoran & Riggs ventured into the business and politics of the Texas debt. They expected to profit from a brief and tidy operation; instead, sporadically over the next six years they had to lobby intensively in Congress and in the Lone Star State. The debt, incurred during Texas' independence from 1836 to 1845, totaled about $10 million at face value, although most of the notes and bonds had been sold by the impecunious Republic at huge discounts. Under the guidance of Nicholas Biddle, the Bank of the United States of Pennsylvania had been the leading financier; its creditors, represented by several groups of trustees, continued to hold about 10 percent of the debt. Further reflecting the Bank's role, Philadelphians held another 15 to 20 percent, giving that city the greatest concentration of ownership. Large amounts were controlled from New York, with a significant scattering elsewhere. Among notable individuals interested in the debt were such close political allies of the defunct Bank as Henry Clay and Daniel Webster; Clay's Kentucky crony, Leslie Combs; Webster's close associates, Richard Blatchford and Biddle's old lieutenant, Samuel Jaudon; and James Hamilton, former governor of South Carolina and personal link between Biddle and the Republic of Texas. But the most important debtholders were the trustees for creditors of Biddle's doomed institution. The Bank had died in 1841, but the corpse twitched on for years.[1]

In the early 1840s the debt of the bankrupt Republic plummeted to below 10 percent of face value. There the price remained, except for sporadic upswings when prospects of American annexation improved. Well-placed politicians and businessmen speculated on this possibility. The most noteworthy transaction was William S. Wetmore's June 1844 purchase of about $650,000 of bonds from trustees of the Bank of the United States. When annexation was accomplished the following year, Whigs and Free-Soilers believed holders of Texas paper were an important force behind it.[2]

Annexation failed to fulfill hopes of payment. In January 1847 Corcoran, believing the federal government would never assume any of the debt, sold his small holdings. But hope was stimulated by one promising possibility: Texas and the federal government were at odds over her uncertain northwestern boundary. Perhaps the state could be induced to cede the disputed region (now New Mexico) in return for federal assumption of her debts. The long-term prospects certainly seemed brighter by October 1848 when Corcoran and Peabody tried unsuccessfully to buy large blocks still held by creditors of the Bank of the United States.

The debt question became inextricably entangled with the gathering struggle over slavery in the territories. During 1849 plans were matured to enlist the influential creditors' interest, with its strong Whig and United States Bank elements, by exchanging federal assumption of the debt for Texas' relinquishment of New Mexico as part of a general settlement of differences between the North and the South. In the middle of January 1850 Free-Soiler Thomas Hart Benton attempted to forestall and break up the incipient coalition, introducing a bill to settle the boundary dispute by paying Texas $15 million of United States 5 percent bonds. This amount was substantially greater than the debt and would have netted the state several million dollars. Two weeks later Clay introduced his famous omnibus compromise proposal. Measurably less generous to Texas, it provided for federal assumption of a portion of the debt.[3]

A flurry in the marketplace accompanied these developments. Corcoran & Riggs' first ascertainable purchase of Texas paper occurred at the end of February (although some may have been acquired in January): $11,300 of 8 percent shares at 25. The total bought during the first four months of the year was probably less than $50,000 to $60,000 face value, mostly for Corcoran's personal account. With congressional action uncertain and the last of the Mexican War loans still to be liquidated, caution remained the rule.[4] Early in May, Clay's measures were reported from committee; the partners bought up to $50,000 to $60,000 more by the beginning of June. However, the compromise was blocked by the opposition of President Taylor. Corcoran stopped buying until the President's sudden death in August, then celebrated the event by placing fresh orders. From August 12 until the end of the month $30,000 face value of the various kinds of paper were bought through his Philadelphia broker, Edward Whelen.

Meanwhile, Senator James A. Pearce of Maryland offered a new bill to pay Texas $10 million of United States 5 percent bonds. Half of the United States bonds under Pearce's bill were to be withheld until creditors holding bonds for which the Republic's import duties had been pledged filed waivers of claims against the federal government. Legally the United States was responsible for debts secured by import duties, since by annexation it had taken over the exclusive constitutional right to levy tariffs. This technicality was to provide a large stumbling block, but for the time being the problem seemed negligible. Upon passage of the Pearce bill as part of the Compromise of 1850 Corcoran enlisted agents in additional cities and stepped up purchases. In early October almost $50,000 of 6 percent notes was acquired at prices rising from 45 to 55. After a brief pause while prices leveled, purchases were resumed in November and continued into the new year.[5]

Once the speculation seemed certain to succeed, Corcoran made it an instrument of favor to politicians. For John W. Davis, Indiana Democrat who had been Speaker of the House of Representatives from 1845 to 1847, he bought a 30 percent interest in a $10,000 Texas certificate. Although he had to wait longer than expected, Davis eventually collected almost twice his $1,250 investment. Francis A. Grund, influential journalist of the Philadelphia *Public Ledger,* was lent more than $4,000 by Corcoran & Riggs to finance the purchase of $10,000 face value. Grund was especially noted for being well informed on financial matters in Washington. This was not the first of Corcoran's favors to him, nor the last.[6]

Even before the passage of the Texas measure, opponents had interpreted it as a gigantic bribe to powerful interest groups and to the state for their support of the Compromise of 1850. Recently it has been suggested that Corcoran's example bore out the charges of the Free-Soilers and their successors. The existing evidence does not reveal any tangible action by him to assist passage of the compromise, and only a relatively small part of his investment was made before then. But he was active in the lobbies, and was interested in the Mexican indemnity, Illinois debts, and various claims dealings which brought him in contact with Stephen Douglas, Thomas Bayly, and other key figures. Moreover, there may well have been contingent understandings; indeed there probably were, in view of the speed with which loans on Texas paper were made to Grund, Davis, and other politicians. Of course, others with larger holdings must have been at least as active.

There is, moreover, a tantalizing mystery in the Corcoran

papers. The surviving correspondence to the banker is relatively sparse, even including material in the Riggs papers. It would have been consistent with his style and position to consider it improper or indiscreet to preserve revealing letters by his correspondents (although some have survived). But his own letters were a different matter. Corcoran wanted very much to perpetuate the memory of his achievements. From 1845 on he preserved an almost complete file of copies totaling some sixty thick letterpress volumes. There is but a single gap—the volume including the Compromise period of the year 1850. Possibly it fell into the wrong hands along the way, but its disappearance could also imply the nature and value of the contents.[7]

Thus, if Corcoran's activities do not support the Free-Soiler interpretation, neither do they disprove it. The evidence in the Corcoran and the Riggs collections indicates an important role for James Hamilton of South Carolina and Texas, who travelled about the country promoting the cause. He shared an interest with Senator Thomas J. Rusk of Texas and was an agent for Wetmore, the largest single creditor. Hamilton himself owned $110,000 of Texas paper which he had verbally pledged as collateral, reportedly several times over to different creditors. In addition, a 10 percent commission was due him from the trustees of the Bank of the United States on a $400,000 loan he had negotiated for the Texas Republic, if and when it was repaid; and the Bank of the State of Alabama, which held $40,000 (including accrued interest) of Texas paper, promised him a 5 percent commission if redemption were achieved. When the debt bill was enacted Corcoran, on Wetmore's endorsement, lent Hamilton $25,000, secured by his forthcoming commissions.[8]

In November 1850 the Texas legislature complicated matters when it accepted the Pearce Act with an interpretation designed to curtail the gains to some speculators. The provision for payment of certificates bearing an explicit pledge of import duties was to be accepted literally, to the exclusion of other classes of bonds and notes. Those adversely affected organized against the decision and, behind Corcoran's leadership, enlisted the federal government to thwart it. In September 1851 Treasury Secretary Corwin ruled, on the basis of an opinion by Attorney General Reverdy Johnson, that the Texas Act of 1840 guaranteed all previous loans equally by its general pledge of revenues, which implicitly included customs. Obtaining Fillmore's approval was a routine matter. To force compliance Corwin required that the United States receive releases for the entire revenue debt before the reserved $5 million of bonds could be turned over to the state.

This struck at the Lone Star State and some of its creditors. Texas had received much less than face value for her obligations, almost all of which had long since passed out of the hands of the original holders and into speculative ownership at still lower prices. On these grounds, early in 1850, the state had scaled down her debts to a rough approximation of the value originally received, with interest to July 1, 1850. The awards to the various classifications ranged chiefly from 20 to 87½ percent, the latter for the Bank of the United States loans, with only a negligible amount allocated at 100 percent. The favored creditors sought modification of the Secretary's ruling to permit payment to creditors who accepted the scaling, while those whose holdings had been drastically devalued refused to sign releases and demanded a uniform rate for all.[9]

In this situation Corcoran resorted to additional bribes. Corcoran & Riggs had extended a loan of $5,000 to Reverdy Johnson upon passage of the Pearce Act in September 1850. Part of this was repaid but $1,500 (plus $400 interest) was ultimately cancelled for "legal advice and services" in connection with the Texas debt. Corwin, a major claims client and ally of the firm, eventually received $8,000 as his Texas "fee." His Assistant Secretary of the Treasury, William L. Hodge, received $1,800. Corwin also induced Corcoran to lend $10,000 on Texas collateral to the hard-pressed Leslie Combs, in addition to the $5,000 already lent at the time of the Compromise. But discord and deadlock prevailed as Texas rejected the stand of the disgruntled creditors and the federal government.[10]

In 1852 the state finally moved to repay the first portion of its debt, $2 million of nonrevenue obligations, i.e., those not explicitly secured by tariff or other revenues. To raise the money it would finally begin disposing of the fourteen-year 5 percent United States bonds, offering a flotation of $2 million of the $5 million already received. Some of the bonds were offered in exchange for nonrevenue obligations at the state's scaled valuations (with the United States bonds valued at a 3 percent premium including accrued interest). The rest was to be sold by competitive bidding at auction. Corcoran hurriedly dispatched an agent to enter a bid. Baring Brothers and Howland & Aspinwall, with whom Corcoran had agreed in 1850 to share the operation, hesitated, then joined the account. Corcoran & Riggs split its share with George Peabody.[11]

Corcoran's agent was William Gouge, the famous Jacksonian publicist. He carried a letter of introduction to W. D. Miller, intimate friend of Sam Houston and other Lone Star notables, who received a loan of $5,000 against Texas paper and later a fee of $1,000. (Gouge also was to buy up as much of the paper as possible at up to 75 percent of scaled value. Fortunately for his principals he would have little success, for widespread expectations of a rapid settlement at a higher rate were to prove mistaken. Gouge also carried with him $25,000 of the nonrevenue debt, reserved by the partners for himself and others, to be traded in for United States bonds under the terms of the Texas offer.)

For Gouge it was a journey with varied attractions. En route he undertook to inspect some of Corcoran's newly acquired land holdings in Mississippi along with some of his own. He found time to write polemics against Senator Robert Hunter's proposal to reduce the silver content of the coinage, pontificating to Corcoran: "As moneyed men and private bankers you have a deeper interest in preventing an alteration of standard." Nominally a Democrat, Gouge, who was intermittently employed in the Treasury until his death during the Civil War, traveled about Texas at the department's expense gathering intelligence on political conditions and checking for the Whig Secretary, Corwin, on the political loyalty of office holders and seekers.

This freelance intellectual also wanted to write a history of the Texas debt as a service to political economists, statesmen, and the creditors, and to strike against repudiation: the *Fiscal History of Texas* was the result. Corcoran (and others on both sides) ascribed to the book considerable influence in determining the final result: "He was mainly instrumental in getting the Texas debt paid by personal efforts in the State and a work he published, 'Gouge's Financial History of Texas,' with frequent essays in newspapers all over the country." Gouge lobbied among politicians and publishers to build up support for a settlement prorated equally among all the creditors, an outcome which, he frankly reported, not one of ten Texans favored. From friendly state officials he obtained for Corcoran confidential lists of creditors, commenting, "An inspection of them has convinced me that some of my friends have even a deeper interest than I supposed in a faithfully written Fiscal History of Texas." He passed along the unsurprising advice of Texas Secretary of State Duvall and his brother-in-law, Judge Paschal, that bribery would be necessary and was the accepted way of doing things in the state legislature.[12]

Meanwhile Gouge completed his immediate task. When the bids were opened early in May, Corcoran & Riggs was awarded $600,000 of the United States bonds. The competition turned out to be more severe than expected. Most of it was provided by Zacharie & Co., partly as agent for the State Bank of Louisiana, partly for New Yorkers. Gouge had to obtain Corcoran's hurried permission to increase his offer. The winning bids were for six blocks of $100,000 each at rates of 105.01 to 105.05 and 105.10, payable at New York.[13]

Attention then turned back to Congress. In August 1852, Senator James Mason of Virginia introduced an appropriations rider to support Texas by turning the reserved bonds over to the state as equivalent releases were obtained from creditors. Simultaneously a bill was prepared by Pearce to replace the reserved bonds with $8.333 million of United States 5 percent bonds to be paid directly to the creditors, pro rata and without scaling.[14] Action was postponed until the next session; in the interim the creditors redoubled their activities. Corcoran & Riggs furnished loans to well-placed individuals for the purchase of Texas paper, which served as collateral. William H. English, Democratic Representative from Indiana, received $8,200. Adam J. Glossbrenner, former Congressman from Pennsylvania and sergeant-at-arms of the House, shared loans totalling $15,000 with William H. Kurtz, Democratic Representative from his state, and probably others. (Glossbrenner and Asbury Dickins, secretary of the Senate, had served for years as middlemen between Corcoran & Riggs and members needing advances against their salaries.) Texas Senator Thomas J. Rusk, who played a leading role throughout and shared an interest with James Hamilton and William D. Miller as early as 1848, borrowed $5,000 jointly with Orsamus B. Matteson, a Seward cohort and Congressman from Utica, New York. In repayment Corcoran eventually accepted some of Rusk's Texas lands at an inflated valuation. A Texas lobbyist, Memucan Hunt, received an advance against the fee that was to be paid on settlement, as in Hamilton's case, by trustees of the Bank of the United States.[15]

Among the most important of Corcoran's pecuniary allies was Jesse D. Bright, unscrupulous and resourceful boss of Indiana politics. Bright had become an intimate friend and collaborator of Corcoran and was united to the Riggs family by his daughter's marriage. He joined Corcoran in a speculation in Texas paper, his share financed by a loan in the usual fashion. Eventually he was to collect $35,000 on the investment, along with an outright bribe of $5,000. It was probably through him that Representative English was interested. Additional payments eventually went to Representative John L. Taylor (Whig, O.), $400; E. H. Thompson, a lobbyist from Michigan, $5,500, much of it almost certainly for distribution to congressmen; James Harrison (presumably the partner of Pierre Chouteau, Jr., who held about $8,000 of the debt), $200, probably to be conveyed to a politician; and one Albert Smith, $500. William A. Richardson, Stephen A. Douglas' influential lieutenant in the House, received a loan of $2,500. A loan of $3,500 of September 30, 1850 to New York Senator Daniel Dickinson ultimately brought a disappointingly small profit of $1,000. Another important politician interested in the debt held by the diligent Leslie Combs was Representative John C. Breckinridge (Dem., Ken.).

Still other political figures who owned Texas paper (to judge from their small contributions to slush funds managed by Corcoran) were Representative Samuel Vinton (Whig, O.); J. W. Denver, elected to Congress from California in 1854; and Sidney Webster, private secretary to President Franklin Pierce. Corcoran also handled some of the accounts set up to finance lobbying activities. Congressmen for whom Corcoran & Riggs as agent later collected Texas paper yielding from a few hundred to $5,000 included George Vail (Dem., N.J., 1853–1857), Miles Taylor (Dem., La., 1855–1861), William O. Goode, (Dem., Va., 1841–1843, 1853–1859), F. S. Spinner (Dem., N.Y., 1855–1861), and Senator Richard Brodhead (Dem., Pa.).[16]

In the spring of 1853 James Mason's bill in support of Texas' scaling of the debts again came before the Senate. He was vocally supported by Sam Houston, who denounced Gouge's recently published book. But Stephen A. Douglas jibed at the dollar patriotism of the bond holders who had saved the Union in 1850 and gotten themselves $10 million, although in the end he demonstrated his live-and-let-live policy and abstained from voting. Mason's bill was beaten, 31 to 13. Bright attempted to have the reserved $5 milion paid directly by the Treasury on receipt of releases from the creditors but was defeated, 25 to 17. Pearce offered his bill as an amendment to Mason's but this lost, 34 to 8. The impasse remained.[17]

Perhaps the senators were hoping the new Attorney General, Caleb Cushing, would spare them the onus of making a decision. Corcoran and others submitted lengthy memoranda in support of an equal pro rata distribution. James C. Christy, a large owner from Philadelphia, offered to send petitions signed by all that city's creditors (except the trustees of the Bank of the United States), holders of $1.65 million. Since the bank debt was among the most favored under Texas' scaling at 87½ percent, this group (and Hamilton, who was to receive a commission as its agent) supported the state's position. Cushing's opinion only further befogged the issue, since he added to the classes of debts covered by the import revenue guarantee while excluding Treasury notes.[18]

Nine months after Cushing's decision, Bright was finally able to bring his bill before the Senate. He had become a Democratic leader with a dominant role in committee assignments. By placing himself and another of Corcoran's old friends, Gwin of California, on the finance committee, he was able to exert the necessary leverage. After various maneuvers he reported a bill to authorize, if Texas consented, a cash distribution from the Treasury to her creditors of $8.5 million. This, Bright argued, was still $3 million less than the debt with interest accrued. A committee minority proposed instead the payment of $6.5 million in any way Texas approved, but Bright whipped his bill through to a 21 to 19 victory late in 1853. During the next session the bill was brought up in the House where John C. Breckinridge managed it smoothly. An amendment by Jones of Tennessee to reduce the amount to $6.5 million passed, 120 to 82, although Texans threatened that this sum was too small to be acceptable. The amended bill passed by 153 to 43. The conference committee compromised on a figure of $7.750 million, which was accepted by the Senate, 30 to 14, and by the House, 123 to 77. The settlement was if anything more generous than the original Act of 1850, in Corcoran's estimation.[19]

The last problem was to gain Texas' acceptance. The chief motive for opposition there was that the scaling under the Act of 1848 would have left the state more than $3 million of United States bonds with which to finance internal development. A lively controversy was under way over whether to have the state build railroads or seek private investment, with many who favored public enterprise relying on the surplus from the indemnity payment.[20]

James Hamilton had publicized a plan to pay the creditors partly in cash and partly, to the face value of the instruments of debt, in land. He added a fillip and promoted a scheme to make part of the settlement in stock of the Harrisburg & Richmond Railroad's extension to Austin, using the cash saved to build the road. No doubt his land speculations would also have benefitted, and he may even have hoped to revive his political career. Corcoran was enraged. He asserted Hamilton was due $150,000 in commissions without ever having advanced a dime, but since the whole was already hypothecated he had nothing further to collect. However, he would lose $12,000 in commissions by reduction of the award to the Bank of the United States from the scaled amount to the pro rata. "Til I read [Hamilton's proposals] I could not believe that any man could be so base," Corcoran exclaimed. Before Hamilton's departure for Texas the financier had refused to pay him $1,200 to promote the Legislature's acceptance of the measure and he afterward rejected requests for additional loans.[21]

The controversial settlement was submitted to popular referendum—which was not binding on the legislature—in the spring elections of 1855. Led by Senators Houston and Rusk, the congressional delegation campaigned for it with more or less subdued enthusiasm. Miller lobbied assiduously, with Corcoran dangling before his nose the carrot of a large loan. Corcoran & Riggs was asked to join the Milbanks, leading New York creditors, and others in raising $5,000 each to influence the Texas legislature—entirely in lawful and proper ways, they of course claimed. Corcoran vigorously rejected such tactics—unless they should become necessary. But $14,250 was set aside out of an earlier slush fund placed at his disposal by Charles Macalester of Philadelphia. The campaign was carried out under James S. Holman, an important creditor who went south from Philadelphia with a war chest raised jointly with E. W. Clark & Co.[22]

Profits aside, among Texans the chief rationale for accepting the congressional settlement was found in the craving for economic growth. Even some, like Governor E. M. Pease, who professed support for state or mixed enterprise, concluded that regardless of the $3 million or more that might become available through implementation of Texas' scaling, private capital would eventually be needed. Proponents of private enterprise, led by Rusk, naturally emphasized this argument. The point was also made bluntly, if not convincingly, by creditor members of the financial community. Corcoran argued that if Texas had promptly carried out the Act of 1850 she would have had 500 miles of railroad already in operation and another 500 within two years instead of the existing void. Finally, there seemed little chance that Congress would enact new legislation.[23]

Despite the support of the state's leading politicians the settlement was rejected at the polls, 13,800 to 11,600, with almost 20,000 abstaining. The referendum was not binding on the legislature, however, and the governor decided to interpret the abstentions as acquiescence and ask for approval. State Senator Palmer, who was in confidential touch with Corcoran, guided the bill through the upper house by 17 to 14. In the House of Representatives the battle was even closer (and no doubt more expensive). The bill was defeated, 40 to 38, then finally passed, 42 to 38, after two full days of debate. Opponents demanded and obtained an investigation of charges of bribery. The result was a whitewash followed by unsuccessful demands for an investigation of the investigators. After six long years the speculators and creditors were able to sit down to the fruits of their efforts.[24]

The $7.75 million allocated paid 76.895 percent of all claims. A total of $1.175 million went to the trustees of the Bank of the United States, who were listed in two groups: Samuel Jaudon and James A. Bayard in one, Charles Macalester and Josiah Randall in the second, with Christopher Fallon and William B. Reed members of both groups. Much, or most, of this money went to William S. Wetmore, who was a member and trustee of both groups. Another $70,000 was collected by Corcoran in April 1861 on paper hypothecated by Hamilton. Of this $30,000 went to Corcoran & Riggs, $15,000 to George W. Riggs, and the rest to the Holford estate, Wetmore, and United States Bank trustees.

The president of the Girard Bank of Philadelphia, C. S. Boker, appears as United States Bank trustee on another payment of $66,000. Other notably large payments included $465,000 to William E. Mayhew, William D. Miller, and James Mason Campbell of Baltimore, surviving partners and assignees of British financier Frederick Dawson, and $409,000 to Milbank & Co. of New York. Some claims were never presented and others delayed for various reasons including litigation by adverse claimants. Congress passed several resolutions postponing the deadline for presentation. The payment to Wetmore in 1861, which had been contested by Hamilton's estate, seems to have been the last. The payment to Corcoran & Riggs on Hamilton's paper in 1861 was $12,000 less than his debt with accumulated interest. Litigation dragged on until finally settled in 1867 by payment of bonds of the James River & Kanawha Co., in which Hamilton had been interested.[25]

The memoranda in Corcoran's papers are not precise and detailed enough to account for the whole Texas speculation but they do indicate that the results were unsatisfactory. The firm collected $625,000 (excluding the delayed receipts of 1861) of which $214,000 was as agent for others. Of the remaining $411,000, $296,000 was finally divided in a 3-to-1 ratio between Corcoran and Elisha Riggs, Jr., former partners of Corcoran & Riggs. Of the $115,000 balance about $40,000 was applied to repayment of loans to politicians and lobbyists, about $35,000 was paid out to them as fees, bribes, and profits, and somewhat under $10,000 was credited to commissions on collections for others. The rest—something over $30,000—appears to have repaid Jesse Bright's loans financing his joint Texas debt account with Corcoran. The politicians, financed by Corcoran and Riggs, netted roughly 20 percent (after deduction of interest) on the money the firm put up. But to Corcoran it was an "unfortunate speculation": the firm absorbed most of the management and lobbying costs, leaving little if any profit, and the money tied up would have been far better employed elsewhere.[26]

Of the $96,000 collected for him, Combs finally received $39,000; the rest offset his debts. Hamilton and Combs were each charged $2,000, apart from commissions, "Due per sealed agreement." Favored congressional contacts like Glossbrenner and Kurtz were charged only ½ percent for collection. Harrison's 1 percent was the lowest among others. Combs paid 2½ percent while financiers like the Milbanks and Robert & William, who had already paid that amount, were surcharged the same for a total of 5 percent. Many complained bitterly at these charges but Corcoran replied that the commissions were still not one-fifth what collection of the debts had cost him. Had an effort been made to hold him to the originally promised 2½ percent, he added, he would have given up the whole affair. The financier also acted to obtain an injunction to compel the Bank of the United States trustees to repay him the commission of $1,700 he had advanced to Memucan Hunt.[27]

But Corcoran's disappointment with the monetary result neglects the unforeseen political profits. The coalition brought together by the Texas creditors maintained a fascinating continuity in the drive to make Buchanan President in 1856 and to elevate Breckinridge after him. A direct link is suggested by an intriguing detail in one of the memoranda in Corcoran's papers on the disposition of Texas debt collections: $113 of the expenses was to pay for his trip to the Democratic convention in Cincinnati. There he and Senators Bright and Bayard, with John Slidell, Judah P. Benjamin, and Samuel L. M. Barlow, led the Democratic party to its decisive nomination of Buchanan and Breckinridge. Slidell and Benjamin were from New Orleans, after Philadelphia one of the key cities in which Texas paper was concentrated; Bayard, a Bank of the United States trustee, had been whipped into line by Bright after initially favoring the Texas scaling so beneficial to his clients. James Guthrie, Treasury Secretary to a President still hopeful of renomination, had cooperated with the Texas creditors to make their money speedily available in time for the convention; after it, when their links to Buchanan became clear, he fought their attempt to obtain an additional appropriation of $300,000.

After the convention Corcoran was one of the major financiers of the campaign against the new Republican party. Bright continued to manipulate closely divided Indiana, while a crucial shift of Whigs of the old Bank of the United States group, led by trustees Josiah Randall and William B. Reed, helped keep vital Pennsylvania barely in the Democratic column. Of course slavery, in various manifestations, fueled the greatest controversy, but the Texas debt—among other relatively narrow interests—was instrumental in the organization and financing of political coalitions.[28]

The California Debt

A similar speculation on a smaller scale was undertaken in California war bonds. The state issued $838,000 of 7 and 12 percent bonds in 1851–1852 and smaller amounts later for emergency financing of Indian wars. On grounds that protection against Indians was a federal function under the Constitution, the state's congressional delegation sought federal appropriations to pay principal and interest.[29]

Corcoran & Riggs began buying California bonds early, chiefly through their San Francisco correspondent, James King. The firm gradually accumulated $50,000 face value, with another $20,000 for Corcoran himself and also put bonds in the hands of influential politicians. Purchases totaling $9,500 of 7 percent shares were made for the account of Presidential nominee Franklin Pierce in August and September 1852 by his secretary, Sidney Webster, with $3,500 added the following spring. Webster also bought $2,000 for himself with money lent by the firm. Bright and his colleague, Thomas G. Pratt of Maryland, were furnished funds to accumulate $10,000 and $7,000 respectively, partly in a joint account. Among others interested were James Buchanan, Andrew Glossbrenner, John Davis, John L. O'Sullivan, and William L. Hodge. The Corcoran & Riggs purchases were all made at about 56 to 62.[30]

California Senator William Gwin introduced the bill to pay the state's Indian war debt. It languished in committee but was finally passed in August 1854 as a rider to a military appropriations bill, making $924,000 available.[31] Delay followed, caused by conflict between California and the federal government. Secretary of War Jefferson Davis insisted on receiving and passing upon vouchers for the expenses claimed by the state, whose accounting was not rigorous enough to satisfy him. He also enforced a cutoff date of January 1, 1854. California wanted to pay the principal and interest on the 12 percent bonds first. This would have left only enough for an 80 to 90 percent settlement of the 7 percent bonds, whose owners, including Corcoran and Riggs and their allies, naturally objected. The creditors wished to receive their money in Washington while the state wanted the funds turned over to her for disbursement. Corcoran was not unduly dismayed, for he mistakenly considered the state reliable for payment of the 7 percent interest accruing.[32]

In the summer of 1856 Senator Weller of California introduced a bill which, with an amendment by Benjamin of Louisiana, would satisfy the creditors by authorizing payment at Washington. A prominent supporter was Robert W. Johnson of Arkansas, another intimate and client of Corcoran who was shortly to receive a large loan partly for the purchase of California war bonds. After being passed by the Senate the bill was tabled in the House, 108 to 77, partly because of the truculence of partisans such as Denver of California, but it was promptly attached as a rider to the civil appropriations bill and passed two days later.[33] Payment was finally obtained in the fall of 1856. The firm's overall profit was better than 40 percent, despite nonpayment of interest from 1854 and exclusion of $10,000 of bonds of late issue.[34]

Florida Debts

In October 1848, Corcoran & Riggs joined George Peabody, William Wetmore, and John Cryder in the purchase of £12,000 of a £30,000 claim against the Bank of the United States in order to secure the collateral, which included £56,000 of Florida territorial bonds and £15,000 of Union

Bank of Florida bonds. These had been repudiated in 1842, but Corcoran believed he could lobby through Congress federal assumption of the debts on grounds that they had been incurred while Florida was still a territory under national jurisdiction. Disappointed when Peabody sold off part of their share, Corcoran tried to increase his holdings: confident as he was he thought the cost in bribes would be justifiable only if the investment were large.[35]

Suddenly there was a Congressman in the ointment. Representative Edward Carrington Cabell (Whig, Fla.) wanted to buy $200,000 of the bonds Corcoran controlled. He warned the surprised banker, who could not understand how the information had leaked out, that any publicity of his interest could be fatal. Cabell wanted the bonds for his uncle, John G. Gamble, who as president of the Union Bank had sold its securities in the Northeast and abroad. Gamble would turn them over to the bank at face value to pay off mortgages on his sugar plantations.[36]

Corcoran remained confident enough to reject Gamble's offer of 40 percent. The approaching assumption of the Texas debt raised hopes that the federal government would perform the same service for creditors of Mississippi, Florida, and Arkansas. It also seemed possible that Wetmore, who was managing the claim against the Bank of the United States, would get it settled in full. All these prospects fell through and the bonds were finally disposed of at about 35, apparently to an English group that planned to carry a suit for their payment to the Supreme Court. The profit was a cool 100 percent. By January 1852 Corcoran, chastened by experience, was less optimistic about repudiated state debts and declined to speculate again in Florida bonds.[37]

Arkansas Bonds and Politics

In 1854 Corcoran declined an ambitious speculation offered by Democratic Senator Robert W. Johnson of "from 5 to

700,000 dolls. *Clear profit* can be made on 3 or 400,000 by an operation (financial) in connection with the affairs of my state (Arkansas) which is not only fair and legitimate and honorable, but will be a benefit to every party that it affects. Others will be on the scene and early action should be had." What the Senator had in mind is not quite clear since Corcoran did not take up his offer, but there are several possibilities. In 1841 Arkansas had defaulted on bonds of her issue or guarantee, but after 1850 the craving for capital to build railroads spurred a movement for resumption of payments of the debt and interest.[38]

Resumption got nowhere in Arkansas. Although Governor Conway, ally of Johnson, obliquely suggested it in 1856, the legislature refused to act. But bonds were a means to another end—land. As was the case with other repudiating states, Arkansas' debt had been incurred to support banks which later failed. Their receivers would accept bonds at face value plus interest for two purposes: to settle debts, or in exchange for mortgaged land taken over from defaulted borrowers. As the state's population grew and the cotton economy boomed, speculators and settlers bought up depreciated bonds to exchange them for land. The process was accelerated by congressional passage of important railroad land grants.[39]

The deepening personal and financial ties between Corcoran and Johnson formed a link in an expanding coalition of politician-enterprisers. Johnson enjoyed the cooperation of Albert Pike, attorney in charge of the liquidation of the banks. A former Whig and leader of the Know-Nothing party in Arkansas, Pike had already helped put Johnson in the Senate over strong opposition within the Democratic party. Johnson was to reciprocate soon and amply enough. Pike was attorney for the Choctaw Indians in prosecuting claims arising from the Treaty of Dancing Rabbit Creek of 1830. Between 1855 and 1861 $1 million was paid in settlement of these claims, of which at least one-third went to Pike—in good part, no doubt, *through* him in the usual way. There was heated opposition to these appropriations in Congress. Pike credited Johnson for piloting them through the Senate, and Breckinridge, as Vice-President and presiding officer, for permitting him to choose the Senate members of the key conference committee.[40] The relationship, with its tie-in of huge Indian claims and state and national politics, is strikingly like that enjoyed by Jesse Bright with Richard W. Thompson in Indiana.[41]

It was natural for Corcoran to aid Johnson in his bond and land transactions. In the summer of 1854 he advanced $31,000 to pay for $44,000 of Arkansas bonds and accrued interest coupons, managing the purchases as well. His experience as government banker told him where to turn, chiefly to former congressman Daniel B. St. John. Then superintendent of banking of New York State, St. John knew which securities were registered as collateral for note issues by banks under state law. Johnson was able to achieve his goal: use of the bonds to pay for a large plantation acreage.[42]

Mississippi Bonds and Politics

Of all the campaigns of aggrieved creditors, perhaps none so radically—if unwittingly—influenced the history of an American state as that in Mississippi. The bonds, issued by the state to promote the Planters and Union Banks, were defaulted in 1841. The Union's were officially repudiated in 1842; the Planters' were in fact just as dead. Still, hope flickered. Some states moved toward resumption of defaulted debts, and in 1848 a tiny sum in the sinking fund of the Planters Bank was distributed to bondholders.

Before year's end Corcoran & Riggs joined Samuel Riggs and Peabody in purchases at a little over 20, and in November 1849 Corcoran bought at least $50,000 face value at the same rate for his own account. Robert J. Walker, who had demagogically advocated repudiation during his Mississippi career, became a speculator and apparently acted in conjunction with Corcoran. Some creditors, including Baring Brothers, considered legal and political action to gain resumption of the

Planters Bank bonds. If the Union Bank bonds were ever to be paid, it could only be in the wake of the Planters Bank's, which had been issued without the grave irregularities attached to those of the Union. By the middle of 1851 Corcoran was unable to find Planters bonds at his limit of 66⅔ percent. The price rose as high as 75, aided by seemingly favorable political developments stemming from the Compromise of 1850.[43]

The compromise, detested by states-rights extremists, led to a series of struggles between incipient secessionists and Unionists. Nowhere were these more intense than in Mississippi where the secessionists, led by Jefferson Davis, controlled the majority Democratic party. A faction led by Senator Henry S. Foote, a leader among southern Compromisers, split off from the party to form a Unionist coalition with the Whigs for the 1851 elections. Although only a small minority in the coalition, the Unionist Democrats were allotted half the nominations for state-wide office. Foote himself headed the ticket as candidate for governor. The Democrats rechristened themselves the States-Rights party. The compromise—or, fundamentally, the Union—was *the* issue over which the campaign was fought. However, to the creditors there appeared to be intriguing possibilities, for Foote and most of the Whigs were sympathetic to resumption. The explosive debt controversy was carefully avoided for the time being. On the sole issue of the Union, Foote was able to draw about 4,000 Democrats with him. Added to 26,000 Whigs, they gave victory to the Unionists by less than 2,000 votes.[44]

The victors celebrated in a curious way: by committing political suicide. Prompted more or less discreetly by agents of the Barings and Corcoran, they revived the debt question in the legislature. It was linked to internal improvements in classic Whig fashion: foreign and northern capital, necessary to build railroads, allegedly could not be attracted without a settlement. Leading New Orleans banker and railroad entrepreneur James Robb (also an important Texas creditor) lent his aid. Foote, a southern Douglas in his Whiggish economic attitudes and middle-of-the-road course on the territorial issue, gave assurances of support.

In February 1852 a bill was introduced in the state Senate to offer to redeem the Planters Bank bonds in equal face value amounts of stock of the New Orleans & Nashville, Mobile & Ohio, Southern, and other railroads. Their construction would be financed out of the revenues of the general property tax, which had just been sharply reduced. The bill was beaten by a 40 to 40 tie vote, the Unionists dividing 31 to 25 in its favor while the States-Rights party opposed it by 15 to 9. The Whigs pressed for enactment of a public referendum on the issue of resumption and got it. The legislation included an egregiously candid amendment. Instead of asking, as originally proposed, "Shall the bonds issued on account of the Planters Bank of the State of Mississippi be paid?" the question was worded, "Will you submit to a direct tax for the payment of the Planters Bank bonds?" The proposal was rejected, 24,000 to 12,000.[45]

Meanwhile the infatuated creditors had brought suit in Chancellor's Court to have the Union Bank bonds declared a valid obligation of the state. These were the bonds which, in contrast to those of the Planters Bank, virtually no one in Mississippi considered legitimate. The lower court ruled them legal, however, and was upheld by the High Court of Errors and Appeals, the highest court of the state. The bond question immediately became the sole political issue as the States-Rights Democrats launched a bitter assault upon the judges, who were predominantly Whig. Union Democrat leaders began to waver and break. Governor Foote came out flatly against payment of the Union Bank bonds while some Democrats who had been cautiously preparing the way for redemption of the Planters' bonds recoiled and became outright repudiationists. The States-Rights Democrats swept the fall elections of 1853 by a majority of about 5,000, regaining almost all the votes lost in 1851 and recapturing full control of all branches of the government including the popularly elected High Court.

The Union coalition had begun to show symptoms of disintegration after its victory in 1851. Impatient Whigs saw the successful use of the Union issue as the means to establish the party's dominance and implement their program of aid and encouragement to business. They ignored warnings not to make redemption a partisan issue, disregarding their Union Democratic allies. It is a measure of their self-delusion that Foote and the Whig leaders were utterly unprepared for the unity, violence, and single-mindedness of the attacking States Rights repudiationists. Too late, they tried to revert to a Unionist campaign, but the Democrats, pretending to full acceptance of the 1851 election decision, successfully branded this a phony issue. The election of 1853 was a disaster not merely for the Whigs but for moderate politics in a state that was soon to become a chief fomenter of secession. Foote later blamed the debacle largely on the "wholly *impertinent*" bond issue. Perhaps he still had it in mind years later when he laid the Civil War not only to the "incessant agitation of sectional factionists" but also to the "unskillful and blundering management of men in power."[46]

Thereafter, with agents of the Barings furnishing most of the initiative, Corcoran & Riggs and other creditors occasionally signed memorials and bought the services of Mississippi newspapers. William Gouge volunteered in 1859 to write another history. In a long letter soliciting employment to prepare a volume on the Mississippi debt similar to those for Texas and Arkansas, William Gouge began with an exposition of the importance of the intellectual. "I am well aware that exertions of another kind were necessary: but I firmly believe that if *somebody* had not drawn up a full and plain narrative of the facts, the creditors would not have gotten their money till this day, if at all." He outlined a plan of campaign and listed his qualifications: the reputation of his publications in Mississippi; "suggestor" of the Independent Treasury system; long experience in the Treasury Department, with knowledge of where to get hold of important documents not easily accessible to others; labors in Texas and Arkansas; wide personal acquaintanceship in Mississippi and among southern men in Washington; continued ownership of 2,700 acres in that state, the remains of purchases made more than 20 years earlier. "If it should become necessary for me . . . to recommend taxation, I can declare that I am willing to bear my part of the burden. . . . My own political interests accord with those of the great body of the people of Mississippi. They profess to be hard-money, anti-bank, Sub-Treasury, free trade, State Rights, Conservative Democrats, and so am I." He asked Corcoran, whom he had known for more than twenty years, to pass the message on to other bondholders, but nothing came of his proposal.[47]

Corcoran, partly motivated by his bond holdings, banked favors with Mississippi congressmen by lending them money and by selling lands through them to their constituents. As late as Reconstruction times, he proposed a joint speculation to J. S. Morgan, successor to Peabody, in the belief the state government might prove obliging. In 1870 the Rothschilds and their agent, August Belmont, accumulated $2 million face value, half the total outstanding. These were futile activities; for all practical purposes, the affair of the Mississippi bonds was over.[48]

Loans to Frontier Towns

During the 1850s Corcoran & Riggs invested in bonds issued by several Iowa cities to finance internal improvements. In 1852 they took large blocks of Burlington municipal 8 and 10 percent bonds which had been turned over as subsidies to the Burlington & Louisa Plank Road Co. and the Peoria & Oquawka Railroad. After his retirement Corcoran kept $20,000 of these, with another $5,000 of Keokuk bonds, but all were defaulted after the Panic of 1857. When repudiation followed, based on fraud or other real or alleged irregularities, Corcoran joined the hundreds of litigants in late nineteenth-century municipal bond cases. Eventually he went to court to obtain judgments, then compromised with the municipalities by taking new bonds for 50 percent of Keokuk's overdue debt and for the whole Burlington debt (including accrued interest).[49]

The Keokuk and Burlington loans were simple business transactions, but a loan to Dubuque also involved political considerations. Corcoran's contact there was Iowa's Democratic Senator, George W. Jones, one of the prosouthern group battling for control of the midwestern Democracy in the fifties and a collaborator in such matters as the Texas debt and railroad land-grant legislation. From 1852 to 1854 the banker lent him $5,000 to finance his operations, chiefly land speculations in Dubuque and Des Moines which were based on the railroad expansion he was trying to help bring about in Congress. Additional loans and interest brought the outstanding balance to $10,000 in 1857. These loans helped Jones carry investments which he valued (probably excessively) at $150,000 in 1859.[50]

Frontier communities still commonly appointed their congressmen to negotiate loans in the East, thus saving expenses for agents. Jones was delegated to negotiate a loan of $100,000 for Dubuque. Corcoran advanced money at 10 percent for twenty years, thus presumably strengthening his portfolio and Jones's prestige. The loan was secured by a mortgage on the city's Central Island, which lay in the Mississippi River, and it was understood that much of the money would be applied to construction of wharves on the island. When Corcoran discovered that this was not being done and that flood damage was going unrepaired he threatened to halt advances, but despite the "remarkable looseness" with which the city was conducting its business he relaxed when assured the lapses were being corrected. Corcoran kept $30,000 of the bonds and allocated the rest to relatives and friends at cost, including $50,000 to the Riggs family, $6,000 to Sidney Webster, and $1,000 to William Gouge.[51]

Disillusionment came quickly. Dubuque, like many other boom towns on the frontier, was borrowing exuberantly. Debt approached $750,000 by the spring of 1858 despite widespread criticism and attempts during the state constitutional convention of 1857 to limit municipal and county borrowing.

The Panic of 1857 and the ensuing depression wrecked the city's finances. The Democrats had profited politically before the panic from booming expansion accelerated by their land grant and borrowing programs; the Republicans gained by their discredit. Jones was among those of the wounded majority party who were swept from office in 1858.[52]

Corcoran finally learned how irresponsible the city fathers were. Dubuque had conveyed rights on the Central Island to the Central Improvement Co. in exchange for its assumption of the debt burden. When the company went bankrupt the city disclaimed responsibility for the bonds. Corcoran also discovered that the improvements which were supposed to be financed by his loan had never been made. To add to his woes, he was informed in 1860 that the island on which he held the mortgage had been largely submerged and was not worth more than $30,000. After several years of sparring Dubuque offered to settle its obligations at 50 percent. Corcoran refused and had the mortgage on Central Island foreclosed for interest due of $77,500, but the sale under the decree only yielded $1,000. Another suit was begun and eventually settled by a refunding of the debt and accrued interest at 7 percent. The whole was finally repaid in four equal installments from 1870 to 1873.[53]

To make matters worse, Jones was not paying his debt. From Colombia, where he went as minister after his defeat in 1858, he tried to sell Corcoran an interest in a get-rich-quick silver mining scheme and was curtly refused. The debt was extended for two years when William Aspinwall guaranteed its payment on maturity. The guarantee was not fulfilled, perhaps because of his death. Despite his exasperation Corcoran leniently carried the debt for some years longer, finally going to court in 1868. Payment in full was received in 1870.

Other cities whose bonds soured in Corcoran's portfolio were Milwaukee and Janesville, Wisconsin; Memphis; Nashville; Covington, Kentucky; and St. Paul. Most of the loans were to finance railroads. The Milwaukee bonds were taken during the firm's active investment banking days in 1850; most were sold at above 107, but Corcoran and his family kept $10,000 which were defaulted in 1859. The loan was to help build the Milwaukee & Mississippi Railroad, then headed by Byron Kilbourn. The Janesville bonds, $8,000, were collateral for a loan to Robert J. Walker. The city repudiated them on a technicality but they were apparently used by Walker to repay a debt to the Chicago, St. Paul & Fond du Lac Railroad. The St. Paul bonds were purchased through a nephew, William M. Corcoran, who left Riggs & Co. to find his fortune in the west. City bonds of $18,000 were taken late in 1856: although the interest was high (12 percent) Corcoran insisted he was chiefly interested in helping his nephew get started. Jesse Bright bought $8,000 of the lot. In addition William entered politics, gaining a postmastership through his uncle's and Henry Rice's patronage and winning election to the Board of Aldermen. Unfortunately, despite all his advantages, William was a loser. His uncle had to bail him out after heavy losses in the Panic of 1857. Still hoping the young man would straighten himself out, Corcoran subscribed for $60,000 of bridge bonds, keeping $25,000 and selling $10,000 to F. R. Corbin of Philadelphia and $25,000 to Royal Phelps in New York. He also added to his holdings of the city improvement bonds. The city defaulted on interest payments, however, and in 1866 Corcoran accepted refunding in 7 percent bonds.[54]

Yulee and the Florida Railroad

Another politician-businessman with whom Corcoran collaborated was David Yulee. His Florida Railroad received various swamp and internal improvement lands donated by Congress to the state, especially a grant of 1856. The route ran from Fernandina, in northeastern-most Florida, southwest to Cedar Keys on the Gulf Coast. In December 1856 Riggs & Co. distributed $250,000 of the company's 8 percent "Freeland" bonds, secured by its lands. Corcoran took $20,000, Elisha Riggs $25,000, and the latter's relatives and agent additional amounts at 65. Subscribers at 70 included such notables as Robert J. Walker, $2,500 (apparently in part a commission for services rendered); lobbyist George Sanders, $2,500; Henry Varnum Poor, publisher of the *American Railroad Journal,* $15,000; and shipping magnate Marshall O. Roberts, $10,000 (of which $7,000 was for himself and the rest at least partly for Yulee). In September 1859 August Belmont, Riggs & Co., and James Soutter, president of the Bank of the Republic (New York) advanced $15,000, $10,000, and $5,000 respectively to pay interest on outstanding bonds, taking notes secured by mortages on the railroad's property and Yulee's slaves. Still unfinished in 1861, the road was left bankrupt and deteriorated by the Civil War.[55]

In the spring of 1867 Corcoran prepared to join other creditors in buying the company's lands with Freeland bonds at a public sale for the benefit of creditors. He drew back when he learned that the railroad's most promising real estate, the terminal townsites of Fernandina and Cedar Keys, had already been privately sold to insider creditor F. Dickinson & Co. for $800,000 of bonds bought up at 18 to 20 percent of par. Angered, Corcoran retained Wilkinson Call, nephew of a former governor of Florida, to sue to invalidate the sale. Nothing seems to have come of these plans and in 1871 the remaining lands of the company were put up for sale at public auction and bought in for the benefit of the bondholders, among whom they were divided whether or not they had agreed. Corcoran's share was 13,587 acres, but, refusing to acknowledge the legality of the proceedings, he rejected the award.[56]

In 1879 Corcoran filed suit against various parties involved in plundering the Florida Railroad during and after Reconstruction. Among the defendants was Yulee, who tried to buy the bonds of Elisha Riggs' estate at 15. A Democrat, he escaped the charges of corruption hurled against the Republicans although he had collaborated with them during Reconstruction. Corcoran was pessimistic about the suit but Call, who had just been elected to the Senate, persuaded him to file and enlisted Senators Benjamin H. Hill of Georgia and Augustus

Garland of Arkansas to assist in the case. After the deal with Garland had been closed Call became Attorney General but he continued to give advice and ultimately received a $500 retainer.[57] While the case was dragging on, the Florida Railway & Navigation Co., successor to the Florida Railroad, began to sell the remaining unclaimed lands. Call belatedly tried to prevent this in Congress on grounds that it would deprive many settlers, without compensation, of land they had improved. The lands, Call argued, should be forfeited back to the United States for failure to complete prescribed improvements within stipulated time limitations. These tardy efforts failed, both in Congress and the courts, marking the evaporation of Corcoran's investment.[58]

The Moral Man Offended

Throughout these wrangles Corcoran never failed to take a high moral position. A quarrel over a private loan perhaps best reveals how rigidly moralistic he could be as a creditor. In 1856 he and Elisha Riggs, Jr. made a large personal loan of $200,000 and $50,000 respectively at 10 percent to Pierre Chouteau, Jr., James Harrison, and Felix Valle of St. Louis against a mortgage on ore-bearing property at Iron Mountain, Missouri. There the borrowers were developing an iron works and preparing to build the St. Louis & Iron Mountain Railroad as a link to markets. The Iron Mountain property suffered vicissitudes of imperfect land titles, depression, and war but despite occasional difficulty and delay, interest payments were maintained. In view of the high return Corcoran was complacent when the debtors were unable to repay the principal due in 1861 and 1862. (But Riggs agreed late in 1862 to lower the interest rate to 9 percent, and a few months later to 8 percent.)[59]

A bitter controversy broke out after Congress passed the Legal Tender Act of 1862, which empowered the government to issue paper money to help finance the war. Corcoran acknowledged that interest could be paid in depreciated paper but insisted that the debt, having been lent in gold, was payable in gold. It was, he reiterated solemnly, a matter of principle; any gentleman would repay gold. At his urging Riggs, who had been more flexible, withdrew an offer to accept paper. The dispute continued for more than a year until J. P. Morgan, handling Corcoran's affairs during his Civil War exile, accepted repayment in paper as the only realistic solution. The elder Charles P. Chouteau, hard pressed but embarrassed by Corcoran's repeated moral strictures, admitted that the settlement was unfair and promised to propose an adjustment. None was forthcoming, despite Corcoran's increasingly haughty reminders, and the long friendship between the two old men was sacrificed to his sense of outrage.[60]

Corcoran's conduct in this episode was unusual. He was more rigid than others with the same interest; more demanding of an old friend than he would have been, perhaps, with someone less close, not that he was hypocritical in maintaining the sanctity of debt. Immediately after his first great coup in 1847, Corcoran had voluntarily paid in full, with 6 percent interest, the debts left by the failure of his and his brother's firm in 1823. Few, if any, of the creditors or their heirs even remembered those ancient debts, which had been legally discharged decades before. The only possible element of calculation in their repayment lay in the widespread favorable publicity, which came at a time when the circumstances of his winning war-loan bid seemed questionable to many; yet the settlement was expensive—$48,000 was a heavy price to volunteer. It was a unique act in an age when bankruptcy was coming to be regarded as not too reprehensible an episode in the education of a businessman.

The ambiguity of Corcoran's conduct lies in the contrast between the harsh rigidity of his position and his usually pragmatic and flexible ethics. Perhaps that seeming contrast is in fact the link. Economics aside, there is an air of subconscious compensation about his moralization of debt, as if he were seeking the refuge of some fixed general standard amidst the tumultuous striving and insecurity, as if seeking something sacred where precious little was sacred.[61]

Widespread conflicts grew out of the attempts to apportion responsibility for the blunders and culpability of lenders and borrowers, speculators and investors, financiers and politicians. The speculator scavenging after the disaster was often neither innocent nor scrupulous; yet he was sufficiently subject to error and resistance to share losses as well as gains, and by maintaining a market sometimes inadvertently enabled the more innocent to recover something. To the historian, however, in government debts as in claims, subsidies, or "pet" banking, the seemingly haphazard political effects are far more intriguing, particularly those following from the gradual coalescing of initially isolated individuals and groups. But the most grandiose arena for these dynamics was furnished by the promise of railroads.

11

The Great Superior Scheme: Continental Ambitions in Townsites, Railroads, and Politics

Turning and turning in the widening gyre. . . .
—W. B. Yeats, "The Second Coming"

Conception

One day in the spring of 1853 Stephen A. Douglas climbed on a chair before a wall-size map and pointed to a spot at the head of Lake Superior. Here, he told a friend, would begin the greatest railroad in the nation, excepting only the southern transcontinental. The Sault Ste. Marie Canal, soon to be completed, would clear a waterway to the Atlantic; the Mississippi River route to the Mexican Gulf was close by; a railroad would link these waterways with other railroads running east and south, and turn westward across the continent toward the Pacific. At the hub of these avenues a great city would grow up, the center of a commerce destined to link Europe and the East. Fortunes, Douglas added, would be made in real estate.[1] He did not need to add that great political fortunes also might be won.

Douglas had vaulted into national leadership in 1850 partly

by mobilizing reciprocal economic interests to compromise the conflicts over slavery. It seemed logical to repeat the strategy when controversy over slavery revived, and to use the Superior scheme as a tactical political instrument. But this time instead of success Douglas was to reap the winds of Kansas-Nebraska, and his strategy, copied by ambitious state and national politicians, would fuel rather than quiet the gathering hostilities.

As the foremost political banker of the day and the most effective at working with diverse factions, Corcoran was one of the first brought into the speculation. His role, however, was to be subordinate, clerical, almost passive, for the fate of the scheme would depend upon more strategically situated politicians and businessmen in Washington and elsewhere. For Douglas, Superior was to be, for a time, a central element in his struggle to organize a controlling national political coalition from the hordes of clashing would-be empire builders across the states and territories. The doom of his efforts was part and symbol of the growing chaos of these forces.

The Superior speculation was launched early in 1853. The population frontier was spreading westward and northward in Wisconsin and Minnesota Territory. Copper had been found around the western Great Lakes. The Sault Canal was being built and would open new areas to through navigation within two years. I. I. Stevens, assigned by the War Department to survey the northernmost of potential rail routes to the Pacific, found it promising and kept Douglas informed. Railroads were being projected. The most ambitious, planned to extend from the head of Lake Superior to Puget Sound, was promoted by Wisconsin, Minnesota, and Oregon politicians, while Chicago and Milwaukee interests were already building northward toward the future location of Superior.[2]

The first claims at the intended townsite were established by Daniel A. Robertson, acting for himself and Douglas. Robertson had entered politics by way of Tammany Hall in New York. After moving to Ohio in 1837 he held various political positions and edited Democratic newspapers, among them the Cincinnati *Enquirer*. In 1850 he looked for room at the top in St. Paul, where he became leader of a minority faction of his party and editor of the *Minnesota Democrat*. Accompanying him to the future Superior were Rensselaer R. Nelson, erstwhile New Yorker and son of a Supreme Court Justice, and Daniel A. J. Baker. Each of these later received one share in the townsite, along with Julius N. Granger, a young relative of Douglas employed in the General Land Office in Washington.[3]

Competitors arrived even while Robertson and his confreres were laying out their claims. The second group was headed by Henry M. Rice, later delegate and Senator from Minnesota and already a prominent and troublesome figure. A Democrat, he was the senior partner of the St. Paul firm of Rice, Hollinshead & Becker, lawyers, moneylenders, and land agents. His brother Edmund shared his economic and political interests, which included wholesale land speculation in Minnesota, Wisconsin and Iowa. George Becker, a Whig, was their brother-in-law. Associated with Rice in the Superior exploration were George and William Nettleton, William H. Newton, Benjamin Thompson, and James Stinson, another large-scale speculator who operated out of Chicago and St. Paul. These took up positions adjacent to their predecessors, upon whose claims they tried to encroach.

At the end of November Robertson and Rice were antagonists in speculation, as they had long been in politics, but having reached a stalemate they were soon united by the logic of the situation: together the two groups might better exclude other speculators who were beginning to appear. It was time to seek a railroad land grant, on which success would largely depend; unity would be vital in local and national capitals. At the beginning of December Rice proposed an alliance and Douglas accepted. Locally, he patched up his quarrels with Robertson and other important politicians. The combined townsite preemption claim totalled 6,000 acres at the mouth of the St. Louis River in Wisconsin opposite what is now Duluth, Minnesota.[4]

The speculators strengthened their position by incorporating a wide spectrum of important Democratic politicians. The original shares in the company numbered twenty-seven, held by nineteen individuals. Henry Rice conveyed one of his shares to his brother Edmund and one to Horace S. Walbridge, prominent merchant and member of Congress from New York. Corcoran, Robert J. Walker, and Douglas each received two shares. Douglas's lieutenant in the House, William A. Richardson, held one share, as did Granger, John Forney, clerk of the House of Representatives and a standard bearer for James Buchanan's presidential ambitions, and rising railroad man George W. Cass of Pittsburgh, nephew of Michigan Senator Lewis Cass. Senator Jesse Bright of Indiana received two shares, Senator Robert Hunter of Virginia and Congressman John C. Breckinridge of Kentucky one each. Two each for Robertson, Baker, Nelson, and Stinson and one each for Newton, Nettleton, and Thompson completed the original twenty-seven shares of the Superior Land Company.

The web of influence was stretched still further. Forney sold fractions of his share to Alfred Nicholson, his partner in publishing the party's national organ, the Washington *Union;* to I. D. Hoover, another House functionary; and to a prominent southerner, perhaps Representative W. W. Boyce of South Carolina. James Buchanan joined in, while Corcoran sold one-quarter share each to Representative John L. Dawson of Pennsylvania and to Elisha Riggs. Robertson sold a fractional interest to Tammany leader Charles P. Daly. Richardson did the same for Congressman John McQueen of South Carolina, and another Representative from that state, William Aiken, bought in, perhaps from Douglas. Breckinridge interested prominent Kentuckians, including his law partner, James B. Beck, and Governors Beriah Magoffin and Lazarus Powell.

Few Whigs were involved. These included James Cooper, Senator from Pennsylvania, who had joined Webster in opposing the Taylor-Seward Whigs and supporting compromise during the crisis of 1850; and his brother David, a Minnesota politician. Alexander Ramsey, former Pennsylvania Congressman and Minnesota's leading Whig, had land interests in or near Superior.[5]

Corcoran performed banking and clerical services for his associates. He acted as trustee for Douglas, Granger, Richardson, Bright, Breckinridge, and Forney, thus keeping their names out of public record.[6] He advanced money to some of the speculators—$5,000 to Bright and Douglas on joint account and $4,125 to Dawson in May and June 1854, when it seemed certain that a vital railroad land grant would be passed by Congress. Richardson borrowed $1,000 and Newton, who succeeded Nelson as resident manager for the proprietors, about $4,000. The more than $11,000 owed Corcoran by Walker in 1854 was partly secured by his two Superior shares. In January 1855 Douglas and Bright increased their borrowing to $5,000 each to share a joint account with Breckinridge and a fourth party. The size of the loans and the burden of paperwork were greater than Corcoran liked. In June 1855 the distribution of the Superior property to the shareholders began and was completed in five stages by July 1857. Corcoran impatiently obtained repayment from some of his debtors as they realized profits, but he also extended further credits up to several thousand dollars each to enable Bright, Dawson, Breckinridge, and Hunter to increase their holdings.[7]

Early in 1854 Rice moved to have the townsite claim legally confirmed. Aided by Senator George W. Jones of Iowa, he prompted the Government Land Office to survey the area, as required by law before claims could be validated, and saw to it that his associates were ready with dummy preemptors. By September the site was platted and the claim officially sanctioned.[8]

Town-building

Town-pioneering quickly got under way. Publicity by advertisements, newspaper reports, personal contacts, and lectures stimulated the beginnings of a boom. The place became something of a regional tourist attraction, especially for the political and speculative sort. Breckinridge built a summer home and entertained prominent passers-by. Even Corcoran seems to have gone there on the only western trip of his life, en route home from the 1856 Democratic convention.

What the visitors saw was doubtless a typical frontier boom town. On June 1, 1855, when the first census was taken, there were 385 inhabitants: 291 males, 93 females, 1 colored male. Sixty-four were foreign-born. By January 1856 the population was almost 600 and at its peak in 1857 it must have exceeded 1,000. The Superior Company made sales to actual settlers on credit with stipulations for improvements. Sales totalled $26,000 in 1854, $87,000 in 1855, and $14,000 January through May 1856, the months when the first migrants of spring appeared. Early in 1856 there were 105 dwellings, 17 stores, 14 shops, 15 offices, several each of shoemakers, blacksmiths, and drugstores, a brickyard, 2 saw mills, a schoolhouse, 2 federal land offices, and a wildcat bank.

The proprietors took the lead in the community's development, making large investments from the proceeds of sales. Lots were set aside for parks, churches, railroads, and other public facilities, and the clearing of streets was begun. Three thousand dollars was advanced to build a hotel. The harbor was dredged, wharves built and a large pier constructed for over $20,000. Steamers called regularly and Nettleton opened a stagecoach service to St. Paul. Two employees of the *Congressional Globe,* Washington Ashton and John C. Wise, were recruited by Douglas to establish a newspaper, the Superior *Chronicle,* whose first edition appeared in June 1855. (Presumably there were inducements to ease the risk.) County government was organized in 1854, with Nelson guiding the lobbying at Madison, and local government by 1856. Thereafter the company shared development costs with the citizens, the proprietors becoming individually liable for taxation and the company's role declining as it was liquidated.[9]

In addition to the proprietary company, individual entrepreneurs, and local governments, the federal government was making needed investments. Minnesotans, like other westerners and Americans generally, were indefatigable in the hunt for congressional appropriations, and foremost among them was Henry Rice with his well-placed contacts at Washington. A lighthouse was built for $15,000 and "military" roads for several times as much. But all this was secondary—what was really needed was a railroad.[10]

Douglas and the Illinois Central Railroad

The route decided on ran from Lake Superior to St. Paul, already a good-sized town, and south to the Iowa line where it was to link with a projected railroad to Dubuque and the Illinois Central. The idea had been born earlier in expansive Minnesota minds. Henry H. Sibley, delegate to Congress in 1852, introduced a bill for a land grant from Lake Superior to St. Paul with branches. Early in 1853 Governor Ramsey glowingly imagined a north-south trunk line through the Mississippi Valley, the "great New Orleans and Minnesota Railroad," and predicted the Minnesota line would also serve as the first step toward the Pacific. More tangible preparations were made in December when Rice offered cooperation at Superior. He plied Douglas with the vision of a railroad over the route laid out in the land grant legislation of 1850 from Mobile on the Mexican Gulf to Chicago and Dubuque, and on to Lake Superior. "One of the greatest works in the world. You know the men to call to your aid in procuring the grant—you know the men to build the road," Rice said, and continued: ["a favorable response] will save me from the regret of applying elsewhere for doubtful aid."[11]

Rice did not have to name the Illinois Central Railroad and its indispensable role in Douglas's rise to national leadership. It had been vital to the solution of the great intersectional crisis of 1850, in which the dangerous issues were those related to slavery. Congress had been unable to agree on a unified compromise, but after long and acrid controversy (and the death of President Taylor) it achieved the goal with a series of measures. As customarily understood by historians, the Compromise of 1850 left the new territories of New Mexico and Utah to legislate as they saw fit on slavery within their borders; admitted California to the Union as a state; ended the slave trade in the District of Columbia; adopted new procedures to assure the return of fugitive slaves to captivity; and settled the Texas debt. Strangely, however, historians have neglected the role of the Illinois Central Railroad land grant (although they have come to recognize the importance of the Texas debt settlement, which was equally irrelevant to slavery). The promise of the land subsidy from Chicago to the Mexican Gulf broke a major deadlock by detaching the crucial votes of Representatives Wentworth of Chicago and Thompson of Mississippi from the northern Free-Soil and southern "ultra" opposition to the compromise, passage of which cleared the way for the railroad grant. If the shift of Thompson and Wentworth reflected the economic interests of developing areas, another key promoter of the compromise, Whig congressman George Ashmun of Massachusetts—with his eminent Senate friend, Daniel Webster—represented the interests of northeastern investors. Ashmun was close to the New England and New York railroad builders who controlled the major midwestern roads. Later his collaboration with the "Little Giant," Douglas, recapitulated his intimacy with the late Whig orator, Webster, as the Illinois senator, like Webster, strove to synthesize economic expansion and national patriotism.[12]

The Illinois Central was not simply an end in itself as constituted. It was a budding empire, cooperating easily if imperfectly with the Michigan Central and the New York Central to the east while harboring ambitions westward. Reciprocally, with its elite leadership and demonstrated political strength, the Illinois Central's support was sought by frontier enterprisers contesting for local railroad mastery and by politicians who emulated Douglas' appeal, under the banner of progress, to both business and the electorate.

Perhaps the first thorough-going repetition of the Douglas–

Illinois Central precedent occurred in Arkansas. Robert W. Johnson was the state's congressman in 1852 when Senator Solon G. Borland introduced a land grant bill for the projected Arkansas Central Railroad from Memphis, Tennessee, to Little Rock. Its backers at home were a coalition of Whigs and the anti-Johnson faction of Democrats. In the House, however, Johnson pushed through a grant from Cairo, Illinois, through southeastern Missouri and via Little Rock to Fulton in the southwest corner of Arkansas. Two branches were provided for. One extended from Little Rock to Fort Smith in northwest Arkansas (reflecting the omnipresent transcontinental visions) and the other eastward to a point on the Mississippi to be chosen by the state—perhaps Memphis, perhaps not; there would be hard bargaining, if not blackmail, over this.

Johnson's tactics were cunning and ruthless. The support gained from Missouri, which shared in the grant, and from other congressmen representing prospective connecting roads (and contractors, suppliers, and investors), probably made possible House passage of the bill. With choice of the southeast branch terminus left open, Memphis and her rivals competed for Johnson's support in the state legislature: there would be no disgruntled opponents while state action was pending, and defeat would disarm the losers afterward. Arkansas Senator William K. Sebastian may have hoped his hometown of Helena would be favored: Johnson's bill was put through the Senate in February 1853 when Sebastian violated a gentleman's agreement not to call it up in Borland's absence, and it passed by voice vote. In the bargaining that followed at the state legislature, Memphis was finally chosen as the southeast branch terminal, but the victorious company was the previously little-noticed Memphis & Little Rock rather than the Borland-supported Arkansas Central. Openly outwitted and with a newly laid basis of statewide political power in enemy hands, Borland accepted a minor diplomatic post and resigned in April 1853. His place in the Senate was taken by his tormentor. Thus did Johnson establish his leadership in Arkansas politics.

The Cairo-Fulton Line would serve as a feeder for the

Illinois Central. But more important, although the Illinois road preferred a transcontinental link further north, it wanted access to a southern route if one became a reality, and such a route was being planned by allied entrepreneurs (although the effort eventually failed). The Arkansas road would provide a connection. When the Cairo & Fulton was organized and took up its land grant in 1854, the Illinois Central furnished its management. Still scrambling to complete its main lines, the Illinois road was not willing to take direct responsibility for any extensions; but it did supply personnel and advice to the new road, and apparently some capital was subscribed by common investors. Changing future circumstances were to force a more binding relationship, but for the time being the alliance was close enough.[13]

Another senatorial affiliate of the Illinois Central group was George W. Jones of Iowa. In 1850, abetted by Iowa Senator A. C. Dodge, Jones had forced Douglas to switch the planned Mississippi River terminus of the land grant from Galena to Dunleith, opposite his own town of Dubuque. Thereafter he made something of a pest of himself to the Illinois Central in pursuing his business and political ambitions, but conflicts were resolved readily enough in favor of the wider community of interests. For several years he lobbied for a grant from Dubuque to Keokuk, Iowa, perhaps hoping eventually to build a great north-south trunk line comparable to the Illinois Central on the west (Iowa) bank of the Mississippi. This aroused opposition in Iowa and Illinois, however, as transcontinental goals quickly asserted priority.

By 1853 the rapidly progressing Illinois Central was planning its next step westward. The Cairo & Fulton was rather too far to the south, although it would be a worthwhile connection if the Arkansas and the southern transcontinentalists could make a go of it; but Iowa, rich in promise, was growing by bounds and was the direct route to the Pacific. The Dubuque & Pacific Railroad was chartered, with management, directors, and investors drawn in large part from the Illinois road. Dubuque voted a $200,000 stock subscription and a grant of depot land. Jones looked forward to a federal land grant, but the Iowa delegation continued to be divided by the competition of cities and projected railroads on different east-west routes. Jones and the Dubuque & Pacific had to bide their time and strengthen their support while the Illinois Central turned to another alternative.[14]

David Yulee of Florida, temporarily out of public office, had no direct stake in the expansion of the Illinois Central, but his alliance typified the intersectional diplomacy of the time. He had once fought to prevent the concentration of power in private hands, in 1844 favoring state ownership of a trans-Florida railroad in preference to a feared investor monopoly. By 1849, driven by the hunger for capital, Yulee acquiesced in private enterprise and solicited northern investments. Largely under his leadership the state was still inclined to place some limits upon railroads: a (generous) ceiling on the rate of profit, a charter of limited life (twenty years), double liability, and a state option to buy the road. In 1851 Yulee and A. G. Benson interested Marshall O. Roberts and George Law, ship operators with important interests in Mexican Gulf and Caribbean commerce, in his Atlantic & Gulf Railroad, but the New Yorkers pulled out because of charter restrictions and Yulee lost control of the road. Thereafter he continued his evolution to the right and ended by embracing the increasingly dominant attitude of his generation of politicians, favoring the utmost possible aid to enterprise from every level of government with minimal or no restraint.

In the mid-1850s Yulee's intersectional alliances centered on two locations, Superior and Kentucky. He was a staunch adherent of Douglas, largely because of the latter's leadership of the land grant movement. In 1853, when Rice and Douglas were joining to promote Superior, Yulee was hard at work for a land grant to his Florida Railroad from Fernandina in the far northeast corner of the state, southwest across the Florida Peninsula to Cedar Keys on the Gulf Coast. His Kentucky connection developed partly by marriage into the powerful Wickliffe family of that state and Louisiana. His lobbyists included the notorious A. R. Corbin and Anson Bangs, who were promoters of a road from Cincinnati to Louisville. Corbin expected assistance from Senator Cass and Congressmen Henry May of Baltimore and Breckinridge of Kentucky and Superior.

The tactics supporting the Florida land grant bill of 1854 were sardonically akin to those which passed the Arkansas grant, thanks to the ministrations of Robert Johnson. As originally introduced the bill called for an eastern terminus at Jacksonville, home of Senator Stephen Mallory and a town competing with Yulee's Fernandina for the area's urban leadership. In House committee the choice of terminus between the two towns was left to the states, thanks to the management of Florida's Representative, Augustus Maxwell, her former Representative, Edward Cabell, and her second Senator, Jackson Morton. In the Senate the ever-ready Johnson brought his talents to bear. In Mallory's absence he effected the elimination of Jacksonville, and the bill passed. It was sent to the House in this form. There the Superior group was promoting a Minnesota land grant with the expectation that the Dubuque & Pacific and Florida bills would follow it through, the supporters of all three cooperating. Despite stiff opposition the whole baggage of the Illinois Central alliance might have arrived safely in the summer of 1854 if not for the Minnesota & North Western and Schuyler scandals.[15]

The clearest evidence of the Illinois Central's influence is the fact that only its allies were able to win land grants before 1856. In addition to those already discussed there were the Hannibal & St. Joseph and the St. Louis & Iron Mountain in Missouri. The former was an extension of the Michigan Central; the latter tapped the iron interests of Pierre Chouteau, Jr. and J. F. A. Sanford, whose American Fur Co. was still important throughout the Northwest and who were directors of the Illinois Central. While the group was not able to achieve all its goals, striking success was achieved until 1854.[16]

Douglas, his eye ever on the path to the presidency, had played the central role in developing this alignment, yet its continuance did not depend on him. The great Senator was keenly aware of this and of the implications for his larger ambitions. Not all of those who cooperated tactically supported him for the presidency. Yulee and perhaps Dodge seemed to be in his camp, but Johnson and Jones were doubtful: they were intimates of Bright, who had been his rival for leadership of the Democratic party in the Northwest. Whether Bright's hostility was dead or only dormant remained to be proved. Douglas hoped the common interest in Superior would contribute to an enduring reconciliation, which would be infinitely more valuable than pecuniary profit. But he had to run to remain leader of the column. There was nothing vague in Rice's challenge to promote the Minnesota bill: Douglas's favorable response "will save me from the regret of applying elsewhere."

Not that Douglas had to be prodded to support the bill. Far from conflicting with his interests and policies, it favored them in every way—assuming, as he did, those interests and policies actually were mutual with those of the Illinois Central. The planned Minnesota line would exploit a promising hinterland and growing towns and would connect the Great Lakes and waterways of the Mississippi. It would give the Illinois Central a head start against potential rivals in the northern Mississippi Valley. Although the Dubuque & Pacific promised the most direct avenue to the Pacific, the Minnesota—with the Cairo & Fulton—would enable the Illinois road to tap other potential transcontinental routes. Finally, a completed Minnesota road would speed the development of adjacent areas to the west and presumably win their allegiance for the Illinois Central group, since rivals would be left behind without a grant. At the least a lead would be achieved. If momentum could be maintained (and with, perhaps, successive land grants), the transcontinental race might be won step by step.

As far as the Illinois Central group was concerned, then, a Minnesota railroad would be part of a three-pronged fanning out designed to straddle all potential Pacific routes. If the avenue was less direct than that through Iowa, at least it was likely to be the first to win a land grant, and if the successful coalition could be held together, it might even pave the way for an Iowa grant later in the session. The Minnesotans, it appeared, had been able to compromise their internal conflicts and unite to pass the bill. Some intersectional support was forthcoming from southerners who hoped the future state's politics might be influenced in their favor, as well as from others seeking land grants. And of course there was the potent Superior coalition.

These ambitious programs were a key element in one of the most bitterly controversial episodes in American history, the Kansas–Nebraska Act. Without plan or desire, the politics of railroad expansion excited and became enmeshed in the slavery conflict. The Illinois Central and other systems, beginning to take discernible shape, stimulated the settlement and political organization of the western frontier areas. Once organized and its institutions functioning, the Nebraska Territory, as projected by the initial version of the bill, might speed the next step westward by land grant lobbying, grants of corporate charters, and other aids. The two territories of Kansas and Nebraska, which emerged from the rewriting of the bill, would increase representation in the national councils and the options available to enterprisers.

One of the many mysteries to historians of the Kansas–Nebraska Act has been Douglas' determination, after momentary hesitation, to force it through in the face of awesome political dangers. When he introduced his territorial bill, proslavery politicians presented a series of demands culminating in the explicit repeal of a universally accepted ground rule that had stood for a third of a century: the provision of the Missouri Compromise of 1820 that excluded slavery from the Western territories of the Louisiana Purchase north of 36°30′. It was clear that this revolutionary demand would rekindle the blaze that had been dampened down by the Compromise of 1850—yet Douglas agreed. Implicitly, his acceptance of the proslavery ultimatum reflected a fundamental assumption of his political career: that the growth and consolidation of regional and national corporations—of far-flung railroad empires—would naturally, almost automatically mold and direct political institutions.

The two aspects of Douglas' miscalculation must be seen together if either is to be judged correctly. If he accepted the risks and dangers of slavery as a moral, psychological, and sectional-patriotic issue it was not simply because he underestimated them but because of his faith in the materialism of his countrymen and in the growing strength and leadership of corporate business. Incomplete and defective as it was, Douglas' vision was nonetheless seductively "sublime," in the vocabulary of his age, in its anticipation of power, prosperity, and harmony. Given the course of future corporate development, Douglas' calculations were perhaps not so much wrong as premature; given the usually—but not always—predominant materialism, his were not merely individual miscalculations but reflect a classically tragic flaw in his civilization.

Such a strategic conception readily accepted the immediate tactical dictates of railroad expansion. If many northerners would resent repeal of the Missouri Compromise, their distaste for slavery would be controlled by the paramount interest in economic development. On the other hand, disappointment of the potent southern-oriented bloc over the Kansas–Nebraska issue might deprive those preoccupied with railroad expansion of crucial support in Congress. If aggressively expansionist or aggressively defensive southerners insisted that the Compromise of 1820 be repealed and new territories legally opened to slavery in order to give national sanction to their paramount interest—"the peculiar institution"—let the price be paid that America might career westward on wheels without delay. The price, the raging conflict over slavery, soon enough proved exorbitant; for the time being, it seemed, the way was clear for a railroad.[17]

The Minnesota & North Western Railroad Land Grant

In February 1854 a land grant bill for a route from the head of Lake Superior via St. Paul to the southern border of Minnesota Territory, with provision for future extension toward Dubuque, Iowa, was introduced in the Senate by Douglas's friend James Shields of Illinois. It passed without opposition, but when it was brought up in the House a month later, it ran into difficulty.

A major problem was the rivalry among budding railroad entrepreneurs and systems. Instrumental in the initial defeat of the Minnesota grant was the Michigan Southern & Northern Indiana Railroad, which was allied with the Chicago & Rock Island in competing against the Michigan Central–Illinois Central group for midwestern traffic and westward expansion. Its spokesman in the House was Hester Stevens, Democrat of Michigan. Advocates of the Minnesota bill had to fend off charges of an Illinois Central coup. Territorial delegate Henry Rice denied knowledge when it was charged that a favored company already was slated to take over the grant. But his disclaimer was false: the charter, to an alliance of Illinois Central and local interests, had already been approved by the Territorial legislature, timed so the news would reach Washington after the expected passage of the grant. Rice's assurances were generally disbelieved and an adroit trick was required to move the bill around the first obstruction in the House. The Public Lands Committee was the usual route for land grant legislation, but it was controlled by friends of the Michigan Southern under Stevens' chairmanship. To bypass this roadblock Representative William A. Richardson, Douglas' lieutenant in the House, had the bill reported by the Committee on Territories, of which he was chairman. By this maneuver supporters were able to push the bill ahead of other land grant seekers, who presumably would want to set a favorable precedent by its approval and would seek reciprocal support.

The competition of states and localities and of politicians were other themes of the struggle. Bills for Wisconsin land grants had had priority in the Public Lands Committee and members from that state resented being set aside. In particular Ben C. Eastman belatedly discovered the parliamentary maneuver and also learned that the grant, ostensibly a Minnesota measure, would terminate at Superior in his Wisconsin district. Confronted by Eastman, Rice feigned surprise, then tried to persuade him to accept the measure as it stood, but Richardson promptly agreed to terminate the grant in Minnesota. Eastman then learned, however, that Rice's friends Nelson and Hollinshead had just procured a Wisconsin charter for a railroad from Superior southward on the route of a projected land grant in which the Congressman himself was interested. Thus the Superior group, seeking to control Wisconsin as well as Minnesota access to its townsite, was encroaching on Eastman's territory both politically and economically.

Increasing the general air of deceit, James H. Lane of Indiana called attention to the Superior scheme (without naming names) when he charged that 6,000 acres around the intended terminus had already been preempted by speculators interested in the measure. Rice virtuously denied knowledge of any such interest: this was perhaps slightly less than a lie since the amended bill moved the terminus across the creek to Minnesota. Lane probably was kept informed by Willis A. Gorman, a former Hoosier recently become governor of Minnesota who was contesting the position of Rice and his allies. In the end the bill could not be defeated outright, but opponents succeeded in raising a new and diversionary issue by attaching a controversial amendment to divide the proceeds of alternate sections of land retained by the federal government in land grant areas among states not receiving grants. Outfoxed, supporters of the bill agreed to table it.[18]

While the first drive in Congress was under way, Illinois Central executives and lobbyists appeared at the territorial capital, St. Paul, in the late winter of 1854 to push through the charter of the Minnesota & North Western Railroad. Legislators were warned that only the Illinois Central had the power to push a land grant through Congress and that speed was necessary to outrace Wisconsin in building to Lake Superior. Governor Gorman was extremely reluctant to agree to the charter: not only were the terms highly favorable to the company; its political allies were his antagonists. Still, Gorman could not veto the bill in view of the universal craving for a railroad and the near unanimity among the numerous political factions. After a few moderate concessions by the promoters the charter was passed and signed. The Minnesota & North Western Company was guaranteed ownership in fee simple of any lands donated to the Territory along its route. Unexpected trouble was to arise out of the time limitations, however: the incorporators had to accept the charter within sixty days and organize the board of directors by the next July 1.

Among the incorporators, those identified with the Illinois Central were the brothers Robert and George L. Schuyler, Morris Ketchum and his partner Edward Bement, Roswell B. Mason, and George W. Billings of New York. New York Central and Michigan Central representatives included Erastus Corning of Albany and his Dubuque land agent, Frederick Jesup, and John Murray Forbes of Boston. Other eastern investors included John Gardiner and Curtis Raymond of Boston and W. E. S. Moore of Bangor, Maine.

The Minnesota incorporators included representatives of the major local political factions. Gorman and J. T. Rosser were members of the territorial administration appointed by Pierce. Henry H. Sibley was represented by his brother-in-law, Franklin Steele, and Charles Borup, merchant and banker of St. Paul. Whig leader Alexander Ramsey was named. The others were James Stinson of the Superior group and Orange Walker and Alexander Wilkin, allies of Henry Rice. Formalities were completed in New York on April 4, when the company accepted the charter.[19]

A swarm of lobbyists was dispatched to join the crowds infesting Washington in quest of land grants and other tidbits. One of the leaders was Billings. Among the most notorious of the breed, he had been a prominent lobbyist for the precedent-setting Illinois Central grant of 1850. He also labored for subsidies and government contracts for domestic hemp interests, among others, and for the resumption of the Mississippi state debt. In the Mississippi affair his loud-mouthed, bull-in-the-china-shop efforts at intrigue and his crass attempt to divert slush funds to his own pocket alienated many. His boasts of manipulating the eminent Douglas and other statesmen disgusted solid businessmen: aside from the question of exaggeration, this was not the way gentlemen discussed these matters. George Ashmun was an outstanding lobbyist. His influence in Massachusetts was especially important since opposition in that delegation had been an important factor in the defeat of the Minnesota grant early in the session. Active Illinoisans included Representative John Wentworth of Chicago and Robert Smith, former downstate Congressman. From Minnesota came additional manpower: the ex-Pennsylvania Whig, Ramsey; Robertson and Newton of the Superior group; Hugh Tyler, erstwhile agent of the American Fur Co. and friend of Sibley; and others. Billings reached lobbyists for other interests, such as steamship magnate E. K. Collins; George Brega, a newspaper correspondent of easy ethics; and E. H. Thompson of Michigan, who represented various midwestern railroads. Another clique of lobbyists, and one of the most potent, was collected around New York Whig leader Thurlow Weed of Albany, whose key lieutenants in this operation were congressman Orsamus B. Matteson of Utica, New York and George Harrington.

These were the appetizer days of the "Great Barbecue," as one historian has called the burgeoning corruption of the late nineteenth century. A few congressional investigations were launched and, although they were carefully checked before much damage could be done, some interesting details were exposed. Representative George Jones of Tennessee could not be brought to vote for the Minnesota bill but was apparently bribed to abstain. Thomas Clingman of North Carolina reportedly received over $10,000 in stock. If the figure is accurate he was probably a "bagman" for others as well. Manuscripts offer more certain insights than do the congressional inquiries. Harrington dispensed at least $5,000 of bribes, including $2,500 to Superior speculator Forney for prostituting his position as clerk of the House. Eastman of Wisconsin typified the general yielding to what John F. Kennedy once charmingly termed "the pressure of opportunity." Offering to "serve," Eastman wrote an intimate:

> I am not disposed to extend my services for pure patriotism . . . if this town on Lake Superior is to be so much benefitted they can afford to give some lots to you for valuable services . . . let them act honorably and liberally. Men who cannot be on the ground there should not lose all chances of benefitting themselves in the speculation. This of course is sub rosa.

He, too, was soon satisfied. Finally, Billings pointed to another factor. Since the passage of the Kansas–Nebraska Act, there were many lame ducks anxious to seize a last opportunity and many survivors hopeful of reelection "& they or their friends come here to *obtain relief.* We are making their wants inure to our benefit."[20]

By the end of June the 850,000-acre Minnesota land grant passed by voice vote in the Senate and by 99 to 71 in the House and was signed by the President. (The troublesome amendment to reserve to nongrant states the proceeds of government-retained alternate sections in the grant area, whose adoption had led to the tabling of the earlier measure in March, was defeated this time by just 85 to 84.) Following established custom, Senator Henry Dodge of Wisconsin (father of the Iowa Senator), Representative J. P. Cook and Senator George Jones of Iowa, and Rice successfully petitioned Secretary of the Interior Robert McClelland to withdraw lands from sale along the route. Indian treaties were pressed to make more land available in the region for the expected increase of immigration. The Minnesota & North Western Company completed its organization and prepared to survey the route. But just when it seemed the territory would have its first railroad the whole process crashed to a halt in the tangles of local politics.[21]

The Struggle for Power in Minnesota

The first of Minnesota's three leading politicians of the 1850s was Henry H. Sibley. For years he had been local manager of the ruling business firm of the rudimentary frontier economy, the American Fur Company, which was controlled by the

Chouteaus of St. Louis. Dominant in the interwoven fur and Indian trades for a generation throughout the northern Mississippi Valley, the company's agents worked hand-in-glove with the federal government, often negotiating and administering the treaties under which the United States paid for provisions furnished to acquiescent tribes. Until 1848, when he was easily elected Minnesota's first delegate to Congress, Sibley was unrivaled chieftain in the territory's business and politics.

Sibley's first and leading antagonist was Henry M. Rice. Also an agent of the American Fur Co., Rice had quit under a heavy cloud when Sibley proved he had diverted tens of thousands of dollars of the firm's funds to his own use. Rivalry, already intense, soured into detestation. In the isolation of frontier winters Rice took advantage of Sibley's absences at Washington to develop his own organization; at the same time his business partners, Hollinshead and Becker, built a following in the Whig Party. In 1850 Sibley won reelection, but by a much-narrowed margin, over Alexander Mitchell, a Whig supported by Rice. By this time the third major figure of the period, Alexander Ramsey, had arrived on the scene, appointed governor of the territory by President Taylor in 1849. Suave and skillful, he carefully maintained friendly personal relations on all sides, sometimes staying out of the combat, sometimes moving smoothly back and forth between Sibley and Rice.

In the early 1850s personal alignments in Minnesota cut across party lines, with interacting national and local ramifications. The 1850 election threatened not only Sibley's Democratic leadership but also Ramsey's control of the Whigs. Mitchell was the candidate of Rice and his Whig partners, Hollinshead and Becker, and of other Whigs such as Judge David Cooper of the Webster-Fillmore wing of the party. In contrast, Sibley and Ramsey worked through Senator William H. Seward and Thurlow Weed of the Taylor Whigs (among others in both parties) to influence Secretary of the Interior Thomas Ewing in territorial matters. Sibley's victory in 1850 was Ramsey's as well, for Ramsey was able to retain his post as governor when Fillmore succeeded Taylor as President, and in 1851 he smoothly but firmly brought the chastened Mitchell and Cooper into cooperation with himself and Sibley. Ramsey politely declined overtures from Rice (although they were business partners in at least one enterprise, a sawmill) and tightened his control of patronage.

For a time the struggle intensified, Indian treaties becoming the major issue in 1852. Rice was allied with George W. and W. G. Ewing of Indiana, fur traders who were challenging the Chouteau interests. They lobbied for the appointment of Richard W. Thompson, important Indiana Whig ally of Jesse Bright, as agent for forthcoming Indian negotiations in Minnesota. At Washington, Rice was supported by Jones of Iowa whereas Sibley was backed by Douglas and by Dodge of Iowa. Ramsey and Sibley won a difficult but clear-cut victory when their Indian arrangements were upheld in Congress.[22]

Early in 1853 the barrel of snakes that was Minnesota politics writhed into a strange new aspect: Rice was reconciled with Sibley and Ramsey. One reason was the expense of the warfare, for in flaying each other the enemies had been skinning themselves. In a profit and loss statement dated July 1, 1852 Sibley (perhaps making the worst of the situation to impress others with his honesty) indicated a net deficit of $31,372.42. Similarly, Rice reportedly had accumulated debts approaching $50,000. (He was to run this to a much exaggerated reputed net worth of $500,000 by the boom spring of 1857.) In addition, Daniel A. Robertson had arrived in the territory and was making his own bid for power as editor-publisher of the St. Paul *Minnesota Democrat.* In the fur and Indian tangles he acted with Madison Sweetser, an agent supported for tactical reasons by Rice in his efforts to gain a share of the business. (The link among these intriguers apparently was Sweetser's brother Charles, Democratic representative from Ohio, where Robertson had been editor of the Columbus *Ohio State Journal,* the state party organ at the capital.)

To restore order and safeguard their position, Ramsey and Sibley presented Rice with a piece of the Indian business by appointing him government agent. Rice, discarding Sweetser, joined Sibley, and they supported each other's claims at Washington. Sibley cut loose from the American Fur Co., which had been under attack for years by Rice and others as a monopoly: with Minnesota emerging from the simple undifferentiated frontier stage the connection was becoming a liability. Continuing their rapprochement, Rice invited Sibley and his brother-in-law, Franklin Steele, to join him and Robert Smith in an important mill development at the Falls of St. Anthony. (Apropos of the forthcoming Minnesota & North Western Company, bankers Frederick Gebhard and J. F. A. Sanford, members of the Falls combine, were associated with the American Fur interests and the Illinois Central and Dubuque & Pacific railroads. St. Anthony's Falls was to be included on the route of the Minnesota & North Western.) Robertson, effectually isolated, tacitly acknowledged defeat in 1853 by selling a half-interest in his newspaper and retiring from its editorship. By the beginning of 1854, when both were busying themselves with the Superior speculation and the land grant was the thing, he, too, restored relations with Rice.[23]

The rapprochement of 1853, subject as it was to the limitless ambitions of many individuals, might have lasted longer if not for the fluidity reintroduced by a new national administration. In that year Ramsey's term expired, and the selection of the new governor rested with Franklin Pierce. In addition to its intrinsic importance, the office carried with it the post of superintendent of Indian affairs for the territory. With prestige, patronage, and profits at stake in the treaties still to be negotiated for cessions of Indian lands, Sibley, formally supported by Rice, lined up fifty-eight congressmen to petition for his nomination. (He thus broke a promise to back a candidate agreed upon with Douglas. Robertson, then still attacking Sibley, Ramsey, and Rice in his newspaper, was also a candidate with the support of the Ohio congressional delegation.)[24]

The President chose to bypass those already on the scene and appointed Willis A. Gorman of Indiana. Despite many shortcomings, the Pierce administration seems to have had greater integrity than its predecessors or the succeeding Buchanan regime. In an age of deteriorating public ethics, there were relatively conspicuous islands of integrity in the Pierce cabinet, although as distance from Washington's oversight increased their influence faded. One able and honest administrator was Robert McClelland, who as Secretary of the Interior was most responsible for territorial affairs. Pierce carefully consulted him when he decided to select someone not already entangled in Indian dealings. In addition, Gorman was a loyal politician and personal friend of the president.[25]

It was a thankless job that Gorman undertook. He set an independent course, ignoring the vested interests of the old Indian traders and attacking them for corruption in letters to Pierce and Douglas. But except for Robertson, who for all his efforts remained a secondary figure, Gorman's influence was virtually confined to his immediate appointees. By January 1854 his administration was completely isolated as Robertson, with Douglas at Washington, joined Ramsey, Sibley, and Rice. This alliance was easily capable of overriding the governor's veto of a railroad charter in the territorial legislature.[26]

Thus, despite a restive governor and national administration, Minnesota politicians appeared closer to harmony early in 1854 when the land grant campaign was put in high gear than at any time in years. Yet sweetness and light were too novel to be relied upon, particularly since the prospective railroad was expected to become the dominant political as well as economic institution in the territory. When Rice sought Sibley's support for the grant the latter was obliging enough, provided his erstwhile enemy was not put in a position to ride the railroad right over him to political domination. With Rice already solidly established in the councils of the projected road, Sibley and Gorman cooperated to safeguard their interests. At their insistence they were allowed to draft the bill, which placed any land grant at "the disposal of any future legislature of the Territory or state of Minnesota" and denied it to "any company constituted or organized before the passage of the act." This provision also allayed the suspicion of members of Congress who were concerned not to strengthen, or publicly appear to strengthen, the Illinois Central. As a further guarantee Sibley was assured of a seat on the board of directors (as was Gorman in his official capacity as governor).

A valuable ally of Sibley was Illinois Whig Congressman Elihu Washburne. Representing the northeastern corner of the state, Washburne resented the Central's bypassing his home, Galena, to make Dunleith, opposite Dubuque, Iowa, its Mississippi River crossing point. Furthermore Washburne considered the Illinois Central to be politically affiliated with his Democratic opponents, a belief that was correct partly because of the background of its top management and directors, but chiefly because the Democrats were the majority party throughout the region, and the corporation had to work within that framework. To secure his own interests, the Congressman demanded and received assurances that the Minnesota & North Western would be independent of the Illinois Central, that he would have a voice in its control, and that the connecting roads to the East through Iowa and his Illinois district would be controlled by his allies. The road favored by Washburne was a project of the Michigan Southern group: the Chicago, St. Charles & Mississippi, which was to link with the Iowa Central Railroad, a planned route from the Mississippi due west to the Missouri River. The concessions to the Michigan Southern interests won the support of Hester Stevens, chairman of the House Public Lands Committee.[27]

Washburne could also help to clear away partisan roadblocks. One of the undercurrents running against the Minnesota scheme was widespread resentment "that Locofocos control all the R. R. organizations—they do generally."[28] That nickname, first given derogatorily to the radical faction of New York Democrats in 1835, was later loosely applied to Jacksonian Democrats generally and to those of the Empire State in particular. In fact the movement of old "Regency" politicians into the ranks of midwestern railroad leadership was striking. John A. Dix was president and Azariah Flagg treasurer of the Rock Island; Erastus Corning was a prominent member of the Forbes group that controlled the Michigan Central, the developing Chicago,

Burlington & Quincy, and other projects; Charles Butler was director of the Illinois & Wisconsin; his brother-in-law William Butler Ogden (with the assistance of Samuel Tilden among others) was to weld that road, the Galena & Chicago Union, and others into the Chicago & North Western system. Not that enterprise was partisan; it was simply that railroad men, who if anything were more likely to be Whigs, had to obtain and defend corporate charters, subsidies, and land grants in legislatures, executive mansions, and courthouses. It was natural for them to recruit or join politicians of the then dominant Democratic party. The leadership of the Illinois Central and its extensions, politically bi- or non-partisan, had to be on good terms with Democrats.

However, with Democratic and railroad politics so factionalized, avid subsidy seekers reached out to willing Whigs for reinforcements. Appeasing Washburne cleared the way for members of the minority party to support the Minnesota bill. Indeed, he took the lead in enlisting the Thurlow Weed lobby group. Moreover, the initial proponents of the measure—the Illinois Central political coalition—were closely identified with the Kansas–Nebraska bill. In a bitter year when politicians threatened to do in each other's land grants to retaliate for stands taken in that savage fight, the anti-Nebraska Washburne and his associates helped to partly neutralize that source of opposition to the Minnesota bill. Such were the interconnected local and national compromises that made possible its passage.[29]

And then success was recklessly risked and lost out of greed for factional supremacy. It is not clear whether the double cross had been planned all along or was the reflex to an illusory opportunity, but in any case the original Illinois Central combine and its newfound Michigan Southern allies betrayed their promises. After the House passed the bill a cabal including lobbyist Billings, Congressman Stevens, Senators Jones and Charles E. Stuart (Dem., Mich. and chairman of the Public Lands Committee), and House Clerk Forney changed the official document. In the section placing the grant "at the disposal of any future legislature" of Minnesota, the word "future" was erased; and where "any company constituted or organized before the passage of the act" was denied the grant, the word "or" was changed to "and." The altered version passed the Senate and was signed by the President. The Minnesota & North Western, already "constituted," then "organized" itself in New York with the selection of officers and directors. Robert Lowber, later notorious for traction ring scandals in New York, was made president and his associate in these and other endeavors, Marshall O. Roberts, appeared in the company. Sibley was denied his promised directorship. Instead Minnesotans Edmund Rice, Lyman Dayton, and Ramsey (who had already given indications of abandoning his alliance with Sibley) were chosen, and the firm of Rice, Hollinshead & Becker was appointed the corporation's attorney.

The conspirators thought they had presented their rivals with a fait accompli. Their power seemed ample, and since railroads were of highest priority to developing areas, the excluded politicians presumably would have no hope in an appeal to the public. Indeed, congressional ethics, and political ethics generally, were such that an outcry was not even dreamed of. For example, the cocky Billings, a classic blabbermouth, had even bragged in advance to Sibley of the changes in the bill. Losers were expected to swallow their chagrin and quietly sue for peace, as Borland and Mallory had in the earlier Arkansas and Florida intrigues, while the winners took credit for cleverness and success.

It was a shattering miscalculation. Sibley, Gorman and Washburne mobilized all their resources in Minnesota and at Washington to expose the fraud. A special committee of the House was organized to investigate. The committee, like a number of other such investigations in the fifties, avoided tracking the trail of corruption too far. It was notorious that much of Congress was for sale or rent; a serious self-investigation was out of the question. (In this instance it must be added that speed was important since the session was to end in a few weeks.) The committee strained itself to abjure questions of ethics. The majority report, written most conveniently by Breckinridge, blandly observed that such alterations were common, if pernicious, and made no recommendation. The minority members, Lewis D. Campbell and G. A. Simmons, asked only that the bill's original wording be restored. It appeared that the company would survive its blunder when the House rejected motions to restore the intended language and to repeal the grant altogether.

But its supporters had gone too far too brazenly. Moreover, the great Schuyler railroad frauds had just been disclosed. Despite efforts to minimize the scandal, a near-panic hit Wall Street and railroads in general came under temporary discredit. The Minnesota & North Western was severely damaged by the fact that Robert Schuyler headed its list of incorporators. On August 3, the last day of the session and just a month after Washburne learned of the skullduggery, Senator Pearce attached a rider to repeal the grant to a minor claims bill. Douglas, supported by Bright, Jones, Stuart, Johnson, and Cooper, tried to salvage the grant by an amendment restoring the original wording of the grant but was defeated by 28 to 15. Instead the repeal was enacted.[30]

It must be emphasized that, to the frontier politician, control of the railroad meant survival and mastery; no Marxist was ever more the economic determinist. With few exceptions, they were relatively little interested in many of the issues, such as slavery and temperance, that exercised many fellow citizens. Most politicians simply utilized those issues as clubs with which to beat opponents. The same can be said of most newspapers, which were by and large integral parts of political cliques. In a bitter attack upon his antagonists, Rice was obviously, and on the whole accurately, reading into their minds his own motivation: "The sole object is to get this left an open question so that some aspirants can feather their nests and control the political complexion of the territory and future state."[31]

Another noteworthy comment appeared in the Washington *Union,* the administration newspaper of which Forney was one of the publishers. The problem was what to say; most of the major antagonists were Democrats and Forney's conduct was most embarrassing, yet the scandal was too conspicuous and the issues too profound to be totally ignored. The solution was anxious generalizing. An editorial which avoided explicit mention of the Minnesota or any other specific affair, warned that

> the power of railroads in the hands of combinations of men, operating upon the politics of the country, will presently assume so startling an aspect as to command the earnest attention of our statesmen. Imagine 16,000 miles of railroads in the United States, in active and constant use, controlled by capitalists, wielding millions of money, every year seeing vast extensions . . . penetrating into most of the states and territories of the Union, and so forming one mighty network.[32]

Unwilling to give up, the Minnesota & North Western planned litigation to overthrow the repeal. Meanwhile Rice pressed the Interior Department to keep lands along the route withdrawn from entry. Secretary McClelland chose this moment to reconsider the department's policy, which had permitted withdrawals along *proposed* land grant routes to the extent of 49 million acres. Settlement on these vast tracts was slowed since it was not widely realized that preemption was still permitted and it was often impossible to add to a preempted tract by cash purchase. The Secretary also believed "that speculators may be more interested in such roads . . . than the people of the state." President Pierce backed him and the Minnesota lands were restored to market. This was but one example of the administration's avoidance of favoritism to special interests. Similar steps were taken in Arkansas, Iowa, Wisconsin, and other states as well. Rice showed his rage, as did railway bloc associates in Congress, and was acidly rebuffed by McClelland.[33]

The Secretary also rejected a proposal to arrange a suit to test the legality of the repeal. This time, however, Rice found a way to bypass the administration. Daniel Baker of the Superior speculators had dissuaded Attorney General Caleb Cushing from appointing a member of Gorman's administration as federal attorney for Minnesota Territory. Instead the post went to John E. Warren of Troy, New York. John Barbour, New York attorney for the Minnesota & North Western, the Rices, and Ramsey arranged things with Warren, who obligingly sued the company for trespass when it cut down trees on the abortively granted government lands. The case was hustled into the district court, where it was dismissed on the grounds that the company owned the property. Warren immediately appealed to the supreme court of the territory, which upheld the lower court decision.

Even while these cases were argued Warren was receiving his payoff. He advertised as agent for real estate at the edge of St. Paul, assuring prospective customers that "there are good reasons for believing that the projected railroads from Lake Superior and Chicago will enter St. Paul" either through or right by the lots. Cushing furnished a different kind of reward. Blithely ignoring department regulations, Warren had proceeded without informing his superiors. When Cushing learned of the case he was outraged, and there was no chance of professional sensibility succumbing to other temptations: he had large investments at St. Croix, Minnesota, which were bypassed by the Minnesota & North Western route. The Attorney General summarily fired his corrupt subordinate. The latter returned east leaving the lots he had advertised to be sold by Emerson & Case, allies of Rice.

The Minnesota & North Western looked forward to the final test before the United States Supreme Court, having enlisted an array of eminent lawyers (Greene C. Bronson, Reuben Walworth, William Curtis Noyes, and Barbour) to argue the case. The company went ahead with plans to survey the route, a display of optimism that benefitted its local supporters in the autumn elections of 1854. Unfortunately for them Cushing refused to allow the government to be sued in the Supreme Court. Since the United States could not be sued without its permission the case was, in effect, in limbo and the company's efforts were nullified. Under redoubled pressure by Rice and his senatorial allies the administration wavered, almost permitting a test case, but in the end another stratagem had to be devised. In 1856 Edmund Rice bought some land on the proposed route from the government; the Minnesota & North Western again chopped down some trees. Rice sued the company for trespassing. The territorial supreme court, reversing the district court decision, found for the defendant on grounds that the land grant had given the company valid title. This case finally was heard by the United States Supreme Court, but not until 1862, and the decision upheld repeal of the land grant.[34]

Meanwhile, the railroad became the outstanding issue in Minnesota politics. Rice vigorously defended himself in the 1854 elections. For years Robertson's St. Paul *Minnesota Democrat* had been a burr under his saddle: he had his allies buy it out. Public letters praising Rice's role were sent by Breckinridge, Bright, Stuart, Alexander Pennington (Whig, N.J.) and Samuel Clark (Dem., Mich.). On the whole the Minnesota & North Western bloc was strengthened by the election but Sibley won a seat in the lower house of the legislature.[35]

Overtures were made to Sibley and his allies, who responded with a counterattack. Supported by Gorman, Sibley introduced in the territorial legislature a memorial asking Congress to annul the charter of the Minnesota & North Western. It was not passed. Simultaneously, at Washington Washburne introduced a resolution to revoke the charter in the House of Representatives; it passed by voice vote. In the Senate the resolution was referred to the Committee on Territories, which was dominated by the railroads' friends: Douglas was chairman and Jones and Cooper were members. Seward and other Whigs working for Lowber and Roberts (with Thurlow Weed as middleman between the businessmen and the politicians) made the company's support bipartisan. Cooper wrote the committee report, grounding its opposition to repeal of the charter on Douglas' doctrine of squatter sovereignty.[36]

By the beginning of 1855 the time limit set by the charter for the company to begin construction was running out. The territorial legislature passed an extension over Sibley's opposition and Gorman's veto. The struggle was repeated a year later when another two-year extension was vetoed by Gorman. Its supporters passed a new bill with tax and other provisions more satisfactory to the territory and the governor acquiesced.[37]

The exasperated Rice, joined by Douglas and others of the Superior group, bore down heavily on the President to remove Gorman from his post. The man the intriguers wanted as governor was Breckinridge, since his appointment would have strengthened the Superior and Minnesota & North Western speculators and enabled Rice to complete the political isolation of his local enemies. But there may have been much more to it, for apparently the Kentuckian was already being groomed for a greater role. He was a friend and protégé of Jesse Bright, whose plantation retreat was in Breckinridge's congressional district—Bright helped him win a tough election campaign in 1852. Breckinridge was a popular orator as well as a smooth operator. By placing him at the head of Minnesota politics, Bright hoped to deny the future state to his party rival Douglas, whose appeal would ordinarily be greatest in such a frontier environment. For the ambitious Breckinridge, the post would have provided an opportunity to build a second base of support in a distinct section of the country. Finally the appointment would have been part of a developing pattern of southern carpetbaggers migrating to the northern and western frontier, not to contest futilely for the institution of slavery there but to build with increasing self-consciousness political machines that would be more reliably prosouthern.

Rice, ironically joined by Douglas as well as others of the Superior group, insisted to the President that Gorman was not only splitting local Democrats, but was corrupt as well. Pierce sent J. Ross Browne, for years a government troubleshooter, to investigate. He exonerated Gorman and sharply criticized his traducers; they promptly expanded their charges of corruption to include Browne and demanded another investigation. This time the President sent out his own private secretary, Sidney Webster. He upheld Browne, but there are indications that he tried to accommodate the speculators for political reasons (and perhaps because he was bribed) without tactlessly denigrating Pierce's old friend. Early in the election year of 1856 the President belatedly tried to soothe disgruntled speculators and politicians by replacing Gorman as Indian superintendent. His retention as governor, however, continued to cause friction.[38]

Bearing out in large measure his belief in the paramount economic motivation of the electorate, Rice was able to ride the Minnesota & North Western to temporary political triumph. The fall elections of 1854 had been close and inconclusive. The following summer Gorman and Sibley bolted the party to suport maverick David Olmsted, Robertson's former partner in the St. Paul *Minnesota Democrat,* for delegate to Congress in opposition to Rice. At first the incumbent's campaign emphasized the land grant almost exclusively. Olmsted, attacking on a broader front, denounced his backing of the railroad and of the Kansas–Nebraska Act, while the third candidate, Republican William R. Marshall, made his major assault on the latter measure. Seizing weapons to counter Rice's economic leadership, his opponents also adopted Nativism and Prohibition (perhaps to their disadvantage). For weeks Rice ignored these issues or denounced them as red herrings while proclaiming his advocacy of the land grant and his success in winning appropriations for road, harbor, and other public investments. Eventually, he felt compelled to meet all his opponents' attacks directly, but continued to reiterate the importance of southern cooperation in Congress to Minnesota's growth through appropriations, land grants, and eventual statehood. Emulating Douglas, he called for unity on a platform of economic development: "Where is the difference between Old Line Whigs and Democrats"? The results were decisive, for the time being, as Rice clearly outpolled both his opponents combined. Several months later his newspaper spokesman could claim that an overwhelming majority of the voters favored the Minnesota & North Western, in contrast with the road's general discredit when the scandal had erupted. Unfortunately for Superior and its backers, all these efforts produced not a mile of railroad in Minnesota before the Civil War.[39]

Another Opportunity: Wisconsin

Although plans for a Minnesota railroad bogged down the Superior boom continued, for it seemed only a matter of time before an alternative materialized. By 1856 a number of roads were progressing toward the region from Chicago and Milwaukee. Then, after two years under a cloud of discredit caused by the scandals of 1854, the land grant idea reemerged into the sunshine of a presidential election season.

There were three important roads in Wisconsin. The most advanced, the Milwaukee & Mississippi, was sending two branches toward Iowa, at Dubuque and further north at Prairie du Chien.[40] The second, pushing toward southern Minnesota, was Byron Kilbourn's La Crosse & Milwaukee. Son of an Ohio Congressman and son-in-law of inventor John Fitch, Kilbourn settled at Milwaukee in the 1830s and since then had envisioned its supplanting Chicago as the commercial center of the Middle West. The Milwaukee & Mississippi, which he headed, was to have fulfilled his dreams, but he was ousted from it in 1852 under charges of incompetence and dishonesty. Remaining in the background to spare his new project the burden of his reputation, Kilbourn hired lobbyist Moses M. Strong for a fee of $2,000 to gain the La Crosse charter. In 1854 his road absorbed the Milwaukee, Fond du Lac & Green Bay, which ran due north along Lake Michigan, but he continued to focus his energies westward.[41]

Unlike these local enterprises, the third westward-bound rival, the Chicago, St. Paul & Fond du Lac, came under the control of out-of-state—"foreign," in the language of the day—interests. It began as a short local line, the Madison & Beloit, which in 1850 was transmuted by merger into the Rock River Valley Union Railroad. Abram Hyatt Smith and John B. Macy, the leading Wisconsin politician-businessmen in the project, enlisted Robert J. Walker, who became fund-raiser in the East and in Britain, lobbyist in Washington, and stockholder (like the others, almost wholly on credit). In 1851 the Illinois & Wisconsin was chartered in Illinois to connect the road with Chicago via the Galena & Chicago Union.

By 1853 William Butler Ogden controlled these roads. He had come to Chicago in 1837 as local representative of his relative, Charles Butler, head of the wide-ranging American Land Co. Wealthy and powerful in real estate, railroads, and timber lands and a popular ex-mayor of Chicago, Ogden had excellent financial connections in the East—corporation lawyer Samuel J. Tilden was one close ally. His first railroad venture had been the highly successful Galena & Chicago Union. This road was in an ambiguous position as both rival and ally of the Illinois Central, which ran on Galena & Chicago Union tracks while building its own parallel line somewhat to the north. Ogden had temporarily left the management of the Galena but, although quietly critical of his successors, he and his friends retained large investments in it. Meanwhile he shifted his attentions northward. In 1855 the Rock River and Illinois & Wisconsin roads were combined into the Chicago, St. Paul & Fond du Lac which, together with the Galena, was destined to become the basis of the future Chicago & North Western system.[42]

By 1854, as railroadmen's eyes glistened toward the Pacific, the three rival Wisconsin companies were wrestling for land grants. Ogden's Rock River mounted the most intensive campaign under the leadership of Walker; one newspaper called it perhaps the greatest lobby effort ever for a single measure. Among the lobbyists were many former or current senators and representatives: Jere Clemens of Alabama, James Westcott of Florida, John P. Hale of New Hampshire, N. P. Tallmadge of Wisconsin (earlier of New York), Joel Sutherland and Lewis Levin of Pennsylvania, William W. Snow of New York, and William Moor of Maine. Hale, originally a Democrat, had become a Free-Soiler and was to become a Republican; Levin had been a member of the American Party; the rest were Democrats.

The Rock River bill passed the Senate but failed in the

House. There was opposition from southern sectionalists, unimpressed by the argument that the grant would link the region economically to the South via the Illinois Central; from advocates of limited government; and from homestead proponents who feared land monopolization by railroad corporations. Failure also was caused by sectional strife within the Wisconsin delegation, for Ogden's road threatened to drain much of the state's commerce to Chicago instead of Milwaukee.[43]

By 1856 competing railroads, sections, and states were beginning to abandon mutual frustration for community of interest. Moreover, it was a presidential election year of more than ordinary importance because of the rise of the Republican party. In land grants, as in Texas and California debts and private claims, the impulse toward logrolling was stronger than usual. This proved to be the best congressional session for land grants before the Civil War: Alabama, Louisiana, Florida (including the Yulee interests), Wisconsin, Iowa, and Minnesota Territory were recipients.

Legislation was lubricated by bribery of such proportions that, despite the customary restraint of congressional self-investigation, four American and Whig party representatives from New York and Connecticut were nominated for expulsion. (Three resigned but one of them, Weed's henchman Orsamus Matteson, immediately won reelection, testifying to the acceptability of such practices to sizable numbers of Americans.) One report, apparently accurate, had it that thirty congressmen had codified a bribery scale of $50 to $5,000 depending on the importance of the particular measure. Newspapermen were also offered large inducements. Bribes might be in cash, securities, land, or land warrants. The Ogden road spent heavily and the La Crosse & Milwaukee appropriated $105,000 (the proceeds of $200,000 face value of bonds sold in New York) to bribe the Minnesota grants through Congress. (In the latter case it was charged that the corrupt Congressmen were double-crossed and the money pocketed by company insiders. If so it was not the only such incident. Thieves' honor was an unstable commodity.)[44]

Some Congressmen were entrepreneurs rather than mere hirelings. Elihu Washburne was promised the desired railroad (supported by a land grant) to his Tête des Mortes properties by William Osborn, the new president of the Illinois Central. Osborn was consolidating his position in the company at the expense of the "old regime" that had, among other things, clashed with Washburne and thrown in with the since discredited Minnesota & North Western. Henry Rice was able to obtain one of the Wisconsin grants to benefit his own townsite of Bayfield, midway on the south shore of Lake Superior. About the Minnesota grant, he wrote that "Everybody here [in Washington] owns land in Minnesota and everybody has something to say in regard to where the roads shall run."[45]

Improved cooperation among the incipient regional systems also helped to break the logjam. The groups gradually forming the North Western, the Illinois Central, and the Chicago, Burlington & Quincy systems had managed to work together reasonably well, but the Michigan Southern was a constant source of friction, and the Rock Island was caught in the middle. A major obstacle to harmony was cleared in 1854 when the Michigan Southern relinquished plans for its own route across Illinois and Iowa. In May 1856 the Illinois Central, Burlington, Rock Island, and future North Western routes each received a congressional land grant westward across Iowa. The Illinois Central's extension, the Dubuque & Pacific, won a grant running north to the Minnesota boundary.[46]

These arrangements concluded, Wisconsin's turn was next. This time, however, community of interests proved to be only a deception. Ogden's Chicago, St. Paul & Fond du Lac bore the heaviest burdens of the lobbying campaign, laboring under the impression that the La Crosse and the Milwaukee & Mississippi companies had agreed to concede the grants to it. They were expected to content themselves with receiving access to the westward route. They pretended to accept the arrangement because Ogden's money and connections were essential if anything was to be obtained from Congress.

The Superior speculation, railroad competition, state politics, and President-making all converged. When Governor William A. Barstow departed for Washington to lobby for the land grant he was pledged to support Douglas for the Democratic nomination. At the capital he found that the real Senate powers were Buchanan's supporters, Bright and company, who were also the Superior speculators, Douglas having given up and sold his two shares in March 1855 when the Minnesota & North Western seemed doomed. The Wisconsin grant passed with provision for two routes, one paralleling the shore of Lake Michigan, the other running northwestward to the Minnesota line, on the St. Croix River or Lake, and on to Superior, with a branch to Rice's townsite speculation at Bayfield. Passage achieved, Barstow went on to the Democratic convention to swing his delegation to Buchanan, then returned home where, controlling the federal patronage after the latter's election, he applied himself to his and his allies' interest in the state.[47]

Kilbourn had no intention of surrendering his imperial ambitions for westward expansion. The Milwaukee & Mississippi joined his La Crosse & Milwaukee in defense against the threatened deflection of commerce to the Ogden road and Chicago. In addition there was a new railroad, the St. Croix & Lake Superior, organized in 1855 with Barstow as president. It was backed by the Superior proprietors, for whom it became the great hope after the bloom was off the Minnesota & North Western. They advanced funds for preliminary surveys and granted rights of way, lakefront facilities, and forty-three acres of terminal grounds. Cooperation among the three roads was signified by interlocking directorates.

The leaders of all three companies were Democrats. Little as they trusted each other they could unite tactically in attacking Ogden, a Republican. But where sectional or factional considerations conflicted with party interest, the former dictated. In Milwaukee, Republican businessmen were urged to abandon their new party lest they contribute to the decline of their city, while Ogden was supported by Josiah Noonan, a Democratic factional leader who feared that if Barstow and Kilbourn gained the grants they would thereby dominate party and state politics for a generation.[48]

Kilbourn, at the head of the coalition, set to work to overcome or buy off his partisan, sectional, and business opponents. Ogden's fellow Republicans controlled the governor's mansion and the legislature; he was likely to win support from Democrats as well along the route of the Chicago road; and "Milwaukee was very apt to be divided, while Chicago always and invariably presented one united front."[49] Kilbourn began by buying out a competitor, the Milwaukee & Watertown, which had begun to build westward and also sought the northwestern grant. A heavy price was paid in stock, while the acquisition brought little of tangible assets to offset its bonded debt of $812,000. The gains were chiefly political, the conciliation of new businessmen and localities, and especially of Republican Governor Coles Bashford, who insisted on the merger as part of his price.[50] Republican support was enlisted with reorganization of the La Crosse board of directors to include leading banker Alexander Mitchell and Rufus King, editor of the Milwaukee *Sentinel*. (These changes were temporary indeed. As soon as the grant was in Kilbourn's hands the new directors left and their predecessors were restored.)[51] Kilbourn then paid Barstow's price in a complicated transaction designed to compel these incorrigible schemers to maintain a degree of unity by inextricably intertwining their two companies. The La Crosse bought the existing property and franchises of the St. Croix & Lake Superior Company for $1 million of bonds. After the expected award of the federal grant, the lands along the St. Croix's route were to be turned over to that company for $1 million of its bonds and $500,000 of stock. The La Crosse was to name the management of St. Croix.[52]

The preliminaries concluded, the agents of the various railroads and the Superior proprietors descended upon the capital. It would be a bland understatement to describe what followed as a saturnalia of corruption. The La Crosse representatives distributed $175,000 among thirteen senators, $350,000 to fifty-eight assemblymen, and $246,000 to twenty-three state officials, railwaymen, editors of the Milwaukee *Sentinel, Wisconsin Banner, Wisconsin Patriot,* and other newspapers, and on and on. If anything these amounts, taken from the official report of the ensuing legislative investigation, are low. Much of the graft was in stock, some cash but by far the greatest part bonds —the recipients preferred what they believed to be the greater security of bonds and there was precious little cash available. They rightly distrusted Kilbourn and his associates and insisted on payment in advance.

The awards were thus pushed through the legislature, but Governor Bashford dropped a fly in the paté by vetoing the bill on various pretexts. Again local patriotism was drummed up. In Milwaukee the noted abolitionist Republican, Sherman Booth, chaired a meeting of conservative Democrats, and a southern sympathizer of the Democratic party presided over a rally of Republican businessmen. In the countryside 2,000 farmers had mortgaged their lands to raise funds for construction of Kilbourn's railroad and many of these added their voices to the chorus. All this was quite unnecessary; it was merely a matter of a few simple concessions. Bashford was awarded $50,000 of bonds with the understanding that they would be exchanged for cash as soon as the land grant was enacted. A shrewder businessman than the other politicians, he emerged from the mess with his profits intact. After a few additional changes the land grant awards were passed and signed.[53]

Events in Wisconsin were related to railroad developments in Minnesota, with the common theme the drive to the Pacific. While it was still anticipated that Ogden's Chicago, St. Paul & Fond du Lac would participate in the Wisconsin grants, a series of companies sharing the name of Northern Pacific was incorporated in Minnesota and Washington Territories and Wisconsin by multipartisan coalitions of railroad entrepreneurs. The Wisconsin incorporators were headed by James D. Doty and included two of his relatives, Governor I. I. Stevens of Washington, other politicians and ex-politicians, and representatives of the La Crosse and the Milwaukee & Mississippi interests. The eastern terminus was to be at the head of Lake Superior or further west at some point of the Mississippi north of the Illinois–Wisconsin line. The Washington company included Stevens and Doty, President John B. Turner of the

Galena & Chicago Union, and Henry Rice, Ramsey and Shields of Minnesota (the last named the former Illinois Senator). The Northern Pacific of Minnesota included William Ogden and Charles Butler and Minnesotans Edmund Rice, William R. Marshall, Ramsey, Steele, and David Cooper. The interlocking of incorporators and, later, directors is clear.[54]

The next step after the Wisconsin coup was a fresh new Minnesota land grant. At the beginning of the congressional session, the Committee on Public Lands favored the Transit Railroad backed by Sibley and Gorman. However, each interest group was in a position to block rival proposals without having the power to enact its own; hence, an omnibus bill to satisfy all groups and sections. After repeated failures, the various political-economic interests were finally harmonized and a network of land grants promising something for all concerned was enacted by Congress in March 1857. The hordes of lobbyists promptly swarmed into St. Paul for the customary rites of dispensation.[55]

So far as the east–west routes were concerned, it was again a struggle of the Kilbourn–Milwaukee group against the Ogden–Chicago. With the former apparently dominant in Wisconsin, the Rice coalition, which had affiliated with the Ogden interests when they seemed to have the advantage, switched sides. Kilbourn and his allies, making the usual payments, were able to seize control of three of Minnesota's westward land grants.[56]

The Bubbles Burst

By this time, the speculative boom of the northwest frontier country was at its peak. Kilbourn continued to build across Wisconsin in the early months of 1857, but he was reaching the end of his resources. It was a case, essentially, of suicide by corruption. The political costs of the railroad were immense and the resulting claims on revenues far into the future made hopeless the already difficult task of raising capital. By the fall of 1856 Kilbourn had already tried to break his agreements with Barstow and the St. Croix & Lake Superior: their purpose had been achieved, and with finances becoming critical a line to Superior seemed a distraction from the prime goal of reaching the Pacific. As a result, when Kilbourn stopped in New York en route to Washington to lobby for the Minnesota grants, he found himself held under $30,000 bond by Barstow's attorney, "Prince" John Van Buren, son of the former President and Regency leader. The Milwaukee promoter was forced to keep his word. To avoid egregious embarrassment, not to mention securing his release, he had to deliver the promised securities. Control of the Minnesota grants was the last illusory success. Kilbourn thrashed about trying to stay afloat, but even before the Panic of 1857 the La Crosse & Milwaukee was bankrupt. Only after a long delay for reorganization (including repudiation of securities issued for graft) was the road finally built west to the Mississippi River. In Minnesota, despite huge (for that frontier) flotations of state bonds, not a mile of railroad was in operation when the Civil War broke out.[57]

A democratic and individualistic political climate, in which discipline dissolved in a general frenzy to seize every available opportunity, bred a profusion of projects, many of which died while others remained stunted in growth by the dissipation of resources. After a brief, flourishing infancy, Superior, that offspring of enterprise in politics, was left a starveling by the same process that had given it birth. In the summer of 1855, when Bright thought the town would outstrip Chicago in twenty years, sales were at the rate of $25,000 cash for one of the twenty-seven full shares of the Superior company. Prices teetered uncertainly until the Wisconsin land grant passed Congress, then soared to $40,000 a share in June 1856. In February 1857 Corcoran offered to sell a quarter share for $20,000, half cash and the rest within a year, take it or leave it. In April, James Beck offered Breckinridge's remaining quarter-share at $25,000 cash (although urged not to sell by Edmund Rice). Prices continued to skyrocket during the summer, a full share reportedly being sold for $160,000 cash and single lots at up to $2,000. Then, at summer's end, the Panic of 1857 struck and prices plummeted more than 90 percent. Within months sales were practically impossible and the place was depopulated. However mixed the results to individuals, from huge windfalls to huge losses (for latecomers, of course), the net effect was wasted effort and loss.[58]

The political results were saturated with irony. The speculation had begun with Douglas' approach to rival factions to assure success, foster good will and unity, and advance his own ambitions. Implicitly, Douglas (and lesser men who emulated him) hoped that personal leadership in harmonizing and promoting material interests, especially by the lavish sharing of land grants, would help prevent or even heal major political divisions. Instead, Superior added but another major disturbing element to the nation's feverish railroad politics, and contributed to the intensification of the struggle over slavery. As for Douglas' personal ambitions, he was the foremost spokesman of "Young America," but his antagonists, too, could find many allies by the same obvious appeal to material interests, and they would not be reconciled.

12

Success

The Making of a President

In 1856 Corcoran savored his greatest political success—he was one of the clique that made James Buchanan President. It was a victory tainted with caprice, owing much to coalitions formed out of trivial and irrelevant materials. The taste of success soon soured for Corcoran, as it turned into a misfortune for his country.

The friendship between the two men had ripened for more than a decade. Corcoran was one of the prosperous Pennsylvanian's investment advisers and gave financial assistance to some of his key lieutenants. Adam Glossbrenner, later private secretary to President Buchanan, had been Corcoran's debtor and his intermediary in Texas debt speculation and in loans to congressmen. Jehu Glancy Jones, Representative from Pennsylvania, was another borrower, and Corcoran also made loans to John Forney and indirectly furnished the bond required when he was elected clerk of the House of Representatives.[1] These men never mistook their leader's protestations disclaiming presidential ambition. Buchanan wrote the banker in 1850:

> For me it is a melancholy spectacle to witness men of 3 score and upwards still struggling on the political arena . . . as though the earth was destined to be their eternal home. I trust in Heaven that I may never present such a spectacle.

He then proceeded to present just such a spectacle.[2]

The most important leaders of the cabal were Senators John Slidell and Jesse Bright. Senators James Bayard and Judah Benjamin also participated, and among lobbyists the foremost were Corcoran and Samual Barlow, the rising Wall Street lawyer. Initially Slidell, Bright, and Corcoran planned to keep away from Cincinnati during the convention (Corcoran staying conveniently close by in Columbus, Ohio), after laying the groundwork the previous week. In the end the two senators decided to attend, equipped with a long and fulsome letter from Buchanan proclaiming his prosouthern sympathies for display to that section's delegates.

The balloting gave political reward to the financier's diverse speculations, most notably the Texas settlement which was finally rushed through Congress in time for the convention. Corcoran charged his convention expenses to the Texas debt account. Stephen Douglas, a major contender for the nomination, attacked the settlement verbally while abstaining from a key vote, recognizing it as a movement of his rivals yet fearing to alienate irreconcilably an influential interest. At the convention the states with the heaviest holdings of Texas paper—Pennsylvania, New York, Maryland, and Louisiana—gave Buchanan fifty-six votes out of seventy-six on the first ballot and fifty-nine on the sixteenth, the last before Douglas' withdrawal. Among states benefitting from the railroad land grants passed just before the convention, Wisconsin's and perhaps Iowa's votes were influenced by the Bright-Corcoran alliance. The former gave three votes to Buchanan and two to Douglas, the latter all four to Douglas on the first tally; thereafter Iowa gave two to each candidate and Wisconsin all five to Buchanan.[3]

Corcoran helped Bright maintain control of his Indiana delegation. As in previous years his loans, endorsed by Bright, helped cement political friendships with such politicians as Graham Fitch, Andrew J. Harlan, C. L. Dunham, and Ashbel P. Willard. Corcoran was a little more difficult than in earlier days. Besides tiresomely insisting a loan is a loan, he became sticky about extensions, since he wanted to clear up the outstanding business of the terminated partnership. Still, when necessary, an extension could be arranged or the financier would advance his personal loan in place of the old firm's. Indiana's thirteen votes remained with Buchanan throughout the convention.[4]

Buchanan and Douglas were both at peak strength, 168 to 122, when Douglas conceded. Stalemate was the best he could hope for. By yielding graciously he might at least build good will for the future. Moreover, if a dark horse were nominated it might have been worse for Douglas, for it was assumed the 65-year-old Pennsylvanian would serve only one term; with a different President the succession might not open up so soon. Douglas' strategic retreat left only the vice-presidential nomination to be decided. On the first ballot seven candidates received from twenty-seven to fifty-nine votes each, but a swing to Breckinridge, who had fifty-one, started immediately. Youth (he was thirty-six), sectional background (southern and border state), political suavity, and popularity as an orator made him an ideal running mate for the elderly Pennsylvanian. And of course there were the potent interests the Kentuckian had cultivated in the Texas debt, railroad land grant, and Superior matters. Withal, the smooth and canny Breckinridge was on good terms with Douglas, who ostentatiously endorsed him when his victory grew certain. Again the "Little Giant" was attempting to ingratiate himself and ride before men and forces he could not control, just as he did in the case of the presidential nomination, and before then in the Superior alignments, railroad land grants, and Kansas–Nebraska policy. It still seemed possible he might win acceptance as leader in his turn; but in fact he was only playing into the hands of his antagonists.[5]

The convention over, Corcoran plunged into the campaign

against the Republican party, which was contesting its first presidential election with John C. Frémont as standard-bearer. Corcoran's greatest services were as fund raiser in the financial centers of the East, where he appealed to old Whigs as well as Democrats. Of his own contributions only $1,000 is explicitly identifiable, but from certain transactions indicated in his correspondence it appears that he gave at least $20,000 more. Democratic Senators, caucusing in Washington, broke into spontaneous applause at the mention of an anonymous individual who had rendered great services: the whisper spread rapidly that it was Corcoran. The campaign against the "Black Republicans" was as expensive as it was bitter and close; the sums spent by the Democrats were unprecedented. Corcoran was a ranking officer in "the Wall Street War."[6]

Another of Corcoran's old specialties, an Indian claim, paid off handsomely in aiding Buchanan's victory in Indiana. Richard W. Thompson, leader of the Native American ("Know-Nothing") party there, had successfully pressed a claim of the Menominee Indians for $242,000, which meant a commission of over $80,000 (one-third) for him. However, Indian Commissioner George Manypenny blocked the fee, calling it outrageous. To enable Thompson to press the claim Corcoran & Riggs advanced $2,000, half of which was endorsed by Fitch, and exerted their influence, for which a commission of $1,000 was ultimately collected. Bright lent Thompson an additional $3,000. Private bills for the pay-off failed in Congress until the summer of 1856, when Bright took charge in the Senate and secured passage by swinging a key vote at the last minute. In return, Thompson prevented the consummation of a coalition in Indiana between his party and the Republicans, thus insuring a Democratic victory in a crucial state.[7]

Thus did James Buchanan become President of the United States, to be lamented ever after as one of the most pathetic figures to occupy that most demanding office. His triumph owed much to his years of assiduous equivocation and evasion of responsibility, but it might never have happened if not for the coalition of men who gathered in pursuit of a Texas debt settlement, of railroad land grants, and assorted individual claims and who perceived how to manipulate their petty and irrelevant interests toward a larger conquest. If it is true that Buchanan's sad presidency contributed to the coming of the Civil War, then that war may be ascribed in good measure to the functioning of the American economy in politics.

For the time being the election of Buchanan left Corcoran with only one regret, the defeat of his friend Millard Fillmore on the Know-Nothing ticket. Responding to indirect requests for aid, he had written the ex-President to explain his course by reference to the sectional crisis over slavery. "I would rather you [were] elected than any man living. Yet I have not supported you for the reason that I have never doubted the success of the Democratic candidate for a moment, and he being the only man who could command strength enough in the North united with the whole South to put down Abolitionist fanaticism in the North. . . . Had you been nominated by the Whig Party *only,* a very different result would have been obtained." The nomination by the divided and disintegrating American party ruined Fillmore's chances when the preservation of the Union required his or Buchanan's election, Corcoran concluded.[8]

After the election Corcoran settled down happily with Bright, Slidell, Benjamin, and Barlow as major arbiters of patronage. His hope for a successful administration was doomed, however, by Buchanan's helplessness in the violent controversy over slavery and the futility of his attempts to appease the South. Corcoran and the rest of the men behind the President shared fully in these failures. His own activities were vulnerable to attack. The sharp-tongued Governor Henry A. Wise of Virginia, his ambitions frustrated and morality offended, called Corcoran a "snob . . . who slaps a big pocketbook" and Bright a "money pimp of Corcoran's." Wise's distrust of these men as corruptionists, excited by his hot personal ambition and temper, soon turned this Buchanan supporter into a bitter opponent.[9]

The fevered temper so common in these tense years was

burlesqued in Corcoran's break with the President. Early in the summer of 1858 his only surviving child, Louise, was being romanced by a Spanish attaché, Muriaga, whom he detested. One evening, while dining at Slidell's, he received word that Muriaga, against his prohibition, had taken the opportunity to visit his daughter. Corcoran rushed home, dragged the Spaniard from behind the piano, and kicked him out of the house. Soon afterward Muriaga, having perhaps collected his wits, presented himself and a pistol before the old banker's door. Corcoran appeared and denounced him as "unworthy of anything but the Penitentiary, where he would have him put." The attaché departed, leaving behind oaths, exclamations, and threats of vengeance.

Corcoran promptly went to Buchanan and demanded that the hapless diplomat be ordered out of the country. Buchanan tried to calm the infuriated Corcoran by agreeing with him and went privately to work with the Spanish minister to have Muriaga quietly withdrawn. This was the proper way to handle the affair, of course, but Corcoran, enraged, would be satisfied with nothing less than a peremptory expulsion. He solemnly believed the minister was Muriaga's "confederate in this crusade against me. . . . To say that I am surprised and mortified . . . would be but a feeble expression of my true feelings," he wrote, letting off steam in a letter which he had the sense not to send. Corcoran never spoke again to his old friend; instead he snubbed him openly and pompously. It was the most absurd episode in his life, Buchanan later recalled.[10]

Civil War, Exile, Return

During the downhill slide toward war, Corcoran held to the attitudes of a typical southern gentleman. He was aware of and—in the early days at least—even horrified by the evils of slavery, and in individual cases attempted to ameliorate them. In August 1835 he had spent two nights under arms with his militia company helping bring under control a mob of race rioters who were pulling down the homes and meeting places of free Negroes. The killer mob even had the nerve to send a group to the White House in search of Negroes, he told his wife. Two years later he wrote in horror of the sundering of a colored woman and her four small children from her husband to be sold down to Georgia: while confined in jail before shipment she strangled the two youngest, then tried to beat out the brains of the others and kill herself. Describing the murder to his wife, Corcoran wrote "It will be a feather in the cap of the Abolitionists. Indeed it has almost made one of me."[11]

Almost, but not quite, and he seems never to have gone as far as that remark again.[12] Rather, he maintained two prime objectives in the slavery controversy: the defense of the South, and the preservation of the Union—in that order. Although usually moderate in style, he supported the aggressive proslavery demands of his extremist friends. In so doing he disregarded moderates like his friend, former Massachusetts Senator Edward Everett, who pleaded with him to help restrain the "succession of unwise and violent measures on the part of the South" that hopelessly embarrassed northern well-wishers.[13]

By the end of 1859, with feelings exacerbated in both the North and the South following John Brown's raid, Corcoran feared the breakup of the country. In 1860 he enjoyed only brief spells of hope that no candidate would receive an electoral majority and the old Whig, John Bell, would be chosen president by the House of Representatives. His certainty of the defeat of Breckinridge and the victory of Lincoln caused him to decline to make campaign contributions.[14]

As the South plunged tumultuously toward secession, the uncomprehending Corcoran hoped for its peaceful accomplishment. His old friend, the aging army commander Winfield Scott, kept him informed of his efforts toward a peaceful division of the country as the only alternative to a long, bloody, costly war. When the war flared Corcoran voiced his bewilderment in unconsciously ironic rhetoric. The people of North and South would get along fine if matters could only be put before them, but "the politicians are corrupt and will ruin the country rather than yield," he solemnly lamented. "What is to become of us? The South should have her rights in peace," he exclaimed; the North was waging a "cruel and unnatural war upon their brethren of the South, who only want to be let alone." It would cost hundreds of millions to conquer, hundreds of millions a year to keep her. It was all the fault of the North: a little forbearance with the border states would have brought the cotton states back by the end of Lincoln's term. "Time may again unite us. War, never!"[15]

Corcoran began to do what he could for the South. There were rumors of his inviting Rebel commissioners and foreign diplomats to dine together with him. His terse, one-sentence resignation from the Union Club of New York was sent in May 1861. He defended the private interests of southern friends. With Bright he arranged the exchange of Slidell's Illinois lands, part of a joint speculation with Elisha Riggs and August Belmont, for the New Orleans and Louisiana bonds of a prosouthern Bostonian.

Despite General Scott's efforts to protect Corcoran, his property "and people," personal life began to grow unpleasant. In August, after the northern defeat at Bull Run, he was arrested and his property began to be harassed. The arrest seemed a shameful act of persecution to such northerners of moderate spirit as Navy Secretary Gideon Wells, and Corcoran was quickly released. In November he was preoccupied with the safety of his son-in-law, George Eustis, Jr., private secretary to Confederate agent Slidell: Eustis, Slidell, and James Mason were taken off the British ship *Trent* in the famous incident that precipitated a diplomatic crisis with Britain. Several of Corcoran's friends in the Boston business community risked the animosity of perfervid patriots to see to the comfort of Eustis before he and his companions were freed to continue to Europe. A more lasting annoyance came to Corcoran when his Washington property began to be occupied by the Federals.[16]

By the end of 1861 Corcoran had given up all hope of reunion "in our time, at least." He worked for peace and the

South by helping conservative Democrats in the North. Francis Grund, reminding the old banker of past devotion to his interests, asked him for aid in establishing a German language newspaper. Late in 1862 Corcoran gave $1,000 and invested a like amount to enable him, with Glossbrenner and Welsh, to publish the Philadelphia *Age*. But the Lincoln administration remained in power and the war continued relentlessly.[17]

The whole fabric of Corcoran's life had been torn. His daughter had joined Eustis, and their family was likely to remain overseas indefinitely. Many of his closest friends, especially the southerners, were gone. Wartime Washington, heavily overcrowded, was growing uncomfortable. To militant Unionists Corcoran was suspect; behind the commandeering and harassment he sensed the threat of confiscation. He decided to join his family in Paris, taking as much of his fortune as could readily be liquidated without substantial sacrifice. By the end of 1861 Corcoran was liquidating some of his stocks, bonds, and real estate, converting the proceeds into sterling and sending the money to Peabody in London for safe keeping. This was done in small amounts at first, but accelerated rapidly early in May 1862. When Corcoran himself sailed for Europe on October 8 he left instructions that liquid funds should be transferred to Europe whenever the accumulation reached $5,000. The shipments were handled in Washington by his secretary, and in New York by Riggs & Co., and (chiefly) by the Bank of America. Peabody was amused by the vastly exaggerated 1862 newspaper reports which had Corcoran removing $1.6 million in gold and paying only 10 percent for sterling. The figure would be nearer the mark, although still greatly exaggerated, for the whole of Corcoran's capital flights (including securities) throughout the war. By the time Corcoran left the country in October 1862 he had forwarded perhaps $300,000 in cash and $100,000 in securities, with perhaps $70,000 or more in cash following in 1863. By April 1864 almost $200,000 of securities had been liquidated. Only after Appomattox did the flight end. Besides the continuing flow of funds, a box of securities was sent across in April

1863 as "Mrs. Eustis's valuables." European friends assisted: securities were shipped under the personal direction of Samuel Cunard of the Cunard Line or one of his captains, or of the French consul. The French ambassador took custody of a large quantity of silver plate, giving it the benefit of diplomatic immunity; the Prussian minister, Gerolt, asked the Secretary of State for the use of one of Corcoran's houses.

The rumored departure of Corcoran's money was denounced in some newspapers as unpatriotic, but to no effect. His old friend of Fillmore days, William L. Hodge, did not believe a word of it and informed him that he was assuring his New York acquaintances to that effect. The latter were more skeptical, but apparently they heard news of Corcoran as of a dim figure from the receding past. His secretary, Anthony Hyde, happily reassured the exile that Washingtonians sympathized with him, irrespective of politics.[18]

The expatriation of capital suited another purpose: avoidance of income taxes. None was paid on the money, which was invested through Peabody (soon to become J. S. Morgan & Co.) in London and Erlanger in Paris. In addition, by fictitious transfers of property, nonreporting of income, and other means, Corcoran was able to reduce his tax eligibility. For 1861 he reported gross and net incomes of $63,000 and $44,000, respectively; for 1862, $75,000 and $57,000; for the next two years, net incomes of $46,000 and $27,000. For the earlier war years Corcoran's returns were probably under two-thirds of his actual income; by the end of the war they must have been well under one-half.[19]

If tax evasion was Corcoran's only anti-Union activity, he might as well have been a northern patriot. There were other services to the Confederacy, however, including subsidization of French journals, advice on financial negotiations, contributions to diplomats, and carrying of messages. Federal intelligence got wind of these activities; even Eustis, who should have known better, boasted of them. There was not enough evidence for legal action but Secretary of War Edwin M. Stanton harassed Corcoran with further seizures of property and confiscation of rents. Even this was incompletely and inefficiently or half-heartedly done, however, with the War Department continuing to pay rent on some of his buildings, although it occupied others rent-free. Hyde deemed it prudent to postpone demands for compensation while vociferously denying allegations of disloyalty.[20]

The war's end left Corcoran and his son-in-law with the disagreeable necessity of liquidating their involvement with the South to protect the family fortune. They took the oath of allegiance and Eustis, advised to do so by Slidell, asked for amnesty. Corcoran, returning home for a brief visit at the end of 1865, received a warm welcome from his fellow townsmen, who sent a delegation to meet him at dockside in New York. He learned that the only important official still hostile to him was Stanton, whom President Johnson would get rid of in due time. He began to gradually repatriate his capital and reverse fictitious property transfers, a process that he cautiously stretched out over five years. He went back to France to rejoin his daughter, whose health, always frail, was steadily deteriorating. When she died at the beginning of 1868, apparently of tuberculosis, Corcoran returned with her remains. Except for brief trips to nearby cities and resorts he never again left Washington.[21]

By the middle of 1866 Corcoran resumed a fairly active part in politics. The radical and Unionist past of Andrew Johnson could not have appealed to him, but he established a friendship with the President and helped procure amnesties for defeated rebels. Friendly articles appeared declaring that he had opposed only the administration, not the country, during the war. For the rest of his life he remained a generous contributor to Democratic campaign chests and newspapers, sometimes donating as much as $10,000 in an election.[22]

Corcoran was most active in Washington politics, where he reverted to the more successful flexibility of earlier times, working with the Republicans who dominated the District of Columbia. At the end of 1872 he loaned $25,000 to Forney, whose Washington *Sunday Chronicle* was a mainstay of Republican rule in the District as well as the national party organ. Aside from the potential usefulness of a good relationship, Corcoran remembered the journalist's defense of him, "creditable alike to your head and heart," against attacks for prosouthern conduct. He continued to help Forney with loans and contributions. There was a close collaboration, marked by a personal loan of $3,000, with Republican boss Alexander Shepherd in his ambitious programs for city development. The two men, with George Riggs and, unknown to them, the notorious Democratic "Boss" Tweed of New York, founded the Washington *Patriot;* John P. Stockton and Eugene Casserly, Democratic Senators from New Jersey and California, were other investors. Another leader of the local Republican machine was Henry D. Cooke, brother of the powerful financier, Jay Cooke.[23]

Corcoran began to dissent from the conduct of the local administration in 1871, opposing plans for a $4 million loan for street improvements. The *Patriot,* charging corruption, became the only daily newspaper to support him. Learning of the notorious Tweed's investment after his exposure and fall, Corcoran bought out his share to maintain the paper and its policy. Nevertheless the $4 million program was inaugurated when the Republicans swept the 1871 elections. The victors tried to placate the District's most prominent citizen. He declined a testimonial dinner but accepted appointment to the Board of Commissioners in charge of the sinking fund for the debt of the old Corporation of Washington. More tangibly, they arranged for the city to pay him $100,000 of 7 percent 20-year bonds for land for a central market. He also bought large amounts of city sinking fund debentures.[24]

For a time these measures helped allay Corcoran's fears and suspicions of the city's finances; also, local patriotism and acceptance of politics as it was made him reluctant to stir. Early in 1873, declining "to be drawn into a newspaper controversy that is, at all times, so distasteful to me," he refused an interview to the New York *Tribune.* When the newspaper fabricated one containing a long and detailed attack on the

District government, he repudiated it. Not until five days after the closing of Jay Cooke & Co. at the beginning of the Panic of 1873 did Corcoran send in his resignation as sinking fund commissioner. Even then he pleaded poor health, and was induced to remain in the post for a time.

But malfeasance could no longer be overlooked. Corcoran was quietly informed by Baltimore financiers of secret loans negotiated by the remaining commissioners. In February 1874, after demanding and failing to receive an explanation of recent debt transactions, he took the offensive against street contract corruption with open letters to newspapers in Washington and elsewhere. (Included in his bill of particulars was an attempt to persuade him to pay $22,000 in taxes, less a 16 percent discount. The money was intended for Forney, he was told, in payment of a government debt. Ordinarily prompt tax payments earned a 6 percent discount and the money went into the city's treasury.) Corcoran thus helped overthrow the Shepherd ring (although he maintained friendly personal relations with the boss, as with Forney, and helped him grapple with heavy personal debts). With this success he retired from Washington politics.[25]

With advancing age Corcoran finally retired from national politics, too. His last personal initiative was to singlehandedly keep alive the Washington *Union* through late 1876 and early 1877, vainly supporting the election of Samuel Tilden for President. In 1882 he declined an invitation to chair, or serve on, the Democratic congressional campaign finance committee. Candidly citing his record of failure, he graciously suggested that younger men were needed.[26]

Passing into the Past

When Corcoran acknowledged failure he meant failure to achieve his goals; he never doubted the wisdom of the goals themselves. Far from believing that he had involved himself in a monstrous blunder, he always justified the South. In this he differed radically from his son-in-law, George Eustis, Jr., who was very well placed to make an informed analysis. His father had been chief justice of Louisiana; he himself had been elected to Congress as a Native American in 1854 and 1856, and during the Civil War he served as secretary to John Slidell, Confederate agent in Paris.

Eustis was a most unusual southerner. Far from blaming the other section for the troubles of his own, he ascribed the catastrophe to southern statesmanship, which he considered not blind but paralyzed. In slavery, he later wrote, the South had been grimly defending a system increasingly alien and repugnant to all of modern civilization. Some saw and feared the perils of this isolation, Eustis recalled. He recounted how Louisiana Senator Pierre Soulé's sensitivity and rationality—if not his cynicism—had been aroused by the slavery issue. He had suggested to John Calhoun that the time had come to modify the system, to reduce or evade the political liability of hereditary involuntary servitude—yet retain its material benefits. Calhoun, preeminent spokesman of his society, was the one to initiate such a change, Soulé argued, possibly the only man in the South with sufficient prestige and stature. The phrasing is ambiguous: reform may have been for Soulé a mask for continued exploitation, or an ideal that had to be approached circumspectly; whatever the motivation, his proposal might have introduced significant changes into a society that was dangerously rigid.

One wonders what passed through Calhoun's mind as he pondered, and what lay behind his answer. Did he overestimate southern strength? Did he consider even himself a prisoner of the fanatic and fearful rigidity of his section? Did he merely seek the most tactful way to reject an unwanted proposal to weaken slavery, which he publicly praised as a "positive good"? Calhoun finally replied, evading the issue, that the South was not yet ready for such a departure.[27]

After the war Corcoran sought to vindicate the South, hoping ultimately to regain by appeal to public opinion what had been lost on the battlefield. He subsidized the writings of historian

A. T. Bledsoe and contributed to the Southern Historical Society.[28] He gave sizable gifts to colleges in the South and may have inspired his friend George Peabody's famous educational philanthropies there. In 1869 he and Peabody responded to the appeal of Robert E. Lee on behalf of Washington (later Washington and Lee) College with donations, large for that day, of $20,000 and $60,000 respectively. As did many cosectionalists, Corcoran looked hopefully to the University of Virginia to counter Yale and Harvard in molding national opinion. He gave over $100,000 to endow two chairs there. At home, his contributions in land and money to Columbian College (later George Washington University) may have exceeded those to the University of Virginia.[29]

In his long old age, Corcoran busied himself increasingly with individual charities, in which his sympathies gave priority to southerners. Much assistance was given tactfully in the form of loans: Henry Wise, erstwhile enemy, received a donation of $500 and loans totaling $1,000, for which he was as fulsome with gratitude as he had once been with vitriol. Robert M. T. Hunter was assisted in reclaiming and selling his Superior property. William Aiken of South Carolina, once one of the wealthiest of planters, borrowed $10,000, and Breckinridge a smaller amount. William H. Trescott of South Carolina was lent $1,500 on condition that he would draw on Corcoran to that extent for any of the latter's old friends whom he discovered in need. The failure to honor this obligation or to repay his debt when he regained his affluence provoked from the old philanthropist the harshest excoriation in all his correspondance. There were large donations for homes for Confederate women and soldiers in Charleston, for which he was much appreciated there. Only one northerner of prominence (apart from Forney) benefited from his largesse: Robert J. Walker, who owed the salvation of a modest estate to Corcoran.[30]

Unlike his friend Peabody, who reportedly felt a strong distaste for alms-giving, Corcoran found it an enjoyable duty. By 1867 he had a private pension list of ten people receiving

$.50 to $5 each per month, totaling $31.50, and the list grew steadily thereafter. Some of the sums would seem absurdly small, except that other rich Washingtonians often aided the same recipients. For Corcoran the practice began after the war, the only earlier instance being the widow of President James Madison.[31]

Most of his charities were nonrecurring, however. By the end of 1871 over seventy of the larger donations totaled almost $20,000. Most were tactfully given in the form of loans, with the notes to be cancelled or returned on Corcoran's death if not voluntarily paid. He made myriad small donations. There was a steadily increasing volume of pleas for alms by mail, fifty to 100 per day by 1888, from all over the country and even Europe—"begging letters," his secretary Hyde sourly called them, upon which the old man lavished personal attention as long as he was able. By 1880 they were withheld by Hyde to ease Corcoran's remaining days, apparently even when from so eminent an acquaintance as James M. Mason.[32]

An important motive of the aging man's philanthropy was the vicarious life-after-death of a perpetuated name. Like another wealthy old man a half-century later, he took to giving coins to small children in the street. Years later, a lady remembered saying she would like to give him something too, and recalled his reply: "Don't give me anything; I have enough already. Only remember me when I am gone." Bathos, but with some judgment and taste it found constructive outlets.

Of all Corcoran's philanthropies the closest to his sentiments was the Louise Home, named after his late wife and daughter. It was built as a residence for elderly ladies in reduced circumstances (or, as Mrs. Henry Adams called it with aristocratic and Adams-like indelicacy, an "alms house for some 40 decayed gentlewomen"). He gave the building, the grounds, and an endowment of $160,000 of notes and bonds yielding an income of $12,500. This undertaking in private social security for the upper classes brought so many applications that admission was made by invitation only. Corcoran had his birthday parties there and visited every New Year's

Day. Even in an undertaking so innocuous and kind, sectionalism was an issue. Preference was given to southern ladies, giving rise to attacks in Congress against a bill to exempt the institution from taxes. Corcoran denied the accusations, claiming that only half the residents were southern. (His own breakdown belied his assertions, revealing nine northern and thirty-two southern women. Nineteen of the latter were from Maryland and the District of Columbia, which were universally considered southern.)[33]

Churches were a favorite outlet for Corcoran's philanthropy. His religious belief was conventional, receiving an impulse from the illness and death of his daughter in 1867 much as it once had from financial panic and from the meditations of his wife. In the late stages of his daughter's illness he decided at last, after sporadic musings over many years, to be baptised and confirmed. A memorial window was commissioned for a church at Cannes, where the Eustises had lived, and another for the Church of the Ascension in Washington. Upon the latter he showered attentions and, by the beginning of 1882, more than $80,000 of gifts.[34]

The old man was to feel even the taste of religion spoiled by cupidity. Corcoran was persuaded by the vestrymen of the Ascension to share the church's cost, he matching their notes to a total of $50,000 to secure a loan. He also made a large donation, but to his consternation Corcoran found his donation used to pay off the debts secured by the other vestrymen's notes. Shocked, he demanded "respectfully, but nonetheless, firmly" that they adhere to the spirit and letter of the agreement. For years the work went on with Corcoran alternately cajoled and resented. In 1876 he finally submitted his "peremptory resignation" as vestryman and dunned the church to complete the gift of a pew to him, voted more than a year earlier.[35]

Corcoran's greatest benefactions were devoted to Washington, and the most outstanding was the art gallery bearing his name. Begun before the war, then commandeered by the government, it was finally completed and opened to the public in 1871. What with building, grounds, his collection, and endowments, Corcoran estimated his lifetime gifts to the gallery at $1.5 million and added a final $100,000 bequest. This was probably more than half of all the donations, great and small, during his long lifetime.

Corcoran took pleasure in an active role in the gallery and exercised some influence in its purchases. He was taken with the sculptures of Antoine Louis Barye. The visitor to the gallery may find himself taken with them also: several dozen such exotically sanguinary pieces as *Bull Attacked by Jaguar, Bear Attacking Bull, Stag Trampling Wolf,* and *Ocelot Carrying Heron,* plus equestrians and other subjects such as *Ape Riding Gnu.* Corcoran was certainly vulnerable to flattery. Albert Bierstadt selected a peak in the Rockies, called it "Mount Corcoran," and painted it large and uninteresting. In a fulsome letter ostensibly addressed to Sam Ward, Bierstadt unreeled a long line about Corcoran being the modern Medici, in whose gallery he would rather place his paintings than elsewhere at double the price. "Mr. Corcoran and the true artists of the world are allies or friends at heart," he gushed. "A dealer is simply a speculator." With impish glee Ward passed the message on to the sentimental old banker to add to "those touching letters you gratified me with a sight of [expressing gratitude for alms] . . . tribute to your genuine inwardness of Conscientious honor. . . ." Ward, the talented scion of a New York banking family, had abandoned high finance to take up the life of Washington lobbyist and bon vivant. In him there must have been, besides a mischievous sense of fun, a touch of the sardonic. The old gentleman was relieved of $7,000 for *Mt. Corcoran.*[36]

It was almost a tragicomedy of good intentions unleavened by taste. Large sums, up to more than $10,000, were paid for paintings by Kauffman (a trustee of the gallery), Burnier, Heilbirth, and others of that caliber, while opportunities furnished by Junius Spencer Morgan, his partner, Levi P. Morton, and State Department officials to buy works of (or attributed to) such masters as Gainsborough, Titian, Ruysdael, and Tiepolo at comparable prices were declined. But it may be said

William Wilson Corcoran, by John Q. A. Ward, 1883. In the Collection of The Corcoran Gallery of Art.

W. W. Corcoran, by G. P. A. Healy, 1884. Courtesy National Portrait Gallery, Smithsonian Institution.

The Original Corcoran Gallery of Art, Washington, D.C. James Renwick, Architect. The building now houses the Smithsonian Institution's Renwick Art Museum. Courtesy Commission of Fine Arts.

Portrait of W. W. Corcoran, artist unknown, c. 1871. In the Collection The Corcoran Gallery of Art. Gift of the United States District Court of Washington, D.C.

for Corcoran that his taste was typical of his generation, and it was his laudable policy to encourage native art. He could be proud that he had made some contribution to the cultural life of the community. At the end of his life the gallery reportedly received nearly 100,000 visitors per year. Although the Corcoran collections were artistically unimpressive (they retain some historical interest), the institution was securely established. Even more to his credit, the gift of an art museum to the public by an individual was unprecedented and helped invigorate a vital tradition in American culture.[37]

Corcoran symbolized his long and active concern for the beautification of Washington by campaigning for a monument to the city's planner, Pierre Charles L'Enfant, whose grave lay neglected across the Potomac. He induced John Kasson of Iowa to introduce a resolution to that effect in the House of Representatives, thus giving homage to the man who laid out what (as Corcoran put it) "was once ironically called the 'City of Magnificent Distances' but which should now be called the Garden City of the World." Before the war, when he had political influence, Corcoran had promoted this transformation by supporting Andrew J. Downing's plan of 1851. (Probably influenced by Downing, whom he retained to design some of his own buildings, he also ornamented his native Georgetown by buying twelve and one-half acres at a cost of $3,000 for the Oak Hill Cemetery. By 1853 his outlay reached $12,000; by 1878, $120,000.) If Corcoran comprehended that Downing's ornate romantic vision would have radically altered L'Enfant's Baroque classicism, he did not allow it to detract from veneration of the father of the city's design.[38]

In 1878 Corcoran joined in one other act of monumental patriotism, as vice-president of the Washington Monument Society and chairman of the commission to complete it following decades of delay. He participated in the wrangling over aesthetics. Deferring to the taste of William Wetmore Story, he agreed with his proposed design changes, venturing only to suggest the substitution of the "segment of a globe, surmounted by the statue of Fame, for the pointed summit proposed by you." Story also wanted something more ornate than the original obelisk design and derided the "chimney." But Robert C. Winthrop, whose influence proved decisive, dissented, partly because he feared there would be "another 30 Years War" over the proposed changes. He rejoiced, too, that Story's plan "contemplates no *pulling down*. . . . Whatever else we do or leave undone, the vandalism of tearing down must be resisted." But most important, Winthrop approved the original design in all its simplicity:

> Story's reiterations about *Chimneys* do not disturb me. When the Bunker Hill monument was proposed Horatio Greenough, the great sculptor prepared the design, and it was approved by Stuart, the great portrait painter and Allston, the grand artist. It was an *Obelisk,* and Webster, Everett, and Judge Story united in sanctioning it! We have never considered it a Chimney, and are entirely satisfied with it.[39]

Story's model was universally admired, but a horde of lobbying designers (or designing lobbyists) wore down the patience of the President and Congress. The matter was transferred from the Committee on Public Buildings and Grounds to that of the District of Columbia, and with Winthrop leading the campaign the original design was approved and the appropriation passed. "Both Congress and the people seemed determined to have the *tallest structure in the World*. I did oppose this decision, but the friends of the chimney prevailed," Corcoran lamented. But he bore no resentment. With his loans in advance of government funding helping to speed the work, rapid progress was made until the completion and dedication of the monument in 1885.[40]

These venerations were performed as Corcoran himself, mellow in his new role, attained the status of patriarch. Militia companies were named after him, perhaps in hopes of donations. Some small ones were made. There were the Corcoran Cadets in Washington, and in Baltimore the Corcoran Rifle Corps and Corcoran Zouaves, the latter chiefly government and newspaper printers disporting themselves in grey uniforms with red trimmings and white and red turbans. The city government of Washington voted to have his full-length portrait painted for the City Hall: he chose for the artist the able G. P. A. Healy. In 1879 Corcoran was the only private citizen invited to President Hayes' official dinner for the diplomatic corps. To ladies such as Mrs. Adams he was "sweet as barley candy," and he was privileged to call upon Mrs. Grover Cleveland informally. (George Bancroft was the only other man so honored.)

Corcoran maintained, on the whole, a decent sense of proportion. A hanger-on who wanted to write a roseate authorized biography was discouraged and genealogies were disdained. Correspondents were asked not to address him by his militia title of colonel. He was restrained in accepting honors and flattery, for example, refusing an offer to change the name of Columbian College to Corcoran University in gratitude for past gifts (and no doubt in hope of further donations, which were obtained). His retainer, the faithful Hyde, ascribed Corcoran's recovery from a serious illness to the prayers offered in Baltimore churches and elsewhere by recipients of his charity, and especially to a woman who "kneeled on the footway facing the Bank wall and prayed for his recovery." But Hyde's liege lord good-humoredly credited an "elegant" brandy sent by a friend.[41]

Corcoran strolled gently down his declining years, a hoary figure from a semilegendary past. He helped create this aura in interviews with newsmen. Born the year of Washington's death, he told of having known all the presidents. Corcoran had once visited the aging John Adams at Quincy. There the old statesman told the young real estate agent that "my physical house is out of order and the landlord has warned me that he will make no further repairs." He had often seen Jefferson drive to the home of his business agent in Georgetown: "He sat his fiery horse well."

Innocent of ironic intent, Corcoran often lamented the decline of statesmanship in the latter days of the Republic. His partisanship and exile during the Civil War era were forgotten. When he died in February 1888, the flags in the District of Columbia were lowered to half-mast in memory of the first citizen of Washington.[42]

13

Disintegration in an Age of Progress

. . . chance, or rather that tangle of secondary causes which we call chance, for want of the knowledge how to unravel it. . . .

—Alexis de Tocqueville, *Recollections*

Corcoran was on the whole an ordinary man, able but not brilliant. His outstanding trait was a keen opportunism that enabled him to make the most of his luck. Birth did not give him wealth, but did provide political and business connections, notably with the Riggs family. One thing led readily to another as he sequentially developed chains of personal and business relationships. Through shared interests and favors he became an intimate of key politicians and of Wall Street's leaders. By the end of the Tyler administration the firm of Corcoran & Riggs was a major government depository, and within months of Polk's inauguration it was practically the exclusive Treasury agency at the seat of government. The shrewdly capitalized opportunities of the Mexican War climaxed its rise to eminence.

For the next half-dozen years Corcoran played a central role in American finance. His firm enjoyed the use of sizable government deposits—even after the Independent Treasury had been established. Corcoran, chiefly through Newbold of the Bank of America, was the link between the Treasury and the New York money market. These men were consulted and relied upon in primitive federal open market operations. Simultaneously Newbold, with the cooperation of Palmer of the Merchants Bank and a few other Wall Street leaders, held in some restraint the exuberant expansiveness of the business community.

The lines and techniques of cooperation were improvised while Walker was at the Treasury, after experience had taught him that the possibilities of an independent or controlling government course were extremely limited under existing conditions. The inherited modus operandi was uneasily acquiesced in during the brief Taylor administration. Meredith at the Treasury and Clayton in the State Department were awed by Corcoran and his allies, although deeply suspicious of the banker's Democratic and southern connections. Evident in their conduct was the belief that Corcoran represented power—power of dubious legitimacy. Suspicious as they were of his ambiguous interests in business, government, and politics, the Taylor Whigs were conservative and cautious or lacked self-confidence when it came to upsetting established patterns. Despite veiled threats there was only a slight erosion of his special position. After Taylor's early death, the last Whig administration under Fillmore worked as closely with Corcoran as if he had been the old Bank of the United States. He was not toppled from his eminence until the Pierce administration, when Treasury Secretary Guthrie deprived the firm of its federal deposits and appointments and of any special role in government operations.

The continuing retreat of government from conscious participation in American finance added to the importance of Wall Street policies, but there centrifugal forces were growing paramount. Newbold had been an important member of the coalition that brought down the Bank of the United States, in which Corcoran was a minor figure; the two had shared largely in succeeding to the bank's functions and opportunities.

But if Newbold labored to assume Nicholas Biddle's central banking role, he had failed to foresee that killing the great rival institution would undermine the very idea of central banking. For a decade and a half Newbold and his allies, at the strategic center of American finance, had the will and the resources to restrain business by tightening credit when overexpansion threatened. The trouble was that Newbold's position was not one of domination, but rather of first among equals. His authority was steadily eroded as the number of his peers increased and his leadership was challenged by the Bank of Commerce.

The turning point was reached after 1854, the last year of effective control under the post-Biddle regime. Profiting from its more expansionist credit policies in a climate of prolonged prosperity, the Commerce passed the America as the largest bank of the community, while the number of rivals approaching parity rapidly increased. Their momentum was fueled by the expansion of credit (in the form of outstanding banknotes and deposits) relative to cash reserves, in proportions often more than double the accustomed ratios of the America and other banking conservatives. Ironically, it was the latters' self-restraint in maintaining relatively high reserves that made possible their rivals' gains without great danger to themselves and the whole community. But as rivals gained, power and leadership were fragmented.

Insidiously, the rapid growth of more expansionist institutions seemed to prove that the Bank of America could safely and profitably emulate its competitors, and *had* to if it were not to fall to second rank. It did so, reducing reserve ratios below earlier standards, and surrendering a degree of control which in any case could not have been long maintained, and thus opened the way to overexpansion and the Panic of 1857. The panic under way, the still powerful but no longer self-assured banking leaders fled from risk by drastically contracting credit, unloading the burdens of responsibility onto an outraged but helpless and deferential community.

Although he made a vain effort to exert a constructive influence on the panic, Corcoran by that time had turned away from finance. Not a Faustian businessman bent on ever-higher peaks of wealth and power, he had long contemplated an early retirement. It followed anticlimactically upon the end of his special government role. But his sizable fortune continued to be spread, if anything more widely, over numerous business and political investments and speculations, partly to minimize risk and partly from that dilettantish diversity of interests which the Barings had earlier criticized. The almost bewildering gamut ranged to lands, claims, political loans, repudiated state debts, transportation, and municipal bonds (not to mention charity and philanthropy).

Corcoran ramified his political influence by loans, bribes, employment of agents, investments, and campaign contributions. Sometimes a specific quid pro quo was the important consideration; always there was the banking of good will. Out of the logrolling over scores of particular issues were improvised informal overlapping alliances that endured through successive controversies and influenced presidential politics. Most far-reaching was the chain opportunistically forged by Corcoran, Bright, and others through claims, Texas debt, Superior speculation, railroad land grants, and other collaborations, leading in 1856 to the frustration of Douglas' presidential ambition, the election of the disastrous Buchanan, and the advancement of Breckinridge.

It is profoundly unsettling to perceive what trivial, frivolous interests, entangled with others more vital, could be so important in making a president—in making such a president at such a time. Many of the social adhesives of other times or places—army, church, educated elites—were weak, fragmented, or irrelevant. The national political structure, rather than successfully containing local interests, was jerry-built and torn down in rapid-fire elections from innumerable, unstable local foundations. Under these conditions success might be won at any given moment by the feeblest combinations if they were shrewdly timed—but such successes could not be secured. In politics as in business, great prizes seemed always within reach but proved always vulnerable when grasped; optimism and insecurity thrived together.

So when the short lines of early railroads began to evolve sequentially into organizations of unheard-of scale, it was as natural as a reflex for politicians to affiliate with and try to control them. Spellbound by visions of organizations without peer in strength and durability, "practical" politicians verged upon economic determinism. Naturally the political potentiality of railroads seemed relatively greatest and the field clearest for newcomers in the less developed areas. (It is symptomatic that Corcoran's modest assistance tended, with maximum leverage, toward politicians from such regions.) Douglas set the leading example in his relationship with the Illinois Central and attempted to extend his political influence step-by-step with its projected extensions through neighboring regions. But there were many would-be corporate giants, each state and locality had its own soaringly speculative businessmen and politicians, and what Douglas saw was obvious to all. He worked ceaselessly to win loyalties by building mutuality of interests, but his assiduous and impressive tactical leadership was futile. His competitors and enemies, the Breckinridges and Brights with their own ambitions and interests, cynically understood his tactics of racing to keep ahead of a following.

To Douglas, fearful of the moral struggle over slavery, material interests were the valid interests of American politics, and coalitions based upon them would properly control other kinds of conflict. If he was accurate in his estimate of his countrymen's motivations, as he was in judging politicians', he was simply premature. The irony of Douglas's career lay in his pursuit of the politics of vested interests before the interests had been vested. The concentrations of economic power so feverishly anticipated were not yet in existence.

As the implications of the railroad grew in men's minds, their hopes expanded explosively and their self-discipline—the discipline men accept or impose upon themselves when they recognize limits—disintegrated. It was still possible—for instance in the general Compromise of 1850 and, with greater difficulty, in the Texas debt and railroad land grant swaps of 1856—to contain the struggle over slavery. But the higher priority of evolving economic and political interests also meant that when they clashed, each faction was likely to occupy positions in the slavery controversy not for the sake of slavery or freedom, but to defend or advance particularist ambitions. Those who rated moral priorities higher, rather than being curbed, in the long run would gain reinforcements from the political economy. The forms in which the fundamental dilemma was brought home varied from Mississippi to Minnesota to Wisconsin and to the grand arena at Washington, where Douglas accepted with fearful determination the risks of 1854. The net result of the chaos of forces was to churn American politics into a maelstrom.

In business as in politics, the same fundamental forces, centrifugal and fragmenting, were at work. Among the turning points of the decade were those at which ambitious men ran headlong against the limitations of resources. The Depression of 1857, partially caused by the fragmentation of finance and the dissipation of resources among too numerous railroad, townsite, and other projects, constricted the economic range of possibilities at a critical moment and thereby helped deflect the nation's tensely balanced momentum toward a desperate and ferocious solution.

This was the meaning of Corcoran's career: representative of a generation of Americans shrewd, opportunistic, determined, pressing with gusto their particular interests; a generation even more atomized than the nation's historical norm, its possibilities of conflict multiplying even as its prosperity grew, dissipating its chance of peaceful resolution.[1]

Abbreviations
Notes
Bibliography
Index

Abbreviations

AB	Letters from Executive Officer, Treasury Department, National Archives, Washington
Alb. Inst.	Albany Institute of History and Art
B Letters	Cabinet and Bureaus, Treasury Department, National Archives, Washington
BB	Baring Brothers & Company
BP	Baring Papers
BPGL	Baring Papers, General Letters
BPLB	Baring Papers, Letter Books
BPOC	Baring Papers, Official Correspondence
BuffHS	Buffalo Historical Society
C	W. W. Corcoran
ChiHS	Chicago Historical Society
ColU	Columbia University
C&R	Corcoran & Riggs
DelHS	Delaware Historical Society

DetPL	Detroit Public Library
DukeU	Duke University
E Letters	Letters and Reports to Congress, Treasury Department, National Archives, Washington
EI	Essex Institute, Salem, Massachusetts
ER	Elisha Riggs (after 1854, Elisha Riggs, Jr.)
ER, Jr.	Elisha Riggs, Jr.
GWR	George W. Riggs
HU	Harvard University
HuntL	Huntington Library
Iowa St	Iowa State Department of History and Archives, Des Moines
K Letters	Miscellaneous K Letters, Treasury Department Archives, National Archives, Washington
LC	Library of Congress
LR	Lawrason Riggs
M&M	Manning & Mackintosh
MassHS	Massachusetts Historical Society
Ms. Div. NYPL	Manuscript Division, New York Public Library
MinnHS	Minnesota Historical Society
NHHS	New Hampshire Historical Society
NYHS	New-York Historical Society
NYPL	New York Public Library
PaHS	Pennsylvania Historical Society
PriU	Princeton University
R	Riggs

SoHC	Southern Historical Collection, University of North Carolina
SR	Samuel Riggs
U.S. Misc. Mss.	United States Miscellaneous Manuscripts, Library of Congress
VHS	Virginia Historical Society
WiscHS	State Historical Society of Wisconsin
YA Letters	Richard Ela, Agent, Treasury Department, National Archives, Washington
YU	Yale University
UChi	University of Chicago
UMich	University of Michigan
UNC	University of North Carolina
UPa	University of Pennsylvania
UPitts	University of Pittsburgh
URoch	University of Rochester
UTex	University of Texas

Notes

Chapter 1

1. The sources for Corcoran's early life are chiefly the bound and unbound materials in his papers at the Library of Congress. See, for example, Nicholas Biddle to Edward S. Whelen, Sept. 19, 1840, C Papers, LC. See also David Maurice Cole, *The Development of Banking in the District of Columbia* (New York, 1959), 3–4, 8, 67, 77–8, 86, 99, 110, 112, 150, 249–50; Wilhelmus B. Bryan, *A History of the National Capitol,* 2 vols. (New York, 1914–1916), I, 410, 596n., II, 160, 210; Ralph C. H. Catterall, *Second Bank of the United States* (Chicago, 1903), 104–5, 368–9; obituaries of W. W. Corcoran, Ms. Div., NYPL, but containing many errors; Kendall to C, Oct. 12, 1830, Sept. 9, 1832, PaHS. A selection of Corcoran's letters, some incomplete and only a few important, is in William Wilson Corcoran, *A Grandfather's Legacy* (Washington, 1879). There are portraits of Corcoran's parents by Charles Peale Polk in the Corcoran Gallery of Art, Washington.

2. See Walter Buckingham Smith, *Economic Aspects of the Second Bank of the United States* (Cambridge, 1953), ch. 3, 236; Thomas Payne Govan, *Nicholas Biddle, Nationalist and Public Banker, 1786–1844* (Chicago, 1959), 1–2, 86–7; Fritz Redlich, *Molding of American Banking: Men and Ideas,* 2 vols. (New York, 1947–1951), II, ch. 6; Bray Hammond, "Jackson, Biddle, and the

Bank of the United States," *Journal of Economic History* 7 (May 1947); John M. McFaul, "The Politics of Jacksonian Finance" (Ph.D. diss., University of California, 1963).

3. Hammond, *Banks and Politics in America from the Revolution to the Civil War* (Princeton, 1957), ch. 12; Charles Grier Sellers, Jr., *James K. Polk, Jacksonian: 1795–1843* (Princeton, 1957), ch. 7.

4. Ellis Paxson Oberholtzer, *Jay Cooke, Financier of the Civil War,* 2 vols. (Philadelphia, 1907), I, 68.

5. Corcoran, Riggs, and twelve others formed a syndicate to purchase practically all of the Bank of the United States' real estate in Washington. The agreement was cancelled after the Panic of 1837. Besides Riggs, the New Yorkers in the group were Robert L. Patterson, J. L. and S. Josephs & Co., and Samuel Swartwout. The Josephs, who failed soon after, preceded August Belmont as American agent of the Rothschilds and intimate of leading New York Democrats. Swartwout, collector of customs of the Port of New York, used government funds to purchase real estate in various parts of the Union and became the most notorious defaulter of the day. Corcoran's share was $10,000 of a total purchase price of $184,000 with 10 percent down. See C to Louise Corcoran, Oct. 13, 17, 1836, C Papers; memoranda and agreement, Sept. 30, Oct. 1, 1836, Feb., 1837, and n.d., C to ER, Jan. 21, Aug. 3, Sept. 30, Oct. 7, 1837, July 11, 1838, May 28, 1839, R Papers, LC; Richard Smith to Charles S. Folwell, Nov. 26, 1842, PaHS.

6. It is difficult to make exact statements about his operations at this time for lack of surviving materials. See C to Louise Corcoran, Aug. 25, Oct. 13, 1836, C Papers; Cole, *Banking in D. C.,* 249–50; Smith, *Second Bank,* 51–63, 180–2; Henrietta Larson, *Jay Cooke, Private Banker* (Cambridge, 1936), 36f, 57–61.

7. Smith, *Second Bank,* 183f; Govan, *Biddle,* 305f; Ralph W. Hidy, *House of Baring in American Trade and Finance: English Merchant Bankers at Work, 1763–1861* (Cambridge, 1949), 205f; George Rogers Taylor, *Transportation Revolution, 1815–1860* (New York and Toronto, 1951), 338–45; U.S. Bureau of the Census, *Historical Statistics of the United States, Colonial Times to 1957* (Washington, 1960), 563–6.

8. Rafael A. Bayley, *National Loans of the United States* (Washington, 1882), 140.

9. Corcoran joined other brokers in attempts to rig the market. Riggs paid a commission of ¼ percent, but agreements were rarely kept for more than a few days. See C to ER, Nov. 12, 15, Dec. 6, 10, 11, 14, 16, 20, 24, 1837, Jan. 25, 1838, and R accounts current book, R Papers; Walter Buckingham Smith and Arthur Harrison Cole, *Fluctuations in American Business, 1790–1860* (Cambridge, 1935), 76–8.

10. Exchange operations were timed with government processes in various ways. While specie payments were suspended, government requisitions made on government funds at other points and sold to individuals provided a form of domestic exchange. Congressional politics occasionally delayed the passage of appropriation bills, causing them to fall to a very low premium, say par to 1 percent rising to 3 percent upon passage. Corcoran was sometimes able to take advantage of these fluctuations. See C to ER, Dec. 17, 1837, Jan. 25, 27, 28, 29, 31, Feb. 2, 9, 1838, Mar. 18, 19, 21, 22, 28, 30, 1839, and R accounts current book, R Papers; Smith, *Second Bank,* 55.

11. The advice of politicians was not foolproof. A losing speculation in Virginia military land warrants was based on Senator William C. Rives' erroneous expectation of new legislation. See C to ER, many letters of 1838, especially Jan., Feb., Apr., May; also Feb. 23, Sept. 20, 27, 1839, and R accounts current book, R Papers.

No evidence has been found of relationships between Corcoran and Democratic politicians while he was with the Bank of the United States.

12. Secretary of the Navy Mahlon Dickerson, undecided on what to sell for the Navy Pension Fund, was talked into letting Corcoran have his choice. In contrast, Secretary of War Joel Poinsett declined a proposed exchange on the grounds that it would set a bad precedent. See C to ER, Dec. 30, 1838, Jan. 2, 5, 8, 16, 26, 31, Feb. 2, 7, 13, 18, 23, 24, Mar. 11, 16, 21–5, 28, 30, Apr. 1, 19, May 30, June 4, July 15, 16, 19, 20, 1839, R Papers. See also C and ER joint account, ER account book, R Papers; ER to C, Feb. 22, Oct. 30, 1840, R Domestic Letters; C account, 1841, C&R ledgers, Riggs Bank; Taylor, *Transportation Revolution,* 344–5; Smith, *Second Bank,* 207–26; Govan, *Biddle,* 336f; Hidy, *House of Baring,* 275; B. U. Ratchford, *American State Debts* (Durham, 1941), 18–20; Paul B. Trescott, "Federal-

State Financial Relations, 1790–1860," *Journal of Economic History* (September 1955), 240.

13. The agents of Arkansas for the disposal of her bonds were Theodore Williamson and Senator Ambrose H. Sevier. They were assisted by a Kentuckian, Richard Mentor Johnson, Vice-President of the United States. The best-known member of a notable political family, one of Johnson's brothers had gone to Arkansas. His nephew, Robert Ward Johnson, was on his way to becoming an important politician there. The Vice-President was listed as a purchaser of thirty of the $1,000 bonds.

A brokerage commission of 1 percent was divided between Corcoran and the president of the North American Bank, Joseph D. Beers. Corcoran also sold $100,000 of Illinois 6 percent shares to Navy Secretary Dickerson as broker for Beers. See Beers to Levi Woodbury, Dec. 8, 1837, Feb. 19, 1838, Woodbury to Beers, Feb. 21, 1838, Woodbury Papers, LC. See also Beers to Woodbury, Feb. 7, 14, Mar. 9, 1838, June 29, 1839, Ambrose H. Sevier and Theodore Williamson to Woodbury, Aug. 6, 1838, Woodbury to C, Aug. 23, Sept. 5, 12, 1838, Woodbury to C and to four others separately, Dec. 27, 1839, K Letters; Butler Letters, passim, Olcott Papers, ColU Library; Reginald C. McGrane, *Foreign Bond Holders and American State Debts* (New York, 1935), 245f; Joseph Dorfman, "A Note on the Interpenetration of Anglo-American Finance, 1837–1841," *Journal of Economic History* 11 (1951); William L. MacKenzie, *Lives and Opinions of Benj'n Franklin Butler and Jesse Hoyt* (Boston, 1845), 146–149; MacKenzie, *Life and Times of Martin Van Buren: The Correspondence of His Friends, Family and Pupils* (Boston, 1846), 179.

Some years later Corcoran became financial adviser to the Smithsonian, serving without pay. Large balances, as much as $200,000 and more, were kept by the institution with his firm. On these balances, interest was allowed at 5 percent per year—an exception to the company rule that no interest be paid for deposits. This was doubtless prompted by Corcoran's desire to make some amends for his connection with the Arkansas bonds, as well as by his philanthropic impulses and perhaps the profitability or usefulness of the deposit even at that rate. See Robert Dale Owen to C, Sept. 13, 1846, C Papers; Smithsonian account, C&R ledgers, 1852, Riggs Bank; Cole, *Banking in D. C.*, 267.

14. See Amos Kendall, *Autobiography,* ed. William Stickney

(New York, 1872), 377–81, 387; Hammond, *Banks and Politics,* 412, 414–23, 466; Frank Otto Gatell, "Spoils of the Bank War: Political Bias in the Selection of Pet Banks," *American Historical Review* (October 1946), 37, n. 8, and passim.

It may be argued, with some validity, that Newbold's leadership would have become vulnerable to challenge if he had refused the huge federal business while potential rivals accepted it. The fact remains that none did, and cogent reasons make this caution understandable. The decision was not purely financial, but rather highly political. A change of administration or of government policy (as with the Distribution Act of 1836) could bring retaliation and loss of deposits and patronage, or simply less severe but still dangerous uncertainty. The Bank of America could accept these risks with little danger. Other institutions with smaller resources, less powerful clientele, and lower liquidity had to be more cautious; they could not risk alienating the America while politics were so unstable. This does not prove the "pet bank" system would not have been set up without Newbold, but at the least it would have been an even weaker system than it proved to be.

15. See Thomas Ellicott to Newbold, Oct. 15, 29, 1833; C. W. Lawrence to Newbold, Nov. 22, Dec. n.d.: rec'd 22, 21, 1833, Jan. 23, Feb. 3, Mar. 26, 1834, Daniel Jackson and John S. Crary to Woodbury, Nov. 21, 1835, Newbold to [Woodbury], Dec. n.d., 1835, Roger Taney to Newbold, Dec. 13, 1833, Apr. 19, 1836, Newbold to William L. Marcy, Feb. 28, 1838, Marcy to Newbold, Mar. 8, 1838, Amos Kendall to Newbold, June 28, 1838, letters, 1834, passim, Newbold Papers, NYHS; Jesse Hoyt to Woodbury, Sept. 15, 16, 1839, Woodbury Papers; James K. Polk to Newbold and others, July 14, 1838, Polk Papers, LC; C to ER, Dec. 17, 1838, Mar. 27, 1839, John J. Palmer to C, Nov. 26, 1845, C Papers; reports of New York State bank overseers listed in Adelaide R. Hasse, *Index of Economic Material in Documents of the States . . . New York, 1789–1904* (Washington, 1907), 43; *Bankers Magazine,* January 1847, 448–9, November 1849, 361–2, July 1851, 84, August 1851, 108–9, December 1853, 445–8, February 1855, July 1856, 12; Robert E. Chaddock, *Safety Fund Banking System in New York States, 1829–1866,* U.S. Congress, *Senate Document 581,* 61st Cong., 2d sess., 1910, 238–40, 296–7; Philip Hone, *Diary,* ed. Bayard Tuckerman, 2 vols. (New York, 1889), II, 155; Redlich, *Molding American Banking,* II, 201, ch. 12;

Margaret G. Myers, *The New York Money Market: Origins and Development* (New York, 1931), 40–1.

16. See Govan, *Biddle,* 348–67; Smith, *Second Bank,* 209f; Hammond, "The Chestnut Street Raid on Wall Street, 1839," *Quarterly Journal of Economics,* Aug. 1947.

17. It should be emphasized that Woodbury was allied, not subservient, to Newbold et al. He had earlier declined a suggestion by Beers and Newbold that he issue notes to the America when he thought he could effect an outright sale elsewhere. Cf. Beers-Woodbury correspondence, as cited in n.13, above. For an important study of Jacksonian banking policy emphasizing its effort to exercise real control, see McFaul, "Politics of Jacksonian Finance." See also Nathan Miller, *The Enterprise of a Free People: Aspects of Economic Development in New York State During the Canal Period, 1792–1838* (Ithaca, 1962), 252, and ch. 11–13 passim.

18. The Bank of America paid Corcoran a ¼ percent commission on his orders. For whom he was agent is not indicated in surviving papers. See Asa Fitch to Newbold, Mar. 6, 1839, Newbold Papers; Newbold to Woodbury, May 9, 13, July 9, Aug. 10, 12, Woodbury to Newbold, May 10, July 10, Aug. 10, Jesse Hoyt to Woodbury, Aug. 10, Oct. 2, Campbell P. White to Woodbury, Aug. 10, Woodbury Papers; C to Richard Ela, May 21, YA Letters; C agreement, May 25, C to Woodbury, May 29, correspondence on Treasury notes; Woodbury to C, Nov. 8, K Letters; ER to C, May 25, 27, 29, 30, June 1, 20, 22, 24, 26, 29, July 3, 8, C to ER, Oct. 22, 23, 25, R Papers.

19. See n. 10, above; see also C to Louise Corcoran, Jan. 14, 1838, C Papers; C to ER, Mar. 30, Apr. 2, 9–11, R Papers; and n. 24, below.

20. At this time, in bidding for note issues the rate of interest was the variable while the price was fixed at par. Another instance shows that Woodbury received as well as gave concessions. Corcoran & Riggs offered 5 percent for notes, payment in New York, preferring these to 5⅖ percent notes payable in Washington because of the risk and expense of transferring specie from New York. When Woodbury insisted on both 5 percent and deposits in Washington, Corcoran acquiesced.

21. ER to C&R, July 3, 8, 10, 1840, R Papers; C&R to Woodbury, July 6, Treasury Note Letters; Woodbury to C&R, July 8, K Letters.

22. Elisha once charged Corcoran with deviousness when he sold notes in Baltimore that the former had committed in New York. See C&R to Woodbury, May 2, July 31, 1840, Jan. 30, 1841, Beers to Woodbury, Jan. 21, 1841, Treasury Note Letters; Woodbury to C&R, May 4, July 24, Nov. 5, Dec. 16, 1840, Jan. 18, 1841, K Letters; ER to C&R, May 19, 20, June 24, 25, 28, July 3, 24, 1840, Treasury note accounts, Apr., 1841, R Papers; Bayley, *National Loans,* 140–1.

23. The earlier books and those for mid-1842 to mid-1845 have been lost.

24. See Woodbury-C&R correspondence, 1840–1841; also C&R ledgers, Riggs Bank.

25. Samuel Riggs, nephew of Elisha, was the resident partner of Peabody, Riggs & Co. (George Peabody, who had left for London in 1837, was soon to terminate the partnership.) Corcoran & Riggs had a volume of $370,000 with the Western Bank, of which Samuel Riggs became a director from 1843–1846. The most important correspondent there, however, was the Bank of Baltimore, with a volume $1 million.

Chapter 2

1. For indications of a similar depository relationship between the Commerce and the Whig administration of New York State, see Stevens to Comptroller John Collier, Aug. 21, 1841, Bank of Commerce Papers.

Other major contractors of the loan were the Bank for Savings (New York), $500,000; Suffolk Bank (Boston), $455,000; Merchants Bank (Boston), $175,000; Ketchum, Rogers & Bement (New York), $125,000; and Cammann, Whitehouse & Co. (New York), $109,000. Morris Ketchum, a Whig broker connected with the Bank of Commerce, was Ewing's agent in the negotiations. See ER to Woodbury, Jan. 15, 1841, Morris Ketchum to Thomas Ewing, Aug. 13, 1841, George Curtis to John C. Spencer, March 6, 1843, K Letters; Ewing to John A. Stevens, July 31, 1841, Stevens Papers, NYHS; Stevens to Ewing, Mar. 5, Apr. 7, 17, 22, May 1, 3, 13, 21, Aug. 24, 1841, Stevens to Ketchum, May 25, 1852, "History of the Bank of Commerce," 30, manuscript in Bank of Commerce Papers, Morgan Guaranty Trust Co., New York; Jonathan Elliott, *Funding System of the United States and Great*

Britain (Washington, 1845); U.S., Congress, *House Executive Document 15*, 28th Cong., 1st sess., 1001f.

2. At that time Newbold incorrectly feared the Treasury would reach agreement with the Bank of Commerce at his expense. He reminded the administration of his continuous cooperation and his acquiescence in the pending Independent Treasury Bill despite his disapproval of it. Newbold's letters again reveal the high value he attached to the depository appointment, his intimacy with leading New York State Democrats, and the fact that the friendly relationship with the Treasury could not be taken for granted. See Newbold to James K. Paulding, Jan. 22, 1839, Newbold to Van Buren, Mar. 11, Newbold to Woodbury, Jan. 19, 30, Newbold Papers; Woodbury to Newbold, Jan. 19, 21, Woodbury Papers, LC; Woodbury to Samuel Ward, Apr. 15, letters to banks, Treasury Archives.

3. Ketchum had suggested the Merchants, Union, and Mechanics Banks, all former Democratic "pet" banks, as additional depositories, thus enlisting support from all major factions on Wall Street. Not only Newbold's bank, but also the Merchants' Washington correspondent, the Patriotic Bank, was ignored in Ewing's plans, probably because it had been aided by Newbold during earlier difficulties. See Palmer to Ewing, Aug. 21, 25, 26, 30, Ewing to Palmer, Aug. 23, letters from banks, Treasury Archives, 1841; Samuel Southard to Ewing, Aug. 25 [1841], Ewing Papers, LC.

4. The firm had not bid for any of Ewing's loans. Elisha advised doing so once, but not in expectation of a contract. He sent offers via Corcoran & Riggs for $375,000, which included $250,000 for John Ward & Co., but intentionally at higher rates of interest than Ewing was willing to accept. The purpose was simply to inflate the young firm's prestige by having it appear at the head of an important clientele. See ER to C&R, Aug. 25, 27, Sept. 4, 7, 1841, ER Domestic Letters.

5. ER to C&R, Sept. 6, 15–17, 1841, ER Domestic Letters.

6. From this time forward the bid price was the variable while the interest rate was fixed. Corcoran & Riggs sold a small amount of the notes ($130,000) through Elisha. By this time commissions between the correspondents had been reduced to ⅛ percent. See ER to C&R, Sept. 27, 29, 1841, ER Domestic Letters; statement, Jan. 1–Mar. 10, 1842, R Papers, LC; Walter Forward to Edward Curtis, Mar. 2, Benjamin Swan to Newbold, Mar. 11, Newbold

Papers, NYHS; Rafael A. Bayley, *National Loans of the United States* (Washington, 1882), 142.

7. See Fitch to Newbold, Apr. 1, 1842, Newbold to William Robinson, Jr., Aug. 11, John Johnston to Newbold, Aug. 19, Robinson to Newbold, Sept. 19, Newbold to Forward, Oct. 17, Nov. 1, Dec. 31, 1842, Jan. 16, 1843, Newbold Papers; Bayley, *National Loans,* 142.

Corcoran & Riggs' participation in the federal loans of 1842 was trifling—little more than $100,000. See C&R to ER, Jan. 31, 1843, R Papers, LC; Elliot, *Funding System,* 1001–2.

8. In 1844, when the security requirement was raised to $500,-000, Palmer made an unusually explicit acknowledgment of the usefulness of the arrangement: he agreed to redeem Treasury notes for use of the funds. See Palmer to Spencer, Mar. 18, 27, Aug. 12, 30, 1843, Palmer to George M. Bibb, Aug. 2, 1844; cf. letters from Bank of Commerce, late 1844, Mar. 17, 1845, letters from banks, Bibb to Palmer and to Newbold, July 10, 1844, and Bibb to Stevens, July 22, letters to banks, Treasury Archives.

9. Corcoran had previously discussed his plans with the America's cashier, who presumably advised Newbold of his error.

10. See C&R to Newbold, Feb. 17, 28, 1843, Newbold Papers; C&R to ER, Feb. 28, Mar. 1–4, 9, 11, 15, 25, 30, R Papers.

Elisha's cautious restraint on Corcoran & Riggs' credit compelled the firm to forego all but $120,000 of the new 6 percent notes, and that was on joint account with himself and his nephew, Samuel Riggs of Baltimore. Corcoran's judgment was vindicated when the entire $500,000 issue was absorbed within a month at more than a 2 percent advance. See C&R to ER, May 4, 5, 8–10, 12, 13, 1843, R Papers; John C. Spencer to C&R, May 19, Riggs Bank.

11. The loan was under the Act of Mar. 3, 1843. Asa Fitch, Jr., was the other director of the America. See C&R to ER, May 23, 29, July 11, Aug. 4, 1843, R Papers; Newbold to Spencer, May 26, 30, June 5, 1843, John Ward & Co. to Newbold, June 6, William H. Aspinwall to Newbold, June 29, Fitch to Newbold, June 30, Newbold to Aspinwall, July 7, Newbold Papers; Fritz Redlich, *Molding of American Banking: Men and Ideas,* 2 vols. (New York, 1947–1951), II, 245–6.

12. Things had become somewhat disagreeable when Fitch squeezed from Corcoran the admission that their friend Newbold was planning to unload without having warned him: Fitch promptly

sold his holdings. These operations, of course, lacked the coordination of the modern underwriting syndicate. The firm's chief broker in New York, after Elisha, was Cammann & Whitehouse, a firm closely linked to the Merchants Bank. (Oswald J. Cammann, cousin of the broker Oswald Cammann, was to become the bank's cashier in 1846.) See David Thompson to ER, July 6, 1843, C&R to ER, June 28, July 11, 26, Aug. 17, 19, 21, Sept. 20, 30, Nov. 24, Dec. 14, 21, 23, 26, 30, 1843, Jan. 10, 23, 1844, R Papers; Fitch to Newbold, Aug. 29, 1843, Newbold Papers; Henrietta Larson, *Jay Cooke, Private Banker* (Cambridge, 1936), 314–5.

Chapter 3

1. See ch. 2, above.

2. The effective head of the Metropolis, cashier Richard Smith, had been in charge of the Washington branch of the Bank of the United States.

3. See Richard Smith to Ewing, Sept. 1, 1841, Ewing Papers, LC; Martin Van Buren, *Autobiography,* ed. John C. Fitzpatrick (Washington, 1920), 13–18; David Maurice Cole, *The Development of Banking in the District of Columbi*a (New York, 1959), 215–6, 218, 239–45, 263, 277, ch. 5 passim; Charles N. Wiltse, *John C. Calhoun, Sectionalist, 1840–1850* (Indianapolis and New York, 1951), 80f., ch. 8, 13.

4. Sometimes Corcoran speculated with favored clients on joint account. See C&R ledgers, Riggs Bank.

5. Other participants included Amos Kendall and his brother, who were expected to be especially useful in lobbying in Congress and executive departments; a Major Armstrong, probably Robert, the Tennessee politican and newspaper colleague of Heiss; Daniel Saffarans, a Memphis merchant; Charles Fisher, former Representative from North Carolina; and various Indian agents and members of the Riggs family. Kendall was the first noteworthy borrower in the firm's record. He received loans of over $6,000 in the year 1840 to 1841 from Elisha Riggs through Corcoran, whom Kendall joined in an Illinois land speculation.

6. ER to C, Jan. 27, 28, 1840, ER to C&R, July 28, 1840, ER Domestic Letters; C&R to ER, Oct. 6, 17, 30, 1843, Jan. 27, 1844, Feb. 18, Oct. 27, 28, 1845, Mar. 16, Apr. 7, 11, Nov. 6, Dec. 14,

1846, Jan. 11, 1847, GWR to ER, Feb. 5, 1846, Riggs, Son & Paradise to ER, Nov. 16, 1843, Riggs, Son & Paradise to C&R, Aug. 22, 1844, William Paradise to ER, Sept. 20, Nov. 18, 1847, John Elliott to ER, various, 1847, Charles Fisher to ER, Dec. 1, 12, 1851, two contracts, Nov. 7, 1843, R Papers, LC; Kendall to C, May 17, Sept. 23, 1841, Jan. 15, 1844, William Gwin to C, Apr. 22, 1845, C Papers, LC; C to F. P. Stanton, Aug. 5, 1854, Jan. 26–28, 1856, C Letter Books; Choctaw Land Scrip, interest and various name accounts, C&R ledgers; twelve Alabama and Mississippi senators and representatives to Walker, n.d., Walker Papers, LC; Jackson to Polk, June 5, 1845, Bancroft Collection, NYPL; Muriel Emmie Hidy, "George Peabody, Merchant and Financier, 1829–1854" (Ph.D. diss., Radcliffe College, 1939), 267; Mary Elizabeth Young, "Redskins, Ruffleshirts, and Rednecks: Indian Allotments in Alabama and Mississippi, 1830–1860" (Ph.D. diss., Cornell University, 1955), 93–100, 217, 222; same author and title (Norman, 1961), ch. 3; James P. Shenton, *Robert John Walker: A Politician from Jackson to Lincoln* (New York and London, 1961), ch. 2, 30–4, 64–7; below, this chapter.

7. Shenton, *Walker,* ch. 1, 3, 4, and passim; James C. N. Paul, *Rift in the Democracy* (New York, 1961), 24–7, 63–5, 94f, 115f, 135–6, 176–7.

8. In consequence, from this time on no summary profit and loss statements appear in the ledgers (although individual name and activity accounts sometimes yield essentially the same information to the researcher). See Bibb to C&R, Aug. 22, 1844, C Papers; Cole, *Banking in D.C.*, 245.

9. Walker, Bibb's successor, adhered to this policy which tended to improve the market for state bonds and therefore had broad political support. By 1846 state bonds accounted for over 90 percent of the firm's collateral. See documents cited in n. 7, below.

10. Riggs charged 2½ percent for the loan of his securities, and kept the interest they earned.

11. A Senate resolution asked the Secretary of the Treasury to report whether the depositories had used or lent public funds and the government had received compensation for such use. Bibb carefully begged the question with a series of irrelevancies, but his 1844 Annual Report, issued about the same time, more candidly acknowledged that the deposits drew no interest. See Palmer to C&R, Sept. 2, 3, 6, 12, 17, 23, 1844, C&R to ER, Sept. 12, Dec.

11, R Papers; ER to C&R, June 15, 1847, ER Letter Book; U.S. 5 percent and 6 percent accounts, C&R ledgers; Bibb to C&R, Aug. 31, Sept. 4, 14, 19, 20, 1844, letters to banks, acting Treasurer to Bibb, Sept. 16, 19, 21, 1844, William Selden (Treasurer of the U.S.) to Bibb, Dec. 27, 1844, letters to Secretary, acknowledgments of collateral, Dec. 30, 1844, Treasury note issues, Treasury Archives; C&R to Peabody, Aug. 29, 1844, Peabody to C&R, June 3, 1845, Peabody Papers, EI; R. H. Gillett to Thomas W. Olcott, Aug. 28, 1845, Olcott Papers, ColU Library; *Treasury Reports,* 1844; Cole, *Banking in D.C.,* 264–5.

Managing the federal deposits was sometimes difficult and inconvenient. For a complex example see the dissertation version of this book, Henry Cohen, "Business and Politics from the Age of Jackson to the Civil War: A Study From the Career of W. W. Corcoran" (Ph.D. diss., Cornell University, 1965), 56–8.

12. See J. B. Nicholson to C, Jan. 8, 1845, Thomas Ritchie to C, July 28, 1847, C Papers; C account, C&R ledgers, Riggs Bank; Wiltse, *Calhoun: Sectionalist,* 223–4; William Ernest Smith, *The Francis Preston Blair Family in Politics,* 2 vols. (New York, 1933), I, 159–62, 177–81, and ch. 15 passim.

13. Woodbury had been returned to the Senate after his term as Secretary of the Treasury and was reportedly still influential in fiscal matters.

14. Burke worked for Corcoran's interests during and after his term in Congress. In December 1845 he called on the Speaker of the House, after seeing Corcoran, and arranged the substitution of Lockport, N.Y., banker Washington Hunt for his fellow New York State Whig, William A. Moseley, on the District of Columbia Committee, at which time he reported, "The Committee is Anti-Bank, if the Chairman, Mr. Hunter of Va. is sound, and I *know* he has been in principle, a hard money man. Both the Speaker and myself believe the Committee as now constituted to be perfectly sound on the bank question." See Edmund Burke to C, Dec. 8, 1845, C Papers; C&R to ER, Dec. 7, 30, 1844, R Papers; Smith to Robert J. Walker, Mar. 7, Apr. 25 (with copies of Smith to Burke, Mar. 25, Burke to Smith, Mar. 31, and others), 1845, letters from banks, Treasury Archives; Jonathan Elliott, *Funding System of the United States and Great Britain* (Washington, 1845), 978; Wiltse, *Calhoun, Sectionalist,* 360–1.

15. Burke to C, June 5, 1872 (in William Wilson Corcoran, *A*

Grandfather's Legacy [Washington, 1879], 391), C Papers; C to Burke, June 10, 1872, C Letter Books.

16. In retaliation for the hostile committee report, the Metropolis called in its loans on U.S. securities, but the resulting price decline was momentary. See C&R to ER, Jan. 4, 13, 14, 16, 17, 20, 21, 23, 1845, R Papers.

17. Walker ordered gradual withdrawals in addition to reduction of balances in displaced banks. His collaboration with Corcoran is egregiously demonstrated in the manipulation of Georgetown banker Francis Dodge, who had $50,000 of United States 6 percent bonds as collateral for government deposits. Corcoran & Riggs happened to have precisely this amount to spare and wanted to buy the bonds or, preferably, to lend on them at 5 to 6 percent. Elisha tried to procure them but Dodge would not agree to his price. Corcoran had the Secretary issue a transfer draft against Dodge for $50,000 in favor of the Bank of America. Dodge was unable to sell the bonds at a satisfactory price, and the fish was netted when the firm lent Dodge $50,000 against them at 5 percent. See C&R to ER, May 28, June 4, 11, 13, 24, 28, 1845, R Papers; Walker to C&R, June 2, letters to Banks, Treasury Archives.

18. The term *broker*, to that generation, included what would be regarded today as investment banker. See Newbold to C&R, May 6, C&R to ER, July 3, 7, 17, 22, Aug. 18, 28, Sept. 1, 4, 8, 20, 22, Dec. 22, 26, 29, 1845, Jan. 11, Feb. 5, 25, 1846, R Papers; ER to C&R, June 4, 1846, R Letter Book; C&R and GWR to Peabody, Aug. 29, 1845, Peabody Papers.

19. In other patronage actions, an agency for payment of interest on outstanding loans in New York was transferred from the Bank of Commerce to the America, and the brother of president William Gunton of the Bank of Washington was dismissed from a Treasury clerkship he had held for twenty-seven years. On the other hand, when another Whig was dismissed from the Treasury after the change of administrations, Corcoran wrote Palmer and Newbold to find employment for "our friend." See C&R to ER, Apr. 1, 5, 12, 17, July 19, 22, Dec. 4, 1845, C to GWR, Apr. 25, 1845, R Papers; Smith to Polk, Feb. 25, 1845, William Gunton to Polk, Aug. 28, 1845, C to J. Knox Walker, Nov. 5, 1845, Polk Papers, LC; Walker to John L. O'Sullivan, June 30, 1845, PaHS; Stevens to Walker, Mar. 17, George Curtis to Walker, June 23, 1845, letters from banks, Treasury Archives; C&R to William H.

Polk, Feb. 15, 1856, C Letter Books; James K. Polk, *Diary,* ed. Milo M. Quaife, 4 vols. (Chicago, 1910), I, 153.

20. On this transaction almost $2,000 additional was earned in commissions. See Newbold to C&R, Dec. 5, 1844, Palmer to C&R, Dec. 13, C&R to ER, Jan. 20, 1845, R Papers; *Treasury Reports,* IV, 674; Rafael A. Bayley, *National Loans of the United States* (Washington, 1882), 142–3.

21. The volume of Treasury foreign exchange business in 1846, the first year, was $200,000. Under the preceding Democratic administration, N. M. Rothschild and Sons had held this account. General Armstrong tried to influence Bancroft in favor of Peabody through the latter's fellow Massachusetts Democrats. He was close to Peabody, perhaps through negotiating sales abroad of Tennessee bonds. McLane was on leave from the presidency of the Baltimore & Ohio Railroad, which the Barings had greatly aided. Secretary of State Buchanan seems to have drifted with the prevailing breezes. See C&R to Peabody, Dec. 29, 1841, Feb. 27, June 27, July 13, 1844, Oct. 11, 1845, ER to Peabody, Oct. 8, 1846, Peabody Papers; ER to Peabody, Nov. 27, 1845, MassHS; C&R to ER, Apr. 27, 29, Sept. 21, 24, 1846, R Papers; Walker to C&R, Jan. 16, 1846, letters to banks, C&R to Walker, June 24, letters from banks, Treasury Archives; Hidy, "Peabody," 212, 266, 326; Ralph W. Hidy, *House of Baring in American Trade and Finance: English Merchant Bankers at Work, 1763–1861* (Cambridge, 1949), 281–8, 350–1.

22. See C&R to ER, Sept. 20, 22, 24, Oct. 2, 6, 7, 1845, R Papers.

23. Corcoran interpreted Washington politics in letters to either Newbold or Riggs, who promptly exchanged information. Palmer, too, was soon included in the correspondence, which evidences Corcoran's growing intimacy with these financial leaders. See C&R to ER, Feb. 14, Apr. 17, 29, June 13, July 17, Nov. 15, Dec. 8, 22, 24, 26, 1845, C to ER, Aug. 25, C&R to Palmer, Apr. 20, 1846, Palmer to C&R May 6, 18, R Papers; see also, undated and unsigned memorandum [late Nov. or early Dec., 1845], C Papers; C&R to Peabody, May 13, Dec. 27, William S. Wetmore to Peabody, Dec. 2, Peabody Papers; Hidy, "Peabody," 167–71: Wiltse, *Calhoun, Sectionalist,* 252; Norman A. Graebner, *Empire on the Pacific: A Study in American Continental Expansion* (New York, 1955), 115–22, 137–49, 202–4, 214–5, and sources cited on 263–4;

Richard R. Stenberg, "The Failure of Polk's Mexican War Intrigue of 1845," *Pacific Historical Review* 4 (March 1935). The exception referred to is noted at the beginning of the next chapter.

Corcoran also tried to soothe sectional financial jealousies, writing to the president of the Bank of Mobile that the collateral required of his institution was not invidiously larger than that required of northern depositories. See C to Hallett, Apr. 21, 1846, C Letter Books.

24. Corcoran repeatedly conveyed to the politicians Wall Street objections transmitted by Palmer and was able to return Tyler's assurances to the businessmen that the Independent Treasury Bill would be vetoed if passed. See C to ER, Nov. 12, 1837, Jan. 31, Mar. 10, Dec. 7, 1838, C&R to ER, Dec. 26, 30, 1844, Palmer to C&R, Dec. 26, R Papers; Charles Grier Sellers, Jr., *James K. Polk, Jacksonian: 1795–1843* (Princeton, 1957), 223–32, 320–1; David Kinley, *The History, Organization and Influence of the Independent Treasury of the United States* (New York and Boston, 1893), 32–3.

25. These warnings were passed along by Corcoran and read to the cabinet by a member, probably Buchanan, who supported them. Late in December Corcoran showed similar warnings to the Secretary of the Treasury and five members of Congress. All agreed with him, he reported, but they declined to act, pleading party unity. This may have been more of a pretext than a reason—a polite way of closing the discussion. On the other hand, there may well have been misgivings about new and unfamiliar kinds of responsibility. See Woodbury to Polk, Feb. 28, 1836, Polk Papers; F. Knithing to Van Buren, May 14, 1845, Van Buren Papers, LC; C&R to ER, Dec. 26, 1845, Mar. 14, 30, Apr. 14, Aug. 1, 6, Dec. 7, 1846, Jan. 2, 1847, R Papers; Daniel Webster to C, n.d., C Papers; ER to C&R, Aug. 4, Dec. 31, 1846, Jan. 4, 1847, R Letter Book; C&R to Palmer, Apr. 13, 14, Nov. 28, 1846, C&R to ER, June 22, C to Whelen, Dec. 29, C Letter Books; Marcy to Stevens, July 24, Stevens Papers; Newbold to C&R, Dec. 10, Newbold to Thomas W. Ward, Dec. 12, Newbold Papers; see also Webster speech, Aug. 1, 1846, U.S., Congress, *Congressional Globe,* 29th Cong., 1st sess., 1174–6.

26. See C&R to ER, Apr. 16, Aug. 13, 1846, R Papers; ER to Palmer, Apr. 7, R Letter Book; C&R to Palmer, Apr. 3, 11, C Letter Books; Washington Hunt to Olcott, Apr. 14, Olcott Papers.

27. See C&R to ER, Oct. 20, 1846, Palmer to C&R, May 21,

1847, R Papers; ER to C&R, Oct. 26, 1846, R Domestic Letters; Treasurer of the United States account, C&R ledgers; U.S., Congress, *House Document 174,* 29th Cong., 1st sess.; Treasurer's statement in Washington *Union,* July 3, 1847; *Bankers Magazine,* December 1846, 328–9; Kinley, *Independent Treasury:* 271–83 (sec. 6, 18–21 of the Act).

28. George Newbold arranged most of the redemptions directly with institutions and a few wealthy individuals. In the open market the usual brokers were Cammann, Whitehouse & Co. in New York, Charnley, Whelen & Co. in Philadelphia, and Gittings, Donaldson & Graham in Baltimore. Corcoran & Riggs continued to act as broker for the Indian trust, the Smithsonian, and other special government funds. These activities provided an outlet for securities in inventory, superior knowledge of market conditions, and ¼ percent commissions. See C&R to ER, Jan. 4, 1847, C Letter Books; Newbold to C&R, May 10, 1847, Oct. 4, 5, 8, 9, 11, 13, 14, 15, 18, 27, 30, Nov. 11, 12, 13, 30, Dec. 8, 1852, C to ER, Jr., Nov. 3, 5, 23, Dec. 2, 1852, C to ER, Nov. 15, 1850, Mar. 17, 19, 1853, Gittings, Donaldson & Graham to C&R, Dec. 2, 1852, C to ER, Jr., Dec. 21, 1852, R Papers; office of the register of the Treasury to C&R, Dec. 30, 1848, Aug. 5, 1850, tin box marked "Loans," R Papers; C&R to Newbold, Dec. 20, 1847, Newbold Papers, NYHS; William S. Hodge to Millard Fillmore, June 2, 1851, Fillmore Papers, BuffHS; accounts of Department of Interior, Commissioner of Indian Affairs, and other agencies, and of Speakers of the House under their individual names, and of dividends on U.S. loans, C&R ledgers, Riggs Bank; C&R to Peabody, Oct. 6, 1851, BPOC; C to Peabody, Oct. 14, 1851; Peabody Papers; statement, Dec. 18, 1844, letters to the secretary, Walker to C&R, Feb. 3, 1847, letters to banks, statement, June 15, 1850, C&R to Meredith, June 18, 22, K Letters, Haines to Meredith, June 22, 1850, AB Letters, C&R to register, Aug. 22, Corwin to register, Aug. 4, 1851, Mexican indemnity 5 percent file, C&R to William L. Hodge, Dec. 18, 21, 24, 30, 1850, Jan. 3, 1851, Corwin to register and to treasurer, Aug. 4, Corwin to Acting Secretary Derrick, Aug. 7, B Letters, statement, n.d., U.S. loan letters, 1852, Treasury Archives; Bayley, *National Loans,* 146–7; Kenneth Wiggins Porter, *John Jacob Astor, Business Man,* 2 vols. (Cambridge, 1931), II, 1006; Cole, *Banking in D.C.,* 267; ch. 4, below.

29. In a typical episode, Corcoran contracted with Walker to

furnish $1.5 million in New Orleans in ten equal weekly installments at ¾ percent, a rate far below rival bids. The firm lent the deposited money on call in the North while exchange was accumulated gradually in New Orleans. Corcoran subcontracted $1 million to J. Corning & Co. of New York and New Orleans, retaining an option to furnish up to 25 percent of this without charge for collection. The remaining $500,000 was subcontracted at ½ percent to New York banker Matthew Morgan on joint account with the Canal Bank of New Orleans. That institution, allied with the Rothschilds and several local private bankers, was perhaps the major factor in the exchange market there.

Matthew Morgan was distrusted by government officials and businessmen as devious and grasping—or perhaps he was simply too competitive.

See Morgan to C, May 22, 1847, C to Morgan, May 24, R. Papers; C&R and Morgan to Walker, June 9, and Walker's reply, June 10, AB Letters. This episode is discussed more fully in Cohen, "Business and Politics," 100–1. Many of the most profitable transfers were made in connection with deposits on account of the great war loan contracts (see ch. 4, n. 17).

30. As shown by the terms of the New Orleans exchange contract, Walker sometimes imposed time limits on transfer operations, especially those directly supporting the military campaigns in Mexico. Private exploitation of other transfers may have been permitted as faits accomplis for purposes of good will or patronage, or as compensation when unusually heavy services were required. Ironically, the rather restrained conduct of houses like Corcoran & Riggs made the greediness of other houses more bearable. See Newbold to C&R, Mar. 1, Apr. 5, 1847, Matthew Morgan and Reuben Withers to C&R, Apr. 24, agreement, C&R and J. Corning & Co., Apr. 23, C&R to Newbold, June 17, 18, C&R to Charnley & Whelen, June 18, C&R to Palmer, June 18, statement, Morgan to C&R, Sept. 8, R Papers; Marcy to Walker, Apr. 13, Maj. Thomas to John Y. Mason, Aug. 18, Walker to Young, Aug. 23, Young to Polk, Aug. 26, Walker to Polk, Aug. 27, Polk Papers; C&R to Walker, Apr. 19, 1847, K Letters (1850); C to C. W. Lawrence, Apr. 28, 1847, C Letter Books; Hidy, *House of Baring*, 583, n. 19; Margaret G. Myers *The New York Money Market: Origins and Development* (New York, 1931), 185.

31. Reduced earnings or losses in the last half (especially the

last quarter) partly reflect the seasonal cycle of non-Treasury deposits, which were fully replenished each year after Jan. 1.

32. See C, ER, Jr., and profit–loss accounts, C&R ledgers.

Chapter 4

1. Wall Street intractability may have stemmed from resentment mingled with fear of the effects of the Independent Treasury.

Elisha had handled Buchanan's investments before introducing him to Corcoran. Perhaps their acquaintance was originally made through Romulus Riggs of Philadelphia. Buchanan was banking good will with Corcoran which was to be repaid in 1856. See C&R to ER, June 22, 1846, Newbold to C&R, Oct. 28, R Papers, LC; ER to C&R, June 24, Oct. 14, 26, R Letter Books; Palmer to Olcott, Dec. 11, Olcott Papers, ColU Library; New York *Courier & Enquirer,* Oct. 13; James K. Polk, *Diary,* ed. Milo M. Quaife, 4 vols. (Chicago, 1910), II, 163–6, 183, 192, 194, 200, 213; Rafael A. Bayley, *National Loans of the United States* (Washington, 1882) 143–4; James P. Shenton, *Robert John Walker: A Politician from Jackson to Lincoln* (New York and London, 1961), 91–2.

2. The firm's bid, and almost the entire loan, was at par. It also subscribed $50,000 for Elisha, $20,000 of which was for third parties. In this operation Elisha apparently cooperated with the Bank of the State of New York. See C&R to ER, Oct. 31, Nov. 6–27, 1846, R Papers; ER to C&R, Oct. 31, Nov. 7, 9, 14, 19, 24, 27, R Letter Book; Polk, *Diary,* II, 221; Muriel Emmie Hidy, "George Peabody, Merchant and Financier, 1829–1854" (Ph.D. diss., Radcliffe College, 1939), 288.

3. See citations in n. 2, above. See also GWR to C, Nov. 27, 28, 1846, R Papers; ER to C&R, Nov. 30, Dec. 2, R Letter Book; John Beverly Riggs, *The Riggs Family of Maryland* (Baltimore, 1939), 328–9.

4. See Robert Dale Owen to C, Sept. 13, 1846, C Papers, LC; C&R to ER, Dec. 6, 7, 1846, Jan. 2, 16, 1847, R Papers.

5. See C&R to ER, Dec. 7, 28, 30, 1846, Jan. 2, 8, Feb. 15, 1847, Newbold to C&R, Jan. 9, 12, 18, 27, R Papers; ER to C&R, Nov. 23, 1846, Feb. 6, 1847, R Letter Book; C&R to Newbold, Jan. 7, 1847, C Letter Books; U.S., Congress, *Congressional Globe,* 29th Cong., 2d sess., 228–31; Secretary Walker's announcement in Washington *Union,* Feb. 10–Apr. 14, 1847.

6. Others included J. Crozier, Charles H. Carroll, R. Chapman, J. Collamer, J. F. Collins, J. C. Dobbin, S. S. Ellsworth, C. Goodyear, S. D. Hubbard, G. W. Jones, T. Jenkins, J. Lawrence (apparently a relative of Cornelius W. Lawrence), T. W. Ligon, W. B. Maclay, J. McCrate, J. W. Miller, W. S. Miller, M. Moulton, A. C. Niven, J. Russel, G. Sykes, H. Wheaton, H. Williams, J. A. Woodward, and J. S. Yost. In contrast, President Polk returned $3,000 of U.S. bonds at cost on grounds of conflict of interest, refusing to accept the profit on a price rise of 4 percent, although the Attorney General assured him the transaction was legal and proper. See John W. Davis to C, June 13, 1847, C Papers; Selden to Young, Sept. 27, 1848, K Letters, individual members of Congress under various dates, E Letters and Letters on Treasury Notes, Treasury Archives; *Treasury Reports,* VI, 164–79; Polk, *Diary,* III, 15–17.

7. See C&R to ER, Feb. 10, 1847, R Papers; memo, Mar. 28, 1849, C to Woodworth, June 2, 1852, C Letter Books; GR to ER, Jan. 24, 1851, Detroit Public Library; Walker to Washington Hunt, Feb. 11, 15, 1847, Walker to W. W. Woodworth, Apr. 15, E Letters, individuals; Woodworth to Walker, Jan. 16, with smudged markings indicating receipt Feb. 15 or 18, McClintock Young to Walker, Mar. 25, Apr. 14, 1847, John L. O'Sullivan to Young, Feb. 18, 1848, letters to the Secretary, Treasury Archives. For Hunt's intimacy with the important Albany banker Thomas Olcott see the Olcott Papers, passim.

8. Morgan's father-in-law was president of the Canal Bank and his daughter was married to Dudley Selden, one of the chief officers of the New York State Bank (not a state institution, title notwithstanding).

9. Just before his shift to Morgan's side, Ward had joined the firm in $220,000 of a 6 percent Treasury note contract, yielding tiny profits. See ER to C&R, Feb. 10, 11, 15, 20, Mar. 24, 25, 29, 1847, ER to GWR, Mar. 23, 31, Apr. 3, ER to C, Mar. 30, Apr. 1, R Letter Book; C&R to ER, Feb. 10, 13, 15, 17, 24, C to ER, Feb. 12, William B. Astor to C&R, Feb. 10, 15, Newbold to C, Feb. 15, Newbold to C&R, Mar. 4, Palmer to C&R, Mar. 31, GWR and ER joint account, Feb. 22 to Apr. 8, John Ward and C&R joint account, Feb. 10 to Mar. 27, R Papers; C to Matthew Morgan, Feb. 13, Mar. 18, 22, C Letter Books; Daniel B. St. John to C&R, Feb. 3, 1848, special account, Mar. 31 to July 9, C&R ledgers, Riggs Bank.

10. See ER to C&R, Apr. 3, 7, 1847, ER to GWR, Apr. 5, ER to SR, Apr. 5, 7, R Letter Books; Palmer to C&R, Apr. 5, R Papers.

11. "The *prudent, cautious* old gentleman [ER] has made an offer that will astonish you," Corcoran wrote. See C&R to Newbold, Apr. 11, 1847, Newbold Papers.

The Winslow & Perkins and Henshaw bids were for $11.3 million at 1/20 percent and $7 million at 1/16 percent, respectively. See ER to C&R, June 9, 1847, R Letter Books; Charnley & Whelen to ER, Apr. 5, 8, 16, 17, Newbold to C&R, Apr. 8, Palmer to C&R, Apr. 8, R Papers; New York *Journal of Commerce,* Apr. 19; *Treasury Report,* VI, 315–8.

12. See ER to C&R, Apr. 19, 1847, R Letter Book; C&R to ER, Apr. 21, Riggs Bank.

13. Winslow, later partner of J. F. D. Lanier was allied with the firm thereafter. See Walker to Morgan, Apr. 3, 1847, Walker Papers, U. of Pittsburgh; Walker to Polk, Apr. 9, Polk Papers, LC; ER to C&R, Apr. 19, R Letter Book; New York *Tribune,* Apr. 6; New York *Journal of Commerce,* Apr. 19; Washington *Union,* Apr. 20, 21. For Newbold's entrée to the *Journal of Commerce,* see Newbold to Spencer, May 2, 1843, Newbold Papers. See also ch. 8, below.

14. Small amounts were sold at 103, sometimes to such foreign accounts as the Suarez Brothers of New York and Mexico. Brokers included the firm's correspondents, Sam Harris & Sons in Baltimore, and Charnley & Whelen in Philadelphia. Winslow & Perkins was made New York broker when John Ward and his banking house, Prime, Ward & Co., failed. On the advice of Newbold and Palmer, Corcoran went to Boston to offer Franklin Haven of the Merchants Bank $1 million at 103, with any profit above that to be divided equally with the firm. "He is represented to be all-powerful there and I believe it," Corcoran wrote. Haven declined. Newbold to C&R, Apr. 13, May 24, June 12, 14, 17, 1847, M. Morgan to C&R, Apr. 13, Palmer to C&R, Apr. 14, C to GWR, Apr. 16, C&R to ER, May 22, Aug. 15, C&R to Charnley & Whelen, May 23, C&R to Winslow & Perkins, May 25, Withers to C&R, Aug. 16, J. N. Barnett, J. Knox Walker, and Samuel P. Walker to C&R, Sept 9, R Papers; ER to C&R, Jan. 7, Aug. 19, R Letter Books; Newbold bank book, Bank of America, 1847, Newbold Papers, NYHS; Corcoran and Riggs interest accounts, C&R ledgers, Riggs Bank; New York *Tribune,* Apr. 24.

15. Of the first $1 million loan, the Merchants Bank furnished $700,000 and the America the rest. Palmer wanted 5 percent but, urged by Newbold, allowed 4½ percent. Corcoran asked 4 percent but was ready to compromise at 4½ percent when Palmer and Newbold, in recognition of his growing importance, deferred and agreed to 4 percent. Thereafter a preferential rate ½ percent under the prime rate became standard on loans to Corcoran & Riggs, at least when money was in ample supply. In September, Corcoran had to go to Albany to borrow $300,000 at 6 percent, 1 percent above the call rate. Corcoran borrowed heavily there during the winter months, when the banks had heavy surpluses because of the closing of navigation on the Great Lakes–Erie Canal transportation route. On December 20, however, Corcoran & Riggs was able to make a six-month loan to the Bank of America. See C&R to ER, Apr. 27, May 7, June 14, 15, 19, July 17, Aug. 4, 5, 15, Nov. 9, 10, 12, 27, Dec. 30, 1847, Jan. 17, 21, 24, 1848, Newbold to C&R, May 3, 6, 8, 1847, John Jacob Astor to C&R, June 14, SR to C&R, June 12, 15, GWR to C&R, June 19, statement, John Ward & Co., May 20 to July 20, C&R to Peabody, Aug. 13, C&R to Newbold, June 12, 14, 15, 1847, Newbold to C&R, June 12, 14, 16, C to ER, Sept. 7, Palmer to C&R, July 8, 10, 12, Oct. 13, memo, interest paid to Merchants Bank, June 17 to Oct. 20, Watts Sherman to C&R, Nov. 27, 1847, Alexander Brown & Sons to C&R, Nov. 27, accounts current, Winslow & Perkins, July 31–Nov. 1, 1847, C&R and ER, Jan. 26–Feb. 2, 1848, C&R and Joseph K. Riggs, Jan. 28–Feb. 1, Palmer to ER, Jan. 27, Taylor to C&R, Jan. 28, Feb. 17, James Taylor to C&R, Dec. 1, R Papers; C to Newbold, May 9, 1847, C&R to Newbold, Dec. 20, Newbold Papers; ER to Peabody, June 15, ER to C&R, Aug. 14, 17, 1847, Feb. 11, 1848, R Letter Books; M. Hidy, "Peabody," 288–9.

16. See ER to Peabody, Apr. 29, May 11, 1847, R Letter Book; C&R to Palmer, May 22, C&R to Newbold, May 22, 28, June 3, Letter Book in R Papers; C&R to ER, July 20, 23, Nov. 12, R Papers; n. 15 above.

17. This was the profit on the loan itself, excluding all other operations. It earned $200,000 on the first $5 million sold. See Loan of 1847, C&R ledgers, Riggs Bank.

Of the $14 million credited to Corcoran & Riggs in an incomplete workbook at the Treasury, about $6.9 million was deposited in New York, most of it in the early months of 1847; $3.1 million in Washington, most of it in late 1847 and early 1848; $1.5 million in Philadelphia; a surprisingly large $800,000 in St. Louis; in the spring of 1847 $500,000 each in Boston, Baltimore, and New Orleans; and a total of less than $100,000 at Charleston and a few other points. See lists of letters concerning, and of issues of, Treasury notes, Treasury Archives; LR to ER, Aug. 6, 1847, C&R to ER, Aug. 14, R Papers; *Treasury Report,* VI, 193; *Treasury Report,* 1849, 661–97; Henrietta Larson, *Jay Cooke, Private Banker* (Cambridge, 1936), 69–71; Margaret G. Myers, *New York Money Market: Origin and Development* (New York, 1931), 185; ch. 3, above.

18. Thomas Baring was also influential in the Bank of England. Walker later called him "the most powerful banker in the world." See Walker to Millard Fillmore, Nov. 7, 1851, Fillmore Papers, BuffHS; Sir John Clapham, *The Bank of England: A History,* 2 vols. (Cambridge, Eng., 1958), II, 168–9. For his influence on diplomatic policy during the Civil War see Lord John Russell to Thomas Baring, Dec. 31, 1861, George Halsted [of Lloyd's] to Baring, Mar. 26, 1863, William Rathbone to anon., Apr. 1, 1863, Baring to Lord Robert Cecil, May 18, 1864, BP miscellaneous correspondence; Aspinwall to Salmon P. Chase, Apr. 8, 18, 1863, Chase Papers, LC; Boston *Daily Advertiser,* Mar. 9, 1864, clipping in BP.

19. Statement read by Ward to Buchanan, Dec. 17, 1847, Ward to BB, Dec. 18, 19, BPOC; Palmer to C&R, Jan. 22, 1848, Newbold to C&R, Jan. 22, 28, R Papers; Polk, *Diary,* III, 221–2; *Treasury Report,* VI, 275–8; Shenton, *Walker,* passim.

20. To prevent a recurrence of the acrimony accompanying the previous loan, the Act included an amendment offered by Whig Congressman Moses H. Grinnell, one of the great merchants of New York City. It specified that advertisements for bids were to be placed in newspapers of the capital or chief city of each state, and included explicit rules for the method and timing of payment. This would avoid the uncertainties of the previous year and dim the lingering suspicion that "persons residing here had an advantage . . . by intimations more or less definite." See C&R to ER, Nov. 10, 1847, Jan. 15, 1848, R Papers; Ward to Abbott Lawrence, Jan. 18, 1848, BPOC; Newbold to Ward, Jan. 19, Newbold Papers; U.S. Congress, *Congressional Globe,* 30th Cong., 1st sess., 370–4, 536.

Despite the advantages of Treasury notes, bonds sold for as much as 1 percent higher: they could be transferred more easily and without showing the names of the principals. See Charnley & Whelen to ER, Apr. 19, 1847, R Papers.

21. The Rothschilds had furnished exchange to American forces during the Mexican War. See Henry P. Jenkins to ER, Sept. 3, 1847, W. S. Wetmore to C&R, Mar. 30, 1848, R Papers; ER to C&R, Mar. 20, R Letter Books; BB to Ward, Sept. 18, 1847, BPLB; Peabody to C, Oct. 18, C Papers; Ward to BB, Dec. 15, 1847, Jan. 26, 1848, BPOC; C&R to Newbold, Mar. 21, Newbold Papers; M. Hidy, "Peabody," 265f.; Ralph W. Hidy, "A Leaf from Investment History," *Harvard Business Review* 20 (Autumn 1941), 68.

22. Of Corcoran & Riggs' share, $350,000 was taken by the Bank of America, by Newbold personally, and by other associates. Profits on the notes sold were about 1 percent. See Newbold to C&R, Feb. 23, 1848, C&R to Newbold, Mar. 8, 9, Newbold Papers; Newbold to C&R, Mar. 2, 3, 7, memo from D. Thompson, June 2, R Papers; C to ER, May 17, 1848, C accounts, C&R ledgers, Riggs Bank; C&R for N. M. Rothschild Sons of London and selves to Walker, Mar. 8, bids on loans, Treasury Archives; Dallas to Walker, Mar. 8, Walker Papers, LC; *Bankers Magazine,* April 1848, 638, 640.

23. See C to Peabody, Apr. 29, 1848, C Papers; BB to T. W. Ward, Apr. 28, May 5, 18, 26, June 2, BPLB; Ward to BB, May 8, 30, Ward to James G. King, June 2, BPOC; Bancroft to Walker, May 26, Walker to Bancroft, June 12, Bancroft Papers; Bancroft to Walker, May 28, Walker Papers, NYHS.

24. Of Baring Brothers' $1.25 million, $100,000 was for William Appleton & Co. and Abbott Lawrence of Boston and even more was apparently slated for sale in America. Other of the firm's subscribers included the Bank of Commerce, $500,000; Winslow & Perkins, $400,000; Elisha Riggs, $645,000 (of which $275,-000 was for himself); $170,000 for seven others; $200,000 for Spofford & Tileston (the latter was president of the Phoenix Bank of New York); James G. King, $250,000; Cammann, Whitehouse, $300,000 (of which two-thirds was for foreign account); C. W. Lawrence, Samuel Riggs, and William H. Aspinwall, $200,000 each; Kernochan & Parish, $150,000; and L. S. Suarez, $125,000 (doubtless for foreign account). These twelve largest subscriptions totaled $4 million. Sixty subscriptions of $100,000 or less totaled

$1.5 million. Matthew Morgan, James Watson Webb, and various others took $100,000 each; George Curtis and John A. Stevens of the Bank of Commerce and Newbold took $50,000 each; Palmer and O. J. Cammann of the Merchants Bank took $20,000 each; and other bank officials took smaller amounts. This list includes subscriptions accepted through September. Corcoran seems to have taken $1 million (to which he may have added later) for his personal account. Winslow & Perkins won $50,000 under their own name, probably submitted by Corcoran in response to a last-minute request. This firm also placed a losing bid of $1.6 million, probably by arrangement with Corcoran to heighten the illusion of a scramble. Aside from E. W. Clark & Co., which took almost $1 million, the only noteworthy successful bids were W. R. Morgan, son of Matthew Morgan, $300,000, and Chubb & Schenck of Washington, $150,000. (J. M. Chubb had been trained as a clerk by Corcoran & Riggs.)

The near disappearance of banks (excepting the Commerce) as large bidders is worth noting. With rising prosperity they turned their resources back into commercial banking, the field of their first priority. For the Merchants and other banks of Boston, loans for industrial expansion may also have had precedence. See King to BB, May 2, June 7, 10, 13, Ward to BB, June 13, 19, C to Ward, June 17, 21, Ward to C, June 20, 1848, BPOC; Peabody to C&R, Apr. 14, June 23, July 7, 14, Peabody Papers; C to Ward, June 16, C to Peabody, June 19, C Letter Books; Peabody to C&R, June 9, 23, James Robb to C&R, June 7, Ward to C&R, June 14, King to C, June 16, Newbold to C, June 16, Curtis to C&R, Sept. 27, numerous other letters, subscription list, and work sheets in box labelled "Loan of 1848," R Papers; SR to C&R, Oct. 17, 1848, DetPL; *Treasury Report,* VI, 325–31; Fritz Redlich, *Molding of American Banking: Men and Ideas,* 2 vols. (New York, 1947–1951), II, 348–50.

25. See C to various, June 24, 1848, C to Peabody, July 3, C to King, July 11, C Letter Books; Ward to BB, July 3, 11, C to Ward, June 26, July 1, 25, Ward to C, July 4, BPOC; BB to Ward, July 7, 28, BPLB.

26. Money commanded 1 to 1½ percent per month on Wall and State Streets. See Peabody to C&R, July 14, 21, 28, Aug. 4, Peabody Papers, EI; Ward to BB, July 11, BPOC; BB to King, July 14, BB to Ward, July 14, 21, 28, BB to anon., Aug. 22, BPLB; M. Hidy, "Peabody," 286f; *Bankers Magazine,* July 1848, 72; *Hunt's*

Merchants' Magazine, March–April 1848, 302, 408f.; Walter Buckingham Smith and Arthur Harrison Cole, *Fluctuations in American Business, 1790–1860* (Cambridge, 1935), sec. 3, and 108, 122, 126; U.S. Bureau of the Census, *Historical Statistics of the United States, Colonial Times to 1957* (Washington, 1960), 428.

Newbold and the Barings agreed that business was not generally overexpanded in America, but feared that it was in Boston: Ward disagreed. See Newbold to Ward, Jan. 19, 1848, Newbold Papers; BB to Ward, July 7, BPLB.

27. The Rothschilds broke off their cooperation following a dispute between Corcoran and Belmont. Belmont had transferred $800,000 to the army at Mexico City in payment for Treasury notes receivable under the March loan contract at 101.26. Corcoran, who had joined him in the loan, received a 2 percent commission for helping to arrange the transfer. There was a disagreement over whether the commission was payable in Treasury notes at par (they were selling at more in the open market); in the end all but $1,000 was paid in cash. Of the $800,000 of notes, $175,000 was turned over to Corcoran at cost. He wanted more, perhaps all, but Belmont politely refused. After the books had been closed, Belmont applied for $300,000 of the new loan, at the subscription price and apparently for export to England. Corcoran abruptly accused him of trying to get cheap stocks at a time when the price was going up. Belmont, bitterly resentful, warned Corcoran that he would get the stocks cheaply if he chose to. It was at that point that the Rothschilds unloaded. See Belmont to C&R, July 1, 1848, R Papers; C to Peabody, July 3, C Letter Books; ch. 6, n. 5, below.

28. In early August the money market verged on panic, with interest on prime commercial paper at upwards of 15 percent (compared with 2½ percent in Europe). A month later the rate on commercial bills was down to 2½ percent, but railroads and "speculators" could not get sufficient funds to meet their calls at 6 to 7 percent. See Ward to BB, July 25, Aug. 8, 1848, BPOC; BB to Lee, Higginson, Sept. 8, BPLB; Walker to C&R, Aug. 2, 5, C to Walker, Aug. 4, Walker to Bancroft, Aug. 9 (two letters), C Letter Books.

29. Ward to BB, July 25, 1848, BPOC.

30. See ch. 3, above. Minister to England George Bancroft had told them of the intrigue; Peabody admitted it although he disclaimed foreknowledge.

31. As will be seen, the Barings worked with Corcoran in a

number of operations, but suspicions were never allayed and the relationship did not mature. William S. Wetmore and George Cryder were other noted merchants the Barings considered "boasters." See BB to Ward, Aug. 11, 1848, BPLB; Bates to Ward, Sept. 25, 1851, Ward Papers, MassHS; Ralph W. Hidy, *House of Baring in American Trade and Finance: English Merchant Bankers at Work, 1763–1861* (Cambridge, 1949), 396–7.

Some years later William Aspinwall reflected on the pitfalls awaiting the aggressive American. He had wanted to submit a proposal to a certain Englishman but knew it would be refused without discussion. He cultivated the man for two weeks before seizing an opportune moment. The Londoner readily agreed, remarking that Aspinwall was the first American he knew who would not have offered forty propositions by then. They subsequently became the closest of correspondents. See John Bigelow, manuscript of diary, May 13, 25, 1863, NYPL.

32. Daniel Webster was considered for the job of emissary, but was rejected as too prominent an opponent of the administration. Davis, after refusing an offer of $500 per month, settled for expenses plus $1,000 for the trip in the unlikely event of failure, or $5,000 in case of success. Minister George Bancroft, his brother-in-law, received an option to buy $5,000 of the loan at the subscription price between Jan. 1 and Apr. 1, 1849. He shared the option with Samuel Hooper (later Congressman) of Boston. See Ward to BB, July 31, Aug. 8, 11, 1848, King to BB, Aug. 17, BPOC; BB to King, Sept. 1, BB to Ward, Aug. 11, 18, 25, Sept. 15, BB to C, Aug. 25, Sept. 1, BPLB; C to John Davis, Aug. 2, 5, C Letter Books; Davis to C, Aug. 6, Ward to C, July 27, 28, Abbott Lawrence to C, July 27, 31, C Papers; Peabody to C&R, Aug. 11, Peabody Papers; Bancroft to C, Dec. 29, Bancroft Papers; Hidy, *House of Baring,* 337.

For the first time the Barings expressed concern about the slavery controversy and Ward had to reassure them.

33. See Nathan Miller, *The Enterprise of a Free People: Aspects of Economic Development in New York State During the Canal Period, 1792–1838* (Ithaca, 1962), 251–2, 294f; Bray Hammond, *Banks and Politics in America from the Revolution to the Civil War* (Princeton, 1957), 480; Clapham, *Bank of England,* II, 164–5, 214. Cf. R. G. Hawtrey, *A Century of Bank Rate* (London, New York, and Toronto 1938), 108–9; Arthur I. Bloomfield,

Monetary Policy under the International Gold Standard: 1880–1914 (New York, 1959), 24, 56–7.

34. Corcoran first planned to hypothecate the bonds but this was out of the question: Peabody, Britain's largest dealer in American securities, had not borrowed on them in years and did not care to try now. The risk for the British would be no greater if they bought the bonds; in fact they would enjoy any resultant capital gains.

When Corcoran first projected the trip to Ward he claimed to control $6 million above subscriptions and sales already made. Incomplete records indicate that the true amount was much greater, as Baring Brothers apparently suspected.

35. Unfortunately only one passing mention of the Paris negotiation seems to survive. For the importance of French cooperation, see Clapham, *Bank of England,* II, 100–1, 169–70, 329–30.

36. Corcoran had already prepared the way by inducing Walker to maintain large deposits, instead of small balances or overdrafts, with the Barings. In 1853 he helped Sam G. Ward (Thomas' son) quash a threat to the Barings' government agency from the new firm of Duncan, Sherman & Co., although the latter was associated with Peabody. He continued to assist Baring Brothers in having the government maintain credit balances as late as 1855. See Ward to BB, July 25, Oct. 3, 1848, King to BB, Aug. 16, Oct. 11, 17, C to Thomas Baring, Sept. 15, 21, Bancroft to BB, Sept. 27, BPOC; BB to Peabody, Sept. 1, BB to Hottinguer, Sept. 7, BB to Ward, Sept. 22, BPLB; Peabody to C&R, Aug. 11, Peabody Papers; Davis to Bancroft, Sept. 6, Bancroft Papers; Walker to Bancroft, Aug. 9, 1848, C to Sam. G. Ward, Apr. 1, 1853, C Letter Books; Peabody to C, Sept. 1, 1848, Marcy to C, Jan. 26, 1855, C Papers; C to ER, Jr., Sept. 22, 1848, Ward to C&R, Jan. 12, 22, 1853, and contract and other materials in box labelled "Loan of 1848," R Papers; C&R to Young, Sept. 8, 1848, letters received, 1843–1895, Treasury Archives.

37. Peabody became involved in the controversy between Corcoran and Elisha when the latter declined to forward his share of the Corcoran-Riggs joint account, wishing to use it to cover his short sales. Annoyed, Peabody pressed them to settle, which they finally did with his arbitration. See Cammann, Whitehouse to C&R, Oct. 3, 1848, Charnley & Whelen to C&R, Sept. 30, Oct. 9, R Papers; C to Peabody, Feb. 5, 1849, ER to Peabody, Feb. 23,

Peabody to C&R, Mar. 9, 23, Peabody Papers; C to Peabody, Jan. 20, Apr. 2, C to ER, Feb. 20, C Letter Books.

38. Sales on the joint accounts with Peabody and Elisha brought a profit of almost 5 percent. The firm still had almost $1 million in its name, of which it had ordered sale of $300,000 at 106 (equal to about 115 in America) through Baring Brothers. It was to be expected that the options would be exercised, but not all were. Morrison, through oversight, seems to have failed to take up his $167,000 in time and Jones Loyd early relinquished his $83,000 to Corcoran & Riggs and Peabody on joint account for 5 percent. These blunders were not imitated by others. Morrison thought he had been badly treated; the details are not clear. See Peabody to C&R, Oct. 13, 1848, Mar. 23, 1849, C to Peabody, Dec. 24, 1848, Jan. 6, 1849, Peabody to C, Nov. 23, 1848, Peabody Papers; King to BB, Oct. 23, Nov. 22, BPOC; BB to C&R, Oct. 20, Nov. 24, BB to King, Nov. 3, 10, BB to Hope & Co., Dec. 1, C to Ward, Dec. 11, BPLB; Davis to C, Nov. 20, Peabody to C, Dec. 29, 1848, BB to C&R, Jan, 12, 1849, C Papers; C&R to BB, Nov. 7, 1848, C to Peabody, Nov. 20, 1848, Jan. 20, Feb. 17, 1849, C Letter Books; Denison & Co. to C&R, Dec. 27, 1848, joint accounts, C&R and Peabody, Oct. 1848–May 1849, Cammann, Whitehouse to C&R, Oct. 7, 12, 23, Dec. 1, 1848, Newbold to C&R, Dec. 6, 9, BB to C&R, Dec. 15, 29, R Papers; and below.

39. See King to BB, Oct. 23, 1848, C to Ward, Oct. 21, Ward to BB, Nov. 1, 6, BPOC; SR to C&R, Oct. 15, 25, 26, 28, Riggs, Babcock to C&R, Nov. 4, Brown Bros. to C&R, Nov. 10, 14–17, Dec. 4–8, 19, R Papers.

Some relief was afforded by government cooperation of the kind that had been enjoyed for more than a decade. Corcoran obtained deposits of $200,000 from the Navy Secretary and $44,000 from the State Department for their accounts with Baring Brothers, making the transfer with his bills on the Barings' loan account. Thus the transfer was made on the Barings' books in London. This procedure was repeated in February. See C to Ward, Dec. 20, 1848, Jan. 19, Feb. 14, 1849, C Papers; Ward to BB, Nov. 14, 1848, King to BB, Nov. 14, C to Ward, Dec. 20, Ward to BB, Feb. 19, 1849, BPOC.

40. C. W. Lawrence, collector of the Port of New York and intimate of Newbold, secretly managed the open-market purchases with Cammann, Whitehouse as broker. See C to Morgan, Nov. 11,

1848, C to Peabody, Nov. 11, C to ER, Nov. 16, C Letter Books; Palmer to C&R, Nov. 18, R Papers; C&R to BB, Nov. 7, C to Peabody, Dec. 23, C Papers; Newbold to C, Nov. 24, Dec. 5, Newbold Papers, NYHS; King to BB, Nov. 8, Ward to C, Dec. 8, C to Ward, Dec. 5, 11, C&R to BB, Dec. 23, clipping of Walker announcement, Nov. 7, BPOC; Walker to Lawrence, Nov. n.d., 26, Dec. 2, Lawrence to Walker, Nov. 21, letters received, 1843–95, Treasury Archives; *Bankers Magazine,* December 1848, 384.

41. These agreements were made partly through Secretary of War William L. Marcy, old intimate of Newbold and Lawrence and a most prestigious politician. From New York Walker, careful to share the onus with Marcy, wrote his subordinate in Washington not to order, but to "recommend" renewal of the loan. See C to Selden, Nov. 9, 1848, C to Morgan, Nov. 11, C Letter Books; R. L. Cutting to Walker, Sept. 23, Walker to Young, Sept. 26, Selden to Young, Sept. 27, W. R. Morgan to Young, Sept. 28, K Letters, W. R. Morgan to Walker, letters to the secretary, Treasury Archives; Newbold to C&R, Dec. 6, R Papers; U.S. Congress, *Congressional Globe,* 30th Cong., 2d sess., 655; *Treasury Report,* 1849, 661.

Cf. the English expedient (but for the opposite purpose of tightening money): Hawtrey, *Century of Bank Rate,* 68–9.

42. See ch. 5, below; Francis DeP. Falconnet to BB, Feb. 5, 1849, BPOC; C to Newbold, Feb. 12, C to Cammann, Whitehouse, Feb. 21, C Letter Books; Walker announcement, Washington *Union,* Feb. 9.

43. Ohio had passed a similar law before the war; Corcoran predicted passage of such a bill in Pennsylvania. (He also thought, erroneously, that the new administration would repeal the Independent Treasury and return to a depository system, with a requirement of United States bonds as collateral for federal deposits or for bank notes.)

In New York, the very helpful purchase of United States government bonds for collateral rose gradually. Deposits with the comptroller were still only $1 million in 1852. The next year they jumped to $5.3 million, more than half the total of state bond collateral, as a large-scale expansion of banking got under way. See the analysis in chapter 7. See Rufus H. King to C, Nov. 1, 1847, Dudley Selden to C, Nov. 8, R Papers; C to Morgan, Nov. 11, 1848, C&R to Peabody, Jan. 10, 1849, C Letter Books;

C&R to Marcy, Apr. 25, Marcy Papers, LC; New York State comptroller, *Annual Report,* 1849, 139; New York State superintendent of the Banking Department, *Annual Report,* 1853 to 1854; New York State *Assembly Journal,* 72d sess., 1084–5, 1113–4, 1452; *Senate Journal,* 610, 652; Comptroller Washington Hunt, circular, May 1, 1849, AB Letters; *Bankers Magazine,* May 1849, 708; Ernest Ludlow Bogart, *Financial History of Ohio* (Urbana-Champaign, 1912), 278–80; Redlich, *Molding American Banking,* II, 100.

44. At the end of Polk's administration the lame-duck Congress authorized government purchases of the Loan of 1847 at the market price. (The original Loan Act had forbidden redemption at above par.) Treasury purchases continued through Cammann & Whitehouse, with C. W. Lawrence temporarily retained as collector in New York by the incoming Whigs to manage the operation. Besides Cammann & Whitehouse, Corcoran used Winslow, Lanier & Co., successor to Winslow, Perkins, as New York broker and often joint account partner. Peabody shared his European business with the Barings for a commission of ½ percent. Of the $14 million of the firm's contract for the Loan of 1848 about half was sent directly overseas, in marked contrast to the previous loans. More, of course, streamed abroad via the firm's domestic subscribers. A sizable proportion of this was repatriated for use as New York State banknote collateral under the Act of 1849.

The only extant description of the firm's holdings of United States bonds after the fall of 1848 shows the following hypothecations as of February 1850 (1848 bonds, face value): Baring Brothers, $600,000; Baltimore & Ohio Railroad, $450,000; Bank of Mobile, $100,000; V. K. Stevenson, $70,000; Bank of America, $30,000 (plus $19,000 of the Loan of 1847). There was $18,000 on hand. Stevenson was president of the Nashville & Chattanooga Railroad, for which some of the iron rails and cash were furnished by Corcoran & Riggs and Peabody on joint account in exchange for its bonds. Until the Nashville & Chattanooga needed it, the money remained on loan with the bankers against collateral of United States bonds. See Peabody, accounts rendered, May 3, June 6, 1849, Winslow, Lanier, joint account statement, June 1849–Apr. 1, 1850, memo, Sept. 30, 1849 (in "Loan of 1848" box), John B. Gossler & Co. (Hamburg) to C&R, Dec. 24, 1849, Cammann, Whitehouse to C&R, Jan. 22, Feb. 22, Mar. 20, 1850, C to ER,

Aug. 14, 15, C to C&R, Mar. 8, Oct. 11, Nov. 8, 15, 1850, May 14, July 9, Sept. 3, 1852, BB to C, Jan. 25, 1850, C. C. Jamison to C&R, Feb. 20, BB to C&R, May 31, Palmer to C&R, June 28, July 1, R Papers; C&R to Peabody, May 28, 1849, C to Peabody, May 6, 1850, Peabody Papers; C&R to BB, May 30, June 2, 25, July 16, Aug. 6, Nov. 1, Ward to BB, June 25, Nov. 20, 1849, S. G. Ward to BB, Apr. 27, 1850, C to Bates, June 17, Ward to BB, Oct. 15, BPOC; BB to Overend, Gurney, Oct. 6, 1849, BB to C&R, Dec. 14, BPLB; Cammann, Whitehouse to Lawrence, June 12, Hugh Maxwell to Meredith, June 13, 14, Meredith to Maxwell, June 14, Meredith Papers; Newbold to C, Mar. 21, Sept. 25, Newbold Papers; C account, C&R ledgers; Richard N. Current, *Daniel Webster and the Rise of National Conservatism* (Boston and Toronto, 1955), 168.

45. The balance in his private account was usually about $10,000 in the early 1840s, perhaps double that just before the war; afterward it was usually maintained at about $100,000 with occasional fluctuations of $30,000 to $40,000 above or below that figure. See C and ER, Jr., accounts, C&R ledgers.

Chapter 5

1. BPOC.

2. See David Hunter Miller, ed., *Treaties and Other International Acts of the United States of America, 1776–1863,* 8 vols. (Washington, 1931–1948), V, 222–3.

3. British Foreign Secretary Palmerston gave the bondholders "unofficial" support. The qualification proved meaningless when the minister to Mexico accompanied the bondholders' representative and at the same time threatening Caribbean fleet movements were carried out.

The budgets vary in reliability, all being open to question but acceptable as approximations. The peso was equivalent to the dollar. See B. Gomez Farias to V. Gomez Farias, May 27, 1850, Gomez Farias Papers, UTex; Walsh to Buchanan, Nov. 13, 1848, in William R. Manning, ed., *Diplomatic Correspondence of the United States: Inter-American Affairs, 1831–1860,* 12 vols. (Washington, 1932–1939), IX, 302; Great Britain, *Parliamentary Papers,* 42: 385; 1854, 69: 33–9, 50–4, 71; New Orleans *Picayune,* July

20, Aug. 31, 1851; Gustavo F. Aguilar, *Presupuestos Mexicanos* (Mexico City, 1940), 43–53; Wilfred Hardy Callcott, *Church and State in Mexico, 1822–1857* (Durham, 1926), 205–9; Edgar Turlington, *Mexico and Her Foreign Creditors* (New York, 1930), 92–6; Edwin M. Borchard, *Diplomatic Protection of Citizens Abroad* (New York, 1925), 314–5; William H. Wynne, *State Insolvency and Foreign Bondholders* (New Haven, 1951), II, *Selected Case Histories* . . . (New Haven, 1951), 3–106; D. C. M. Platt, "British Bondholders in Nineteenth Century Latin-America—Injury and Remedy," *Inter-American Economic Affairs* 14 (Winter 1960).

4. See Ward to BB, Nov. 6, 1848, M&M to BB, Mar. 14, Ward to Falconnet, Jan. 15, 1849, newspaper extracts, unidentified, Jan. 14, 1848, N. Y. *Journal of Commerce,* Feb. 11, BPOC; BB to M&M, Apr. 28, BB to Ward, Sept. 29, Oct. 13, BPLB; C to Ward, Nov. 7, 1848, Jan. 19, 1849, C Letter Books.

5. W. S. Wetmore and three others may have been associated with Belmont and Corcoran & Riggs at one stage of the 1848 transfer, when payment was taken partly or wholly in United States Treasury notes as described in the previous chapter. See above, ch. 4, n. 27; Wetmore to Peabody, Feb. 19, 1848, Peabody Papers; Belmont to C&R, May 30, R Papers, LC; Belmont to [C], Feb. 21, 1849, C Papers, LC; Clifford to Buchanan, July 2, 1848, in Miller, *Treaties,* V, 421–2; James P. Shenton, *Robert John Walker: A Politician from Jackson to Lincoln* (New York and London, 1961), 98; Robert Greenhalgh Albion, *The Rise of New York Port, 1815–1860* (New York and London, 1939), 175.

Louis S. Hargous first went to Mexico in 1833; Peter A. was a permanent resident there from 1838. They began with little capital but, trading shrewdly on ample credit, were reportedly clearing $75,000 a year before the Mexican War. Louis was related by marriage to Ignacio Trigueros, a former finance minister of low repute. Much of the Hargous profits came from government contracts. See U.S., Congress, *Senate Report 182, Mexican Claims,* 33d Cong., 1st sess., 41–55, 99–100; this chapter, below.

6. Hargous Bros. had handled over a million dollars of the 1848 payment. In the first eight months of 1849 the Hargouses spent at least $11,000 lobbying in Washington. At different times influential lobbyists such as S. L. M. Barlow and George Ashmun worked for their Tehuantepec and other interests. See C to Ward, Nov.

27, 1848, BPOC; C to Ward, Nov. 28, C Letter Books; Hargous Bros. to M&M, M&M Papers, UTex; Hargous Bros. to M&M, Dec. 28, 1848, Jan. 13, Feb. 22, Apr. 4, 19, May 4, June 22, Sept. 15, Nov. 22, 1849, M&M Papers; B. Gomez Farias to V. Gomez Farias, Nov. 16, 1850, Gomez Farias Papers; text and n. 9 and 10, below; Ann G. Wightt to S. L. M. Barlow, June 7, 1850, Barlow to L. E. Hargous, Mar. 15, 1841, George Ashmun to Barlow, Jan. 24, Feb. 1, n.d., 31, 1853, Barlow Papers, HuntL.

7. Walker was later willing to accept an offer to pay the $720,000 interest through Hargous at the much higher premium of 16⅔ percent. This antagonized the contractors, but the offer was evidently only a canard and nothing came of it. See C to Ward, Nov. 28, 1848, Jan. 19, 1849, C Letter Books; Walker to BB, Nov. 17, 1848, U.S. Misc. Mss., 1840–1860, LC; C to Ward, Nov. 27, Ward to Walker, Feb. 24, 1849, Ward to BB, Mar. 3, 13, BPOC; BB to Ward, Oct. 13, 1848, BPLB; Forstall to Falconnet, Mar. 1, 1849, Falconnet to BB, May 12, BPOC; Peter A. Hargous to Walker, May 18, 1850, Walker Papers, LC.

8. Corcoran also argued, with support from northeastern businessmen, that advances would relieve the tight American money market. See C to Ward, Feb. 16, 1849, BPOC; C to Ward, Mar. 10, C Letter Books.

9. American control of the Tehuantepec Isthmus transportation route was not pressed, perhaps because of hostility in Congress. See Thomas Ewing Cotner, *Military and Political Career of José Joaquin Herrera, 1792–1854* (Austin, 1949), 200–20; Clifford to Buchanan, June 26, Aug. 8, 1848, Otero to Clifford, Aug. 7, Oct. 10, in Manning, ed., *Dip. Corr.*, VIII, 1089–91, IX, 3–6.

10. Senator Thomas Hart Benton of Missouri, a bitter antagonist of Polk, divulged the protocol. A battle almost resulted when Henry S. Foote of Mississippi castigated him on the floor of the Senate for perfidy. Apparently Foote viewed the indemnity installments (or the promise to speed or threat to refuse their payment) as a useful lever to obtain the widest possible transit rights in Tehuantepec. For this and other less-relevant reasons Benton, who wanted a transcontinental railroad from St. Louis, was hostile to the protocol. Enmity between Foote and Benton flared again during the crisis of 1850. See Falconnet to BB, Feb. 4, 1849, BPOC; Benton to C, n.d., C Papers; George M. Dallas, manuscript diary, Dec. 18, 1848, Jan. 30, 31, 1849, PaHS; Manning, ed.,

Dip. Corr., VIII, 226–7; Clayton to Letcher, Sept. 18, 1849, ibid., IX, 34–6; Miller, ed., *Treaties,* V, 243–4, 251–2, 378–81; *Senate Journal,* 30 Cong., 1 sess., March 9–10, 1848, 335–40; "Correspondence Relating to, and Proceedings of the U.S. Senate . . . Treaty of Guadalupe Hidalgo," *Senate Executive Documents,* 30 Cong., 1 sess., 52 (serial 509); Buchanan to Clifford, Dec. 22, 1848, Manning, *Dip. Corr.,* IX, 6; U.S., Congress, *Congressional Globe,* 30th Cong., 2d sess., Feb. 3, 5, 6, 10, 1849, 437–8, 442, 448, 454, 456–7, 498–502; James K. Polk, *Diary,* ed. Milo M. Quaife, 4 vols. (Chicago, 1910), IV, 319–21, 326, 328, 353; New Orleans *Picayune,* Feb. 15, 1849; Henry S. Foote, *A Casket of Reminiscenses* (Washington, 1874), 331–6; Arthur W. Thompson, "David Yulee; A Study of Nineteenth Century American Thought and Enterprise" (Ph.D. diss., Columbia University, 1954), 307–8; J. Fred Rippy, *United States and Mexico* (New York, 1931), 49; Holman Hamilton, *Prologue to Conflict: the Crisis and Compromise of 1850* (New York, 1966), 50, 90, 93.

Earlier there had been some sympathy for Mexico because of the difficulties imposed by the Senate's changes. See James E. Harvey [Independent], Philadelphia *North American,* Mar. 13–15, 1848.

11. It does not appear that Corcoran & Riggs' allies were informed of the payment in notes instead of cash or shared in the resulting profits. See C to Ward, Nov. 28, Dec. 11, 1848, Jan. 19, Feb. 3, 16, Mar. 1, 1849, C&R to BB, Feb. 5, C Letter Books; Walker to Falconnet, Feb. 10, U. S. Misc. Mss.; Falconnet to Baring, Feb. 5, 16, Ward to Falconnet, Mar. 27, BPOC; Ward to Bates, July 17, Ward Papers, MassHS; Thomas H. Bayly in U.S., Congress, *Congressional Globe,* 31st Cong., 1st sess., Sept. 18, 1852.

12. In private life Taylor was a Louisiana planter. The Webster group may have also been backed by James G. King, New York correspondent of Baring Brothers. See Edward Curtis to [Samuel Ruggles], Feb. 28, 1849, Curtis Papers, LC; C to Ward, Mar. 28, Apr. 5, 16, C to Newbold, April 3, C Letter Books; C&R to BB, Apr. 2, 16, Ward to BB, May 1, copy, M&M–Arrangoiz agreement, Mar. 27, BPOC; Webster to BB et al., Sept. 12, 1850, State Dept. Domestic Letters, National Archives; J. N. Dox to George Ashmun, J. Watson Webb Papers, YU.; Seward Papers, passim, URoch. See also the support for Corcoran as government banker in the northeastern business community, ch. 6, below.

13. The Barings finally advanced up to $2.5 million. See C to Ward, Mar. 19, 1849, C to Newbold, Apr. 3, C Letter Books; Lawrence to Meredith, Apr. 2, Webb to Meredith, Apr. 6, Meredith Papers, PaHS; Bates to Ward, May 17, 26, 29, 30, Ward Papers; C&R to BB, Mar. 4, June 2, C&R to Meredith, Apr. 20, Ward to BB, May 1, Falconnet to Forstall, Mar. 31, Falconnet to BB, Apr. 13, May 14, BPOC; Meredith to Hall, June 2, B Letters, Treasury warrants 5016, 5944–5, National Archives.

14. The finance minister, Francisco de Arrangoiz, proved hostile: Falconnet reported he was allied with opposing interests. The minister had led him to believe the later advances would be accepted in London and turned over to foreign creditors, thus easing the exchange problem, but at the last minute he demanded payment in Mexico. Arrangoiz later figured openly as a representative of Mexico's internal creditors; possibly, too, he was working with financiers who offered loans to Falconnet at 1½ percent per month. See Falconnet to BB, Apr. 11, May 12, June 12, July 26, 1849, Falconnet to Bates, June 6, C&R to Ward, Apr. 28, memos, Feb.–Apr. (Falconnet), May 13 (M&M), June 12, BPOC.

15. See C&R to Ward, Apr. 28, 1849, Falconnet to BB, May 12, BPOC; C to Ward, Apr. 5, 16, C Letter Books; BB to Ward, Sept. 7, BPLB; Ward to C, May 4, 1850, R Papers, LC; Ralph W. Hidy, *House of Baring in American Trade and Finance: English Merchant Bankers at Work, 1763–1861* (Cambridge, 1949), 583 n. 20.

16. Corcoran's acceptance of Treasury advances was expected to cost the account $4,000. The fact that Corcoran & Riggs shared equally with Baring Brothers while the associated Mexican house had a lesser share was considered unjustified, since that was the most difficult part of the operation. The memory of Corcoran's effort to get the State and Navy Department accounts for Peabody still rankled. Still, Bates commented, "I like him notwithstanding his blunders," but he instructed Ward to remain in direct touch with the administration instead of communicating indirectly by way of "a man however amiable of moderate abilities." Ward to BB, Feb. 16, Apr. 3, July 9, Sept. 3, 12, 24, 1849, C&R to BB, July 2, 9, Ward to C&R, July 7, 9, C&R to Ward, July 6, BPOC; Ward to Bates, July 23, Sept. 11, Bates to Ward, Aug. 3, 24, Sept. 7, Ward Papers; BB to Ward, Jan. 3, 5, 1850, BPLB.

17. As jockeying began Hargous Brothers seemed sufficiently

formidable for the Barings to consider an alliance. The London house thought the former rich and respectable and, perhaps most important, closely linked with the Secretary of the Treasury. Corcoran opposed, rating their financial standing only "fair." The idea was abandoned when Baring agent Edmond J. Forstall learned the Hargouses had no ties to Meredith. See BB to Ward, Oct. 13, 1848, C&R to BB, July 9, 1849, Ward to BB, Jan. 9, 23, Aug. 13, 20, 27, Ward to Clayton, Aug. 15, Ward to Lawrence, Aug. 19, Lawrence to Clayton, Aug. 20, Ward to Meredith, Aug. 20, Falconnet to Charles Baring Young, Aug. 27, BPOC; Bates to Ward, Sept. 7, Ward Papers.

18. The Baring consortium was represented by Abbott Lawrence. Because of the Alphonse-Gaston act between Clayton and Meredith, Attorney General Reverdy Johnson had to handle part of the 1850 installment. Ward considered him a friend of Howland & Aspinwall. See Clayton to Meredith, Apr. 19, 1849, Meredith Papers; Clayton to John J. Crittenden, Aug. 23, Crittenden Papers, LC; Meredith to Clayton, Aug. 21, Clayton Papers, DelHS, Wilmington, Del.; Forstall to Ward, Nov. 17, C&R to BB, Nov. 26, Dec. 10, Goodhue & Co. to BB, Nov. 27, Ward to BB, Dec. 24, 1849, July 1, 1850, BB to Ward, Dec. 28, 1849, BPOC; Duff Green to Millard Fillmore, Dec. 19, 1850, with enclosures, State Dept. Misc. Letters.

19. Clayton engaged in an elaborate deception to delay and discourage the erstwhile contractors, assuring them the installment was still open to competition.

Corcoran, anxious to retain the Barings' friendship, offered them a half interest in any arrangement Parrott might make but hedged by also agreeing upon cooperation with Belmont and the Rothschilds. Corcoran estimated Parrott's wealth at upwards of $150,000. Resigning as consul soon after arriving in Mexico, he was to operate in exchange and, moving on to California, in gold dust and moneylending with a credit on the Barings guaranteed by Corcoran & Riggs. See Ward to BB, Aug. 13, 20, 1849, Forstall to Ward, Nov. 13, C to Ward, Dec. 15, BB to Ward, Dec. 14, Jan. 9, 1850, Feb. 22, Mar. 3, Ward to BB, Dec. 18, 19, 1849, Jan. 19, 1850, Feb. 17, Apr. 27, Ward to C, Dec. 18, 1849, BPOC; Bates to Ward, Sept. 7, 1849, Ward Papers; R. P. Letcher to John Parrott, Jan. 3, 1850, Parrott to C&R, Feb. 14, R Papers.

20. It seems probable—considering the timing of legislative approval and the quality of public life prevalent then—that the

authorization was given only because it was too late, and to embarrass the negotiators.

The Rothschild agents (Davidson and his associates, Garruste and Drusina), may have taken on the indemnity on their own account. In view of the risks incurred Letcher and the new contractors attempted to reconcile their antagonists with a half interest, but were rebuffed. Ironically, Mexico did not accept advances as rapidly as money accumulated and the contractors held idle funds until May 31.

As will be seen shortly, there may have been other, more tangible reasons for the Secretary's unhappiness. See BB to Ward, Jan. 25, 1850, Ward to BB, Jan. 8, Feb. 17, Apr. 1–2, 27, June 25, 1850, Forstall to BB, April 12, 1854, BPOC; Letcher to Meredith, Feb. 13, 15, Mar. 11, Apr. 8, 1850, Forstall to Letcher, Apr. 2, Meredith Papers; Parrott to C&R, Feb. 14, 15, Mar. 3, Apr. 8, June 1, R Papers; Letcher to Clayton, Feb. 15 (with enclosures), Apr. 11, [n.d., rec'd May 30], State Dept. Dispatches.

21. The Aspinwalls had long been correspondents of the Barings. Their firm was heavily interested in the Panama Railroad and Pacific shipping.

Corcoran sent the Barings a copy of one of Belmont's overtures. Ward, mentioning Corcoran's "underhanded work" during the previous installment, doubted his position with the current administration although "admitting his value with a certain class of people." See Forstall to BB, Apr. 15, 1850, Feb. 4, 1852, Ward to BB, Apr. 30, 1850, June 11, 12, 16, 25, BB to Ward, May 24, Belmont to C, Sept. 7, BB to Hottinguer & Co., Sept. 11, 1851, Falconnet, memo on Mexican houses, July 26, 1849, BPOC; Ward to Bates, June 14, 1850, Ward Papers; Forstall to C&R, June 18, 1853, R Papers; Albion, *Rise of N.Y. Port,* 174–5, 365.

22. Belmont argued that the large Treasury surplus should be put to work earning 6 percent on advances while relieving the recurrently tight money market. If the government had to borrow later (an extremely unlikely contingency unless in connection with the Texas Settlement of 1850, examined in a later chapter) he promised a heavy Rothschild investment. Prompt action was desirable; the Mexican export duty on silver would soon decline, making capital flights easier and raising the cost of exchange. See Ward to BB, July 1, 1850, BPOC; Belmont to Ewing, n.d., Ewing Papers, LC.

Belmont was somewhat naively eager to use this sort of financial pressure to achieve great diplomatic goals. For an example involving Cuba a few years later see Allan Nevins, *Ordeal of the Union,* 2 vols. (New York and London, 1947), II, 64f.

23. Marks was the ally of Mexican financiers Juan and Antonio Suarez. Either Marks or the Suarezes may have been merely agent for the other; the language is not entirely clear. See I. D. Marks to B. E. Green, Feb. 26, 1846, Jan. 4, 6, 1850, B. E. Green to D. Green, Jan. 5, 1849, Marks–D. Green contract, Feb. 6, 1850, Marks to D. Green, Feb. 14, 1850, D. Green to Clayton, Mar. 12, Payno to Marks, Oct. 18, Duff Green Papers, SoHC; Reverdy Johnson to Meredith, Mar. 12, 1849, Meredith Papers; Green to Meredith, Mar. 19, 1850, letters to the Secretary, Treasury Archives; memorials, Green to Fillmore, Dec. 19, 1850, Jan. 4, 1851, with enclosures, State Dept. Misc. Letters; Rosa to Webster, Feb. 17, with enclosures, State Dept., notes from foreign legations; Mexico City *El Universal,* Apr. 25, May 13, translations in R Papers; Green to Clayton, Mar. 12, Marks to B. E. Green, July 13, in U.S. Congress, *Congressional Globe,* 32d Cong., 1st sess., Jan. 21, 1852, 339–40; 31 Cong., 1 sess., Sept. 24, 1850, appendix, 1373.

24. Falconnet memo on Mexican houses, July 26, 1849, Forstall to BB, Nov. 14, BPOC.

25. The connection between Tehuantepec and the indemnity plan aroused both support and hostility in Washington, for the Hargouses were affiliated with New Orleans interests seeking to wrest Pacific commerce from New York–controlled routes. See D. Green to Meredith, Mar. 19, 1850, D. Green to Marks, Mar. 24, W. A. Bradley to R. W. Latham, n.d., Latham to Green, Apr. 5, Marks to D. Green, May 13, Marks to B. E. Green, July 13, Green Papers; Marks to B. E. Green, July 13, 1850, in *Congressional Globe,* 32 Cong., 1 sess., Jan. 21, 1852, 339–40; Sept. 24, 1850, appendix, 1373; New Orleans *Picayune,* Mar. 11, Aug. 1, 12, Oct. 5, 30, 1849, Apr. 5, 27, May 8, 12, Oct. 10, 11, 13, 14, 19, 25, 26, 1850, Mexico City *Monitor Republicano,* Aug. 16, 1850, July 1, 13, 1851.

26. Hargous Brothers held claims against Mexico which Payno was in a position to support. See Marks to D. Green, May 13, 1850, Marks to B. E. Green, July 13, Payno to Marks, Oct. 18, Green Papers; Green to Fillmore, Jan. 4, 1851, with enclosures, State Dept., Misc. Letters; Manuel Payno, *Memoria . . . de Su*

Manejo en el Desempeno del Ministerio de Hacienda (Mexico City, 1852), 14–5, 23–5, *Resena Sobre el Estado de los Principales Ramos de La Hacienda Publico* (Mexico City, 1851), 43–9; Jose Ignacio Esteva, *Esposicion . . . [del] Ministerio de Hacienda* (Mexico City, 1851), 88f.

27. Webster to Franklin Haven, Mar. 9, July 12, 1850, Harvard University Library, Cambridge, Mass; Ward to BB, Jan. 15, 1846, April 30, June 11, Aug. 11, 1850, C&R to BB, July 15, 22, C to Ward, Aug. 2, 5, C to Bates, July 29, Webster to Ward, Aug. 5, BB to Ward, Aug. 19, BPOC; U.S., Congress, *Congressional Globe,* 31st Cong., 2d sess., Feb. 25, 26, 1851), 685f; 32 Cong., 1 sess., Jan. 23, 1852, 371; New York *Post,* Mar. 4, 1851, citing Albany *Argus;* Bates to C, Aug. 16, William Wilson Corcoran, *A Grandfather's Legacy* (Washington, 1879), 89; Henry Cabot Lodge, *Daniel Webster* (Boston and New York, 1899), 347–8; Ralph W. Hidy, *House of Baring in American Trade and Finance: English Merchant Bankers at Work, 1763–1861* (Cambridge, 1949), 100, 284, 321, 553 n. 23; Richard N. Current, *Daniel Webster and the Rise of National Conservatism* (Boston and Toronto, 1955), 93–4, 136–9.

28. See C to Bates, July 29, 1850, Ward to BB, Aug. 11, Howland & Aspinwall to BB, Aug. 14, Aspinwall to Bates, Aug. 19, C&R to BB, Sept. 16, 1850, Aspinwall to Ward, Nov. 17, 1851, BPOC; BB to Ward, Nov. 8, 1850, BPLB; Ward to Webster, July 24, Aug. 9, 30, Corwin to Webster, July 30, Green to Fillmore, Dec. 19, with enclosures, State Dept., Misc. Letters; Webster to BB et al., Aug 10, Sept. 12, State Dept. Domestic Letters; C to C&R, Oct. 23, R Papers; Miller, *Treaties,* V, 424.

29. Dickinson and others of both houses were co-speculators with Corcoran in Texas securities. See Ward to BB, Sept. 17, 1850, Aspinwall to Ward, Sept. 19, C to Ward, Sept. 21, BPOC; Payno to Marks, Oct. 3, 1850, Green Papers; *Congressional Globe,* 31 Cong., 1 sess., 1851f (Sept. 18, 1850), appendix 1373f; 32 Cong., 1 sess., 354f; Hamilton, *Prologue to Conflict,* 121; ch. 10 below.

30. The internal debt, underestimated because of administrative confusion, was actually about 40 million pesos. The agreement gave the government a 5½ percent "premium": this was apparently to be charged to recipients of debt payments in lieu of the identical tax on export of specie, which was nominally relinquished. Among the favored interior creditors were Hargous Bros., who held nearly

$700,000 of claims. See Jecker, Torre to Forstall, June 13, 1850, BPOC; London *Times,* May 16; New Orleans *Picayune,* Sept. 8, Oct. 18; Mexico City *Monitor Republicano,* July 21, Sept. 7, Oct. 5–8, 10, 12, 29, Nov. 9, 12, 13, 25–27, 30, Dec. 2, 4, 13; Turlington, *Mexico,* 95–9.

31. Much of the $700,000 was lent by Mier y Teran, and his was the suggestion that modified the interior debt agreement. See Jecker, Torre to Forstall, June 13, 1850, BPOC; Washington *National Intelligencer,* Sept. 28; Esteva, *Exposicion,* 29; Cotner, *Herrera,* 219.

32. Webster's stand is reminiscent of Woodrow Wilson's on the controversial Article X of the League of Nations Covenant.

The bearers of Payno's appeal were Marks and Antonio Suarez. President Arista rather grossly wished his friend Suarez a speedy return to take advantage of the many opportunities for speculation in the building of Mexico. The latter was also promoting a trans-Mexican railroad with government support. See Payno to Marks, Oct. 3, 18, 1850, Green to de la Rosa, Oct. 9, 18, Payno to Corwin (copy), Oct. 21, Arista to A. Suarez, Oct. 23, Payno to de la Rosa, Nov. 3, Payno to A. Suarez, n.d., Green Papers; Green to Fillmore, Oct. 4, 1850, Fillmore Papers, BuffHS; Payno to Corwin, Oct. 21, C Papers; BB to Ward, Dec. 20, BPOC; Webster to Letcher, Aug. 24 (also including a threat of unilateral action on behalf of holders of the Garay grant), Dec. 4, State Dept., Instructions, Mexico, Letcher to Webster, Oct. 22, Dispatches, Mexico, Green to Fillmore, Nov. 29, 1850, Jan. 4, 1851, and enclosures, Misc. Letters, State Dept. Archives; Forstall to Ward, Jan. 26, R Papers; Rippy, *U. S. and Mexico,* 55.

33. Mier y Teran, who had lent the government $250,000, of course cooperated. This support, with Jecker, Torre's, made Forstall's position in the money market practically impregnable. Some of Forstall's Mexican opponents were on the Junta del Credito Publico. Soon afterward they and the government forced Mier y Teran to resign from that body. See citations to n. 34.

34. The unforeseen outpouring of California gold raised the price of the silver coin required for payment. Despite cooperation from Lionel Davidson, profit on the entire exchange account for this installment was cut to a mere 1 percent. The interest account took up the slack, advances to the government being supplemented by call loans to businessmen. See BB to Ward, Sept. 7, 1849, BPLB;

Ward to BB, July 26, 1850, Forstall to Ward, Aug. 24, Forstall to BB, Dec. 11, 1850, Jan. 2, 14, 25, Feb. 3, Mar. 20, May 5, 1851, BPOC; Forstall to Ward, Dec. 14, 21, 24, 28, 1850, Jan. 16, 1851, BB to Forstall, Feb. 7, Forstall to BB, Feb. 15, Ward to C&R, Feb. 1, 3, R Papers; J. Suarez to A. Suarez, Dec. 28, 1850, Green Papers; B. Gomez Farias to V. Gomez Farias, Apr. 10, 1851, Gomez Farias Papers; Mexico City *Monitor Republicano,* Dec. 19, 1850; Esteva, *Exposicion,* 29; Hidy, *House of Baring,* 583 n. 20.

35. In Washington, Duff Green referred to Mexico's entangled debt and development problems in his pleas to President Fillmore. See Payno to Marks, Oct. 18, 1850, Green to Fillmore, Jan. 4, 1851, State Dept. Misc. Letters; B. Gomez Farias to V. Gomez Farias, Mar. 31, 1851, Gomez Farias Papers; Manuel Payno, Ramon Olarte, and Jose Joaquin Pesado, *Cuestion de Tehuantepec* (Mexico City, 1852); Payno, *Memoria,* 14–5, 23–5; *Resena Sobre el Estado,* 43–9; Esteva, *Exposicion,* 31–5, 78.

Some observers reported growing hostility to foreigners because of the debt situation. For objections to the favoring of foreign over internal debts see Mexico City *Monitor Republicano,* Apr. 25, June 9, 14, Oct. 26, Nov. 3, 23, 1851. But Payno's wish to carry out the British bondholders agreement was reasonable, considering his friends the Suarezes were to receive a commission for negotiating it. Falconnet commented that bribery was the most effectual way for the creditors to accomplish anything. See Falconnet to BB, June 12, 1849, BPOC; Payno to Marks, Oct. 18, 1850, Green Papers.

36. See Rippy, *U. S. and Mexico,* 55. (I have substituted the word "ability" for an awkward translation.)

37. To prevent misunderstanding Forstall reread the letter to Arista before forwarding it. It appears, from some of the detail, he even helped write it. See Forstall to Webster, Nov. 17, 1850, Webster Papers, LC; Manning, *Dip. Corr.,* IX, 420–3; New Orleans *Picayune,* Aug. 17, 1851; Monticello (Miss.) *Southern Journal,* June 25, 1853; Jose F. Ramirez, *Memorias, Negociaciones, y Documentos para Servir a la Historia de las Diferencias . . . entre Mexico y los Estados Unidos* (Mexico City, 1853).

Webster was often overbearing in dealing with Mexicans. He expressed his opinion in the Senate in 1848: "I think very badly of the Mexican character, high and low, out and out." See U.S., Congress, *Congressional Globe,* 30th Cong., 1st sess., 531, 535.

A year after his retirement from the presidency Fillmore reportedly said Mexico wanted to enter the Union and should be welcomed. Citing other examples of rising Whig expansionism, a Douglas Democratic organ wondered who would have expected it three years earlier. See Springfield *Illinois State Register,* May 5, 1854. Certain southerners were rumored to be scheming, with British connivance, for an independent confederacy uniting their section with Mexico. See column by James Harvey [Independent], Philadelphia *North American,* Aug. 5, 9, 1850.

38. See Falconnet to Baring, June 12, 1849, Nov. 1, 1850, BB to Ward, Dec. 20, 1850, Aug. 1, 1851, Ward to BB, Feb. 19, 24, C to Ward, Apr. 30, BPOC; Green to Fillmore, Nov. 29, 1850, State Dept. Misc. Letters; Webster to Letcher, Dec. 4, 1850, State Dept., instructions; Letcher to Crittenden, Jan. 3, 12, Sept. 6, 1851, Crittenden Papers; Forstall to Ward, Jan. 18, 26, March 1, Forstall to BB, Jan. 25, Ward to C&R, Feb. 1, R Papers; Bates to Ward, Feb. 14, Ward Papers; Webster to Arista, May 1, Webster Papers, NHHS; C to Ward, May 5, C Letter Books; Whittlesey to Hodge, June 26, AB Letters; Webster to Fillmore, Dec. 19, Fillmore Papers; W. Selden to D. Green, Jan. 7, 1852, Green Papers; Arista to Webster, June 2, 1851, in Manning, *Dip. Corr.,* IX, 396; Letcher to Crittenden, May 6, 1850, in Mrs. Chapman Coleman, ed., *Life of John J. Crittenden, with Selections from His Correspondence and Speeches,* 2 vols. (Philadelphia, 1871), I, 370; New York *Post,* Feb. 27–8, and other newspapers and congressional debates cited in n. 24 above; also U.S., Congress, *Congressional Globe,* 31st Cong., 2d sess., Feb. 26, 27, 1851, 694f, 109; 32 Cong., 1 sess., Jan. 20–4, 1852, especially the speech by Meade of Virginia, 316f, 338f, 354f, 371f, 379f, Jan. 28, Feb. 2, 411f, 440.

One vituperative defender of Webster and the contractors was James Harvey. This well-informed but not incorruptible journalist, who had given his friend, Clayton, pause in his quest for patronage, praised Corcoran as a patron of "American" artists. In 1852–1853 he was permitted to open an account with Corcoran & Riggs and overdraw by more than $2,000. See James E. Harvey [Independent], Philadelphia *North American,* Mar. 1, 1851; Harvey to Meredith, June 18, 1849, Meredith Papers; Harvey to Robert M. Bird and Clayton to Bird, passim, Bird Papers, UPa Library; Harvey account, C&R ledgers.

39. An investigation was also launched by the Whig administra-

tion into the role of a Hargous partner in the disappearance of a claims payment from Mexico to the United States in 1844. See [Thomas W. Ward] manuscript and printed copy of pamphlet, "Mexican Indemnity Payments," Jan. 27, 1851, BB to Forstall, Mar. 14, Ward to C&R, June 7, Nov. 27, Howland & Aspinwall to C&R, Nov. 20, R Papers; Luis de la Rosa to Webster, Feb. 17, 24, Webster to de la Rosa, Feb. 21, State Dept., notes, Mexico, Green to Webster, Mar. 20, Misc. Letters, Webster to Green, Mar. 22, Domestic letters, B. Smith to Webster, Apr. 1, dispatches; Green to Fillmore, Mar. 20, Fillmore Papers; Whittlesey to Hodge, June 26, AB Letters; Forstall to BB, Feb. 3, Mar. 20, Ward to BB, Aug. 12, BPOC; *Congressional Globe,* 32 Cong. 1 sess., cited in n. 37, above, 33 Cong. 1 sess., *Senate Report 182,* passim; Mexico City *Monitor Republicano,* Mar. 10, July 9, 10; Mexico City *El Universal,* Apr. 25, translation in R Papers; London *Times,* July 28; Enrique Sarro, "La Deuda Exterior de Mexico," *Revista de Hacienda* (Mexico) 4 (August 1939).

40. In the abortive negotiation of December 1847 the Barings suggested payment of the indemnity to the bondholders as a condition for a loan to the United States. Walker was willing to purchase British support for the annexation of all Mexico by assuming the whole debt. See ch. 4, above.

41. See Falconnet to Clayton, Aug. 8, 1849, State Dept. Misc. Letters; Clayton to Falconnet, Aug. 14, Domestic Letters; Letcher to Webster, Oct. 22, 1850, Jan. 2, 1851, and enclosures, State Dept., Dispatches, Mexico; Manning, *Dip. Corr.,* IX, 65 n. 370.

42. In view of the delayed start in the exchange operation better terms were expected. See Ward to BB, Oct. 7, 1850, Forstall to BB, Mar. 1, 1851, BB to Ward, May 16, Howland & Aspinwall to Ward, May 16, June 26, C&R to Howland & Aspinwall, Jan. 10, 1852, BPOC; Ward to BB, Mar. 7, 10, 1851, Ward to Forstall, Apr. 11, Ward to C&R, June 24, ER, Jr., to ER, Jan. 21, 1852. Howland & Aspinwall to C&R, Feb. 21, Mar. 12, 17, R Papers; speech of John McClernand, *Congressional Globe,* 31 Cong., 1 sess., Sept. 18, 1850, 1853.

43. See Jecker, Torre to Forstall, June 13, 1850, Forstall to Ward, Aug. 24, 1850, Mar. 1, 8, 1851, C to Ward, Apr. 30, Ward to C, May 2, 1851, Forstall to BB, Feb. 25, 1852, BPOC; BB to Ward, June 13, 1851, BPLB; Marks to B. Green, July 9, 1851, Green Papers; Howland & Aspinwall to CR, Feb. 19, 21, 1852,

Forstall to Ward, Mar. 7, 15, Apr. 12, R Papers; C to Ward, May 5, C Letter Books.

44. See Ward to BB, Jan. 20, July 9, 1851, BPOC; BB to Ward, July 11, 18, BB to Forstall, June 10, BPLB.

45. More than £10,000 derived from the agency which had been undertaken for the bondholders; the rest came chiefly from exchange. See BB to Ward, Nov. 7, 11, 1851, BPLB; Ward to BB, Feb. 5, 9, 1852, S. G. Ward to Ward, Feb. 12, 14, C&R to Ward, Oct. 17, 1851, Howland & Aspinwall to Ward, Oct. 21, Ward to BB, May 27, BPOC; F. H. Story to C&R, Oct. 29, 1852, Ward to C&R, June 1, 1853, statement, Sept. 26, Dec. 31, R Papers. For later examples of the character of Fillmore's friendship with Corcoran, see his begging for the latter's company on a trip to Europe: Fillmore to C, Mar. 10, 17, Apr. 17, May 3, July 23, 1855, C Papers.

46. In the lucid and outspoken Forstall the gears adjusting intellectual discernment to self-interest ground still more raspingly than they do in most men. See Forstall to BB, May 6, 1852, BPOC.

47. The bondholders asked for payment at Washington but Webster, looking over his shoulder toward Capitol Hill, decided to adhere to the letter of the treaty and make delivery in Mexico City.

Forstall complained that Howland & Aspinwall accepted Iturbe's receipt at excessively favorable rates at the expense of their partners. The total of pledges by the Mexican government exceeded the amount of the final installment by $33,000. See BB to Ward, Dec. 13, 1850, June 10, 1851, Mar. 5, 9, 1852, BPLB; Falconnet to BB, June 12, 1849, Ward to BB, Oct. 24, 28, 29, 1851, Nov. 21, Feb. 17, 1852, Forstall to Howland & Aspinwall, Mar. 25, Forstall to BB, Mar. 6, 30, June 3, Forstall to Thomas Baring, Apr. 1, 1853, Oct. 31, 1854, BPOC; Ward to C&R, June 4, 1851, Aug. 1, Nov. 6, Mar. 19, 1852, Aug. 27, Ward to Howland & Aspinwall, Apr. 3, Howland & Aspinwall to C&R, Feb. 19, 21, Mar. 3, 6, 8, Ward to Jecker, Torre, Aug. 24, R Papers; Letcher to Webster, June 18, State Dept., dispatches; Manning, *Dip. Corr.*, IX, 107; Thomas R. Lill, *The National Debt of Mexico: History and Present Status* (New York, 1919), 38.

Two years later, when Mexico sold territory to the United States (the Gadsden Purchase), payment was made in New York by terms of the treaty. See M. Olasagarre, *Cuenta . . . de los Diez Millones de Pesos que Produjo el Tratado de la Mesilla. . . .*

(Mexico City, 1855); Marks to B. Green, Aug. 14, Nov. 12, 29, Dec. 4, 16, 1851, Mar. 11, 1852, Marks to Letcher, Nov. 14, 1851, Letcher to Marks, Nov. 14, Green Papers.

Hargous, preoccupied with Tehuantepec, had given up bidding for the indemnity in deference to Webster. Marks was interested in both plums, and Duff Green continued to attack Webster, the contractors, and the Tehuantepec treaty. Since this embarrassed Arista by revealing his inside dealings, he desperately turned elsewhere, renouncing the Greens, Suarezes, Marks, et al. The episode petered out in 1854–1855 in a brief and inconclusive congressional inquiry into Green's charges of impropriety against Bayly for his conduct in the indemnity matter. The rumors were that Corcoran had offered Bayly financing for a speculation in United States bonds, but the latter had refused on grounds of propriety. Bayly, of course, denied there had been such an offer. See U.S., Congress, *Congressional Globe,* 33 Cong., 1 sess., 1835–1836; *House Report 354* (series 744), "Hon. Thomas H. Bayly"; U.S., Congress, 33d Cong., 2d sess., *House Executive Document* 142 (series 808), "Case of Hon. Thomas H. Bayly."

48. I believe a careful study of the Central American diplomacy of the Taylor and Fillmore administrations would support this view of their divergent attitudes toward Britain.

49. See Lechter to Crittenden, Nov. 17, 1849, Sept. 15, Oct. 20, Nov. 12, 1850, Nov. 20, 1851, Webster to Letcher, Dec. 23, Crittenden Papers; Letcher to Corwin, Aug. 31, 1851, Corwin Papers; Rippy, *U.S. and Mexico,* 55 and ch. 3–5 passim; Shenton, *Walker,* 70–1.

Chapter 6

1. Among allies not heretofore identified by party, Cammann, Whitehouse, and J. S. Gittings can be definitely established as Democrats. See Toland to Blair, June 4, 1845, Blair-Lee Family Papers, PriU; Cammann, Whitehouse to C&R, June 21, 1848, R Papers, LC; C to Ward, Mar. 13, 14, 28, 1849, C Letter Books; Charnley & Whelen to Meredith, Mar. 14, E. W. Clark & Co., Garrick Mallory, John Towne, J. B. Mitchell (president of the Mechanics Bank of Philadelphia), Paul Furnum and John Tacker to Meredith, Mar. 15, Chubb & Schenck to Meredith, May 24 (two letters), George Richardson to Meredith, June 23, J. Meredith to

Meredith, June 24, K Letters; Henry Toland to Meredith, Mar. 3, C. H. Fisher to Meredith, Apr. 21, 1849, Meredith Papers, PaHS; Newbold to C, Mar. 21, Newbold Papers; Robert Toombs to George W. Crawford, Mar. 17, Toombs to C, Mar. 17, C Papers. The Newbold letter with accompanying signatures is reproduced in William Wilson Corcoran, *A Grandfather's Legacy* (Washington, 1879), 71–2; the draft, with corrections, is in the Newbold Papers.

For a Whig newspaper attack see James E. Harvey [Independent], Philadelphia *North American,* January 26, 1849. This correspondent was later won over by Corcoran. See ch. 5, n. 38, above. A sample of favorable publicity is the New Orleans *Picayune,* March 22, praising Corcoran & Riggs as government bankers, upholders of national credit, and "most liberal and charitable bankers to the poor" of Washington.

2. See ch. 5 above and ch. 9 below. Corcoran was especially close to Assistant (and often Acting) Secretary of the Treasury William L. Hodge, publisher of the New Orleans *Commercial Bulletin,* to whom he lent almost $6,000 during his term of office. See memos, May 23, 1853, June 13, 1854, C Letter Books.

3. The Treasury may have lost slightly in higher prices paid under the new debt repurchase arrangements. Note also Guthrie's civil service reforms in U.S., Congress, 33d Cong., 1st sess., *Treasury Report, House Executive Document 3:* 5–7, 13–4, 31–41; cf. Sir John Clapham, *The Bank of England: A History,* 2 vols. (Cambridge, Eng., 1958), II, 253–5, for a sympathetic trans-Atlantic vibration.

For an anonymous, exaggerated but informed diatribe against Corcoran and his alleged tool, Hodge, by someone claiming to be a Congressman-elect and promising to meet Guthrie, see anon. to Guthrie, Mar. 3, 1853, Guthrie Papers, Filson Club, Louisville, Ky.

4. The details of Corcoran's proposal are obscure. He may also have wanted resumption of Walker's loans on federal securities, having once favored special legislation to permit it.

5. By this time Walker was—literally—deeply indebted to Corcoran. Lawrence had become president of the Bank of the State of New York, a change conducive to harmony in Wall Street.

6. Senator Thomas J. Rusk of Texas, another old ally of Corcoran, also evaded his call. See C to Newbold, Mar. 23, 1853, C to Rusk, Apr. 26, C Letter Books; Lawrence to Marcy, Mar. 24, July 23, Marcy Papers, LC; Rusk to C, June 28, C Papers, LC.

7. See C to Cammann, Whitehouse, Apr. 27, 1849, C Letter Books; Carter Goodrich, *Government Promotion of American Canals and Railroads, 1800–1890* (New York, 1960), ch. 3–5; B. U. Ratchford, *American State Debts* (Durham, 1941), ch. 5.

8. See Walker to C, Sept. 27, 1850 [misdated 1856], C Papers.

9. Defaulted state debts were also on the agenda. See James Shields to C, Sept. 30, 1850, in Corcoran, *Grandfather's Legacy,* 91.

10. See Ward to BB, Oct. 15, 1850, BPOC; Walker to C, Aug. 16, 1851, C Papers; C to Walker, Aug. 1, 2, 1851, C Letter Books; Corcoran, *Grandfather's Legacy,* 100–1; Ralph W. Hidy, *House of Baring in American Trade and Finance: English Merchant Bankers at Work, 1763–1860* (Cambridge, 1949), 338–9, 413–4, 430–2, 595 n. 43.

11. Apparently Corcoran's sole participation in the Illinois Central was $25,000 of a loan of $2.7 million in February 1854, which he soon liquidated. He refused requests to support Pacific railroad schemes, several of which came from Texans and apparently including a later vision of Walker's. In one proposition George Paschal, referring to "the Great Pacific Rail Road" projected through 32 degrees north latitude, claimed the support of an influential brother in the Texas senate and of "confidential friend Enoch Jones and Judge Thomas J. Devine of San Antonio who were the contractors for the San Antonio & Mexican Gulf Rail Road" and were in New York at the home of Jones' brother-in-law, wealthy merchant Henry Sheldon. Paschal's father-in-law, Governor Duval, was to call on Corcoran in Washington; his son, also influential, was the secretary of state of Texas. Senator Rusk visited Albany capitalist Erastus Corning in behalf of the enterprise. Others to be approached were General Orville Clark and "Mr. Greely," who had been in Austin recently. It was hoped that Secretary of the Treasury James Guthrie could be brought in: he "is one of the Texas Land and Immigration Co. whose attorney I [Paschal] have been for several years" and which owned more than one million acres of land through the center of which the road was to run. The object was to gain a congressional grant and charter. The colorful Duval, reputedly influential with many members of Congress, had been a Representative from Kentucky and Governor of Florida before moving to Texas. He died with his boots on in pursuit of this prize at Washington in March 1854. See GWR to C, July 8, 1853, George Paschal to C&R, Aug. 13, 19, W. D. Miller to C&R,

Sept. 28, Dec. 8, R Papers; C to P. S. Buckingham, May 2, 1854, C Letter Books; H. M. Watterson to R. J. Walker, Nov. 2, 1853, Walker Papers, NYHS.

12. The firm was already active in Tennessee railroad finance. In 1849 it joined George Peabody in his first venture in procuring and advancing iron for the Nashville & Chattanooga. Remittance to England was by exchange or American securities, depending on the markets. On Peabody's suggestion cotton bills were sometimes sent, the firm granting credits to southern houses for their purchase. Two years later the account was closed with surprising profits of more than £5,000 each. See Polk to Flagg, Feb. 7, 1839, Flagg Papers, NYPL; Pickett, Perkins & Co. to C&R, Jan. 22, 1850, R Papers; C account, 1848f, C&R ledgers; H. W. Conner to C, Sept. 18, 1851, Peabody to C&R, Oct. 31, C Papers; C to Conner, Oct. 4, C Letter Books; *Bankers Magazine,* November 1851; Muriel Emmie Hidy, "George Peabody, Merchant and Financier, 1829–1854" (Ph.D. diss., Radcliffe College, 1939), 328.

13. In 1852 Corcoran & Riggs granted Walker a $20,000 credit, secured by $21,000 of Memphis 6 percent bonds. At the same time the firm took $175,000 of Nashville & Chattanooga bonds with the state's guarantee, with an option for an equal amount more at 103 and accrued interest. Later the firm joined William Hoge & Co. of New York, each taking three-eighths. Walker and architect Robert Mills, a friend of Corcoran's, took $400,000 of Tennessee 6 percent bonds at about the same rate, plus $200,000 of Memphis 6 percent bonds and $54,000 of Nashville & Chattanooga securities guaranteed by the Memphis & Charleston Railroad at 85½, reduced to about 84½ by deferred payment. Brown Brothers and August Belmont bought $300,000 of the Tennessee bonds. The profit on the $400,000 was $11,500, with Corcoran & Riggs's share $4,300. The return was higher on the Memphis 6 percent shares, which sold at from 90 to 92½ and yielded $5,000.

Early in 1853 Corcoran & Riggs joined Hoge for another bond purchase: $400,000 of Tennessee and $210,000 of Memphis. The two houses shared with Peabody half of a joint iron account for the Memphis & Charleston, undertaken despite Peabody's misgivings. A federal trust fund bought $512,000 of state-guaranteed Nashville & Chattanooga 6 percent shares at par, while Corcoran & Riggs took $20,000 for investment and recommended purchase to others. They proved relatively good investments, thanks to state and municipal governments taking over payments of interest, except during the dislocations of the Civil War. See C to ER, Sept. 8, Oct. 22, 30, 31, Nov. 2, Dec. 21, 31, 1852, Nov. 11, 1853, Samuel P. Walker to C&R, Aug. 10, 1852, Feb. 26, Apr. 8, 1853, James Knox Walker to C&R, Oct. 28, 1852, Jan. 18, 1853, contract, C&R and Stevenson, Oct. 30, 1852, William Hoge to C&R, Jan. 3, 5, 10, 19, 24, 29, Feb. 24, June 1, 14, 21, 1853, R Papers; C&R to William D. Nutt, Apr. 18, 1856, C to president, Nashville & Chattanooga Railroad, and (separately) to mayor of Nashville, Oct. 10, 1860, C Letter Books; Aspinwall to Marcy, July 10, 1856, Marcy Papers.

14. J. F. D. Lanier had begun his career as a clerk in the Indiana legislature. Corcoran's friend Senator Jesse Bright, a political power there, may have been useful in establishing the close connection between the two houses.

15. Additional demand was expected from the vicinity of the railroad. Corcoran & Riggs was relied on to ply the southern retail market. Winslow, Lanier allotted their associates $50,000 of Little Miami (Ohio) Railroad bonds at 90, the prime cost. Corcoran & Riggs had refused that much additional at 91, but when the issue proved attractive another $20,000 was turned over to the firm at 90 although 95 was the current price. See Winslow, Lanier to C&R, July 10, 14, 18, 1851, R Papers; New York *Express,* July 10, cited in *Bankers Magazine,* August 1851; Alfred D. Chandler, *Henry Varnum Poor, Business Editor, Analyst, and Reformer* (Cambridge, 1956), 76f, 117f.

16. See C&R to ER, Feb. 9, 12, 1853, Whitehouse to C&R, Feb. 11, 15, R Papers; C to Newbold, Apr. 5, 1853, C to public treasurer, Rawley, N.C., Dec. 21, 1854, C to James Courts, public treasurer of N.C., Jan. 31, Mar. 31, 1859, C Letter Books.

17. Part of the issue was obtained but the rest slipped through the fingers of the hypercautious Elisha when the price rose toward 90. See C&R to ER, Sept. 22, 24, 26, 29, Oct. 16, 18, 20, 23, 30, Dec. 10, 1845, May 1, 6, 12, 1846, ER & C&R joint account statement, May 12, R Papers; C to John S. Gittings (president, Chesapeake Bank of Baltimore), May 14, 15, 1846, C&R to Palmer, May 12, 1846, C to Palmer, Mar. 19, C Letter Books.

In another collaboration, Corcoran & Riggs and Winslow, Lanier used manipulative techniques which Corcoran had practiced before the Mexican War in bidding for federal issues. They planned to bid for a $500,000 issue of the Ohio & Pennsylvania Railroad, with Corcoran & Riggs taking half and Winslow, Lanier, joined by Moran & Iselin of New York, the balance. Highly reputed friends such as J. F. A. Sanford, Samuel Riggs, and Edward Whelen were enlisted to file lower bids to stoke demand. Whelen was brought in to manage sales in Philadelphia for a ⅛ percent commission. Corcoran, away from the scene of action, underestimated the market and wanted to offer at 89 and fractions but, as managers, Winslow, Lanier raised the bids. The allies received $347,000 of the total, which was taken almost entirely at 91.15 to 92½. They seem to have obtained a reduction in price to 87: presumably there was some such arrangement as in the case of the Wilmington & Manchester. Newbold and John Palmer were also mentioned and may have taken part. Sales began according to plan at 93 and the price was gradually raised. See Winslow, Lanier to C, Dec. 2, 4, 5, 6, 10, 14, 23, 24, 26, 28, 1850, Whelen to C&R, July 7, Aug. 11, Oct. 4, 1852 (with circular of Sept. 25), R Papers; Chandler, *Poor,* 94.

His own occasional slipperiness did not deter Corcoran from a sanctimonious dudgeon when he felt himself victimized. See, for example, the perhaps questionable conduct of his debtors, Chouteau et al., ch. 10 below.

18. Early in 1849 Corcoran acknowledged that he had been "bamboozled" in a purchase of Philadelphia, Wilmington & Baltimore Railroad bonds. In March 1854 he lobbied against an effort to decrease federal payments for carrying the mails. He decided to liquidate his holdings at about 42 but changed his mind when one of the Thayer brothers of Boston, who had a large investment, told him the price would reach par by the beginning of 1856. Instead it fell to 20 and Corcoran bought more.

Typically, Corcoran preferred to find a modus vivendi with potentially hostile interests rather than engage in outright conflict. In October 1860 he attacked a proposal to guarantee $215,000 of the bonds of the Delaware line to enable it to extend southward. The purpose, he wrote, was to forestall an "imaginary air line railroad from New York to Norfolk." Previous advances based on the same argument had cost the company $50,000 per year, he complained, predicting the opening of a line of steamers to Norfolk or elsewhere to make the proposed extension pay. This would arouse the bitter hostility of Baltimore and probably all Maryland, whose favor he thought should be conciliated by every possible means. Baltimore people were already aroused, he added, and the diversion of resources would delay completion of the Philadelphia-Baltimore line which was far more important. The road was doing well and would do still better if it confined itself to its legitimate business. It's bonds would soon pay a regular 8 percent dividend, the retired financier concluded, and the line could put aside enough in four years to build a much-needed bridge over the Susquehanna River. Corcoran parted company with President Felton over the issue. He did not think the board of directors had the right to undertake such an investment without first obtaining the consent of the stockholders, and considered it "extraordinary, as well as offensive . . . making us mere automatons" when Felton threatened to resign unless his policies were accepted. Corcoran began to dispose of his holdings, liquidating the last when the Civil War began. See C to Charnley & Whelen, Jan. 24, 31, 1849, C to S. M. Felton, Dec. 28, 30, 1853, Mar. 29, 1854, July 13, 1857, C to J. L. Gardiner, Jan. 24, 1856, C to Edward Everett, Feb. 8, C to Whelen, Feb. 21, Oct. 29, 1856, July 16, 1860, C to J. E. Thayer, Oct. 21, 1856, C to N. Thayer, Oct. 19, Nov. 25, 1860, Nov. 29, 1861, statement, Mar. 14–15, 1862, C Letter Books; Thomas S. Bayard to James A. Bayard, Dec. 16, 1857, Bayard Papers, LC.

19. Early in 1853 Corcoran & Riggs joined William Hoge in contracting $200,000 of Maysville & Lexington bonds at 87¼. By mid-June only $29,000 had been sold and Hoge, who wanted to unload, had the syndicate dissolved. The firm eventually disposed of most of its bonds—at a loss, in the case of some $10,000 to Elisha Riggs at 70 in July 1854. By the fall of 1854 the company was forced into receivership. Corcoran ultimately organized a majority of the first mortgage bondholders to buy into the road at a bankruptcy sale for $123,000. Bonds were traded for stock, assessments of 6.2 percent of face value were levied, and by the end of 1856 the road was earning a 5 percent net profit. Arrangements were made with Leslie Combs, who had earlier been kept afloat financially by heavy loans from Corcoran & Riggs against his Texas securities, for traffic agreements with his Covington & Lexington Railroad. By December 1856 the road paid a 2 percent dividend. However, the investment was sharply deflated by the Civil War. In the fall of 1865 the Riggs and Corcoran holdings apparently still totaled $135,000 par of stock, of which at least two-

thirds soon was sold at 22. See Hoge to C&R, June 1, 14, 1853, ER ledger, 1854–1856, R Papers; C to J. Johnson, Oct. 7, 1854, C to ER, Dec. 1, C to Cammann & Co., Oct. 6, Feb. 12, 1855, Mar. 22, 1856, Apr. 14, 16, 28, May 7, C to Dangerfield and others, Apr. 14, Nov. 3, C to Gen. J. S. Stoddert, Dec. 1, 1854, Mar. 27, 1855, Oct. 16, 1856, C&R to B. C. Williams, Apr. 1, 1855, C&R to A. Bowie Davis, Feb. 20, 1856, Apr. 16, 1858, C&R to Hoge, Feb. 25, 1856, C to Grammer, May 3, 1856, Anthony Hyde (Corcoran's private secretary) to [brother], June 26, memo, July 9, C&R to W. W. Hunter, July 12, Hyde to C, July 19, C to Leslie Combs, Jan. 28, Feb. 5, 14, 1857, C to B. Wilson of Cammann & Co., Jan. 28, Feb. 3, Dec. 18, 1857, C to anon., Oct. 31, Nov. 2, 1860, Hyde to Riggs & Co., N.Y., Oct. 13, 14, Nov. 3, 1865, C Letter Books.

The Maysville & Lexington tangle was the most troublesome of the railroad investments, but there were others. Corcoran tried to sell his $5,000 of Concord & Claremont (New Hampshire) bonds after learning there would be a delay in payment of interest. Later, using an attorney recommended by Senator John P. Hale, he brought suit to force redemption with interest and attorney's fees. Eventually he settled for 90 percent. See C to John L. Gardiner, Sept. 27, 1852, C to Joseph Low (mayor of Concord, N.H.), Jan. 22, 1855, C to Cammann & Co., Jan. 22, 1855, C to Whitehouse, Jan. 18, 1855, C to John P. Hale, Feb. 29, 1856, C to Tappan & Bailey, Mar. 1, 1856, C to J. E. Thayer, Feb. 23, 1858, C to S. E. Guild, Apr. 27, July 15, 28, Aug. 18, C Letter Books.

Having paid a 20 percent installment on stock in the projected Mississippi & Atlantic Railroad he refused further payments without an accounting for the first. See C to Palmer, June 17, 1854, C to Winslow, Lanier, March 25, 1855, C Letter Books. The firm took $30,000 of Michigan Southern bonds in December 1852 and at least $45,000 more the following February with Elisha Riggs. In the next year, Corcoran came to share Edward Whitehouse's distrust of James Joy's management of the road and disposed of his holdings. See C&R to ER, Jan. 26, Feb. 17, 18, 22, 1853, Whitehouse to C&R, Feb. 11, R Papers; C to Whitehouse, Oct. 10, 1854, C Letter Book; C account, 1852, C&R ledgers; *Bankers Magazine,* December 1850, 515.

20. By the fall of 1857 Corcoran (in retirement) had ceased buying rails and had begun a slow liquidation. Holdings ranging up

to $100,000 (with more by Bright and other friends) in the Lake Erie, Wabash & St. Louis and the Toledo & Illinois proved particularly "unfortunate." See C to C&R, Oct. 24, 1850, C to Winslow, Lanier, Mar. 12, 1851, July 23, 1852, Feb. 21, June 15, 1853, C to Cammann, Whitehouse, July 6, 1852, C to Whitehouse, Feb. 27, 28, Mar. 2, 1854, Oct. 1, 1856, memos, July 17, Nov. 25, 1857, C to Russell Sage, Dec. 5, 10, 1857, Mar. 11, 1858, C to E. D. Morgan, Feb. 10, Mar. 11, 1858, C to Michael G. Bright, Aug. 11, 1858, Hyde to R. R. Springer, Aug. 20, 1856, Hyde to J. M. Forbes, July 30, 1858, C to R & Co. (N.Y.), May 3, 1849, Jan. 4, 1852, C to Samuel Vinton, Dec. 28, 1851, C Letter Books; J. F. A. Sanford to C&R, May 5, 9, July 23, 1852, R Papers; C account, 1852, C&R ledgers.

21. In 1852 Corcoran joined others in lending up to $80,000 to repair damage caused by a flash flood, stipulating that this loan be given first priority of payment after wages and other operating expenses. By 1854 he was one of five trustees of the canal, and when two of his colleagues died he took the initiative in naming their successors. He also lobbied in the Maryland legislature. After the Civil War Corcoran, holding bonds of $40,000 face value selling at 18, resumed his participation in the company's affairs. "We must be very circumspect in keeping the control of the company . . . in the interest of the bondholders," he wrote. Later he added to his holdings and tried to make the company's administration independent of Maryland politics, which, he asserted, had long damaged it. He supported Henry D. Cooke, Republican boss of District of Columbia politics and brother of Jay Cooke, among others nominated to the board. See C to Selden, July 9, 1845, C to Samuel Henshaw & Son, Nov. 25, 30, 1848, C to Worthington, Mar. 27, 1849, C to Grayson and Fist, July 21, 1852, C to Horatio Allen, July 2, 1854, C to Morey and J. P. Poe, Aug. 3, C to J. B. H. Smith, Sept. 7, C to clerk of the court, Rockville, Montgomery Co., n.d., Nov. 17, C to George Morey, Apr. 27, 1855, C to Alexander, Mar. 3, 1856, C to George Peters, Board of Public Works, n.d., memo, Jan. 21, 1857. See also C to Thomas Clemson, Sept. 6, 1866, C to R. H. Maury & Co., Mar. 23, June 6, 1867, C to J. B. H. Smith, Mar. 28, C to Burke, Herbert & Co., May 31, Hyde to C, July 7, 1868, C to Thomas Swan (gov. of Md.), June 1, C to Smith, to Allen, and to Poe, Nov. 9, 1869, C Letter Books; ER to Peabody, Dec. 31, 1847, R Letter Books; C to William B.

Beverly, Jan. 25, 1856, Beverly Family Papers, VHS; Hidy, *House of Baring,* 327; Goodrich, *Government Promotion,* 81.

22. Corcoran's statement that this would be his income appears to have been exaggerated. See ch. 4, above, for his major gains from banking; M. Hidy, "Peabody," 267.

23. The Anglo-American banker, Baring partner Joshua Bates, described Jenny Lind as "a great personage although small in stature and knows as well as any of 'Sam Slick's' family on which side her bread is buttered." See GWR to ER, May 2, 27, 1850, DePL; P. T. Barnum to BB, Apr. 30, 1850, Baring Papers; C to Bates, Sept. 5, BPOC; Bates to C, Aug. 16, notebook with guest lists, C Papers; Corcoran, *Grandfather's Legacy,* 64–5, 158–60; Marian Gouverneur, *As I Remember* (New York, 1911), 197; Allan Nevins, *Ordeal of the Union,* 2 vols. (New York, 1947), II, 55.

24. See C to mayor of Georgetown, July 17, 1848, Feb. 4, 1861, C to Rev. Brooke, Nov. 1, 1851, C to Skinner, Dec. 16, C to Henry Erben, Dec. 20, C to James A. Hamilton, Aug. 11, 1852, C to Dorothea Dix, Mar. 23, 1853, C to Sarah Grimke, Mar. 24, 1854, C to trustees, Corcoran Charity Fund, Jan. 26, 1857, C to Schmidt, Nov. 13, C to Mrs. Eliza Chubb, Nov. 1, 1859, C Letter Books; Mrs. Noon and others to C, Dec. 16, 1851, GWR to C, July 22, 1855, E. N. Gurley to C, Apr. 10, 1858, Mrs. Chubb to C [1859], C Papers; C to Dorothea Dix, July 27, 1854, Dix Papers, HU Library; Richard X. Evans, "The Ladies Union Benevolent and Employment Society, 1850," *Records of Columbia Historical Society,* 162; Corcoran, *Grandfather's Legacy,* 92, 162; Nevins, *Ordeal,* I, 126.

25. Corcoran also bought more than $4,000 worth of books through the secretary of the Legation in London. In contrast, Dorothea Dix tried unsuccessfully to sell him works of more substantial artists obtained at the same time by Rome Vice-Consul Freeman, himself a well-known artist: a Poussin for $600, a Salvator Rosa, a painting of the school of Guido. See C to William G. Ouseley, Aug. 20, Sept. 29, 1852, C to C. B. David, Aug. 23, C to ER, Jan. 6, 1853, C to Lewis Cass, Jr., Sept. 23, C to W. Bucknell, Oct. 28, 1854, C to R & Co. (N.Y.), Dec. 21, 1855, C to Edward Hildebrandt, Mar. 7, 1856, C to Rauch, Oct. 28, C to A. B. Mathausen, Nov. 24, C to H. B. Möllhausen, Nov. 22, 1859, C to Meade, Jan. 14, 1860, memo, Apr. 18, 1853, C Letter Books;

Thomas G. Clemson to C, Aug. 24, 1850, Cass to C, Dec. 5, Dix to C, May 30, 1851, Rauch to C, Aug. 23, 1856, C Papers; ch. 12 below, sec. 3.

26. See C to Möllhausen, Nov. 22, 1859, C Letter Books; Möllhausen to C, June 1, Oct. 24, 1859, J. Lenox to C, Aug. 1, Baron Gerolt to Henry, Aug. 2, Henry to C, Sept. 3, C Papers; Robert Taft, *Artists and Illustrators of the Old West, 1850–1900* (New York, 1953), ch. 2.

27. Through his friend Edward Everett, Corcoran later negotiated for Powers' *America.* The price of $12,000 was high, Everett said, but within European standards for a first-class work. Congress had appropriated $25,000 to buy it but the purchase had been defeated by President Pierce's indecision "and some sinister and adverse influences." Everett had a copy, "semi-draped, entirely suitable for a private home." Apparently Corcoran withstood the temptation. See Selden to C, June 6, 1851, Sidney Brooks to Everett, May 9, 1860, Everett to C, May 30, C Papers; scrapbook, passim, and miscellaneous material, Corcoran Gallery; New York *Courier and Enquirer,* March 1, 1851.

Typical of the range of prices (with most near the lower end) were $70 to G. D. Brewerton for a *Prairie Scene* and $2,500 to Emanuel Leutze for *Cromwell & Milton* (although Corcoran expressed some disappointment with the latter). See C to Robert Mills, May 14, 1852, C to Boston Atheneum, Mar. 22, 1853, C to G. D. Brewerton, Feb. 6, 1854, C to B ——, Mar. 16, C to William D. Washington, July 11, Dec. 15, C to Miss Margaret G. Meade, Jan. 24, 1855, C to Loehner, Feb. 9, C to Peabody, Dec. 17, C to Miss Emma Richards, Mar. 7, 1856, C to Clemson, Jan. 5, 1857, C to M. F. Maury, Feb. 6, C to Eastman Johnson, Mar. 14, C to Clark, Apr. 17, C to John C. King, Nov. 11, 1858, C to D. W. Alvord, Oct. 13, 1859, C to Field, Mar. 27, 1860, C to Joseph Henry, passim, and memos, Dec. 13–14, 1857, Sept. 14–16, 1861, C Letter Books; D. Huntington to C, Aug. 28, 1850, Charles Lanman to C, Sept. 16, 1850, Nov. 20, 1861 (expressing the wish to do for Corcoran what Washington Irving had done for John Jacob Astor—request declined), Clem. West to C, Jan. 23, 1855, Washington to C, July 3, Alvord to Everett, Feb. 17, 1856, Clemson to C, Jan. 3, 1857, Everett to C, Mar. 15, 16, 1858, Richards to C, Dec. 1, 1856, May 7, July 11, 1860, S. R. Meiklehan to C, Aug. 13, 1857, J. D. Bruff to C. Oct. 5, 1860, C Papers; Corcoran,

Grandfather's Legacy, 134; Nevins, *Ordeal,* II, 527; ch. 12, below. For comparison, see also description of the collection of August Belmont, New York *Times,* Dec. 19, 1857.

Chapter 7

1. In Baltimore, the Chesapeake and Baltimore banks were regular sources of credit. For a time the Bank of Philadelphia was an important correspondent. Its president, Joseph R. Evans, was an old ally of Newbold's, having secretly kept him informed of the plans of Philadelphia financiers in the late stages of the Bank War. See C&R ledgers; Evans to Newbold, May 3, July 5, 1838, Newbold Papers, NYHS.

A symbiotic relationship between commercial banks and investment houses was common. In Corcoran's circle the outstanding example was Cammann, Whitehouse and the Merchants Bank, whose cashier was Oswald J. Cammann, cousin of the broker. See Philip G. Hubert, Jr., *The Merchants National Bank of the City of New York . . . 1803–1903* (New York, 1903), 122–3.

2. When Walker left office the Whig New York *Courier and Enquirer* editorially denigrated his record and credited Corcoran's management, among other things, for saving him from the consequences of the sub-Treasury and the lower tariff. The article, despite its factual blunders, found its way into Corcoran's scrapbook with evident approval, and into Walker's papers as an example of the malice of his detractors. See Jaudon to Webster, Apr. 5, 1849, Meredith Papers, PaHS; clipping, Samuel H. Porter to Walker, May 1 or 2, 1849, Walker Papers, LC; John L. Aspinwall to C, June 25, 1851, R Papers, LC; Corcoran Scrapbook, Corcoran Gallery of Art, Washington; William Wilson Corcoran, *A Grandfather's Legacy* (Washington, 1879), 104; James P. Shenton, *Robert John Walker: A Politician from Jackson to Lincoln* (New York and London, 1961), 116. Cf. Richard Henry Timberlake, Jr., "Treasury Monetary Policies from Jackson to Lincoln" (Ph.D. diss., University of Chicago, 1959), 62.

3. See, for example, Newbold's confident observation in 1848 that the money market was difficult but firmness would control it: Newbold to Ward, Jan. 18, 1848, Newbold Papers; n. 5, below. But the bankers were also denounced for operating with a cleaver

instead of a scalpel in 1851: "The Bank People have acted with little wisdom, contracting in a week what wise & judicious Bankers would have taken six weeks to accomplish, making a sort of panic, & forcing people to large sacrifices when there was no necessity for Either." Winslow, Lanier to C, Aug. 5, 1851, R Papers, LC.

4. See Walter Buckingham Smith, *Economic Aspects of the Second Bank of the United States* (Cambridge, 1953), 61; Fritz Redlich, *Molding of American Banking: Men and Ideas,* 2 vols. (New York, 1947–1951), II, 7 and ch. 10 passim; Bray Hammond, *Banks and Politics in America from the Revolution to the Civil War* (Princeton, 1957), ch. 21.

5. See Newbold to [Woodbury], Dec. n.d., 1835, extract from Spring Rice to Jacob Harvey, Jan. n.d., 1839, Newbold to Ward, Jan. 19, 1848, Olcott to Newbold, May 1, 1852, Newbold Papers; ch. 4, n. 26, and n. 3, above.

Bray Hammond misses the point when he says that even such outstanding bankers as Nicholas Biddle and Albert Gallatin understood "very imperfectly" the need for liquid reserves against deposits as well as notes. When Wall Street's leaders opposed fixed legal reserve requirements on deposits while accepting them against notes it was because they *did* understand their identity as liabilities. If Newbold is representative of most bankers on this point (and it is difficult to think otherwise), they were hostile to substantial government regulation. When public opinion favoring regulation grew too strong, the bankers advocated measures that would appear effective but in fact would leave them maximum freedom from control. See Hammond, *Banks and Politics,* 689–90; Olcott to Newbold, Dec. 13, 20, 1828, Newbold to Olcott, Dec. 17, Newbold Papers.

6. The discussion of the ratio of loans to net deposits plus circulation in Smith and Cole, *Fluctuations in American Business,* is somewhat beside the point, given the decline of loans and the spectacular recovery of gold. The authors ascribe the specie gains to events that could not have been foreseen, e.g., unusually heavy shipments from California. This overlooks the fact that the banks did not merely restore accustomed sound reserve ratios, but prolonged ratios that were sensationally higher than any in memory. See references in n. 8 below.

The cashier and future president of the Bank of America later blamed the foreign exchange situation for the banks' course, but an eminent British financier thought this factor may have favored the Americans. Cf. James Punnett to Olcott, Dec. 27, 1860, Olcott Papers, ColU Library; Elmer Wood, *English Theories of Central Banking Control, 1819–1858* (Cambridge, 1939), 161–2 and reference cited therein, n. 81.

Defensive against severe strictures from Boston, the New Yorkers irrelevantly revived earlier attacks on State Street's use of bank credit to finance fixed investment. See John A. Stevens to Nathan Appleton, Oct. 2, 1857, Bank of Commerce Papers, criticizing Boston's long-term developmental "credits ramified to the last degree." Cf. Newbold to Ward, Jan. 19, 1848, Newbold Papers; BB to Ward, July 7, BPLB.

7. See C to Newbold, Sept. 18, 19, 26, 29, Oct. 6, 7, 10, 1857, C Letter Books; U.S. Bureau of the Census, *Historical Statistics of the United States, Colonial Times to 1957* (Washington, 1960), 712, 721; Roy F. Nichols, *The Disruption of American Democracy* (New York, 1948), 132–4.

8. There was a common assumption that, in the leaders' place, most bankers would have done the same. See Stevens to S. Mercer, Sept. 24, 1857, Apr. 30, 1861, Stevens to N. Appleton, Oct. 2, 1857, Bank of Commerce Papers; Aspinwall to Newbold, Oct. 15, Newbold Papers; George Templeton Strong, *Diary,* eds. Allan Nevins and M. H. Thomas, 4 vols. (New York, 1952), II, 263; *Bankers Magazine,* 1857–1858, 406–20, 566–7; reports of New York State bank overseers listed in Adelaide R. Hasse, *Index of Economic Material in Documents of the States . . . New York, 1789–1904* (Washington, 1907), 43; New York State superintendent of banking [James M. Cook], *Annual Report,* 1858; J. S. Gibbons, *The Banks of New York . . . and the Panic of 1857* (New York, 1858), ch. 19; Walter Buckingham Smith and Arthur Harrison Cole, *Fluctuations in American Business, 1790–1860* (Cambridge, 1935), 130–5; Redlich, *Molding American Banking,* II, 5, 273 and ch. 12; Hammond, *Banks and Politics,* 68f; Ralph W. Hidy, *House of Baring in American Trade and Finance: English Merchant Bankers at Work, 1763–1860* (Cambridge, 1949), 454.

Baring partner Joshua Bates drily remarked that the strangest thing about the Panic of 1857 was its occurring without a Biddle, a Bank of the United States, or a Jackson. See Bates to Buchanan, Nov. 5, 1857, Buchanan Papers. Cf. Newbold to Olcott, Feb. 5,

1838, Newbold Papers; Hoyt to Woodbury, Sept. 23, 1839, Woodbury Papers, LC; Hammond, *Banks and Politics,* 477.

9. Among recent overviews of the monetary history of this period, Thomas D. Willett, "International Specie Flows and American Monetary Stability, 1834–1860," *Journal of Economic History* 28 (March 1968), 38–40 and n. 33, has grasped the theoretical possibility of banking atomization but, lacking historical perspective, he does not recognize it as a changing, dynamic factor. Some reformulation will be necessary if accurate causal relationships are to be established, for many causes of monetary and cyclical change must be traced back to the structure of institutions and the behavior of the entrepreneurs. The same point applies to Willett's later remarks about "decision-makers" in the abstract. The "pessimism" that struck a vulnerable banking structure derived in part from the same kind of political-economic atomization and exuberance that affected railroad-building described in ch. 11, below.

Chapter 8

1. Lewis Coryell, Richard M. Cox, Secretary of the Treasury Walker, and George W. Strong (counsel for the line) were among the successful lobbyists. See C&R to ER, Apr. 5, 12, 1845, Apr. 7, 1846, June 24, Oct. 1, 5, 1847, R Papers, LC; ER to C&R, Oct. 2, 4, 7, ER to Collins, Oct. 7, 8, ER Letter Book; Cave Johnson to C, Feb. 14, 1849, C Papers, LC; Collins to Lewis Coryell, Mar. 16, Coryell Papers, PaHS; New York *Herald,* Sept. 27, 1850; John G. Dow, "The Collins Line" (Master's thesis, Columbia University, 1937), 3–19. For a concise discussion of the Collins Line, see John G. B. Hutchins, *American Maritime Industries and Public Policy, 1889–1914* (Cambridge, 1941), 351–8.

2. Joseph Riggs, Elisha's son, was a junior partner in Collins' agency. Corcoran kept $24,000 of bonds personally and, with Elisha Riggs, became a director. Peabody, dubious of the high costs of the liners, later said that he took $10,000 of bonds only to please Wetmore and Riggs. The shipbuilders were paid $300,000 worth of bonds. See ER to C&R, Sept. 29, 1847, ER to Peabody, Nov. 18, Dec. 31, ER to SR, Dec. 20, 23, ER Letter Books; C&R to ER, Jan. 26, 1848, GWR to C&R, July 28, 1852, R Papers; C to M. Livingston, Nov. 28, 1854, Jan. 23, 1855, C Letter Books;

Peabody to ER, Jan. 3, 1851, Peabody Papers, EI; C to Bates, June 17, 1850, BPOC; C, GWR accounts, C&R ledgers; Dow, "Collins Line," 23–6.

3. The influence of the Cunarders was feared. The Russian minister to Washington, Alexander de Bodisco, a good friend of Corcoran, assisted him in the lobby. See Wetmore to ER, Feb. 21, 27, 1851, ER, Jr., to ER, Mar. 1, Jan. 21, 1852, R Papers; Buchanan to Cave Johnson, Sept. 3, Dec. 3, 1851, Buchanan Papers, PaHS; New York *Courier & Enquirer,* Mar. 5, 1851; U.S., Congress, *Congressional Globe,* 31st Cong., 2d sess., 833, 834, 836; Dow, "Collins Line," 41–2, 50–1.

4. The *Union* began a long series of articles with the declaration they would examine both sides of the question; however, all but one or two favored the Collins Line. See Washington *Semi-Weekly Union,* Jan. 31, Feb. 7, 14, 21, Mar. 20, 27, Apr. 3, May 1, 8, 1852; see also New York *Courier & Enquirer,* Jan. 24, whose publisher, James Watson Webb, was a friend and sometimes debtor of Corcoran. C to Webb, July 1, 1847, May 9, 1851, Apr. 25, 1853, C Letter Books; Webb to William H. Seward, Nov. 27, 1849, C Papers.

5. Edward Mott Robinson (New Bedford, Mass.) to C&R, Mar. 4, 1852, E. Corning (Albany) to C&R, Mar. 13, Samuel P. Walker (Memphis) to C&R, Apr. 2, V. K. Stevenson (Nashville) to C&R, Apr. 4, Collins (with petititions from New York and from Fall River and Fairhaven, Mass.) to C&R, Apr. 20, G. Brown to C&R, June 26 (with the assurance that Rep. Thos. Walsh of Md. would be a supporter), R Papers; Alex. Brown & Sons (Baltimore) to Wetmore, Feb. 28, Brown & Sons to C&R, Mar. 1, June 22, 1852, Brown & Sons to Collins, May 30, 1853, Alex. Brown & Sons Letter Books, LC.

6. The names of the eventual recipients among the members were left discreetly unrecorded, except for Representative David S. Kaufman (Dem., Texas) who received $2,000 of bonds. Benjamin B. French complained mildly of receiving only $300 for inducing an opposing Congressman to absent himself from the vote. Corcoran's personal account only erratically specifies names and very rarely purposes. Some entries may represent notes rather than bribes (e.g., Vinton), or derive from other lobbying efforts, or originate from ordinary business transactions (although perhaps indirectly related to lobbying). With appropriate caution, therefore,

each of the following entries may (some certainly do) pertain to the Collins Line subsidy.

Debits			*Credits*		
Recipient	*Date*	*$*	*Depositor*	*Date*	*$*
Glossbrenner	7/23	1,000	Corcoran	7/31	3,000
Corcoran	7/24	2,000	J. K. Walker	8/16	3,000
Armstrong	8/6	3,000	Bright	8/18	5,000
Sullivan	8/6	1,000	Wetmore	9/1	13,000
Wetmore	8/8	2,000	Wetmore	9/3	7,200
Burke	8/12	1,000			
James Whitcomb	8/12	5,000			
Corcoran	8/31	5,000			
S. F. Vinton	9/7	3,000			
Sullivan	9/29	4,000			
L. C. Levin	9/30	2,500			
J. K. Walker	9/30	3,000			

There were three deposits of $30,000 to $40,000 each by Brown Brothers in this period, but these may represent the usual exchange or other transactions with this large house. There were, as usual, many credits and debits whose sums were noted without names. Finally, some entries before and after this peak period of activity might prove relevant if the details could be known. See Brown Bros. to C&R, Apr. 22, 24, 1852, Charles O. Waters to C&R, June 15, F. J. Grund to C&R, Apr. 15, 1853, George Clapp to C&R, Apr. 30, Oct. 3, R Papers; C to Collins, July 23, C Letter Books; B. B. French to H. F. French, Sept. 5, French Papers, LC; C, Burke, and J. K. Walker accounts, C&R ledgers.

7. For the Texas debt see ch. 10, below.

There was some internal dissension over company policy with Elisha Riggs and other directors expressing a dislike of Collins, but this was kept quiet. See Wetmore to ER, Jan. 27, Apr. 12, 1852, ER, Jr., to ER, Apr. 7, 17, Brown Bros. to C&R, Apr. 19, 22, 24, James Brown to C, Apr. 29, R Papers; C to Peabody, Jan. 31, ER to Peabody, Apr. 17, Peabody Papers; C to Samuel Lawrence, Apr. 3, C to Brown Bros., Apr. 28, C to ER, May 12, C to James Brown, Aug. 28, C Letter Books; Cave Johnson to Buchanan, May

20, Buchanan Papers; U.S., Congress, *Congressional Globe,* 32d Cong., 1st sess., 1146f, 1376f, 1489f; Roy F. Nichols, *The Democratic Machine,* 1850–1854 (New York, 1923), 110–1.

8. That perceptive critic, Congressman R. K. Meade (Dem., Va.), saw through the earlier pretenses that the line was losing money. See Thomas J. Rusk to Meade, July 11, 1852, Rusk Papers, UTex; report of New York and Liverpool United States Mail Steamship Co. (official name of the Collins Line), Sept. 15, 1852, GWR to ER, Apr. 19, 1853, R Papers; C to Dangerfield, Apr. 8, 15, C to Wetmore, July 25, Aug. 3, 1853, Apr. 16, 1855, Mar. 3, 1858, C to James Brown, Nov. 26, 1853, C to Collins, Apr. 24, Nov. 20, 24, 28, Dec. 1, 1854, Hyde to C, Jan. 4, 1855, statement, Mar. 22, Apr. 16, 1855, C to ER, Nov. 30, 1854, Mar. 20, Apr. 12, 1855, ER to C, Jan. 5, C to Peabody, Jan. 26, C to R&Co. (N.Y.), Apr. 12, C Letter Books; ER and C accounts, C&R ledgers; GWR to Peabody, Dec. 6, 1853, Nov. 14, 1854, Peabody Papers; ER private ledger, Mar.–Apr., 1855, R Papers; Collins to A. D. Mann, Dec. 1, 14, 1858, NYHS; Dow, "Collins Line," 72–101; Robert Greenhalgh Albion, *The Rise of New York Port, 1815–1860* (New York and London, 1939), 326.

9. See C to Jefferson Davis, Mar. 8, 16, Oct. 13, 1854, C to Col. Craig, Oct. 14, C to Robert McLane, Mar. 8, 1855, C to ER, Jr., Nov. 17, 1856, Apr. 30, 1857, C to Col. Freeman, Sept. 25, 1857, Hyde to Freeman, July 23, Hyde to C, July 23, 1857, May 15, 1858, C to John B. Floyd, Oct. 28, 1857, Hyde to Maynard, Jan. 15, 20, Dec. 19, 1859, memo, Apr. 21, 23, 1858, Oct. 8, 1860, Apr. 6, 1861, C Letter Books; C account, C&R ledgers.

10. Others mentioned as lobbyists were J. B. Steward, James Christie (presumably the Texas creditor), and John Hayes; Amos Davis received over $4,000 "for services." See memos, Apr. 1853, Barlow Papers; C to Appleton, Feb. 24, Apr. 21, 23, 1855, C to William Chauncey, Feb. 17, 1857, powers of attorney to Corcoran, Sept. 23, Hyde to Isaac Toucey, Oct. 5, C to George Badger, Oct. 31, C to fourth auditor, Nov. 27, C to De Launay, Iselin & Clark, Dec. 5, C to D. R. Martin, Ocean Bank, New York City, Dec. 5, C to Groesbeck & Co., Dec. 9, 11, C to Edmund Monroe, Dec. 7, C to Thomas A. Dexter, Dec. 9, C to Samuel R. Brooks, Dec. 9, C to Solomon Foot, Dec. 20, receipt, Dec. 19, C to George W. Hodges, Jan. 20, 1858, C Letter Books; U.S., Congress, 35th Cong., 1st sess., *Senate Executive Document* 57. Note also George

Harrington to Thurlow Weed, Apr. 17, 1856, Weed Papers, URoch.

11. "I had hoped and expected that a fair proposition would have been made and accepted which would have enabled us to move on in peace and harmony for mutual benefit," Corcoran characteristically commented. See C to B. B. French, Aug. 17, 1847, C to Kendall, May 7, 1851, Nov. 17, 1852, Jan. 22, July 12, 1853, C to George H. Hart, Jan. 19, 1853, Oct. 21, 1856, C to Abel R. Corbin, Jan. 19, 1853, Oct. 21, 1856, C to Abel R. Corbin, Jan. 19, 1853, C to Cyrus W. Field, Dec. 22, 1857, Hyde to Kendall, Dec. 1, 1857, memos, July 14, 1851, Oct. 21, 1859, C Letter Books; St. Paul *Pioneer & Democrat,* June 17, 1858; Washington *National Intelligencer,* Feb. [c. 24, 27], 1869, clipping in scrapbook, Corcoran Gallery of Art, Washington; William Wilson Corcoran, *A Grandfather's Legacy* (Washington, 1879), 292.

12. During the preceding decade the federal government had taken possession of scattered tracts from defaulted debtors. Many had been entered on a large scale by land office or other officials such as William Linn in Illinois, William and Gordon Boyd in Mississippi, the Rectors in Arkansas and elsewhere, Lucius Lyon and Henry R. Schoolcraft in Michigan, and Samuel Swartwout of New York. In 1845 an influential Pennsylvania businessman, Lewis Coryell, tried to buy an iron establishment in Maryland and lands in Texas and Illinois formerly owned by Swartwout, who was perhaps the most notorious federal defalcator of the time. Coryell was supported by some Treasury officials, including Secretary George M. Bibb, but not Solicitor Charles B. Penrose who had jurisdiction: he thought the offers too low. Bibb decided to overrule Penrose but the deal could not be consummated before Polk became President.

The squabble resumed in the new administration. Secretary Walker's Pennsylvania father-in-law, Vice-President George M. Dallas, supported Coryell while the new solicitor, Barton, took his predecessor's position. A deal was apparently worked out between Barton and Coryell's agent, ex-Secretary of the Treasury Samuel D. Ingham, but in the spring of 1847, after long delay, Barton was overruled. That worthy servant loyally resigned, as on taking office he had promised to do in case of policy disagreement; he was rewarded and removed with assignment as chargé to Chile. His successor was Gillett, previously register of the Treasury, former congressman from New York, and a trusted courier and adviser of Polk before his nomination for the presidency. Gillett promptly advertised all the lands possessed from defaulted debtors for sale to the highest bidders. See William Young to Lewis Coryell, Feb. 28, 1845, Bibb notations on foregoing, Mar. 3, Swartwout to Walker, Mar. 19, Young to Seth Barton, Apr. 18, Barton to Charles Penrose, Apr. 16, Barton to Young, Apr. 19, Penrose to Barton, May 19, Dallas, opinion, May 10, Barton to Walker, May 23, S. D. Ingham to Coryell, Nov. 4, J. N. Barnett to Walker, Sept. 16, 1847, Walker to Gillett, Sept. 28, Gillett to Walker, Oct. 11, AB Letters; Gillett to Polk, Dec. 9, 1845, Barton to Polk, May 27, 1847, Polk Papers, LC; Dallas to Walker, June 6, 1846, Walker Papers, LC; Gillett to C, Nov. 26, 1847, C Papers; Swartwout to D. Green, Dec. 2, 1847, Green Papers, SoHC; C to James Drane, Mar. 10, 1851, C to solicitor, Apr. 19, 1858, C to Cleghorn & Harrison, Apr. 19, May 10, copy, memo of July 26, 1869, Sept. 16–17, 1869, C Letter Books; Simon L. Sommers to Schoolcraft, Sept. 24, 26, 1859, unbound letterpress copies, C Papers; Leo Hershkowitz, " 'The Land of Promise': Samuel Swartwout and Land Speculation in Texas, 1830–38," *New York Historical Society Quarterly* (October 1964), 308, 312, 319.

13. I have discussed Corcoran's land dealings in "Vicissitudes of an Absentee Landlord: a Case Study," in David M. Ellis, ed., *The Frontier in Western Development: Essays in Honor of Paul Wallace Gates* (Ithaca, 1969).

14. Walker to Gillett, Sept. 28, 1847, B Letters; opinion of Attorney General Nathan Clifford, Oct. 25, on Gillett to Walker, Oct. 11, AB Letters; Swartwout to Coryell, Jan. 14, 1848, Coryell Papers; C to Gillett, Nov. 26, 1847, July 11, 1848, C to James Conkling, Feb. 4, 1848, C to Selden, Feb. 15, C to James B. Murray, Mar. 14, C to William Woodruff, Mar. 25, C to Meek, Apr. 1, C to John Wentworth, April 1, C to William Thomasson, May 24, C to Swann, Sept. 12, C to various collectors in Mississippi, Mar. 10, 11, 1851, C to John A. Jones, Apr. 1, C to C. S. Morehead, July 30, 1852, Hyde to C, Oct. 10, 1853, C to R. H. Maury, Nov. 1, 1854, Hyde to collector, Hackensack, N.J., Oct. 5, 1855, C to Sommers, June 22, 1868, copy, memo of July 26, 1869, Sept. 16–17, 1869, Hyde to Green & Wise, Jan. 18, 1874, C Letter Books; advertisement, Washington *Union*, Aug. 17f. 1847.

15. To the politicians, these transactions represented everything from routine business and favors for constituents to patronage and

the strengthening of machines through recommendations of agents. All stripes and parties are represented in the correspondence in these contexts. The names of pertinent politicians are mentioned in parentheses where they are not apparent from the references themselves. References are to C Letter Books unless noted otherwise.

Arkansas: C to Woodruff (Chester Ashley), Mar. 25, May 23, 1848, C to Solon Borland, Feb. 6, 1849, C to Rev. John Bruton, Feb. 6, 1849, C to S. J. Brandenburg, Dec. 8, 1854, C to Thompson B. Flourney (Robert W. Johnson), Feb. 10, 1855, C to Sommers (Thomas B. Hanley of the state supreme court), Jan. 5, 1858, C to Shall & Miller (chosen as successor to Woodruff, despite the latter's recommendation and because of Johnson's), May 13, 1867, C to Gouge (hiring the Jacksonian monetary publicist to inspect lands in Texas, Arkansas, and Mississippi, in the last of which he had absentee holdings), Apr. 2, 1851 (also Gouge to C&R, passim, R Papers);

Indiana: C to John G. Davis, Jan. 20, 23, Feb. 7, 8, 1854, C to John L. Robinson, May 28, 1855, C to James Hughes, Apr. 20, 1857, C to David Turpie, Feb. 24, 1858 (also C to Caleb B. Smith, Apr. 1, 1850, N. W. Johnson to Smith, Nov. 12, 1849, C. B. Smith Papers, LC);

Mississippi: C to Albert G. Brown, July 24, 1848, Feb. 23, Mar. 9, Apr. 13 (concerning renewal of loan to Brown of $650), 1854, Feb. 6, 11, 1856, July 11, 1857, notation, Apr. 11, 1854, C to William S. Barry, Mar. 22, 1854, C to Otho R. Singleton, Apr. 10, June 29, July 5, 1854, C to Thomas Presley, Sept. 14, 1853, Feb. 11, 1854, C to Lewis Presley, Oct. 13, 1857, C to Jefferson Davis, Aug. 11, 1854, C to William Barksdale, Jan. 3, 1859, C to Jacob Thompson (the following Mississippi references also pertaining to him), Oct. 13, 1857, C to Wade, Aug. 28, 1848, C to William Cochran, Sept. 12, 1848 (also ch. 9, below);

Illinois: C to John McClernand, Feb. 7, 1849, C to J. C. Robinson, June 7, 1860, C to Stephen B. Moore, July 16, 1860, Hyde to E. C. Ingersoll, June 18, 1864, C to Owen Lovejoy, Feb. 16, 1867, list for Senator Lyman Trumbull, July 18, 1867;

Michigan: C to J. N. Rogers (Sen. Charles Stuart), June 17, 1848, C to Osmond D. Smith (Sen. Alpheus Felch), June 10, 1848, C to George M. Peck, Feb. 12, 1856;

Others: C to Presley Ewing (Ky.), Jan. 24, Apr. 4, 15, 1854; C to James D. Doty (Wis.), Oct. 14, 1852, C to S. R. Curtis

(Iowa), Dec. 23, 1858, C to James W. Grimes (Iowa), Dec. 24, 1858, Jan. 5, Feb 3, 26, 1859, C to Wamsley (Va., the later W. Va.), Dec. 1, 1853, C to Gillett, May 7, 1851, C to John C. Clarke, solicitor of the Treasury, June 4, 1851, C to Joshua Van Sant, Jan. 27, 1855, C Letter Books. With Bright, Corcoran was to join Sen. George W. Jones of Iowa in an investment of $5,000 each, apparently in land there, but the deal fell through. He declined an offer by Lincoln Clarke of Iowa to join in an operation using forthcoming land warrants. See C to Clarke, May 24, 1855, C Letter Books; Bright to Jones, Nov. 10, 1853, Jones Papers, Iowa State Dept. of History and Archives, Des Moines. Earlier, Woodruff, a prominent newspaper editor, had been Arkansas agent for Romulus Riggs of Philadelphia. Woodruff to John Elliott, Jan. 30, 1849, R Papers.

16. Others interested in the Stoddard Addition included W. H. Tilghman, Virgil Maxcy, Clement Biddle, Samuel Burche, and C. J. Coots. Perhaps these tracts were also remnants of the Bank of the United States. See William T. Sherman to Ewing, June 5, 1851, Ewing to Ewing, Jr., Sept. 14, Ewing Papers; C to Ewing, Sept. 4, Dec. 3, 15, 1851, C to LR, Oct. 18, C to James Bolton, Sept. 27, 30, Nov. 3, Dec. 10, 1851, Aug. 11, 1852, C to collector of taxes, St. Louis, May 24, 1852, memos, Feb. 9, 1852, Jan. 31, 1855, Apr. 26, 1864, Hyde to C, Sept. 18, 1855, C to Charles Mason, Mar. 10, 1856, C to county tax collector, Washington, Feb. 24, 1858, Hyde to Henry D. Cooke, July 20, 1863, Hyde to C, May 4, 25, 28, 1863, Hyde to Commissioner of Internal Revenue, May 11, 1863, memos, Oct 29, 1868, July 6, 1871, C Letter Books.

17. But an undefined request from J. D. B. DeBow of *DeBow's Review* was refused. Smith Homans, editor and publisher of *Bankers Magazine,* was obviously ill-informed when he asked Corcoran to help him secure a minor job with the Taylor administration. (His journal did not pay $500 per year, he complained in 1849. Soon afterward he moved it from Baltimore to Boston.) Burnley had former Treasury Secretary George M. Bibb as cosigner of many of his notes. Commenting on the accession of Donelson and Armstrong as publishers of the *Union* in 1851, Francis P. Blair showed a continuing and well-informed bitterness in singling out Corcoran among "the Polk inheritors," whom he characterized as steamer and land speculators and "borers for

claims." Perhaps another wisp of smoke from smoldering enmities was Corcoran's having to sue John C. Rives, Blair's old partner, in 1851 for payment of an old $1,000 note. Toombs, a leader in the Galphin raid (below, ch. 9), also discounted with Corcoran a note for $750 from Representative E. C. Cabell of Florida. Apparently he was a leading congressional middleman for political loans, although ordinarily he would probably have obtained them from Whig bankers. See Homans to C, Mar. 21, 1849, Ritchie to C, Mar. 8, 11, 12, 1851, Donelson to C, Mar. 11, Cass to C, Mar. 26, 1851, Toombs to C, Sept. 6, 1853, C Papers; C to Heiss, May 18, 1849, C to J. B. H. Smith, Sept. 13, 1851, C to S. G. Haven, Apr. 3, 1852, C to Rives, Apr. 8, C to DeBow, Oct. 12, C to Burnley, memo, Aug. 5, 1854, Aug. 5, Oct. 13, Hyde to R & Co., Aug. 31, Hyde to C, Apr. 7, 1855, C Letter Books; Burnley to Crittenden, July 22, 1849, Crittenden Papers, LC; Burke to Douglas, Feb. 13, 1850, Douglas Papers, UChi; Blair to Van Buren, Mar. 10, 15, 1851, Van Buren Papers, LC; Rives to Blair, Dec. 10, Blair Papers; C and other accounts, C&R and R&Co. ledgers; Corcoran, *Grandfather's Legacy,* 64, 112, 119; Allan Nevins, *Ordeal of the Union,* 2 vols. (New York, 1947), I, 236, 242, 273; Nichols, *Democratic Machine,* 32; William Earl Parrish, *David Rice Atchison of Missouri, Border Politician* (Columbia, Mo. 1961), 101, 139–40. I have discussed other politicians' loans elsewhere in connection with specific issues.

Chapter 9

1. Waddy Thompson, holder of a claim shared by another South Carolinian, A. P. Hill, and one Lanphier, thought ¼ percent should satisfy the banker for simply collecting and transferring an award. Corcoran insisted he would have refused the agency at less than 5 percent, the lowest commission ever charged on claims. He had to threaten suit to obtain payment. Apparently the going rate declined by 1854, when Corcoran charged 2½ percent for commissions on a claim for which he forwarded a Treasury draft to California. See C&R to ER, Dec. 26, 1843, W. C. Pickersgill & Co. to C&R, Jan. 13, 1848, A. P. Hill and Waddy Thompson to C&R, Aug. 18, 24, 27, 1848, statement, Jan. 18, 1849, C to James King of William, Nov. 3, 1854, C Letter Books; Walker to C&R, Sept.

4, 1846, K Letters; Roy F. Nichols, *The Democratic Machine, 1850–1854* (New York, 1823), 108–10.

2. Corcoran bought one $20,000 claim for $18,000 and lobbied it through the Treasury within a month. He and Riggs were offered another. The commissioners who were sent out to investigate the case appear to have been interested, but Corcoran hesitated too long. (One Kurtz was involved, possibly the future Pennsylvania congressman in the pay of Texas creditors: below, next chapter.) A third time Crawford advised him to buy a claim against the Cherokees in Arkansas, adding that the representative of the Bank of the United States in Little Rock had offered to advance funds. See C to ER, May 2, 3, 8, 10, 25, 28, June 4, July 15, 16, 19, 20, 1839, R Papers, LC.

In 1841 a claim pressed by Corcoran & Riggs (in association with Richard S. Coxe and Matthew St. Clair Clark on behalf of Clements, Bryan & Co.) gave rise to a curious doctrine of bureaucratic particularism, a kind of counterpart within the administration of the doctrine of states rights. A decision on the case was disputed within the Treasury Department and referred to President Tyler. He consulted Secretary of War John C. Spencer and was so impressed by his opinion that he circulated it to the rest of the cabinet as official policy. To summarize, the President declined to intervene between subordinate officials (as requested by the claimant) on grounds that no law explicitly permitted him to do so in contravention of the independence of and balance of power among government offices. See J. C. Spencer, circular, Oct. 19, 1841, AB Letters, 1851, I, 1.

3. The Choctaw speculation dragged to a conclusion during the Fillmore administration. Corcoran lobbied in the Interior Department and the Bureau of Indian Affairs for $25,000 to satisfy W. B. Hart's claim for Indian removal expenses. A dispute over division of the proceeds led to court action in the District of Columbia and Boston and a settlement by arbitration. The account was finally closed at the end of 1853, Corcoran & Riggs receiving $3,000 and Senator Gwin $1,000. Hart had already overdrawn his share. See ch. 3, above; W. B. Hart to C&R, July 14, 1851, C to C. P. Curtis, Apr. 17, May 1, 1852, Hyde to C, Sept. 13, C to GWR, Sept. 28, 1852, Oct. 20, 21, 24, 1853, C to A. H. H. Stuart, Nov. 20, 1852, C to George Manypenny, Apr. 25, 1853, C to J. M Carlisle, Apr. 26, C&R to Joseph Bryan, May 6, C to Gwin, Dec. 14, C Letter Books.

4. See Hyde to Gwin, Aug. 29, 1848, C to Gwin, Feb. 7, 1849, C Letter Books; Gwin to C, Feb. 17, 1849, C Papers, LC; Gwin claim account, C & R ledgers; undated memo, Edmund Burke Papers, LC; James E. Harvey [Independent], Philadelphia *North American,* Jan. 26, 1849; U.S., Congress, 31st Cong., 1st sess., *House Report 489, "Indian Claims Investigation;"* James P. Shenton, *Robert John Walker, A Politician from Jackson to Lincoln* (New York and London, 1961), 32–4, 65–7; ch. 12, below.

5. If the papers of other Washington political bankers were available, especially Selden, Withers, and R. W. Latham, the picture could undoubtedly be made more complete. Latham worked for the Chickasaw interest. See Francis P. Blair to Martin Van Buren, 1851 passim, Van Buren Papers, LC; Blair special account, C&R ledgers.

6. Lawrason Riggs decided not to join his father and brother in New York; instead he founded a prominent St. Louis family. See ER to C&R, June 18, 1841, R Domestic Letters; C&R to Woodbury, Oct. 8, 1842, Woodbury Papers, LC; C&R, ER and SR joint accounts, 1843, ER accounts current book; C&R to ER, May 11, 13, 21, 29, July 11, Dec. 26, 1843, Jan. 30, Dec. 18, 1844, Jan. 11, 14, Feb. 14, 18, 24, Apr. 1, 29, July 11, 1845, Apr. 3, 9, May 1, 6, 12, 15, 20, 21, June 1, 13, 15, 1846, Aug. 14, 1847, GWR to ER, Mar. 22, 1844, Chouteau, Jr. & Co., memorandum of agreement of sale, Sept. 12, 1844, LR to ER, Aug. 23, 1845, July 10, 1847, C to ER, Oct. 29, R Papers; ER to C&R, Mar. 31, June 16, 1846, R Letter Book; C&R ledgers; Kenneth Wiggins Porter, *John Jacob Astor, Business Man,* 2 vols. (Cambridge, 1931), II, 1013.

7. Conclusion of the episode in detail is reserved to ch. 12, below. The affair also seems to have deepened the developing friendship between Corcoran and Jesse Bright. Later Corcoran bought shares of other sizable claims represented by Thompson. See Chouteau, Jr., & Co. to C&R, Aug. 2, 1847, R Papers; C to Benton, Jan. 2, 19, 1856, C Letter Books; anon., memo, Feb. 6, n.d., C Papers; C account, C&R ledgers; 31 Cong., 1 sess., *H. Report 489;* Paul Wallace Gates, "Introduction," *The John Tipton Papers,* eds. Nellie Armstrong Robertson and Dorothy Riker, 3 vols. (Indianapolis, 1942), I, 10f, 41f, 53; Charles Roll, *Colonel Dick Thompson, The Persistent Whig* (Indianapolis, 1948), 166f.

8. Whittlesey, however, did oppose paying interest on the Galphin claim (below). He alone of this group is untainted by loans

or payments in the Corcoran & Riggs ledgers. Thomas Ewing was apparently a more-or-less distant relative of the Indiana Ewings: he described himself as "no immediate relation." Of course there were broader political considerations in the Ewing-Corwin rapprochement, but self-interest was an important lubricant. The speculative Corwins were financially the most desperate and vulnerable of the Ohioans; Whittlesey and Vinton probably the least. See Corwin to C, Oct. 5, 1849, June 21, 1853, C Papers; C to Corwin, Mar. 29, 30, 1854, C to R. G. Corwin, June 5, Dec. 27, 1855, C to L. D. Campbell, Mar. 3, 1855, C to Thos. Ewing, Jr., Nov. 15, 1871, C Letter Books; R. G. Corwin and Thomas Ewing accounts, C&R ledgers; Ewing to Fillmore, July 18, 1850, Webster to Fillmore, July 10, W. G. Ewing to Fillmore, July 20, Fillmore Papers, BuffHS; GR to ER, Mar. 5, 1851, DetPL; C to Peabody, Apr. 11, 1851, Peabody Papers, EI; J. W. Allen to Corwin, Mar. 27, 1852, J. Probasco, Jr., to Corwin, Aug. 31, Corwin Papers; L. D. Campbell to C&R, July 22, 1852, R Papers; 31 Cong., 1 sess., *H. Report 489*.

9. One of the Galphin attorneys was Corcoran's old claims associate, Joseph Bryan. A Georgia Whig Senator, William Dawson, received $2,000 of loans from Corcoran. Within a month of the payment to Gwin the House of Representatives initiated an investigation, which terminated with a committee report condemning the transaction. A. G. Brown was one of the majority; Samuel Vinton signed a dissent. Jacob Thompson also joined the attack. Although evidence corroborated at least one accusation that Ewing was dispensing patronage to newspaper correspondents to buy off their opposition, nothing further resulted from the report. See Orlando Brown to Crittenden, Jan. 11, 1850, Crittenden Papers; C&R to William C. Dawson, Apr. 21, 1855, C to George Dawson, Feb. 25, 1858, C Letter Books; C account, C&R ledgers; 31 Cong., 1 sess., *H. Report 489;* Holman Hamilton, *Zachary Taylor, Soldier in the White House* (Indianapolis, 1951), ch. 27.

10. The Hargous claim was bought from B. Juan Domergue in 1847 and represented the alleged worth of tobacco confiscated and damaged during a siege. The action of an executive department seems sometimes to have been all that was needed; for example, Acting Treasury Secretary Hodge approved an item for Corcoran on behalf of S. & D. Fowler in 1851. But usually the Treasury contacts were useful for expediting payments authorized and ap-

propriated by Congress. Corcoran's attorney before the War Department claims board (and for other Washington matters) was James M. Carlisle. A much larger item, concerning land grants of Lord Selkirk, proved abortive for lack of necessary documents, although an Indiana congressman, Democrat Daniel Mace, expressed an interest in purchasing it for a constituent. See C&R to Marcy, Apr. 20, 1849, Marcy Papers, LC; C to F. & D. Fowler, July 21, 1851, C to King of William, Nov. 18, 1852, memo, July 22, 1854, C to Royal Phelps, Aug. 7, 1854, C to P. A. Hargous, Mar. 31, 1855, Hyde to C, Apr. 7, 1855, July 19, 1856, Hyde to Robert S. Chew, July 18, 1856, C to Daniel Mace, Dec. 20, 1856, C Letter Books; Phelps to C, Mar. 5, 1855, C Papers; Maitland, Phelps & Co. to C&R, Feb. 4, Mar., May 18, Sept. 9, 1853, R Papers; C account, C&R ledgers; U.S., Congress, 33d Cong., 2d sess., *Congressional Globe,* appendix, 420.

11. That is, of King William County in Virginia. The style was still commonly used to distinguish between individuals of identical names.

12. On the general account Corcoran & Riggs charged 1⅛ percent for drafts on New York, 1 percent for others. King thought this rather severe but deferred. The firm limited him to $20,000 per month, forcing him to seek additional outlets. There was also an unprofitable joint specie account involving shipments of gold dust to the East. See King to C&R, Jan. 31, May 14, 15, 31, June 15, 26, and passim, 1852, R Papers.

California banks competed for federal business much as Corcoran & Riggs had. King, and Corcoran & Riggs as correspondent, briefly enjoyed the quartermaster general's patronage but lost it to Gwin's allies, Palmer, Cook & Co.

13. Fremont also paid Corcoran & Riggs and King $2,000 and other creditors $2,500 for legal expenses. Francis P. Blair sometimes acted for Benton and Fremont. A proposed settlement which would have strengthened Fremont's Mariposa claim was refused by Corcoran as a fraud upon other creditors. See first auditor to Corwin, Jan. 29, 1852, AB Letters; King to C&R, May 1, Oct. 15, Nov. 30, Dec. 15, 31, 1852, Apr. 29, Aug. 30, 31, 1854, R Papers; contract, July 28 or 29, C to Blair, Sept. 7, C to King, Dec. 15, 1854, Apr. 17, 26, 1855, C to Fremont, Mar. 31, Apr. 13, C Letter Books; Allan Nevins, *Ordeal of the Union,* 2 vols. (New York, 1947), II, 463, 496–7, and *Fremont, Pathmarker of*

the West (New York and London, 1939), ch. 24; Cardinal Goodwin, *John Charles Fremont: An Explanation of His Career* (Stanford University 1930), 189–90.

Another large claim collected by Corcoran & Riggs was Mariano G. Vallejo's for an alleged $108,000 of supplies furnished to (or commandeered by) Fremont while he was an army officer during the Mexican War. The claim was conveyed in 1851 to Robert McLane, prominent young Maryland politician and son of a former Secretary of the Treasury. McLane had gone to California to make money and run for the Senate. He was defeated in the election: among other things the "natives" were becoming sensitive about electing such recent arrivals. Caring little for his new home, he was soon to return to Maryland, but meanwhile he made money as agent and attorney for King, Corcoran & Riggs (who extended credit), and others: $53,000 was collected. Others involved were Phillip Hamilton, son of the famous Alexander; F. Argenti, formerly of Alex. Brown & Sons of Baltimore, their correspondent in San Francisco; and one Randall. Argenti had a $20,000 interest and King $18,000. The commissions included more than $5,000 to McLane and Hamilton and $4,000 to Randall. This claim and five others were filed for the Marylander by a Maj. Gillespie; presumably some officers were moonlighting. See Brown & Sons to C&R, Dec. 15, 1850, Alex. Brown & Sons Letter Books, LC; Hyde to C, Aug. 11, 1854, memo of contract, Sept. 2, C&R to Whittlesey, first comptroller of the Treasury, Aug. 31, C&R to Phillip Hamilton, Sept. 5, 13, 1854, June 15, 1855, C&R to third auditor of the Treasury, Sept. 29, 1854, C to McLane, Oct. 14, 1854, invoice, Jan. 15, 1856, C Letter Books; McLane to C, Oct. 4, 13, 1852, Apr. 7, 1853, C&R Papers, Riggs Bank; William Wilson Corcoran, *A Grandfather's Legacy* (Washington, 1879), 116; Nevins, *Fremont,* 345, 447.

Peachy, Billings, Wilson, and Sanders were California attorneys mentioned in connection with other claims. For details see C to Charles Atherton, Feb. 22, 1849, C to Jefferson Davis, Apr. 1, 1853, C to William Appleton, Mar. 25, Apr. 25, C to S. Burt, third auditor, June 12, 1854, Hyde to Wilson, June 15, C to Wilson, July 19, Aug. 2, memo, Dec. 12–13, Hyde to L. Sanders, Sept. 13, C to John A. Sutter, Sept. 28, Hyde to Carlisle, Mar. 31, 1855, C Letter Books; C account, C&R ledgers; King to C&R, Nov. 15, 1854, R Papers.

14. Thomas Corwin's interest was bought by George Law, influential operator of subsidized shipping lines, at the request of Governor Young; Jacob Little, famous Wall Street speculator, appeared as broker in the transaction. Law shortly sold the Corwin interests at cost to his partner, Marshall O. Roberts. Edwin Harriman, correspondent for the Washington *Telegraph* and the New York *Herald,* was prevailed on by Washington banker Robert W. Latham to discontinue attacks embarrassing to such leading Whigs as Corwin and Alexander Stuart. In exchange he received the "indulgence" of a $60 loan considered lost anyway. (This must have been the cheapest rent in Washington.) The Corwins' Mexican claims equities were estimated to be worth $80,000 each; Lally's $50,000 to $60,000. Other insiders included S. L. M. Barlow, Charles March, James S. and John Thayer, and the clerk of the commission, Barnard. Asbury Dickens, clerk of the Senate, collected some commissions. Clearly the success of a claim depended on hiring the right agents and sharing the gains.

15. Pertinent information may have disappeared with the Corcoran Letter Book for 1850: see ch. 10, below. There was some infighting as well as cooperation among the insiders: Barlow suspected Thompson of secretly trying to sabotage Hargous. See Marcy to C&R, Feb. 7, 1849, C&R to Marcy, Apr. 20, 25, Marcy Papers; C to Hart, May 3, 19, 23, 26, 30, 1849, C to R. G. Corwin, May 12, 1851, C to Whittlesey, May 13, 14, C to Parrott, May 13, C to Bright, June 18, C Letter Books; Ann G. Wightt to Barlow, June 7, 1850, Barlow to L. Hargous, Mar. 15, 1851, Barlow Papers, HuntL; Otis March to Webster, Apr. 17, Webster Papers, NHHS; R. to T. Corwin, Sept. 3, Corwin Papers; U.S., Congress, 32d Cong., 2d sess., *House Report 1, Gardiner Investigation;* 33d Cong., 1st sess., *House Report 369, Gardiner and Mears Cases; Senate Report 182, Gardiner, Mears, and Other Mexican Claims;* John Basset Moore, *History and Digest of the International Arbitrations to which the United States Has Been a Party,* 6 vols. (Washington, 1898), ch. 27; David Hunter Miller, *Treaties and Other International Acts of The United States of America, 1776–1836,* 8 vols. (Washington, 1931–1948), IV, 488f.

Claims before the Mexican War were originally recognized by treaties of 1839 and 1843. "Scrip" or 5 percent bonds were issued for them by Mexico. For earlier Mexican claims bond speculations by Corcoran see C&R to ER, Jan. 18, Apr. 6, 13, 1843, Feb. 14,

Apr. 5, 1845, C&R to Corning & Co., Apr. 6, 10, May 21, 1843, R Papers; "Letters and Receipts, Mexican Indemnity 5 percent Stock," Record Group 53, Treasury Archives; Miller, *Treaties,* IV, 497–8.

A similar treaty of 1841 with Peru brought settlements totaling $300,000 pro rata with interest at 4 percent. Corcoran & Riggs had an interest in the largest set of awards, three aggregating $142,000 for confiscation of the ship *General Brown.* The awards were adjudicated by Attorney General John Y. Mason in 1846. The firm also collected the commissions of 1 percent allowed Mason and ½ percent for the American envoy who negotiated the treaty, J. C. Pickett. The payments were made in ten annual installments. The sources thus developed probably led Corcoran into a profitable speculation in Peruvian bonds which netted the firm and George Peabody a good profit in 1852. See anon. to C, undated memo (about 1851), R Papers; C&R to Peabody, Aug. 14, Oct. 1, 1852, Peabody to C, Sept. 3, Peabody Papers; Muriel Emmie Hidy, "George Peabody, Merchant and Financier, 1829–1854" (Ph.D. diss., Radcliffe College, 1939), 297; Moore *International Arbitrations,* V, ch. H.

Corcoran also invested in almost $50,000 of Spanish indemnity scrip. See C to Palmer, Sept. 10, 1857, Nov. 4, 1861, C Letter Books. In the last years of his life he and Edward Whelen were lobbying for a few thousand dollars of French spoliation claims a half-century or more in age, part of the Washington assets of the Bank of the United States acquired in 1847. See C&R to Richard Smith, Nov. 21, 1857, Hyde to Whelen, Feb. 11, 1885, C to Louisa B. Smith, Feb. 20, C to Whelen, Apr. 7, 30, Oct. 16, C to Sen. Bayard, Apr. 7, C to K. M. Blakiston, Oct. 16, C Letter Books.

16. By his prompt cooperation with the government Corcoran spared himself the discomforting criticism to which Corwin, Smith, and others were subjected. His conduct was praised in the House committee report written by Congressman F. P. Stanton, who had earlier assisted the banker in obtaining Collins Line subsidies. Gardiner's suicide was by poison. See C to J. Parrott, July 24, 1851, Hyde to Volney Howard, Sept. 11, 1852, C to J. C. Gardiner, Nov. 20, 1852, memo, Dec. 26, 27, 28, 1854, C to anon., Nov. 29, 1852, C&R to Samuel Casey, Jan. 20, 1855, C to Casey, Mar. 28, Hodge to James M. Carlisle, Mar. 7, C to Carlisle, Mar.

21, C Letter Books; Peabody to C, Aug. 8, 1851, Peabody Letter Books; R. G. to T. Corwin, Sept. 3, 1851, John C. Gardiner to W. Thompson, Nov. 12, 1852, Corwin Papers; C to ER, Oct. 28, 1852, R Papers; Clayton to Bird, Feb. 3, 1853, Bird Papers, UPa Library; 33 Cong., 1 sess., *H Report 369;* Springfield *Illinois State Register,* May 13, 1854; Nevins, *Ordeal,* I, 166.

In 1898 the eminent international lawyer John Bassett Moore fulsomely excused the eminent men of high reputation involved in this scandal, accepting their self-justifications at face value on grounds that they were eminent men of high reputation. This, of course, was the tendentious reasoning of a determined defender of established authority. See Moore, *International Arbitrations,* 1251f.

17. An exception was made for George Peabody. In 1855 Corcoran lobbied a $13,000 payment through Congress, reimbursing most of $14,000 his friend claimed for advances to finance the American exhibit at the Crystal Palace in London the year before. See C to Peabody, April 15, 1853, Peabody Papers; Hyde to C, Sept. 19, 1854, C Papers; C to Peabody, Feb. 24, Mar. 26, 1855, C Letter Books.

18. See ch. 6, above.

19. The Ewings, Robert Corwin, Caleb Smith, R. W. Thompson, and F. P. Stanton continued to be among the important lobbyists of the 1860s. See Paul W. Gates, *Fifty Million Acres: Conflicts over Kansas Land Policy, 1854–1890* (Ithaca, 1954), 120–1, 130.

Chapter 10

1. Philadelphia attorneys represented important foreign creditors of the Bank, e.g., Josiah Randall, agent for Hope & Co. of Amsterdam and others, and Christopher Fallon for Frederick Huth & Co. of London. See F. S. Lyon, Bank of the State of Alabama, to C&R, Aug. 18, 1852, R Papers, LC; list, Dec. 17, 1852, Bank of the United States of Pennsylvania (in liquidation) papers, PaHS; Walter Buckingham Smith, *Economic Aspects of the Second Bank of the United States* (Cambridge, 1953), 225, 229–30; William M. Gouge, *Fiscal History of Texas* (Philadelphia, 1852); Edmund Thornton Miller, *A Financial History of Texas* (Austin, 1916), 59–82; Elgin Williams, *The Animating Pursuits of*

Speculation: Land Traffic in the Annexation of Texas (New York, 1949), ch. 4.

2. See Charles Macalester to Nicholas Biddle, Oct. 30, 1843, Biddle Papers, LC; C&R to ER, Feb. 14, 20, Mar. 3, 6, 13, 14, 15, 30, Apr. 3, 6, 1844, R Papers; Gabriel Shaw to Peabody, Apr. 17, Morrison, Sons & Co. to Peabody, June 17, Peabody Letter Book, LC; Webster to Samuel Jaudon, June 11, NYHS; Crittenden to A. T. Burnley, Dec. 28, Crittenden Papers, LC; C to Cammann, Whitehouse [Jan. 24, 1847], C&R to ER, Jan. 28, C Letter Books; Robert L. Bloom, "The Philadelphia *North American:* A History, 1839–1925" (Ph.D. diss., Columbia University, 1952), 122; Ernest Paul Muller, "Preston King: A Political Biography" (Ph.D. diss., Columbia University, 1957), 309; Muriel Emmie Hidy, "George Peabody, Merchant and Financier, 1829–1854" (Ph.D. diss., Radcliffe College, 1939), 279; Williams, *Animating Pursuits,* 161f.

3. Clay's proposal would have had the United States assume the debts secured by the Republic of Texas' import tariffs. See C to Peabody, Sept. 16, 1850, Peabody Papers, EI; Miller, *Financial History of Texas,* 120–1; Holman Hamilton, "Texas Bonds and Northern Profits: A Study in Compromise, Investment, and Lobby Influence," *Mississippi Valley Historical Review* 43 (March 1957), 583–4.

4. The prime supplier was Charnley & Whelen in Philadelphia. The totals given are, if anything, overstatements of the early sales. The figures are based on scattered letters and statements in the Riggs papers (possibly incomplete) and on the certificates in the Treasury Department Archives which indicate the *earliest* date at which a purchase might have been made. The assignment, with date, was usually written at the time of sale by original holders, with a blank space for the name of the ultimate assignee. The certificates might have passed through the hands of intermediate purchasers before coming to rest with Corcoran and his confreres, possibly at much later dates than indicated. See below, text to n. 8; see also Charnley & Whelen account current, Mar. 1, 1850, J. Corning & Co. to C&R, Mar. 9, 14, E. S. Whelen & Co., statement, Oct. 31, R Papers; C account, C&R ledgers; Texas debt claims papers, Treasury Archives.

5. Writing of Taylor's death Corcoran expressed the hope that "good will grow out of evil," then crossed out "evil" and sub-

stituted "the change." See C&R to BB, July 15, 1850, BPOC; T. J. Rusk to Fillmore, July 24, Fillmore Papers, BuffHS; Whelen & Co. account current, Aug. 31, Oct. 31, C to C&R, Oct. 8, 11, C to ER, Jr., Oct. 10, Nov. 9, 11, Edward Martin to C&R, Sept. 13, 19, 24, 27, J. F. May to C&R, Sept. 30, Whelen to C&R, Apr. 9, 10, 12, 1851, R Papers; Miller, *Financial History of Texas,* 121.

Whelen cautioned Corcoran against deceptively low quotations in the Philadelphia *Public Ledger,* alleging that brokers offering [and journalists publishing?] these quotations did so to entice buyers but would sell only at as much as 15 percent higher. In Philadelphia then, as elsewhere and at all times, there were divergences between the stock exchange and the over-the-counter market.

6. See John W. Davis to C&R, June 21, 1849, Sept. 8, 24, 1850, Mar. 6, 1855, Feb. 27, 1856, R Papers; C to Francis J. Grund, Mar. 25, May 8, 1851, Sept. 6, 1853, memo, Aug. 2, 1854, C Letter Books; Davis and C accounts, C&R ledgers; Ellis Paxson Oberholtzer, *Jay Cook, Financier of The Civil War,* 2 vols (Philadelphia, 1907), I, 73–4.

In September 1850, when Douglas became certain his Illinois railroad land grant bill would pass Congress, he put into effect an arrangement worked out with Corcoran to buy as much of the state's debt for him as the banker would extend credit for. Little seems to have become available then, but over the next few years Corcoran purchased several hundred thousand dollars of new Illinois internal improvement bonds at prices ranging roughly from 45 to 65. Most was in his own name, some was for the firm, and about $6,000 face value was for Francis Grund on credit in return for services rendered. The profit on all these transactions reached 50 percent. See Douglas to C, Sept. 10, 16, 1850, C Papers, LC; C&R to BB, Sept. 23, 1850, BPOC; clipping, BB to C&R, Oct. 11, Dec. 27, 1850, R Papers; C to Wetmore & Cryder, Apr. 13, 1851, C to Cammann, Whitehouse, July 25, 1851, Dec. 2, 1852, C to Francis J. Grund, Sept. 4, 1851, C to Winslow, Lanier, Dec. 2, 1851, Apr. 2, May 13, 1852, C to Wadsworth & Selden, Nov. 28, 1852, C to Thomas Mather, Dec. 19, 1851, memos, May 13, Dec. 4, 1852, C to Whitehouse, Feb. 4, 1854, C to Cammann & Co., Feb. 23, Jan. 15, 1855, C to James C. Conkling, Dec. 11, C Letter Books; C account, C&R ledgers.

For possible log-rolling between the Texas and omnibus compromise and the Illinois Central land grant, see Holman Hamilton, *Prologue to Conflict: The Crisis and Compromise of 1850* (New York, 1966), 121.

7. Fortunately, vital memoranda of loans and "fees," including dates, survive. See Preston King to Flagg, Aug. 15, 1850, A. C. Flagg Papers, ColU Library; Philadelphia *North American,* May 17, 1850; George W. Julian, *Political Recollections* (Chicago, 1884), 95; Muller, "King," 481; Hamilton, "Texas Bonds," 580–1; *Prologue to Conflict*, 120–1, 131, 179.

8. See Wetmore & Cryder to C&R, Mar. 15, 16, 1850, James Hamilton to C, Nov. 3, Lyon to C&R, Aug. 18, 1852, R Papers; Hamilton to Rusk, Sept. 27, 28, 1850, Rusk to Hamilton, Sept. 20, 21, J. Y. Mason to Rusk, Feb. 21, 1852, Rusk Papers, UTex; Hamilton to Corwin, Dec. 1, 1850, Corwin Papers, LC; H. R. W. Hill to Crittenden, Nov. 2, 1851, Crittenden Papers; C to W. D. Miller, Jan. 28, 1856, C to Wetmore, Mar. 6, C to Carlisle, Oct. 16, 1858, C Letter Books; also index under "Hamilton" in Williams, *Animating Pursuits.*

9. See U.S., Congress, 32d Cong. 1st sess., *Senate Miscellaneous Document 72;* Miller, *Financial History of Texas,* 82, 118f.

10. Combs, a former Bank of the United States representative under Biddle, had had John M. Clayton and Henry Clay as endorsers of his loans on Texas paper. He held $125,000 face value and interest, representing an actual investment of perhaps 10 percent of that sum. His wheedling letters may be found throughout the historical collections of the country. He wrote touchingly to Corwin, "You have been a debtor and know the feelings of a sensitive man." See Leslie Combs to Bird, Nov. 25, 1848, Bird Papers, UPa Library; Reverdy Johnson to C, Sept. 6, 1850, C Papers; C to Johnson, Apr. 11, Nov. 12, 1851, C to C. Ellis, May 17, C to Whelen, June 2, C to William D. Lewis, June 4, C to Grund, July 21, Sept. 4, 1851, C to James B. Shaw, Aug. 10, Sept. 18, 1854, receipted statement, June 3, 1856, memo, Feb. 17, 1857, C Letter Books; Whelen to C&R, Aug. 22, 1851, R Papers; Combs account, 1851–1852, C&R ledgers; Combs to Corwin, Dec. 9, 1851, Mar. 20, Sept. 17, 1852, Burnley to Corwin, Mar. 27, Corwin Papers; Hodge to Barlow, n.d., 1853, Barlow Papers; Miller, *Financial History of Texas,* 123f.

11. Corcoran & Riggs, among others, sought appointment as sole agent for the loan as soon as the compromise was passed. Treasury

Secretary Corwin and ex-Secretary Walker wrote glowing letters of recommendation to the Texas delegation. Corcoran, confident of success, was inclined to counter Baring Brothers' suggestion of an alliance, of which they expected to have two-thirds, by offering them the European agency on a commission basis. Meanwhile, however, the New York firm of Howland & Aspinwall, also enjoying strong Texas connections and under the same optimistic expectations as Corcoran & Riggs, made the same reply to the Barings' overtures. Thus it was the latter who learned of the conflicting promises, for the parties in New York and Washington had been out of communication. (This was the period of the Mexican indemnity operation in which the alliance among the three had practically disintegrated in mutual suspiciousness.) The Barings worked to restore the coalition, with success—by the end of November it seemed that Texas would ask for competitive bids and the erstwhile allies wanted first of all to overawe and forestall competition. While the other two firms were still half-inclined to play a lone hand if there were any hope of success, Baring agent Thomas Ward tentatively planned for a subscription on the same terms as the abortive indemnity operation, with August Belmont and other banks and individuals to be invited to join. These schemes had to be abandoned because of the squabbles involving Texas and the various groups of creditors. Meanwhile Corwin refused to allow payment to Texas of interest on the United States bonds until the wrangle was resolved. See C&R to BB, Sept. 16, 1850, Ward to BB, Oct. 15, 24, Nov. 15, 25, Dec. 6, 20, King & Sons to BB, Nov. 26, C&R to Ward, Nov. 30, Ward to Howland & Aspinwall, Dec. 3, Howland & Aspinwall to Ward, Dec. 5, S. G. Ward to BB, Dec. 3, 1850, Jan. 6, Dec. 25, 29, 1851, BPOC; Walker to Rusk et al.,. Sept. 21, 1850, Rusk to C&R, Sept 23, W. D. Lewis (in favor of C. S. Boker of the Girard Bank) to Rusk, Sept. 24, C&R to Rusk, Sept. 26, Howland & Aspinwall to Rusk, Sept. 27, H. H. Williams to Rusk, Sept. 28, Rusk to Corwin, Oct. 2, C to Rusk, Oct. 15, J. L. Aspinwall to Rusk, Nov. 30, 1850, R. W. Latham of Selden, Withers & Co. to Rusk, Jan. 27, 1851, Corwin to Shaw, Feb. 12, Rusk Papers; BB to Ward, Oct. 29, Nov. 19, 29, 1850, Oct. 3, 1851, Jan. 6, 1852, BB to C&R, Dec. 13, 1850, BPLB; S. G. Ward to Ward, Oct. 28, 1850, Ward to Bates, Dec. 15, Ward Diary, Jan. 14, 1851, Ward Papers, MassHS; Walker to C, Sept. 21, 1850, Walker to Houston, Rusk, Kaufman and Howard, Sept. 21, C Letter Books; Rusk to C, June 28, 1853, C Papers; William Wilson Corcoran, *A Grandfather's Legacy* (Washington, 1879), 91–2.

Ward was optimistic in his expectations for the new federal bond flotation. Although he had never met him, he was inclined in favor of Corcoran's agent William Gouge, noting however that the discretion given him was greater than he ordinarily allowed. Aware that Corcoran was heavily involved in Texas paper, he was suspicious lest he become entangled in the state's bargaining with its creditors. Ward suggested that since Corcoran had not consulted the other parties he might go ahead on his own while they retained options on one-third each. Corcoran would not accept this: he was not going to share the expected profits after assuming the whole risk.

Peabody and Howland & Aspinwall had an advance order of $200,000. Corcoran & Riggs' agent wrote with amazement of the stupidity of Texas legislators, quoting a high state official: they intentionally required shipment there of the bonds, most of which would have to be returned to the East, in order "that some little of it may stick to the fingers of the people of Texas!" He estimated the cost would be (exaggeratedly) 2 to 3 percent in compensating reduction of the value of the bonds (unless the Texas administration, which was willing enough, found some way of evading the stipulation). Of the $2 million of debt payments then being made, $700,000 remained to be financed in cash by sale of the remaining United States bonds; the balance had been settled directly by payment in bonds. (Citizens of the state were to receive $250,000 to $350,000 of this.) See Peabody to C, Apr. 11, 1851, C Papers; S. G. Ward to BB, Jan. 19, 29, Feb. 9, May 4, 1852, S. G. Ward to Ward, Jan. 30, Feb. 1, C&R to Ward, Feb. 26, Ward to C&R, Feb. 28, Ward to BB, Mar. 5, 23, 30, Apr. 2, 6, 23, BB to Ward, Apr. 16, 20, BPOC; Ward to C&R, Feb. 18, 28, Mar. 25, Apr. 5, 6, Howland & Aspinwall to C&R, Apr. 1, Gouge to C&R, May 7, 21, R Papers.

12. As a starter Gouge arranged for the dissemination of anti-scaling propaganda in the Texas *Wesleyan Banner* and the Houston *Telegraph*. Gouge reported that S. M. Swenson was buying paper for Sheldon, a New York merchant, and John N. Swisher for Chubb Brothers, bankers of Washington. See Gouge to C&R, Jan. 28, Feb. 13, 22, 26, Mar. 1, 28, Apr. 6, 10, 26, 28, May 21, 23,

1852, W. D. Miller to C&R, June 14, Aug. 10 R Papers; Gouge account, C&R ledgers; Gouge to Corwin, May 28, June 25, Corwin Papers; C to Houston, Sept. 1, 1852, C to Miller, Apr. 24, 1856, May 29, Sept. 23, Oct. 27, 1857, C&R to Miller, June 9, 1856, Hyde to Miller, July 3, 1857, C Letter Books; C to Peabody, Dec. 29, 1858, Peabody Papers; Austin *Texas State Gazette,* Mar. 15, 1856; Benjamin G. Rader, "William M. Gouge, Jacksonian Economic Theorist," *Pennsylvania History* 30 (October 1963).

13. Corcoran, who had been unavoidably vague in his instructions, was angered when Gouge exceeded expectations in his winning bids. It quickly became apparent to all, however, that he had done well for his principals. His pay for managing the bid was a modest $600, in addition to a large expense account and further remuneration from Corcoran for other services. See Gouge to C&R, Feb. 13, 20, 22, 24, Mar. 1, Apr. 6, 26, May 1, 3, 4, June 21, 1852, S. B. Shaw to C&R, May 3, Ward to C&R, May 21, Sept. 1, Miller to C&R, June 14, R Papers; C&R to Gouge, Jan. 27, Ward to BB, May 21, 25, June 8, 11, 25, BPOC.

14. See 32 Cong., 1 sess., *Congressional Globe,* 2380–2; Miller, *Financial History of Texas,* 122.

15. This was a year of heavy railroad land grant campaigning, in which Matteson was interested. Kurtz apparently had been a Treasury official in 1839, auditing Corcoran's Indian claims. A New York lobbyist, Ausburn Birdsall, and Ohio Congressman L. D. Campbell had small interests on Corcoran & Riggs' books. See Corcoran to Crawford (commissioner of Indian Affairs), Feb. [26], June 25, 1839, Treasury Archives; W. D. Miller to Rusk, May 20, 1848, May 20, 1850, J. C. Christy to Rusk. Mar. 21, 1853, memo of conversation with James Holman, Oct. 20, 1854, Hamilton to Rusk, Dec. 10, anon. to Hamilton, June 10, 1855, Rusk to C, June 17, Rusk Papers; A. J. Glossbrenner to C&R, July 3, Sept. 27, 1850, Grund to C&R, Apr. 27, 1853, R Papers; C to Glossbrenner, July 19, 1853, C to Asbury Dickins, Jan. 14, 26, 1854, Aug. 14, 1861, Mar. 25, 1879, Hyde to C, Aug. 19, 1854, June 9, 1856, Hyde to William Kurtz, Aug. 22, 1854, C to Kurtz, Mar. 8, 1855, Apr. 24, 1856, C&R to Whelen & Co., Mar., 16, 21, 1855, C&R to Memucan Hunt, Apr. 19, May 24, June 7, 11, 1856, C to Fallon, June 21, C to Rusk, Apr. 23, 1856, Hyde to F. B. Riggs, Apr. 8, 1887, memos, June 2–3, 1856, Sept. 25, 1857, C Letter Books; Hunt, Kurtz and Rusk accounts, C&R ledgers; Amelia Williams and

Eugene C. Barker, eds., *The Writing of Sam Houston,* 8 vols. (Austin, 1938–1943), V, 503–4; ch. 9 above.

16. It should be added that the Texas debt was not the only one which Congress was being asked to pay. Men such as Senator Thomas G. Pratt of Maryland, assiduous in supporting the Texas creditors, would hardly ignore their own interest in the California debt. English came from a politically active family with relatives in Kentucky and Illinois. See English to R. J. Walker, Jan. 23, 1849, NYHS; Combs to Breckinridge, Dec. 4, 25, 1852, Jan. 3, May 27, July 4, Feb. 18, July 4, 1854, Feb. 18, 1855, Breckinridge Papers, LC; Combs to Caleb Cushing, Jan. 4, 1854, Cushing Papers, LC; Hyde to Combs, Aug. 14, 1854, C to Secretary of Treasury, Apr. 16, 1856, memos, Mar. 27, June 2, July 5, 1856, Feb. 17, 1857 ("Disposition of moneys received on account of the Texas Debt"), C Letter Books; A. Mitchell to C&R, Dec. 7, 1852, R Papers; register of claims on account of Texas debt, Act of 1850, Treasury Archives; Van der Weele, "Bright," 196.

17. See ER, Jr., to ER, Feb. 9, 1853, R Papers; U.S., Congress, 32d Cong., 2d sess., *Congressional Globe,* 959f.

18. Cushing later appeared in Corcoran's correspondence as a borrower of $4,000, but not in the table of Texas debt expenses. See C to Cushing, July 28, 1853, May 1, 1856, Hyde to Cushing, Sept. 4, Nov. 16, Dec. 13, 1855, statement, June 4–5, 1856, C Letter Books; James Christy to C&R, Sept. 3, 1853, R Papers; U.S., Congress, 33d Cong., 2d sess., *House Miscellaneous Document 17;* Miller, *Financial History of Texas,* 122–3.

19. This was the Congress in which Bright, Breckinridge, and their allies were abortively pushing through the Minnesota & North Western land grant. Representative Francis B. Cutting of New York was conspicuous in opposing the clique on both measures. He also delivered a denunciation of Breckinridge, citing the inflow of funds to aid his election to the House over Robert P. Letcher in 1852. Among other curiosities of the voting, Douglas abstained after his somewhat incongruous derision of interested parties; James A. Bayard (Dem., Del.), who was related to one large creditor, associated with others, and a backer of Buchanan in 1856 switched from opposition to support with various specious explanations; English, Kurtz, and a number of Texans made a show of voting against the measure when its passage was assured with plenty to spare and after they opposed motions to reduce the

amount of money. See ch. 11, 12 below. See also C to B. Phelps, Mar. 16, 1854, C to J. & R. Milbank & Co., Apr. 17, C&R to Samuel B. Finley, Sept. 13, C to Finley, Feb. 21, 1855, C to William Douglass, Feb. 22, C to Lyons, Oct. 30, 1854, memo, July 24–25, 1854, C Letter Books; Combs to Breckinridge, Dec. 15, 1854, Van Dyke to Breckinridge, n.d., Breckinridge Papers; U.S., Congress, 33d Cong., 1st sess., *Senate Report 334; Congressional Globe,* 1403f, 1462, 1806f, 1832f, 1844f; 2 sess., 275, 593f, 615f, 752, 863f; Van der Weele, "Bright," 128–9.

For Bright's progress as Senator beginning during the Polk administration see Bayard to C, July 10, 1848, C Papers; Van der Weele, "Bright," 53, 130, 189. D. C. Bright, presumably a relative, was for some years the Treasury depository in Jeffersonville, Ind. *Bankers Magazine,* October 1847, 256.

20. See Gouge to C&R, Feb. 26, 1852, R Papers; Austin *Texas State Gazette,* Aug. 19, 26, Sept. 16, 1854, Mar. 3, 10, 17, 24, Aug. 1, 1855.

21. See C to Hamilton, Nov. 26, 1851, Dec. 16, 1854, May 19, 1855, May 2, 22, 24, 1856, Hyde to Hamilton, May 27, 30, C to Rusk, Mar. 25, June 28, 1855, Hyde to Robb, Sept. 13, C to Miller, Jan. 14, 1856, C to Wetmore, Mar. 6, May 2, C&R to Wetmore, Apr. 26, C Letter Books; Austin *Texas State Gazette,* Mar. 24, 1855, Mar. 22, 1856; Washington *Tri-Weekly Intelligencer,* May 29, 1856.

22. While Washington politicians were normally higher priced, the expenses in the provinces this time may have approached those at the capital. See Christy to C&R, Sept. 25, 1853, R Papers; Bright to C, May 18, 1855, GWR to C, Sept. 24, Oct. 22, Combs to Hyde, Nov. 21, C Papers; C&R to Miller, Mar. 27, C to Miller, May 11, Hyde to Miller, Sept. 25, Oct. 22, Hyde to C, May 12, Sept. 17, Oct. 1, 8, 15, 22, C to Macalester, Mar. 28, C to Hamilton, May 19, C to M. Birdsall, June 23, C to Lewis Cruger, June 26, 28, C to J. E. Thayer & Bro., Sept. 11, ER to J. & R. Milbank & Co., Oct. 10, 1855, C to Belmont, June 5, 1856, C Letter Books; New Orleans Contributions account, Aug.–Sept. 1853 (of $4,000 contributed more than half came from J. W. Maury and funneled through one major there), J. S. Holman account, 1845–1847, C&R ledgers; Austin *Texas State Gazette,* May 19, 26, June 16, Nov. 10, 1855, Feb. 23, 1856.

23. Robert & William to C&R, Apr. 21, 1852, R Papers; John

V. L. Pruyn, manuscript journal, Mar. 25, 1854, Alb. Inst.; C to Miller, Jan. 19, 1856, C Letter Books; Austin *Texas State Gazette,* June 2, 9, 30, July 18, 21, 25, 28, 1855; Williams and Barker, eds., *Writings of Sam Houston,* V, 375f; VI, 180–4.

24. Austin *Texas State Gazette,* Jan. 26, Feb. 2, Mar. 22, 29, 1856; Texas *House Journal,* Aug. 5, 25, 28; Miller, *Financial History of Texas,* 126–8.

25. There was controversy over the disposition of unclaimed appropriations. The Texans and their congressional representatives wanted the money turned over to the state. Much to the surprise and mortification of Corcoran, Bright, and other allies of the Buchanan cabal, John Slidell supported Texas. Corcoran noted also that his old antagonist, Secretary of the Treasury James Guthrie, favored the Lone Star State. As a result about 5 percent of the appropriations were absorbed by padded claims from Texas. By September 1856 Corcoran made up his mind to "let Texas bonds . . . notes and Railroads alone." See R. W. Milbank to C&R, Dec. 28, 1853, R Papers; C to Robb, July 11, 22, 1856, C to Bright, Sept. 23, Hyde to J. Milbank, Oct. 9, C to Davis, Dec. 22, C to Combs, Nov. 26, 1858, Jan. 4, 1869 (the latter was apparently still trying to get money out of Texas), Hyde to C, Jan. 30, 1860, C Letter Books; Bright to C, July 17, 1856, C Papers; registers of claims and warrants, Texas debt papers, Treasury Archives; U.S., Congress, 34th Cong., 1st sess., *Congressional Globe,* 2071, 2181, 2184, 2189, 2237; 3d sess., 126f; *Treasury Report,* 1856, 278f.

For the Hamilton case see also C to Carlisle, Nov. 14, 18, 1856, C to Wetmore, Jan. 4, 1858, Cryder to C, Feb. 19, 1861, C to Cryder, Feb. 20, Apr. 9, 11, 12, C to Thomas Ellis, Dec. 12, 1866, C to Carlisle & McPherson, Jan. 11, 14, 1867, C to W. A. Maury, Apr. 3, 11, 15, 22, Aug. 19, Sept. 6, 12, 1867, May 18, 1870, C to Robert Ould, Apr. 3, Aug. 17, 1867, statement, June 19, 1867, Hyde to Ould, Apr. 15, 1868, Hyde to ER, Apr. 15, C Letter Books; Hyde to C, Sept. 16, Oct. 24, Nov. 25, 1867, unbound letterpress copies, C Papers; Hyde to C, Dec. 17, 1862, C Papers; Miller, *Fiancial History of Texas,* 129.

A study of the liquidation of the Bank of the United States, in its branch locales as well as its headquarters, might be most revealing both for local history and the Bank's.

26. I have used the figures from memoranda in the Corcoran letter books. Unfortunately there are discrepancies and ambiguities

in these; consequently the disposition outlined in the text is probable, not certain. In addition to the firm's collections, George W. Riggs, Corcoran's first partner, drew $64,000 from the Treasury and Corcoran drew $45,000 in his own name. See Hamilton, "Texas Bonds," and sources therein.

27. See C&R to Hunt, Apr. 19, May 24, June 7, 1856, statements, May 31, June 3, C&R to Finley, June 11, C to Harrison, June 16, 26, C to ER, June 16, C&R to Robert & William, June 19, 27, Hyde to D. S. Dickinson, June 20, C to Davis, July 3, C to B. Christian, July 10, Hyde to Harrison, July 15, C to Milbank & Co., Nov. 17, memos, Feb. 18, 19, July 21, Sept. 12, 1857, C Letter Books; Bright to C, July 17, 1856, C Papers; ER, Jr., account, Aug. 28, 1856, C&R ledgers.

28. Slidell puzzled and astonished his allies by voting against additional appropriations for the creditors—after the nomination. Glossbrenner became President Buchanan's confidential secretary. See Hamilton, "Texas Bonds," 590f; ch. 12, below.

29. William M. Gwin, manuscript, "Memoirs on the History of the United States, Mexico and California, 1850–1861," Bancroft Library, University of California, photostat in LC; William C. Fankhauser, *Financial History of California* (Berkeley, 1913), 311–3. For the Fremont-King alliance and the connection with the defaulting firm of Palmer, Cook & Co., see ch. 8, above, and Allan Nevins, *Fremont, Pathmarker of the West* (New York and London, 1939), 447.

30. Buchanan's interest, $15,000, was obtained by August Belmont. Curiously, he paid 85 at about the time the firm was making its purchases; apparently Belmont was not very astute or attentive in this case, whereas Corcoran was able to seek out the cheapest sources in a thin market. The price rose still further, apparently into the 90s in New York; Corcoran bought chiefly in San Francisco and small amounts in Cincinnati and elsewhere. E. W. Clark & Co. of Philadelphia, a house of prime importance in the Texas debt affair, was the largest known holder—over $100,000, some of which may have been in street name for third parties. Its Washington correspondent, Chubb Brothers, held $16,000 and ultimately collected $75,000 for others. Other large holders were bankers William Hoge of New York, John L. Gardiner of Boston, and the partnership of Sweeny, Rittenhouse & Fant. See King to C&R, June 29, 1850, Jan. 31, Mar. 19, Apr. 3, 17, 1852, William B.

Hale to C&R, Jan. 28, R Papers; Belmont to Buchanan, May 16, June 3, 15, 1853, James Buchanan Papers, PaHS; C to Thomas G. Pratt, Dec. 5, 1854, Sept. 29–30, 1856, C to Bright, Sept. 29–30, C to Hodge, Mar. 10, 1855, C to Gardiner, Sept. 30, 1856, Hyde to Davis, June 8, 1857, C to Glossbrenner, Feb. 15, 1858, C to O'Sullivan, Dec. 14, 1860, memos, Sept. 17, 1853, Aug. 25–26, Sept. 12, 1856, C&R to Smith and Denver, commissioners of California, Aug. 28, 1856, C Letter Books; Buchanan to C, n.d., C Papers; 34 Cong., 3 sess., *H. Report 243;* California Indian War Papers, Treasury Archives; C and ER accounts, R & Co. ledgers, Riggs Bank.

31. After passage in the House, Sidney Webster wrote Corcoran "Of course the Senate will not fail to receive your attention now." Senator Brodhead borrowed a $100 bond and "forgot" to return it until dunned repeatedly. See S. Webster to C, July 20, 1854, C to Brodhead, Aug. 8, C Letter Books; U.S., Congress, 33d Cong., 1st sess., *Congressional Globe,* 1, 14, 33, 1828, 2184.

32. Senator James A. Pearce (Whig, Md.) obstreperously supported California. See C to Gardiner, Dec. 19, 1854, Mar. 31, 1855, Jan. 24, July 10, 1856, C to Pratt, June 8, 1855, Hyde to C, Sept. 17, C to Hodge, Feb. 25, 1856, Hyde to Robert H. Ives, Sept. 18, C Letter Books; Fankhauser, *Financial History of California,* 312.

33. See Hyde to C, Aug. 1, 15, 16, 1856, memos, Apr. 4, 1857, Oct. 18, 1860, C Letter Books; 34 Cong., 1 sess., *Congressional Globe,* 1567, 1581, 1777f. A similar operation was commenced by Corcoran and Elisha and George W. Riggs, who advanced $50,000 to E. A. Turpin, an associate of Bright in Indiana, to buy the Indian War scrip of Washington and Oregon territories. Turpin was to receive 5 percent of the profits beyond expenses and interest at the legal rate. Further developments are not indicated in the records. See agreement, March 17, 1857, R Papers; memo, Sept. 24, C Letter Books; 34 Cong., 1 sess., *Congressional Globe,* 445, 1834, 1930. Weller, who had obligingly yielded to Johnson and Benjamin in the California matter, introduced the bill for the territories. It died in committee.

34. Sporadic attempts were made over the decades to get California or Congress to pay the outstanding balances. Most of the principal was recovered with the last payment, $1,300, received by Riggs & Co. in 1895. These creditors were certainly tenacious. See

Hyde to Pratt, Sept. 1, 2, Oct. 6, 13, Dec. 4, 1856, Hyde to C, Sept. 1, 2, 1856, memos, Oct. 6, Nov. 7, 17, 1856, Feb. 16, Mar. 31, June 30, 1858, Dec. 7, 1860, Aug. 15–16, 1871, Hyde to Floyd, June 30, 1860, C to Bright, Jan. 24, 1861, Hyde to Hoge, Feb. 28, Hyde to Joseph P. Gardiner, Apr. 13, June 9, 1868, Hyde to J. W. Clark & Co., May 15, June 2, 1868, Aug. 17–18, 1871, Feb. 13, 24, 1882, Nov. 17, 30, Dec. 8, 1885, Hyde to third auditor, July 9, 11, 1870, Hyde to Latham, May 20, 1873, Hyde to C. H. Reynolds, Aug. 15, 1871, May 19, 1873, Dec. 29, 1880, Feb. 7, June 2, 1881, C to Sen. Casserly, Jan. 17, 1874, Hyde to Casserly, Feb. 26, 1874, Hyde to London & San Francisco Bank, Sept. 16, Oct. 21, 1880, Nov. 29, 1881, Dec. 5, 1885, C Letter Books; Hyde to C, July 11, 1868, Aug. 5, 8, 11, 12, 15, 1871, unbound letterpress copies, Hyde to C, Dec. 17, 1862, C Papers; auditor for War Department to Secretary of Treasury, Jan. 8, 1904, Treasury Archives; U.S., Congress, 51st Cong., 1st sess., *Senate Executive Document 122.*

35. Baring Brothers almost joined in. It was hoped, in any case, they would be able to buy for the speculators large additional amounts of the bonds in England. See C to Peabody, Nov. 6, 11, 20, 1848, Jan. 10, 20, 1849, C Letter Books; Peabody to Wetmore, Nov. 10, 17, 24, 1848, Peabody to C&R, Nov. 24, Peabody to King & Sons, Nov. 24, Peabody Letter Book, LC; BB to C&R, Nov. 24, C&R to BB, Dec. 23, 1848, Mar. 4, 1849, BPOC; Peabody to C, Dec. 29, 1848, BB to C&R, Jan. 12, 1849, C Papers; C to Peabody, Sept. 16, 1850, Peabody Papers; Hidy, "Peabody," 275–9. For the origins of the Florida bonds consult McGrane, *Foreign Bondholders,* ch. 1.

36. See C to Wetmore, Mar. 13, 1849, C Letter Books; C&R to BB, Apr. 2, BPOC.

37. See John G. Gamble to Peabody, May 5, 8, June 15, 1849, Peabody Papers, LC; C&R to Peabody, May 28, 1849, Jan. 31, 1852, Peabody Papers; C to ER, Aug. 16, Nov. 15, 1850, R Papers; Ward to BB, Oct. 15, 1850, BPOC; Florida account, C&R ledgers.

38. Gouge later performed the same service in Arkansas that he had in Texas, this time fruitlessly. See Robert W. Johnson to C, Apr. 24, 1854, C Papers; Walter Lee Browne, "Albert Pike, 1809–1891" (Ph.D. diss., Texas, 1955), 293, 302–14; William M. Gouge, *Fiscal History of Arkansas* (Little Rock, 1858); Reginald C. McGrane, *Foreign Bondholders and American State Debts* (New

York, 1935), 261–2; B. U. Ratchford, *American State Debts* (Durham, 1941), 112.

39. Conway's secretary was Richard H. Johnson, brother of the senator and editor of the Little Rock *True Democrat*. In the two years ending Sept. 30, 1856, almost $1 million of bonds (including interest) was cancelled by the state treasurer under these arrangements, and much more thereafter. It was at this time that Robert Johnson became a close friend of Corcoran. See Johnson account, 1853, C&R ledgers; Rufus K. Turnage to C&R, Sept. 29, 1852, R Papers; Dallas T. Herndon, ed., *Centennial History of Arkansas* 3 vols. (Chicago and Little Rock, 1922), I, 270–1.

40. Daniel Clark (Rep., N. H.) and James R. Doolittle (Rep., Wis.).

41. See London *Times*, July 22, 1850; Browne, "Pike," 381–2, 400–1, 429, 439–40, 454; this work, ch. 8–12 passim.

42. Johnson's banker in Memphis was J. Knox Walker. California war bonds were also bought through St. John for urgent shipment to the Johnsons in Arkansas. The loan was largely repaid by 1859, when another $30,000 was lent, two-thirds by Corcoran and the rest by George Riggs. This time 9 percent was charged instead of the earlier 6 percent (although Johnson got back some of it by gains on exchange since the interest was payable semiannually at New Orleans). Secretary of the Interior Jacob Thompson of Mississippi guaranteed the second loan. As in the case of the first, this one was backed by a mortgage on land and slaves. Johnson was not candid with Corcoran: contrary to his assurances there was a prior mortgage, to John C. Rives. The Civil War left Johnson bankrupt and Corcoran, after some entanglement with the Rives heirs, became the owner of the estate through years of trouble and loss. See R. W. Johnson to Rives, Aug. 15, Sept. 9, 1854, PaHS; C to Cammann & Co., Sept. 5, 1854, Hyde to C, Sept. 22, 1854, May 25, 1858, Sept. 5, 1865, Benjamin S. Johnson to C, Sept. 26, 1854, C to GWR, Sept. 27, C to Daniel B. St. John, Sept. 29, Oct. 10, 16, 20, C to B. S. Johnson, Sept. 29 (c/o Smith & Shotwell, Louisville, Ky.), Oct. 16 (c/o Bullitt, Louisville), C to R. W. Johnson, Oct. 7, 20, Dec. 30, 1854, Jan. 10, 1856, Jan. 20, Mar. 27, May 26, 1860, June 27, 1866, Hyde to B. S. Johnson, Oct. 20, 1854, C to clerk of circuit court, Napoleon, Desha County, Ark., Dec. 28, 1854, memos, Jan. 3, 1856, June 6, 7, 1859, C to William L. Jenkins, cashier, Bank of America, Jan. 19, 20, 1860,

C to Duncan, Sherman, Jan. 20, Hyde to R. W. Johnson, Feb. 23, 1860, C to Watkins & Rose, Sept. 7, 1869, Apr. 2, 1870, C to Sommers, Mar. 28, 1870, C to Bradley, Apr. 20, memo, Apr. 25, C Letter Books; *Bankers Magazine,* March 1855, 712–3.

43. These bonds, too, were part of the later history of the Bank of the United States. Prices given include accrued interest. See SR to C&R, Oct. 28, 1848, C to C&R, Oct. 23, 1850, BB to C, Aug. 15, 1851, R Papers; C to Peabody Nov. 11, 1848, C to James B. Murray, July 22, 24, 28, 1851, C Letter Books; BB to Ward, Oct. 26, 1849, Feb. 22, 1850, Feb. 7, Mar. 14, 1851, BB to C&R, Dec. 13, 1850, BPLB; C&R to BB, Nov. 23, 1850, Jan. 8, 1851, BPOC; Peabody to C&R, Apr. 26, 1850, Peabody to W. M. W. Cochrane, May 16, 1851, Peabody Papers; Peabody to C, May 23, 1851, Walker to C, Aug. 16, C Papers; C account, 1849–1850, C&R ledgers; Claiborn to Gwin, Mar. 4, 1879, Gwin Papers, LC; McGrane, *Foreign Bondholders,* ch. 10. The last is a useful but more narrowly focused history of Mississippi bonds.

44. See Natchez *Courier,* Jan. 10, Apr. 8, Nov. 18, 1851; Monticello (Miss.) *Southern Journal,* Mar. 20, 1852; Washington *Semi-Weekly Union,* Mar. 13, 1852.

45. In this election Franklin Pierce won the presidential vote, 27,000 to 13,000. Both the legislative and popular votes were along class and sectional lines, with the richer and more market-oriented plantation areas favoring resumption. The repudiators won greater majorities than Pierce in the counties he carried. Correspondingly, the counties supporting Winfield Scott favored the debt settlement by heavier votes. See C to James Lee, Apr. 29, 1852, C to Jaudon, Aug. 12, C Letter Books; Jackson *Flag of the Union,* Feb. 13, July 30, Aug. 6, Nov. 26, 1852, Feb. 13, 1853; Houston *Southern Argus,* Dec. 1, 1852; Monticello *Southern Journal,* Dec. 4, 1852; Mississippi *Senate Journal,* Mar. 15, 1852, 639–40.

46. See S. G. Ward to BB, Oct. 4, 1853, Daniel W. Adams to S. G. Ward, Nov. 15, Adams to Forstall, Nov. 15, 19, S. G. Ward to Adams, Dec. 6, BPOC; Cochrane to Peabody, Jan. 23, 1854, Peabody Papers; Jackson *Flag of the Union,* Apr. 2, 23, 30, June 25, July 30, Aug. 6, Oct. 8, Nov. 26, 1852, Feb. 25, Mar. 18, Apr. 1, 8, 22, Aug. 12, 19, 26, Sept. 16, 1853; Houston *Southern Argus,* Sept. 15–Oct. 20, 1852, Mar. 16, Apr. 13, June 29, Sept. 7–Oct. 26, Dec. 7, 14, 1853; Cleo Hearon, *Mississippi and the Compromise of 1850,* vol. 14 of *Publications of the Mississippi Historical So-*

ciety (University of Mississippi, 1914), 224–5; Dunbar Rowland, *History of Mississippi, The Heart of the South* 2 vols. (Chicago and Jackson, 1925), I, 737–45; Thomas Pressly, *Americans Interpret Their Civil War* (Princeton, 1954), 284.

47. See Gouge to C, Mar. 28, 1859, C Papers; S. G. Ward to Ward, Jan. 25, 1852, BPOC; C to Peabody, Dec. 29, 1858, Peabody Papers.

48. In 1854 Josiah Randall, one of the trustees for creditors of the Bank of the United States, suggested that part of their receipts from the Texas debt settlement be devoted to the same cause in Mississippi, but nothing seems to have come of this. Sam G. Ward distrusted his intentions. Among the lobbyists dabbling in the debt at various times were Edmond J. Forstall, Abel Corbin, and the improbable George W. Billings, whose antics (such as boasting he had used Stephen A. Douglas in 1850) did more harm than good. After the Civil War the Anglo-American banker, in setting up the George Peabody Fund to aid southern education, included in his donation almost $1.5 million of repudiated bonds of Mississippi and Florida. These states were denied any benefits from the fund for some years. See S. G. Ward to BB, Aug. 5, 1851, Apr. 14, 15, 22, May 6, 10, June 17, July 15, 1853, Feb. 17, 21, 28, Mar. 28, Apr. 25, 1854, Mar. 11, Sept. 16, Oct. 21, 1856, King and Sons to BB, Sept. 26, 1851, Forstall to BB, Apr. 12, 1853, King & Sons to S. G. Ward, Apr. 25, 26, 1853, S. G. Ward to Ward, July 3, Aug. 24, 1855, BPOC; Duncan to Hodgson, June 23, 1870, BPGL; C to S. G. Ward, July 6, Sept. 20, 1853, C to ER, Oct. 28, 1854, Nov. 1, 1869, memo, Jan. 21, 1857, Hyde to James Ogden, Oct. 25, 1859, C Letter Books; Peabody to C, Jan. n.d., 1854, Dec. 10, 1862, C Papers; C to J. S. Morgan, July 13, 1869, unbound letterpress copies, C Papers; Hidy, "Peabody," 284–5.

49. Corcoran originally took $65,000 of Burlington bonds, selling $25,000 to A. C. Harding. The rest was distributed to friends. See statement, C account, May 1, 1852, Sept. 30, 1894, C Papers; A. C. Harding and C&R agreement, June 4, 1852, R Papers; C to Punnett, Oct. 30, 1854, C to mayor of Burlington, Apr. 12, 1855, C to mayor of Keokuk, June 15, 1859, C to J. Cooke (E. W. Clark & Co.), June 9, 1860, C to William Gunton, July 18, 1861, C to E. W. Clark & Co., Feb. 16, 1861, Hyde to mayor of Burlington, Dec. 16, 1862, Jan. 10, 1863, Hyde to Ives, Dec. 16, 1862, Hyde to Messrs. Kelly, July 28, 1863, C to Sidney Webster, Dec. 4,

1865, C to David Rorer, June 6, 24, 28, 1867, June 15, 1868, July 10, 1869, Feb. 28, June 3, Sept. 13, 26, 1870, C to LR, June 12, Dec. 6, 1869, Oct. 10, 1870, Hyde to Rorer, Oct. 26, 1867, Aug. 5, Nov. 17, 1870, Rorer to C, Aug. 25, 1868, copy, Sept. 19, C to city treasurer, Burlington, Mar. 21, 1871, Hyde to ER, June 18, 1863, C Letter Books.

50. Included were an undivided one-sixth of a boat franchise at Dubuque and a terminus for the expanding Illinois Central Railroad across the river at Dunleith; 3,500 acres of unimproved farm land in Iowa; $100,000 par value of Dubuque and Wabash [railroads] stock; and important blocks of real estate in and around Dubuque, Iowa City, Omaha, and Sioux City.

For the rise and decline of the relationship between the two men, see especially C to Jones, Nov. 15, 1852 (cordiality and anxiety to serve), Sept. 29, 1853 (acknowledging mortgage), July 14, 1854 (offering 320 acres of land scrip just received, to be charged to Jones' account), Mar. 31, 1855 (regretting inability to extend additional credit until Texas affair consummated), Apr. 13 (reiterating desire to serve but pleading retirement and denying that promises were made in connection with passage of the Texas bill), Jan. 22, 1856 (asking interest payment and renewal of note), Jan. 7, 15, 1857 (extending overdue debt, now $10,000, and setting schedule of four semiannual payments), Oct. 9 (dunning for overdue notes and suggesting "you can send an order on your pay and mileage, say $3,000, which I can use"—it was the time of the Panic), Nov. 2 (insisting "the matter *must be attended to* without further delay"), Hyde to Jones, Sept. 24, 1858 (threatening foreclosure unless $3,000 paid at once), and below; also Hyde to Jones, Oct. 10, 1854, June 23, 1855, Aug. 21, 25, Sept. 8, 1856, July 8, 1857, Sept. 24, 1858, Feb. 25, 1859, Hyde to C, Feb. 13, 1860, C to treasurer, Chickasaw County, Iowa, Mar. 29, 1862, C Letter Books; Jones to C, Jan. 19, 1859, deed, Sept. 14, 1860, R Papers.

51. Corcoran had ample warning that all was not well. Among other things, Dubuque's debt was misrepresented to him as $20,000 when it was actually over $500,000: there was a single loan of $450,000 abroad which was selling at 75 percent of par. The financier also inquired, "Why is it, in view of the great excitement at the time on the subject, that in a population of 13,000 the whole number of votes polled only amounted to 144 (44 of which were adverse, and 97 in favor of it)." He was satisfied by the explana-

tions, which presumably drew distinctions between city and county loans, and railroad and other purposes. The letter of the law was carefully observed to avoid the sort of irregularity seized upon by Mississippi and Arkansas to justify their earlier repudiations. Corcoran insisted on refunding the 2½ percent commission, sent to him even after he decided against the charge as contrary to law, and Dubuque was to pay interest from day of receipt of the money rather than from date of the contracts. (The city did assume the cost of exchange, taking the full par payments at New York.) Apparently the favorable advice of J. F. A. Sanford, a prominent New York broker and connection of the Chouteaus, contributed to his making the agreement. See C to Sanford, Feb. 21, 27, Mar. 10, 1856, C to Jones, Feb. 16, Mar. 11, Apr. 2, Nov. 3, C to N. A. McClure, Feb. 18, 1856, Feb. 23, 1857, memo, Feb. 19, 1856 (with a curious estimate of the $100,000 as yielding $719,044 when due November 1876 at 10 percent compound interest, but the loan was made on a regular coupon basis), C to Nightingale and Samuels, Mar. 13, Apr. 2, C to mayors of Dubuque, Apr. 2, May 23, June 4, 18, Oct. 20, Nov. 4, Nov. 21, Hyde to Jones, Aug. 16, Hyde to Mayor Wilson, Aug. 19, Sept. 5, Oct. 18, C to clerk of court or recorder of deeds, June 19, C to R & Co., Nov. 21, C to Fox, Nov. 24, Hyde to ER, Nov. 25, 1856, June 18, 1863, C Letter Books.

52. Carl H. Erbe, "Constitutional Limitations on Indebtedness in Iowa," *Iowa Journal of History and Politics* 22 (July, 1924), 397–9, 415–6; Franklin T. Oldt, ed., *History of Dubuque County* (Chicago, n.d.), 145f.

Failure in internal improvements policy compounded the discredit suffered by the Democrats as a result of Buchanan's perverse land policy. See Paul Wallace Gates, *Fifty Million Acres: Conflicts over Kansas Land Policy, 1854–1890* (Ithaca, 1954), ch. 3.

53. See C to mayor of Dubuque, Nov. 5, 15, Dec. 21, 1858, Jan. 18, 1859, C to Jones, Jan. 10, Mar. 29, 1860, Mar. 29, 1862, C to H. Williams, May 11, 1860, C to Joseph Wilson, May 12, Hyde to Jones, Oct. 22, 1860, Nov. 12, 1863, June 22, July 5, 1865, copy, Donelan to C, Jan. 28, 1861, C to Donelan, Feb. 21, C to Babbage & Co., Mar. 29, C to Fox, Apr. 21, Hyde to ER, Jan. 22, Feb. 16, 1864, Nov. 2, 1869, Hyde to C, Mar. 7, Apr. 25, May 6, July 23, 1864, Hyde to Babbage & Co., June 15, Hyde to S. Webster, Nov. 30, 1865, C to Webster, Dec. 5, 11, 1865, Apr. 17,

1868, Jan. 25, 1869, Mar. 31, 1870, Jan. 31, 1871, Hyde to Smedberg, Aug. 24, 1869, C to Rorer, Apr. 4, Sept. 26, 1870, C to ER, May 15, 20, Hyde to Rorer, Nov. 17, C Letter Books; Oldt, *History of Dubuque County,* 145–7, 150, 161, 168–9, 172.

54. See C to William M. Corcoran, Nov. 8, 13, Dec. 18, 20, 1856, Jan. 28, July 7, Sept. 10, 24, 29, Nov. 17, 1857, Oct. 7, 22, Dec. 7, 1858, Jan. 18, 1859, C to anon., Nov. 13, 1856, memos, Apr. 1, 1857, Sept. 1, 1865, C to Rice, Oct. 26, Nov. 9, 1857, June 29, 1858, Hyde to C, July 28, 1857, Apr. 30, 1860, Hyde to Mrs. Call, Dec. 8, 1858, C to Newbold, Apr. 27, May 3, 4, 1858, C to Richard Clayton, July 20, Sept. 5, 1859, Jan. 13, Mar. 1, 17, Apr. 4, May 13, 1862, C to F. P. Corbin, Aug. 6, Oct. 7, 1858, C to treasurer, St. Paul, May 19, June 27, 1860, C to Charles Mackubin, July 9, 22, 1861, C to Berry, Dawson & Co., Mar. 10, 1866, C to president, First National Bank of St. Paul, May 14, 25, July 30, C to mayors of Janesville, Feb. 18, 1856, Milwaukee, May 11, 1859, Oct. 6, 1860, Covington and Nashville, Oct. 10, Memphis, Mar. 12, 1861, C to R & Co., May 20, 1859, C Letter Books; Phelps to C, Dec. 15, 1858, Annie D. Corcoran to C, Aug. 21, 1862, C Papers; Punnett to C, July 22, 1850, W. M. Corcoran to ER, Feb. 7, 1857, R Papers; C account, 1850, C&R ledgers; ER account, R & Co. ledgers.

55. The higher price of 70 was paid by those subscribing on credit; most paid less than half at the outset. The Bank of the Republic was also active in railroad investment in the Middle West during this period. See memo, Sept. 1, 1857, C Letter Books; Elias Yulee account, 1856–1857, R & Co. ledgers; papers in box 223, R Papers; John E. Johns, *Florida During the Civil War* (Gainesville, Fla. 1963), 134, 136, 139; ch. 11, below.

56. A Riggs agent suggested employing Joseph Finegan, a prominent local politician who reportedly owned $51,000, but Riggs and Corcoran insisted on Call. In an odd letter of 1887 an Ocala, Florida, attorney reported finding in the street a memo of tax returns for 1874 on 3,800 acres in Levy County in the name of W. W. Corcoran. "Singular," the old financier commented, and turned it over to his attorney. See C to James F. Soutter, Mar. 11, 15, 12, 23, 1867, Hyde to Smedberg, Mar. 23, Apr. 10, 1867, Oct. 27, 1871, C to R. L. Anderson, Apr. 7, 14, 1887, C Letter Books; Hyde to C, Sept. 16, Oct. 24, 31, Nov. 12, 1867, unbound letterpress copies, C Papers.

57. Call wanted to avoid using local attorneys. See C to ER, June 7, 1879, C to Wilkinson Call, June 7, Hyde to Call, Jan. 22, 24, 1880, Dec. 15, 1881, Sept. 30, 1884, Hyde to G. W. Riggs, Oct. 6, Dec. 14, 23, 1881, Hyde to F. B. Riggs, July 10, 1882, Oct. 20, Nov. 3, 1884, May 2, 25, Dec. 4, 15, 21, 1885, Hyde to John Walker, Oct. 20, 1884, Hyde to R & Co., May 15, 1885, A. T. Brice to C. Morton Stewart & Co. (Baltimore), Nov. 4, Call-Corcoran agreement, Nov. 23, 1885, C Letter Books. Cf. William Watson Davis, *The Civil War and Reconstruction in Florida* (New York, 1913), 657f, 698. Davis, one of the old school of Southern historians, insisted that corruption was purely Republican.

58. Hyde to Call, Apr. 1, 1885, Hyde to F. B. Riggs, Feb. 7, 1888, C Letter Books; speech of George W. Call, Mar. 13, 1885, clipping in C papers; U.S., Congress, 48th Cong., 2d sess., *Congressional Globe,* 226–7, 1831, 2278, 49th Cong., 1st sess., 28–36, 233, and index under "Florida."

59. See C to Sanford, Feb. 27, Mar. 10, Apr. 30, May 27, 29, June 3, 1856, C to LR, May 27, June 3, Oct. 31, 1856, Feb. 7, Oct. 3, Nov. 7, 1857, Hyde to LR, June 11, 1856, F. A. Dick to C, Sept. 12, 1857, C to W. A. Murdock, Oct. 5, 1857, C to Murdock and John H. Thompson, Dec. 11, C to Thompson, Dec. 17, 1857, C to Chouteau, Dec. 11, 1860, Jan. 16, 1862, Mar. 7, 1863, C to Dick, Mar. 25, Apr. 8, 12, June 4, Oct. 25, 30, Nov. 4, 1861, Jan. 16, Feb. 15, 25, Apr. 28, 1862, Feb. 9, June 5, 24, July 20, Aug. 14, 1863, C to Chouteau, Harrison & Valle, Oct. 9, 30, 1861, Feb. 25, Apr. 24, May 26, 1862, Jan. 16, Mar. 7, 1863, Hyde to C, Mar. 7, Hyde to Harrison, July 18, C Letter Books; Peabody to C, Dec. 10, 1856, Hyde to C, Dec. 31, 1862, C Papers; ER ledger, June 30, 1865, R Papers.

60. In the end Riggs wrote off a loss of $27,500 on his original $50,000. Individual morality aside, Corcoran later acknowledged to E. G. Spaulding, on receiving the gift of a copy of his financial history of the war, that making the federal issues legal tender was a vital measure that made possible continuation of the conflict. See Hyde to Dick, Sept. 28, Oct. 1, 1863, Hyde to Chouteau, Harrison & Valle, Oct. 23, 1863, June 14, 1864, Hyde to J. P. Strong, Oct. 24, 1863, Hyde to Nov. 20, 1863, June 30, Aug. 8, 1864, C to Levering, Nov. 27, 1869, C to Chouteau, Nov. 27, C Letter Books; Hyde to C, Dec. 3, 1863, C to E. G. Spaulding, Sept. 13, 1869,

unbound letterpress copies, C Papers; Peabody & Co. to R & Co., Nov. 26, 1864, R & Co. to Peabody & Co., Feb. 21, 1865, C Papers; ER ledger, June 30, 1865, R Papers.

61. Nationalism was a refuge for many, but in Corcoran, who had abandoned his during the Civil War, its return was tinged with expediency. See C scrapbook, Corcoran Gallery; *Diary of Philip Hone, 1828–1851,* ed. Allan Nevins, 2 vols. (New York, 1927), 800; David Maurice Cole, *The Development of Banking in The District of Columbia* (New York, 1959), 250; ch. 12, below.

Chapter 11

1. See John W. Forney, *Anecdotes of Public Men* (New York, 1873), 19.

2. See J. W. Foster and J. D. Whitney to Wilson (commissioner, General Land Office), Jan. 14, 18, 1853, copy, Alpheus Felch Papers, DetPL; Lewis H. Haney, *A Congressional History of Railways in the United States,* 2 vols. (Madison, 1906–1910), II, 54; Frank A. Flower, *The Eye of the North-West . . .* (Superior, 1890), 47f; Alice E. Smith, *James Duane Doty, Frontier Promoter* (Madison, 1954), 327–8, 432 n. 27; George Fort Milton, *The Eve of Conflict: Stephen A. Douglas and the Needless War* (Boston and New York, 1934), 104–5; Allan Nevins, *Ordeal of the Union,* 2 vols. (New York and London, 1947), II, 86. See also Robert W. Johannsen, "Reporting a Pacific Railroad Survey: Isaac Stevens' Letters to Stephen A. Douglas," *Pacific Northwest Quarterly* (October 1956), 100, for Douglas' keen interest in the northern transcontinental route.

3. See Henry H. Sibley to Alexander Ramsey, Apr. 13, 1850, Ramsey Papers, MinnHS; William Allen to Daniel A. Robertson, Feb. 25, 1853, clipping, and other materials passim, Robertson Papers, MinnHS; John McClelland to Julius N. Granger, Apr. 15, 1853, Interior Department, National Archives; Granger account, 1853, C&R ledgers; Henry M. Rice to commissioner, General Land Office, Mar. 6, 1854, Rice Papers, MinnHS; St. Paul *Minnesota Democrat,* Oct. 26, Dec. 14, 1853, Feb. 1, 1854; Walter Van Brunt, ed., *Duluth and St. Louis County, Minnesota: Their Story and People,* 3 vols. (Chicago and New York, 1921), 67f; Nevins, *Ordeal,* II, 86.

4. See Robertson to Douglas, Nov. 21, 1853, Rice to Douglas, Dec. 8, Douglas Papers; Land abstract books, Hudson and Willow River Offices, General Land Office records, National Archives; St. Paul *Minnesota Democrat,* Oct. 5, 1853; St. Paul *Pioneer and Democrat,* Apr. 9, 1856; Van Brunt, *Duluth,* 68f.

5. Corcoran, Riggs, and Rice later put some of their holdings into a joint account and bought more. Cass was related to Dawson by marriage, as was Beck to both Breckinridge and Corcoran. The Kentuckians and Rice also collaborated in other land speculations in Wisconsin, Minnesota, and perhaps elsewhere. During the next few years a small migration, chiefly Kentuckians, from below the Mason-Dixon line gave the politics of Superior and Douglas County a pro-southern cast. Forney had lent Rice $700 in 1852, discounting the note with Corcoran. See Rice to Robertson, Feb. 1, 1854, Rice Papers; Alfred Nicholson to Forney, May 26, 1854, Forney to Nicholson, Aug. 26, 1855, NYHS; L. P. Rankins to John C. Breckinridge, May 28, 1854, Feb. 2, 13, 15, 1855, Douglas to Breckinridge, Sept. 7, 1854, Rice to Breckinridge, Sept. 10, 17, 1854, July, 30, 31, Nov. 23, 25, 1855, Beriah Magoffin to Breckinridge, Sept. 18, 1854, Gov. Powell to Breckinridge, Sept. 19, 27, Oct. 18, 1854, June 5, 1855, Wilson to Breckinridge, Feb. 17, 1855, George Becker to Breckinridge, Apr. 23, R. B. Carlson to Rice, August 6, Breckinridge Papers, LC; Robertson to Charles P. Daly, n.d., Nov. 16, 1854, memos in box labelled "Land Papers," Daly Papers, NYPL; Aiken and Magoffin accounts, C&R ledgers; C to Forney, June 3, 10, 1852, Hyde to C, May 15, 1854, C to D. Cooper, Apr. 20, 26, 1855, C to C. E. Rittenhouse, Apr. 26, C to Breckinridge, May 9, C to E. Rice, June 22, memo, June 30, C to Douglas, July 2, Hyde to Douglas, July 13, 1855, Hyde to Forney, May 14, 1868, C Letter Books; Wallace B. White to Ramsey, Nov. 2, 1858, Ramsey Papers; Philip R. Cloutier, "John C. Breckinridge, Superior City Land Speculator," *Register of Kentucky Historical Society* (January 1959); also see below for the Compromise of 1850 and n. 12.

There were probably other influential men whose names do not appear in the existing manuscripts. Not all interests were represented, however, either nationally or locally. Some (perhaps the South Carolina congressmen) may have been brought into the speculation too late to influence votes (if votes were in fact subject to such influence). In the end even this powerful combination was not quite able to control events in the hectic summer of 1854.

6. Dawson's notorious penchant for land speculation led to his rejection for the post of governor of Kansas Territory. See Hyde to C, Aug. 6, 1855, C Letter Books.

7. By the spring of 1855 Corcoran refused to sign deeds of conveyance unless those for whom he acted agreed to a division of the property and relieved him of the trusteeship. Some still wanted their names kept secret. The result was further inconvenience and irritation, including litigation against Corcoran by Richardson in 1856. See Cooper to Breckinridge, Apr. 16, 1854, Rice to Breckinridge, Apr. 28, James Beck to Breckinridge, June 29, 1854, Newton to Breckinridge, Oct. 10, 28, 1855, Bright to Breckinridge, Apr. 9, 1857, Rankins to Breckinridge, July 5, 7, 1857, Breckinridge Papers; C to Walker, Nov. 21, 1854, C to William A. Richardson, Dec. 7, 13, Hyde to Bright, Jan. 3, 1855, memos, Jan. 26, Mar. 5, C to John L. Dawson, Apr. 24, C to Breckinridge, Apr. 26, Hyde to C, July 7, 16, Aug. 20, Oct. 8, 15, 29, Hyde to Dawson, July 10, Hyde to E. Rice, July 13, Hyde to Newton, Sept. 10, Oct. 6, 1855, C to Hunter, May 6, 1856, Hyde to William Newton, Aug. 9, C Letter Books; Robert M. T. Hunter to C, Feb. 17, 19, 1858, C Papers, LC; C account, 1858, R&Co. ledgers; Dawson to Hunter, Aug. 10, 1855, in Charles H. Ambler, ed., *Correspondence of Robert M. T. Hunter*, vol. 1 of *Annual Report of the American Historical Association for the year 1916* (Washington, 1918), 169.

8. Rice also laid out an adjacent area west of Superior as "Superior City." His agents fought off another local group of speculators with some violence, barely avoiding bloodshed. The rivals appealed to the Interior Department at Washington, bringing on years of litigation. Rice was to receive no cooperation in the case from the Pierce administration, toward which he and his cronies at the capital were increasingly hostile, but this had no bearing on Superior, which was launched during their uneasy truce in support of the Kansas–Nebraska Act. See Rice to surveyor general, Dubuque, Jan. 30, 1854, Rice to Robertson and Stinson, or Newton, Jan. 30, Rice to Nelson, Apr. 19, Rice Papers; Letters of John O. Sargent, Register of letters received, Interior Dept. Archives; St. Paul *Minnesota Democrat,* Apr. 23.

9. In July 1856 the company was reportedly spending $1,800 for streets, the town $2,300. The county commissioners were to spend $1,800 on roads. The year's general and road taxation for the proprietors as individuals ranged from $70 to $160. See Hyde to

C, Aug. 13, 1856, C Letter Books; Beck to Breckinridge, July 4, 1857, Breckinridge Papers; St. Paul *Minnesota Democrat,* Oct. 10, 1855; St. Paul *Pioneer Democrat,* Aug 25, 1856; James S. Ritchie, *City of Superior, Lake Superior* (Superior and Philadelphia, 1859), 9f; Flower, *Eye of North-West,* 66f.

10. Daly's agent believed the profit on a road contract of $400 per mile (excluding bridges) was well over 100 percent. See J. H. Simpson to Sibley, Aug. 11, 1854, Sibley Papers, MinnHS; Rice to Breckinridge, Apr. 7, 1856, Breckinridge Papers; Newton to George W. Jones, Apr. 21, Jones Papers, Iowa St.; Trott to Daly, Apr. 2, 1857, Daly Papers; St. Paul *Pioneer Democrat,* Feb. 16, Apr. 4, 1856; Van Brunt, *Duluth,* 105.

11. See Sibley to John H. Stevens, Jan. 29, 1852, Stevens Papers, MinnHS; Rice to Douglas, Dec. 8, 1853, Douglas Papers, UChi; St. Paul *Minnesota Democrat,* Oct. 5, 1853; Nevins, *Ordeal,* II, 86; n. 2, above.

12. During the compromise preliminaries Ashmun and Douglas were also involved in the related negotiations to settle Illinois' long-defaulted debts, and in Illinois Central matters. This complex of issues furnished the first occasion for cooperation between Douglas and Corcoran. The cooperation of Thomas Bayly also links the broad compromise measures (especially the Texas debt and the land grant) with the Mexican indemnity. See ch. 5 and 10, above.

More narrowly, Ashmun tried to arrange a tariff increase advantageous to eastern industry, but this was aborted. Although a Whig and later a Republican, he continued to link his party with the Democratic leader in times of crisis, e.g., on Lincoln's behalf at the outset of the Civil War. In 1850 James Cooper, Whig senator from Pennsylvania, was with Webster from the beginning of his departure from Taylor-Seward Whig policy. See Illinois Central Archives, Newberry Library and James Joy Papers, UMich Library, passim, and M. C. McConkey, "James F. Joy," manuscript biography in latter, 298–300; John Wentworth, *Congressional Reminiscences* (Chicago, 1882), 39–42 and passim; J. Madison Cutts, *A Brief Treatise upon Constitutional and Party Questions . . .* (New York, 1866), 193f; Allen Johnson, *Stephen A. Douglas* (New York, 1908), 475–7; Carlton J. Corliss, *Main Line of Mid-America: Story of the Illinois Central* (New York, 1950), 12–20, 46–7, 56; Paul Wallace Gates, "Disposal of the Public Domain in Illinois, 1848–1856," *Journal of Economic and Business History* 3 (February 1931), 231–3; Howard Gray Brownson, *History of the Illinois*

Central Railroad to 1870 (Urbana, 1915), ch. 2, 68f; Holman Hamilton, *Prologue to Conflict: The Crisis and Compromise of 1850* (New York, 1966), 80, 81, 120–1, 164–5, 179; Irene D. Neu, *Erastus Corning, Merchant and Financier, 1794–1872* (Ithaca, 1960), 73f; John Bell Sanborn, *Congressional Grants of Land in Aid of Railways* (Madison, 1899), 23–37; Henry Greenleaf Pearson, *An American Railroad Builder: John Murray Forbes* (Boston and New York, 1911), passim; Thomas C. Cochran, *Railroad Leaders, 1845–1890; The Business Mind in Action* (Cambridge, Mass. 1953), ch. 3; Richard C. Overton, *Burlington Route: A History of the Burlington Lines* (New York, 1965), part 1, ch. 3–4.

Westward strategy and tactics and some of the major alliances and rivalries are discussed in Arthur M. Johnson and Barry E. Supple, *Boston Capitalists and Western Railroads: A Study in the Nineteenth-Century Railroad Investment Process* (Cambridge, 1967), ch. 4, 6, 7, 8, 9, 16, with much pertinent detail. Although the book became available too late to be assimilated herein the findings in each work correspond on many points, which is particularly interesting since different primary sources were used.

13. Fulton, Arkansas was to be the junction with the Atlantic & Pacific Railroad envisioned by Robert J. Walker and promoted in the East and at Austin, Texas, by Senators Thomas Rusk (Dem., Texas) and William Gwin (Dem., Cal.). Walker was authorized by the company's directors to subscribe in his own name for all available stock of the Cairo & Fulton. Erastus Corning, New York State Democratic leader and one of the New York Central–Illinois Central interlock, stood ready to assist (if federal subsidies could be obtained) with others unnamed, but whose identity may be surmised from his general affiliations. Rusk also was lining up politicians and contractors in Georgia and other "Southron" states. But there were antagonists too and the project proved premature. Unable to secure federal or state aid or private investment, it died while still on paper.

R. B. Mason was outstanding in top operating management, moving back and forth among the Illinois Central, Cairo & Fulton, and Dubuque & Pacific (for which see directly below in text). He was sometimes connected with several of these roads simultaneously.

See copy of speech of Solon Borland, Feb. 18, 1853, and other material, Felch Papers; J. W. Duncan to Rusk, Mar. 7, 1853, Rusk to Truman Smith, Apr. 19, Rusk to Jefferson Davis, Apr. 21, Simeon

Draper to Rusk, Apr. 23, Corning to Rusk, Sept. 24, copy, Atlantic & Pacific Railroad minutes, Nov. 25, Dec. 15, 16, 1853, Walker to Rusk, Feb. 22, June 21, Aug. 5, 1854, Rusk to E. M. Pease, Mar. 30, 31, June 25, Rep. Wm. B. Dent (Ga.) to Rusk, Mar. 31, Rusk to Draper, Matteson, Stryker and Taylor, May 12, Houston to Pease, June 22, Rusk to M. T. Johnson, July 9, Thos. Butler King to Rusk, Aug. 18, 1854, Thos. B. Lincoln to Rusk, July 9, 1856, Rusk Papers, UTex; McClelland to Robert W. Johnson, May 19, 1853, McClelland to Franklin Pierce, Jan. 20, 1854, Interior Dept. Archives; B. F. Johnson (for R. B. Mason) to Roswell Beebe, Feb. 8, 1854, Gov. Elias Conway to Edward Cross, Aug. 7, 1855, Thomas A. Hendricks to Cross, Nov. 25, 1856, David A. Neal to Mason Brayman, Mar. 26, 1857, Hendricks to Brayman, July 18, Brayman Papers, ChiHS; John V. L. Pruyn, Mar. 25, 1854, journal in Pruyn Papers, Alb. Inst.; *American Railroad Journal,* April 11, Aug. 8, 22, 1857; Walter Lee Brown, "Albert Pike, 1809–1891" (Ph.D. diss., University of Texas, 1955), 332f; Frank H. Hodder, "Railroad Background of the Kansas-Nebraska Act," *Mississippi Valley Historical Review* 12 (June 1925), 13; Robert R. Russel, "The Pacific Railway Issue in Politics Prior to the Civil War," *Mississipi Valley Historical Review* 12 (September 1925), 196; Alfred D. Chandler, *Henry Varnum Poor, Business Editor, Analyst, and Reformer* (Cambridge, 1956), 76–7, 111–12; Corliss, *Main Line,* 39–41, 148–9; William Adams Brown, *Morris Ketchum Jesup: A Character Sketch* (New York, 1910), 32; Clark, *Then Came the Railroads,* ch. 3–5 passim, 63; Sanborn, *Congressional Grants,* 64–5; James P. Shenton, *Robert John Walker, A Politician from Jackson to Lincoln* (New York and London, 1961), 129f; Nevins, *Ordeal,* II, 82–7.

14. See Langworthy to Jones, Feb. 7, 1852, Jan. 10, 1853, John Clark to Jones, Nov. 15, 1852, Jones to Cheever, Nov. 4, 1853, Jones Papers; articles of incorporation, Dubuque & Pacific Railroad, Apr. 28, 1853, Jonathan Sturges to John Wentworth, May 5, 11, 1854, Illinois Central Archives; Sturges to Joy, March 11, 13, 1854, Joy Papers; Franklin Oldt, ed., *History of Dubuque County* (Chicago, n.d.), 243f; Washington *Union,* May 29, 30, June 10, 12, 23, 1852; Corliss, *Main Line,* 77, 142–4, 149.

15. See text and correspondence in Arthur W. Thompson, "David Yulee: A Study of Nineteenth Century American Thought and Enterprise" (Ph.D. diss., Columbia University, 1954), 56, 72, 77–85, 99, 101f, 361–80; Roy Franklin Nichols, *The Disruption of*

American Democracy (New York, 1948), 244; below, this chapter.

Another such ally, seeking capital rather than federal land grants (the state owning its public domain), was Senator Thomas J. Rusk of Texas. See the sections on the Collins Line, ch. 8, and the Texas debt, ch. 10, above; also see Orsamus B. Matteson to Weed, Mar. 30, Apr. 22, 1854, Weed Papers URoch; Rusk to Matteson, Dec. 29, 1856, Rusk Papers.

16. See U.S., Congress, 32d Cong., 1st and 2d sess., *Senate* and *House Journals,* Indexes of Bills, H. R. 347; Paul W. Gates, "The Railroads of Missouri, 1850–1870," *Missouri Historical Review,* 26 (Jan. 1932), 131, 134–41; William W. Ackerman, *Historical Sketch of the Illinois Central Railroad* (Chicago, 1890), 36–7; Ira G. Clark, *Then Came the Railroads: The Entry from Steam to Diesel in the Southwest* (Norman, 1958), 26, 63–4; Corliss, *Main Line,* 279; ch. 10, above, on Yulee.

17. There is a possibility, suggested by the situation rather than by explicit evidence, that the bitter Kansas-Nebraska struggle could have been postponed or its outcome altered had the Minnesota & North Western land grant gone forward on schedule. In that case, perhaps the Illinois Central and its supporters would have accepted a delay for itself and its rivals in reaching westward through Kansas or Nebraska. Such a delay might have permitted the Illinois Central to consolidate its lead as construction of already-projected lines went forward. If that possibility ever existed it died when the Minnesota grant was stalled fortuitously before the Kansas-Nebraska bill came up. See the following section of the text.

For a survey of attempts to understand the Kansas-Nebraska controversy, see Roy F. Nichols, "The Kansas-Nebraska Act: A Century of Historiography," *Mississippi Valley Historical Review* 43 (September, 1956), and citations therein, and the same author, *American Leviathan* (New York, 1966), ch. 6. Compare especially Nevins, *Ordeal,* II, ch. 3.

There is an apt formulation of Douglas' general attitude in Thomas E. Felt, "The Stephen A. Douglas Letters in the State Historical Library," *Journal of the Illinois State Historical Society* (Winter 1963), 684:

> On the issues of the 1850's, the Illinois Senator's strength lay in his consistent effort to search out and build with the cohesive forces in American life—the rapidly improving transportation systems, the drive for national expansion, and the mood of speculative optimism—rather than to offer final solutions to the issues that were dividing

the nation into antagonistic sections. He hoped not so much to solve the basic problem of slavery as to survive it.

See also Douglas' later assertion that he consulted only Jesse Bright and one other northwestern Senator before introducing the Kansas-Nebraska bill, in Johnson, *Douglas,* 229 n; also 239.

18. Robert Johnson was chairman of the Senate Public Lands Committee, through which the Minnesota bill rolled. Soon after Lane made his hostile speech he was refused renewal of a note to Corcoran, endorsed by Forney, for $2,000. Stevens later was to help pass the bill. The Rock Island-Michigan Southern alliance was not so solid and harmonious as the rival, and the Rock Island was inclined toward cooperation. See Langworthy to Jones, Feb. 7, 1852, Jones Papers; W. Cockle to Henry Farnam, Jan. 4, 1853, Farnam to Cockle, Jan. 17, Joseph E. Sheffield to Farnam, Jan. 21, Nov. 7, Jonathan Sturgis to Farnam, Nov. 12, Henry Dwight, Jr., to Gov. Matteson, Dec. 23, 1853, Thomas C. Durant to Farnam, May 13, 1854, John A. Dix to Sheffield, July 3, Farnam Papers, YU Library; Wentworth to Burrall, Jan. 23, 1854, Illinois Central Archives; Rice to Becker, Jan. 31, Rice to Billings, Feb. 3, Franklin Steele to Hercules Dousman, Feb. 2, Dousman Papers, WisHS; J. P. Owens to Ramsey, Mar. 8, Ramsey Papers; Ben C. Eastman to Sibley, Mar. 11, Sibley Papers; Wentworth to Joy, Mar. 11, May 8, Joy Papers; C to James H. Lane, June 12, C Letter Books; U.S., Congress, 33d Cong., 1st sess., *House Journal,* 321–2, 374; St. Paul *Minnesota Democrat,* Feb. 1, 15, Mar. 15, 29; Sanborn, *Congressional Grants,* 54; William Watts Folwell, *A History of Minnesota,* 4 vols. (St. Paul, 1956), ch. 12.

Land grant advocates and proponents of legislation to make free homesteads available to farmers worked against each other. See Matteson to Weed, Mar. 26, 1854, Weed Papers.

19. But Steele later switched to Rice's side. See Charles W. Borup to Sibley, Feb. 18, 1851, Steele to Sibley, Feb. 18, Sibley Papers; White to Ramsey, Mar. 5, 1854, Ramsey Diary, Apr. 4, Ramsey Papers; F. S. Jesup & Co. to Joy, Mar. 13, Joy Papers; Sturges to Burrall, May 15, Burrall to Sturges, June 3, Illinois Central Archives; St. Paul *Minnesota Democrat,* Feb. 22, Mar. 1, 8, 15, 22, Apr. 23; 33 Cong., 1 sess., *House Report* 352 (series 744), "Alteration of the text of House Bill 342," 40; U.S., Congress, 33d Cong., 2d sess., *House Executive Document 35,* "Suit against the Minnesota and North Western Railroad Company."

20. At one point the debate took on a certain mountain style. William Churchwell (Dem., Tenn.) vituperated against William Cullom (Whig, Tenn., and later clerk of the House; his nephew Shelby M. Cullom was about to begin a long career leading to Republican Senator from Illinois). As Rice described it "Cullom jumped over seats & desks & made for Churchwell. The latter drew a pistol and a general commotion ensued. When I saw the pistol *I* was fearful that the *Minnesota Railroad bill would be killed,* altho *some* thought Cullom was in the most danger."

Rice credited Ramsey with influencing the Pennsylvania delegation and denigrated the work of Sibley and Gorman. He urged his Whig ally to buy lots in Superior, remarking, "I had to sell all of my interest for influence." Apparently both men were paid well by Billings. Rice's profits from Superior apparently pulled him out of deep debt for the first time in years. He did not reinvest there but his brother retained an interest.

One lobbyist observed that it was strange how many Congressmen voted against all other land grants but supported the Minnesota & North Western. He cited Jones of Tennessee as an example, widely commented on, of a member absenting himself while opposing all other grants. See D. B. Holbrook to Douglas, June 17, 1850, Douglas Papers; Webster to Fillmore, Aug. 22, 1850, Hiram Ketchum to Fillmore, Feb. 27, 1851, Fillmore Papers, BuffHS; James G. King & Sons to Baring Brothers, Sept. 26, 1851, Apr. 25, 1853, Ward to BB, Aug. 5, 1851, Apr. 22, May 6, June 17, July 15, 1853, Forstall to BB, Apr. 12, BPOC; Billings to Brayman, Dec. 17, Brayman Papers; Wentworth to Burrall, Jan. 14, Mar. 19, Apr. 16, 1854, Illinois Central Archives; Ramsey to Sibley, Jan. 20, Eastman to Sibley, June 6, Sibley Papers; Wentworth to Joy, Mar. 11, McConkey, "Joy," 361–70, Joy Papers; Rice to Stevens, Mar. 27, Rice Papers; Robert Smith to E. B. Washburne, Apr. 8, Washburne Papers, LC; Matteson to Weed, Apr. 30, June 25, 30, Weed Papers; F. S. Jesup & Co. to Jones, May 22, Jones Papers; Billings to Ramsey, May 27, Washburne to Ramsey, June 6, 28, Rice to Ramsey, June 20, July 4, Ramsey Diary, May 7, Ramsey Papers; 33 Cong. 1 sess., *House Report* 353, 69, 72, 78, 80, 87; Brownson, *Illinois Central,* 29f; Nichols, *Disruption,* 533 n. 9. An editorial in the *Wall Street Journal,* Dec. 17, 1963, is the source for the Kennedy quotation.

21. Matteson camouflaged himself by voting against the bill,

with the consent of his allies, when passage was assured. Other Wisconsin Congressmen, including Eastman, protested the withdrawal from market of public land in their state for the Minnesota project. See Matteson to Weed, July 2, 1854, Weed Papers; Billings to Ramsey, July 14, Rice to Ramsey, July 15, McClelland to Jones, H. Dodge, Rice and J. P. Cook, July 8, McClelland to Pierce, July 12, Interior Dept. Archives; St. Paul *Minnesota Democrat,* Aug. 2, 16; Madison *Wisconsin Weekly Argus and Democrat,* Aug. 22, 29; 33 Cong., 1 sess., *House Journal,* 1025–32; Folwell, *History of Minnesota,* I, 306, 324.

22. See J. Cooper to Henry White, Mar. 30, 1849, Meredith Papers, PaHS; Clayton to Crittenden, Apr. 18, 1849, Crittenden Papers, LC; A. M. Mitchell to Ramsey, Jan. 28, 1850, Sibley to Ramsey, Apr. 23, May 18, Dec. 19, 21, 1850, Feb. 9, Dec. 26, 1851, Hollinshead to Ramsey, Sept. 5, 1850, Stevens to Ramsey, Feb. 16, 1851, Ramsey to J. Cooper, Mar. 4, Rice to Ramsey, Apr. 5, Ramsey Papers; Sibley to Stevens, May 15, 1850, Mar. 3, 1851, Ramsey to R. C. Winthrop, Jan. 23, 1851, Ramsey to Stevens, May 28, Stevens Papers, MinnHS; J. Cooper to Fillmore, Aug. 23, 1850, Becker to Fillmore, Sept. n.d., 1850, Mitchell to Fillmore, Oct. 25, 1851, Fillmore Papers, BuffHS; Ramsey to Sibley, May 15, 1851, Sibley Papers; A G. Chatfield to Jeremiah Black, Apr. 4, 1857, Black Papers, LC; New York *Weekly Tribune,* Oct. 10, 1857; Folwell, *History of Minnesota,* I, ch. 10–11.

23. Robertson maintained his newspaper influence. Besides retaining a half-interest he recruited his successor from his Ohio base. Sweetser was an old Indian claims antagonist of Thompson and Bright in Indiana. After the rapprochement he too was served a slice of the Indian pie. Charles D. Fillmore, brother of the President, was involved in local politics and Indian affairs. See Sibley to Hollinshead, Jan. 7, 1853, Dousman to F. B. Sibley, Jan. 14, 25, Smith to Sibley, Feb. 1, Rice to Sibley, Feb. 3, Sibley to Mitchell, Feb. 8, copy, petition by fifty-eight members of Congress, Feb. 21, J. Van Etten and Madison Sweetser to William K. Sebastian, Feb. 26, copy of Robertson deposition, March 19, Ramsey to Sibley, Mar. 8, Steele to Sibley, Mar. 30, Frederick C. Gebhard to Sibley, May 9, Sanford to Sibley, May 9, Dousman to Sibley, May 15, J. J. Noah to Sibley, June 1, profit (loss) statement, July 1, 1852, Sibley Papers; copy, Ramsey statement, Mar. 2, 1853, Sibley to Ramsey, Dec. 23, endorsed drafts, etc., of treaty payments of $593,000, Ramsey Papers; Rice to Robertson, Apr. 19,

1854, Robertson Papers; C to Sanford, June 23, 1855, C Letter Books; Chatfield to Black, Apr. 4, 1857, Black Papers; Folwell, *History of Minnesota,* ch. 10–11; Charles Roll, *Colonel Dick Thompson, the Persistent Whig* (Indianapolis, 1948), 116–22; ch. 12, below.

24. Sibley, whose roots were in Michigan, had favored Lewis Cass for president in 1852. Rice's support may have been perfunctory: his friend Senator George W. Jones was the only member of the neighboring Iowa and Wisconsin delegations to oppose Sibley.

25. For McClelland and his department see below, and Paul W. Gates, *Fifty Million Acres: Conflicts over Kansas Land Policy, 1854–1890* (Ithaca, 1954), index under George Manypenny and passim. (Note the strictures on page 5; but I doubt that the Pierce administration at the Cabinet level should be identified in corruption with the Buchanan.) Compare also the course followed by Guthrie in Treasury, to whom the same variety of interpretations may apply as to Gorman and McClelland: ch. 6, above.

26. Nor was adequate help to be found in Washington. Gorman came out of an Indiana Democratic faction which was at odds with Bright. The latter lost no time in attacking the new governor, whose appointment contributed to his venomous hatred of Pierce. Bright was temporarily able to reconcile his Indiana opponents, cutting Gorman off from possible support there. More broadly, the isolation (if not irrelevance) of Gorman in Minnesota paralleled that of Pierce in national politics. See Sibley to Douglas, Mar. 16, 1853, Willis A. Gorman to Douglas, Nov. 25, Douglas Papers; A. C. Dodge to Pierce, Mar. 16, 1853, Sibley to Marcy, Mar. 16, Sibley to Pierce, Mar. 16, Dodge to Sibley, Mar. 31, June 25, Stevens to Sibley, Aug. 11, Rice to Sibley, Oct. 3, 1853, Jan. 7, 1854, Ramsey to Sibley, Dec. 23, 1853, Jan. 8, 1854, Eastman to Sibley, Dec. 9, 24, 1853, Jan. 1, 5, Feb. 3, 9, 1854, Van Etten to Sibley, May 21, 1853, Sibley Papers; Sibley to Ramsey, Apr. 1, Dec. 7, 23, Richard M. Young, draft of report, Dec. 20, 1853, Billings to Ramsey, Jan. 6, 1854, D. Cooper to Ramsey, Jan. 11, White to Ramsey, Jan. 12, 1854, Ramsey Papers; Dodge to Sibley, Apr. 1, 1853, Robertson Papers; Gorman to Caleb Cushing, Jan. 10, 1854, Cushing Papers, LC; St. Paul *Minnesota Democrat,* Feb. 15, 1854; Wayne J. Van der Weele, "Jesse David Bright, Master Politician from the Old Northwest" (Ph.D. diss., Indiana University, 1948), 119f, 130; Roy F. Nichols, *Franklin Pierce:*

Young Hickory of the Granite Hills (Philadelphia, 1958), 403f.

27. Among the Michigan Southern crowd in the St. Charles company were Edwin C. and Electus B. Litchfield, John Stryker, George Bliss, and Henry Dwight, Jr. Alvah Hunt lobbied for it at Washington and for the Iowa Central as well. This campaign reveals the tensions between the Michigan Southern and the Rock Island, which was led by such figures as Henry Farnam, Joseph Sheffield, Azariah Flagg, and Thomas Durant. The latter road was planning to cross Iowa from Davenport, opposite Rock Island, to Council Bluffs by means of the Missouri & Mississippi Railroad. See proof, newspaper advertisement, Feb. 1, 1853, F. Street to H. Price, Oct. 3, W. G. Woodward to Farnam, Oct. 5, Sheffield to Farnam, Oct. 21, Nov. 2, 7, Dec. 2, George B. Sargent to Farnam, Nov. 17, 1853, Feb. 4, 1854, John P. Cook to Farnam, Dec. 15, 1853, Jan. 26, 1854, H. Dwight, Jr., to Governor Joel A. Matteson, Dec. 23, 1853, Thomas C. Durant to Farnam, May 13, 1854, Farnam Papers; Alvah Hunt to Weed, Mar. 12, July 7, Weed Papers.

Washburne went so far as to ask that George Billings, chief Illinois Central and Minnesota & North Western lobbyist at Washington, give personal security for fulfillment of the stipulations, but relented after referring him to Alvah Hunt for further discussions. To help clear the way for the Minnesota grant (and to win support from Washburne's locale) Illinois senators Douglas and Shields yielded a lesser interest of the Illinois Central and sought government mail contracts for a steamer line based at Galena instead of at Dubuque. In return for Washburne's aid in its quest for access to the West the Michigan Southern men promised to build a branch line in Iowa to Tête des Mortes, where he owned large tracts of timbered land.

28. In the words of Alvah Hunt, chief Washington lobbyist for the St. Charles and Iowa Central roads. See Hunt to Weed, July 21, 1854, Weed Papers.

29. Flagg had been comptroller of New York State; Butler, himself only briefly in politics, was brother of Benjamin F. Butler, Attorney General under Jackson and eminent corporation lawyer; Corning had been mayor of Albany and state senator and would later enter the House of Representatives; Dix, former Senator, was to become governor. A business "genealogy" of the Regency might make an interesting study.

Washburne was also concerned with "Locofoco" boasts (by Douglas, Cass, Wentworth, and Jones) that the (initial) defeat of the Minnesota land grant would hurt him in his own district, but he preferred this risk to that of a railroad allied with hostile politicians. He counted on Weed to help safeguard his interests by the selection of friendly New York directors when the company was organized. See Hunt to Weed, Mar. 12, 26, 30, Apr. 30, June 25, July 2, 4, 21, 1854, Matteson to Weed, Mar. 26, 30, Weed Papers; Dix to Sheffield, July 3, Farnam Papers; Bessie Louise Pierce, *A History of Chicago,* I, 483–4; compare 506–8.

30. Senator Stuart was from Rice's hometown of Kalamazoo. A land grant bill for the Iowa Central Railroad was supposed to follow the Minnesota bill through Congress but instead was derailed in its wake. See C. C. Washburn to [Israel] Washburn, Apr. 24, 1853, Cyrus Woodman Papers, WisHS; Matteson to Weed, Mar. 30, July 2, 4, 1854, Harrington to Weed, June 25, Matteson to Draper, July 6, Hunt to Weed, July 7, 21, Draper to Weed, July 8, Weed to Senator Edwin B. Morgan (Whig, N.Y.), July 8, Billings to Ramsey, Apr. 11, July 5, 1854, Washburne to Ramsey, June 6, 28, Rice to Ramsey, July 4, 31, Aug. 3, 14, Ramsey Diary, July 20, Aug. 16, Ramsey Papers; Rice to Robertson, Apr. 19, Rice Papers; Wentworth to Joy, May 19, July 28, Joy Papers; Sibley to Dousman, May 28, Dousman Papers; Eastman to Sibley, June 23, Hugh Tyler to Sibley, Aug. 1, Washburne to Sibley, Aug. 18, 29, Sibley Papers; King to BB, July 11, BPOC; Wentworth to Brayman, July 13, Jesup to Brayman, Aug. 11, Brayman Papers; Atwater to Washburne, July 25, Sibley to Washburne, Aug. 24, Washburne Papers; 33 Cong. 1 sess., *House Report 352,* "Alteration"; *Congressional Globe,* 2171–8; *House Journal,* 133, 1194, 1302; St. Paul *Minnesota Democrat,* July 28, 1854, Mar. 21, 1855; St. Paul *Pioneer Democrat,* Jan. 28, 1856; Chandler, *Poor,* 112–3.

Interestingly, Douglas had once discovered and combated the same fraudulent technique when rivals for the prospective Illinois Central land grant falsified the manuscript of an act amending the railroad's charter. See Cutts, *Brief Treatise,* 189–93.

31. Sibley to Stevens, May 15, 1840, Stevens Papers; N. P. Tallmadge to Fillmore, Nov. 7, 1851, Fillmore Papers; Eastman to Sibley, Jan. 11–12, 1854, Sibley Papers; Rice to Ramsey, July 24, 1854, Ramsey Papers.

32. Washington *Tri-Weekly Union,* July 28, 1854. Compare the

culminating observations in the essays by Charles F. Adams, Jr., "A Chapter of Erie," and Henry Adams, "The New York Gold Conspiracy," in Adams and Adams, *Chapters of Erie* (Cornell University Press edition, Ithaca, 1960), 96–100, 135–6.

33. Rice applied himself to land matters along the intended route. He negotiated a treaty of cession with the Chippewa Indians, with provision for rail and road rights of way, and the sale by the government at $1.25 per acre of part of Fort Snelling (now part of St. Paul) to squatters and speculators. At the same time the Superior speculators gained title to tracts disputed by squatters. See Douglas to Breckinridge, Sept. 7, 1854, Bright to Breckinridge, Sept. 3, Oct. 30, D. Cooper to Breckinridge, Apr. 11, 1855, Breckinridge Papers; Bright to Hunter, Sept. 2, 1854, Ambler, *Corr. of Hunter;* Minneapolis *North Western Democrat,* Apr. 28, 1855; 33 Cong., 1 sess., *Congressional Globe,* appendix, 1122; 33 Cong., 2 sess., appendix, 375–6; Dwight E. Woodbridge and John S. Pardee, eds., *History of Duluth and St. Louis County, Past and Present,* 2 vols. (Chicago, 1910), 69; Folwell, *History of Minnesota,* I, 306.

After the repeal Bright placed articles in Indiana, Kentucky, and Ohio newspapers supporting Hunter's proposal that state-chartered railroad companies be permitted to preempt federal lands along their routes. See Rice to Ramsey, Aug. 14, 1854, Ramsey Papers; Bright to Hunter, Sept. 2, Ambler, *Corr. of Hunter;* Rice to Wilson, Aug. 14, McClelland to Pierce, Aug. 16, McClelland to Wilson, Aug. 29, Sept. 4, Wilson to McClelland, Sept. 4, Interior Dept. Archives; Nichols, *Pierce,* 541.

34. Warren was well connected in both parties. A few years earlier, when he sought an appointment through Senator William Seward and publisher James Watson Webb, he was described by Democrat Erastus Corning as a Whig in whom "we are all" interested. Sibley was allegedly connected with an east-west railroad chartered through St. Croix. Perhaps discouraged by the legal and political problems, Douglas cashed in the profits on his 2/27 share of the Superior company on Mar. 30, 1855. Edmund Rice was the buyer. See Warren to Seward, Apr. 7, 1849, Corning to Seward, Dec. 5, Seward Papers URoch; Ramsey Diary, Oct. 7, 1854, Rice to Ramsey, Aug. 14, John M. Barbour to Ramsey, July 31, 1855, Ramsey Papers; D. A. J. Baker to Cushing, Aug. 1, 1854, and box of papers on investments at St. Croix, Cushing Papers; John E.

Warren to Marcy, Jan. 12, 1855, Marcy Papers, LC; passim, John Barbour Papers, DukeU Library; deed records, Douglas County Courthouse, Superior, Wisconsin; St. Paul *Minnesota Democrat*, Dec. 6, 13, 20, 1854, Jan. 3, 10, 17, 24, Feb. 21, Oct. 3, 10, 17, 1855; Minneapolis *North Western Democrat*, Nov. 4, 1854; St. Paul *Pioneer Democrat*, Jan. 28, Feb. 16, 1856; Nichols, *Pierce*, 403–4; Woodbridge, *History of Duluth*, 98; Folwell, *History of Minnesota*, I, 349–50.

The alignments of businessmen and politicians may also be seen in the advertisements of land agents. For example, Carlos Wilcox of Minneapolis gave as references at St. Paul Gorman, Rosser, and Ramsey (who, as noted, was the only one of these politicians able to maintain his ties among all camps); A. B. Cornell of Owatona, later elected to the state legislature on Henry Rice's ticket, gave the names of Rice and Emerson & Case. See Rice to Breckinridge, June 30 or 31, 1854, Breckinridge Papers; St. Paul *Minnesota Democrat*, Oct. 10, 17, 1855.

35. Clark was from Rice's and Stuart's home of Kalamazoo. See Rice to Ramsey, Aug. 7, 1854, Ramsey diary, Oct. 22, Ramsey Papers; Ramsey and sixteen others to Breckinridge, Aug. 21, Breckinridge Papers; Eastman to Sibley, Aug. 26, Washburne to Sibley, Sept. 30, Sibley Papers; Bright to Jones, Sept. 14, Jones Papers; Eastman to Dousman, Oct. 4, Dousman Papers; St. Paul *Minnesota Democrat*, Sept. 9, 27, Oct. 4, 11, 25, 1854, Aug. 15, 1855; Minneapolis *North Western Democrat*, Oct. 21, 1854; St. Paul *Pioneer Democrat*, Aug. 19, 1858, Apr. 28, 1859.

36. See Rice to Ramsey, Dec. 9, 1854, Ramsey Diary, Dec. 12, 22, Ramsey Papers; A. J. Morgan to Douglas, late January 1855, James Shields to Douglas, Mar. 13, Douglas Papers; 33 Cong., 2 sess., *Senate Report 547; House Journal*, 262–4, 273–41; Minneapolis *North Western Democrat*, Jan. 27, Feb. 3, 10, 1855; St. Paul *Minnesota Democrat*, Mar. 10, 21, 1855.

37. Sibley to Washburne, Feb. 10, 1855, J. B. H. Mitchell to Washburne, Feb. 19, Washburne Papers; Noah to Sibley, Apr. 27, Sibley Papers; St. Paul *Pioneer Democrat*, Jan. 24, 1856.

38. When Rice asked for a copy of Browne's confidential report McClelland replied, "Regarding it not as a paper which any gentleman has a right to demand, I must respectfully decline acceding to your request." Rice's control of territorial patronage had to wait until Buchanan became president.

Breckinridge's election to Congress in 1852 must have been especially pleasing to Corcoran, for the defeated candidate was one of his Mexican indemnity antagonists, Robert P. Letcher. Since Letcher was a popular political humorist-campaigner in the frontier vein, the victory was impressive. Webster is recorded as acquiring twenty-five lots in Superior on Mar. 29, 1855, for the nominal sum of $1 from the proprietors. In contrast Charles Stuart (presumably the senator) paid a total of $400 for four lots Mar. 16. See Bright to Breckinridge, May 10, 1853, Breckinridge to C, May 23, Bright to C, Aug. 7, C Papers; C account, 1853, C&R ledgers; Bright to Breckinridge, June 5, 1853, July 26, 1856, Mar. 30, 1857, John L. Robinson to Breckinridge, n.d., Mar. 30, 1857, W. V. McKean to Breckinridge, June 17, 1853, Forney to Breckinridge, June 17, 1853, Apr. 17, 1855, McClelland to Rice, Jan. 5, 1854, Apr. 23, 1855, Interior Dept. Archives; Gorman to Douglas, May 4, 1854, Mar. 31, 1856, Douglas Papers; I. D. Hoover to Breckinridge, Aug. 6, 1855, Edwin Croswell to Breckinridge, Jan. 18, 1855, V. H. Willson to Breckinridge, Jan. 18, Robert W. Lowber to Breckinridge, Jan. 18, Rice to Breckinridge, Mar. 18, 20, 24, 26, 28, Apr. 12, 15, 21, 30, May 6, 8, 9, Oct. 11, 14, Nov. 25, 1855, Jan. 27, 1856, Mar. 23, Apr. 6, 28, May 13, 1857, F. P. Blair to Breckinridge, Mar. 26, 1855, Guthrie to Breckinridge, Mar. 30, 31, George H. Martin to Breckinridge, Apr. 16, Emerson to Rice, Apr. 19, Sidney Webster to Breckinridge, May 16, Douglas to Breckinridge, May 25, 1855, J. T. Rosser to Breckinridge, Dec. 13, 1856, John B. Floyd to R. J. Breckinridge, Jr., June 8, 1857, Beck to Breckinridge, July 5, Breckinridge Papers; E. M. Willson to Black, Feb. 24, Chatfield to Black, Apr. 4, Black Papers; Rice to Dousman, Dec. 16, Dousman Papers; Deed records, Douglas County courthouse, Superior, Wis.; St. Paul *Minnesota Democrat,* Oct. 24, 1855; Nichols, *Pierce,* 209–10, 403f; Erling Jorstad, "Minnesota's Role in the Democratic Rift of 1860," *Minnesota History* 36 (June 1960); William Wilson Corcoran, *A Grandfather's Legacy* (Washington, 1879), 113–5; ch. 12 and 13, below.

For southern politicians in other frontier territories and states compare Gates, *Fifty Million Acres,* 4; Nichols, *Disruption,* 104f, 264–5; David A. Williams, *David C. Broderick, A Political Portrait* (San Marino, 1970), passim.

39. See Rice to Breckinridge, July 30, 31, Aug. 17, Oct. 11, 14, Nov. 25, 1855, Breckinridge Papers; Rice to Jones, Oct. 14, Jones

Papers; Rice to Stevens, Jan. 7, 1856, Stevens Papers; St. Paul *Minnesota Democrat,* July 25, Aug. 1, 8, 15, 22, 29, Sept. 12, 19, Oct. 3, 31, 1855; St. Paul *North Western Democrat,* Aug. 25, Oct. 6, Nov. 17, 24, 1855, Jan. 5, 19, 26, Feb. 2, 9 (particularly blatant in its cupidity, this article first attacked Rice's spokesman, the *Pioneer Democrat,* for not sharing patronage, then went on to vituperate against the Minnesota & North Western), 1856; St. Paul *Pioneer Democrat,* Feb. 18, 21, 22. One of the losers' journals declaimed, "We have met the enemy and we are theirs."

40. See E. H. Brodhead to Dousman, Apr. 9, 29, 1854, Edward D. Holton to Dousman, July 26, Dousman Papers; S. G. Strong to George H. Paul, Jan. 23, 1855, Paul Papers, WisHS; Madison *Argus and Democrat,* Apr. 16, 1853; Milwaukee *Sentinel,* June 10, 20, 1854; Herbert W. Rice, "The Early History of the Chicago, Milwaukee & St. Paul Railway Company" (Ph.D. diss., State University of Iowa, 1941), 69; August Derleth, *The Milwaukee Road: Its First Hundred Years* (New York, 1948), 42, 51, 68–73, 265.

41. Kilbourn also had political ambitions. An ex-mayor of Milwaukee, he was to lose a bid for the Senate in 1855. The Milwaukee and the La Crosse ultimately became segments of the Chicago, Milwaukee, St. Paul & Pacific system. See La Crosse & Milwaukee minute books, Jan. 1854, Chicago, Milwaukee, St. Paul & Pacific Railway archives, Chicago; Rice, "Early History," 52, 59–62; Derleth, *Milwaukee Road,* 21–4, 42–4, 51, 265–6; A. M. Thomson, *Political History of Wisconsin* (Milwaukee, 1900), 119; Kenneth W. Duckett, *Frontiersman of Fortune: Moses M. Strong of Mineral Point* (Madison, 1955), 112–6; Bayrd Still, *Milwaukee: The History of a City* (Madison, 1948), 137f, 168f.

42. See M. C. Darling to John B. Macy, Apr. 21, 1850, A. Hyatt Smith to Macy, Apr. 22, Macy to Walker, May 20, Thompson & Forman to Walker, Jan. 16, 1852, Maclean, Maris & Co. to Walker, May 3, 1853, Walker Papers; Isaac T. Greene to Moses M. Strong, Jan. 7, 10, 1852, Smith to Strong, Jan. 10, Macy to Strong, Jan. 12, Moses M. Strong Papers, WisHS; Henry D. Gilpin to William B. Ogden, Nov. 1, 1852, Ogden to Edward A. Russell, Oct. 22, 1855, Ogden Papers, ChiHS; Woodman to Ogden, May 18, 1853, Woodman Papers, WisHS; statement, Nov. 24, 1856, C Letter Books; Rock River Valley Union Railroad records, Chicago & North Western Railway Archives, Chicago; Madison *Argus Democrat,* Apr. 30, May 2, 10, 17, 1853; Minneapolis *North*

Western Democrat, Dec. 15, 1855; *Bankers Magazine,* November 1853, 441; Gates, "Land Policy and Tenancy in the Prairie States," *Journal of Economic History,* I (May 1941), 67; [W. H. Stennett], *Yesterday and Today: A History of the Chicago and North Western Railway System* (Chicago, 1910).

43. John Letcher (Dem., Va.) and Francis B. Cutting (Dem., N.Y.) were prominent in opposing this grant, as later they opposed the Minnesota & North Western. See Walker to Douglas, Jan. 27, 1854, Douglas Papers; Daniel Wells, Jr., to Paul, Feb. 13, Paul Papers; Walker to Coryell, Feb. 25, Coryell Papers; 33 Cong., 1 sess., *House Report 353,* 20; Milwaukee *Sentinel,* Mar. 2, 8, 9, 11, 14, 22, 28, 1854; Madison *Argus Democrat,* Apr. 25, May 2, 16.

44. The other three Congressmen were William A. Gilbert (Whig, N.Y.), William W. Welch (American, Conn.), and Francis S. Edwards (American, N.Y.). See U.S., Congress, 34th Cong., 3d sess., *House Report 243,* 20–6, 32–8, 154f, 206, and passim; Chicago, St. Paul & Fond du Lac Record Book B, Chicago & North Western Archives.

45. See W. H. Osborn to J. N. Perkins, Mar. 20, Oct. 4, 5, 6, Nov. 12, 1856, Osborn to Washburne, Apr. 21, Illinois Central Archives; Rice to Breckinridge, May 21, Breckinridge Papers; Rice to Dousman, July 9, Dousman Papers; St. Paul *Pioneer Democrat,* June 4; Madison *Wisconsin Patriot,* Aug. 23; Oldt, *History of Dubuque County,* 245.

46. Senator Jones, who assisted in the Iowa railroad compromises, hoped the policy of something for everybody would strengthen him at home against sharp opposition within his own party and a rising tide of Republicanism. He was temporarily successful. (It is questionable whether his success could have continued even without being overtaken by the Panic of 1857.) The Minnesota & North Western, gasping toward its last, failed to win repassage of its land grant despite the usual exertions and the assistance of Thurlow Weed. The Illinois Central gave up on it and turned its attentions to the Dubuque & Pacific, whose extension toward St. Paul was the one Washburne was most concerned with. The Michigan Southern's hope, the St. Charles, was taken over in 1854 by the Galena and later became part of the North Western. See above on the Regency railroad entrepreneurs, whose common heritage doubtless smoothed the paths of compromise. See James W. Grimes to Joy, Jan. 7, 1852, Apr. 16, 1853, Corning and J. W.

Brooks, trustees, Detroit & Pontiac Railroad to president et al., Detroit & Milwaukee Railroad, Nov. 26, 1856, McConkey, "Joy," 193, 299, 478f, 493–4, Joy Papers; Brayman to Schuyler, Feb. 7, 1853, Wentworth (probably) to Burrall, Sept. n.d., 1853, Ogden to Osborn, Jan. 17, 1855, Osborn to executive committee, Jan. 16, 1856, Sturges to Osborn, Mar. 19, Osborn to Perkins, Jan. 30, Mar. 20, 21, 22, 24, 25, Apr. 1, 15, 16, Dubuque & Pacific Minute Books, June 2, July 24, Illinois Central Archives; McClelland to Dix, Jan. 31, 1854, Interior Dept. Archives; Galena & Chicago Union records, Feb. 1, 2, 1854, Chicago & North Western Archives; E. Langworthy to Jones, Jan. 14, 1855, Jones Papers; Jesup to Strong, May 9, Strong Papers; Bernhart Henn to Breckinridge, Dec. 10, 1855, Breckinridge Papers; Stone, Boomer & Bouton to C. D. Cooke, Dec. 25, 1855, Cooke Papers, WisHS; Dix to Douglas, March 24, May 13, 1856, Douglas Papers; Osborn to Jones, Apr. 22, Jesup to Jones, May 13, Sturges to Jones, July 7, Jones to La Cossitt, July 28, Francis L. Smith to Jones, Oct. 15, 1856, Jones Papers; Dix to Ogden, Jan. 31, 1857, Ogden Papers; Madison *Argus Democrat,* Dec. 11, 1855; Dubuque *Express and Herald,* Apr. 19, June 26, 28, 29, July 1, 11, 1856; *Railroad Record* (Cincinnati), Mar. 3, Sept. 13, Nov. 1, Dec. 6, 1855; *American Railroad Journal* (New York), Apr. 4, 1857, Oct. 23, 1858; Leonard Floyd Ralston, "Railroads and the Government of Iowa, 1850–1872" (Ph.D. diss., State University of Iowa, 1960), 27–8, 33–9; Oldt, *History of Dubuque County,* 243–48, passim; Corliss, *Main Line,* 144–6; Jack T. Johnson, *Peter Anthony Dey* (Iowa City, 1939), 64f; Jacob R. Perkins, *Trails, Rails and War: The Life of General Grenville M. Dodge* (Indianapolis, 1929), 39; Allan Nevins, *Abram S. Hewitt, with Some Account of Peter Cooper* (New York, 1935), 156f, 252; Glyndon G. Van Deusen, *Thurlow Weed, Wizard of the Lobby* (Boston, 1947), 220–30; Pierce, *Chicago,* II, 483f; Stennett, *Yesterday and Today,* 17, 25, 37; Nevins, *Ordeal,* II, 205, 239. For the Iowa routes of the developing systems see the map in Overton, *Burlington Route,* 88. For the political scramble in Iowa see Morton M. Rosenberg, "The Kansas-Nebraska Act in Iowa: A Case Study," *Annals of Iowa* (Fall 1964), 450, 456–7; "The First Republican Election Victory in Iowa," Ibid. (Summer 1962), 359, 364f.

47. Douglas' sale of his shares was not recorded officially (publicly) until June 17, 1856, when the convention was out of the

way. See I. Woodle to Douglas, May 8–18, 1856, Douglas Papers; George Smith manuscript diary, Mar. 14, 18, 19, 23, 28, Apr. 1, 1857, WisHS; Byron Kilbourn memo, WisHS; deed records, Douglas County; St. Paul *Pioneer Democrat,* May 19, 1856; New York *Tribune,* May 23; Milwaukee *Sentinel,* Sept. 16; Sanborn, *Congressional Grants,* 98–9.

48. Among Barstow's friends were Isaac V. Fowler of New York, a venal Tammany leader who invested in the St. Croix & Lake Superior after the grant was obtained. Corcoran apparently declined to invest, apart from the proprietors' grant. He had already put $20,000 or more into Milwaukee & Mississippi and Milwaukee City bonds, partly at Kilbourn's solicitation, and wanted to limit his risk. See D. V. N. Radcliff to Barstow, May 31, 1855, Radcliff to Attorney General Smith, May 31, Kilbourn to Strong, Apr. 2, 1858, copy, memo for investigating committee, Strong Papers; Hyde to C, July 10, 1855, Oct. 13, 1863, Hyde to Kilbourn, July 12, 1855, Hyde to Otis Hoyt, Sept. 6, C to Beck, Aug. 1857, C to R&Co., Oct. 9, 1860, C Letter Books; Newton to Breckinridge, Apr. 10, 1856, Breckinridge Papers; Josiah Noonan to Horace A. Tenney, June 10, 1856, Tenney Papers, WisHS; Barstow to I. V. Fowler, Aug. 6, WisHS; Receipt, Nov. 7, 1856, George B. Smith Papers, WisHS; Kilbourn memo; Madison *Argus Democrat,* Jan. 17, 1854, May 28, 29, 30, 1856; *American Railroad Journal,* Mar. 24, 1855; St. Paul *Minnesota Democrat,* Aug. 22, Oct. 24, 1855; Milwaukee *Sentinel,* Apr. 17, June 27, Sept. 25, 1856, June 3, 1857; St. Paul *Pioneer Democrat,* May 20, 1856; *Railroad Record,* June 26; Madison *Wisconsin Patriot,* Aug. 2; Van Brunt, *Duluth,* 107; Van Deusen, *Weed,* 228.

49. Kilbourn letter, Milwaukee *Sentinel,* June 3, 1857.

50. Madison *Argus Democrat,* Sept. 8, 12, 23, 1856; Milwaukee *Sentinel,* Sept. 22, 23, 24, 27, 29, 1856, June 3, 8, 1857; *American Railroad Journal,* Nov. 8, 1856.

51. It is not certain whether the arrangement was intended to be temporary on both sides, or the new directors were driven out cynically or in retaliation for loss of power in the other grant (see n. 53 below), or they resigned after gaining better insight into the shaky state of the company. See La Crosse & Milwaukee minute books, Sept. 20, 30, Oct. 15, 22, 1856, Jan.–Apr. and passim 1857, Milwaukee System Archives.

52. Milwaukee *Sentinel,* Sept. 20, 1856; *American Railroad*

Journal, July 11, 1857, Feb. 20, 1858; John M. Bernd, "The La Crosse and Milwaukee Railroad Land Grant, 1856," *Wisconsin Magazine of History* 30 (December 1946).

53. It was rumored that enmity between Barstow and Bashford was a serious obstacle. In the 1855 gubernatorial election Barstow was originally counted the victor but Bashford won after he appealed to the courts on grounds of voting frauds. Business was business, however. The go-between was doubtless B. H. Hopkins, a director of the La Crosse and private secretary to Bashford.

Among other changes, the governor was authorized to name two directors of the Wisconsin & Superior Railroad, an amalgamation of Ogden, Kilbourn, and other interests just formed to exploit the northeastern grant. Bashford's brother was one of those named; the other was a close associate. He then mended his fences; his appointees to the Wisconsin & Superior joined to throw its control to the Ogden interests. This may even have been Ogden's first priority, for he, Samuel Tilden, and other associates had large land holdings, believed rich in iron and other ores, in northeast Wisconsin and the northern peninsula of Michigan. Moreover, the Ogden group could retain some hope for a Pacific link since the charter route of the company took it to Superior, although by a roundabout route. The cost to the Chicago, St. Paul & Fond du Lac was substantial, although small in comparison to its rivals: perhaps not more than $200,000, mostly in bonds and including expenditures in Washington.

See Smith diary, June 20, 1855, June 11, 12, 14, July 18, Aug. 5, 6, 7, Oct. 7, 13, 16, 17, 18, Nov. 8, 23, 1856, Feb. 22, 23, 24, Mar. 5, 11, 12, May 5, 1857, Apr. 20, 1858 (or, Hell hath no fury like a politician hipped away from the trough; and a Brechtian touch in the last entry), Smith to Alex Gray, Sept. 4, 1856, Smith to Newton, Oct. 31, Smith Letter Books; Newton to Daly, Oct. 14, Daly Papers; David ("Hose") Nozzle to Tenney, Nov. 19, 1856, Noonan to Tenney, Jan. 1, Feb. 4, 23, June 17, 1857, H. W. Tenney to Tenney, Feb. 14, Tenney Papers; memo, n.d., 1857, Otis Hoyt Papers, WisHS; Ogden to Samuel J. Tilden, Oct. 18, 25, 1857, Tilden Papers, NYPL; La Crosse & Milwaukee minute books, Nov. 12, 1858, Milwaukee System Archives; Kilbourn memo; Milwaukee *Sentinel*, May 5, 8, 23, Sept. 12, 30, Oct. 1, 9, Nov. 14, 15, 1856; Madison *Argus Democrat*, Oct. 2, 3, 8, 9, 11, Milwaukee *News*, Sept. 25, Oct. 7, 8, 31, Nov. 1, 2, 4, 14, 16, 23, 28; Madison *Wisconsin Patriot,* Oct. 4, 18, Dec. 27, 1856, June 13, 1857, Apr. 10, May 1, 29, 1858; Wisconsin Legislature, *Report of Joint Select Committee,* "Alleged Frauds . . . ," 1858; Charles Whittlesey, *Railway Connections with Lake Superior: Letter to the Hon. Truman Smith* (Cleveland, 1853), 3–12 (indicating the Ogden–Michigan southern interest in a road to the northern peninsula); Smith, *Doty,* 337–41; Duckett, *Frontiersman,* 127–30; Thomson, *Political History of Wisconsin,* 121–9; Bernd, "La Crosse Grant."

54. Late in 1856 the proprietors' manager at Superior had high hopes for a Pacific railroad land grant from that point. See Newton to Daly, Oct. 30, 1856, Daly Papers; G. W. Strong to Strong, May 1, 2, 1857, with clipping from St. Paul *Advertiser,* Apr. 25, Strong Papers; Milwaukee *Sentinel,* Apr. 17, 1856; Madison *Wisconsin Patriot,* Sept. 27, 1856, May 9, 1857; St. Paul *Pioneer Democrat,* Dec. 5, 1856; Smith, *Doty,* 337f.

55. The land grant question threatened to become entangled in the complexities of a dispute over the boundaries of the new state, but this was averted by solution of that question. Among those at St. Paul for the standard distribution ceremonies were the ubiquitous Ashmun, Congressmen Sheppard Leffler (Dem., Iowa), James Thorington (Whig, Iowa), Daniel Mace (Dem., Ind.), and the "Formerly Miss. Rose Walker," as well as a host of Wisconsin promoters. For the sake of appearances Rice chose to absent himself from St. Paul until the festivities were concluded. See Rice to Breckinridge, Apr. 28, 1857, Bullock to Breckinridge, July 31, 1856, Breckinridge Papers; Rice to Ramsey, Oct. 1, Dec. 20, 1856, Jan. 19, Mar. 7, Apr. 5, 1857, Horace Greeley to Ramsey, May 22, Ramsey Papers; C to Mrs. S. E. Thom, Dec. 22, 1856, C Letter Books; Shields to Daly, Jan. 16, May 6, 1857, Daly Papers; Shields to Sibley, Jan. 12, Dousman to Sibley, Jan. 31, Sibley Papers; Sibley to Dousman, Feb. 14, Dousman Papers; G. W. Strong to Strong, May 17 (indicating fruitless efforts by La Crosse & Milwaukee agents in Iowa to gain subsidies for extensions into that state), clipping from Milwaukee *Sentinel,* Apr. 10, Strong Papers; Milwaukee *News,* Apr. 28, May 6, 1856; St. Paul *Minnesota Democrat,* Nov. 22; Milwaukee *Sentinel,* Apr. 10, 1857; Madison *Wisconsin Patriot,* May 30; 34 Cong., 3 sess., *House Report 243,* 110–1, 180–1; Ritchie, *Superior,* 1–4, 15f; Folwell, *History of Minnesota,* I, 405f passim, map, 487.

56. Dillon, Jackman, Jannett & Co. of Pennsylvania were the

contractors for the St. Croix & Lake Superior road and were among the lobbyists at St. Paul. They had earlier been linked to Robert J. Walker and the Rock River Valley Union Railroad in Wisconsin. See James Gamble to Ramsey, Apr. 27, 1857, W. R. Marshall to Ramsey, May 8, Ramsey Papers; Kilbourn to Strong, May 12, G. W. Strong to Strong, May 14, draft of citation accompanying gift of $50,000 of La Crosse & Milwaukee securities to Kilbourn, June 3, Strong Papers; Noonan to Tenney, May 24, 1858, Tenney Papers; Kilbourn memo; Milwaukee *Sentinel,* Oct. 13, 15, 1856, April 22, May 3, 27, June 15, 1857; St. Paul *Pioneer Democrat,* Nov. 5, 14, 1856, Mar. 11, 18, 25, 1858; Madison *Wisconsin Patriot,* May 16, June 20, 1857.

57. See Trott to Daly, Oct. 15, 1856, Daly Papers; Dawson to Breckinridge, Oct. 29, Newton to Breckinridge, Oct. 30, Beck to Breckinridge, June 29, July 5, 1857, Breckinridge Papers; C. C. Washburn to Woodman, Nov. 7, Dec. 7, 1856, Woodman Papers; Kilbourn memo; Milwaukee *Sentinel,* May 14, 1856; Madison *Argus Democrat,* Sept. 24, Oct. 2; Milwaukee *News,* Nov. 25; *American Railroad Journal,* July 11, 1857, Feb. 20, 1858; Rice, "Early History," 160, 167.

58. Henry Rice, detecting signs of monetary pressure and pessimistic about the early construction of a railroad, disagreed with his brother and shrewdly advised Breckinridge to sell his quarter-share at even less than the going price in the spring of 1857. Rice's contention was that, even if he were wrong, Breckinridge would still have plenty left in individual lots and that, above all, he must not be hampered by financial difficulties—an indication of Rice's hopes for Breckinridge's elevation. Bright, although surprised to learn of poor agricultural conditions in the West, remained bullish about Superior. He urged friends not to sell and took $18,000 for his quarter-share because of need and with genuine reluctance. (Bright also sold fifty lots to Elisha Riggs, Jr., for $12,500.) In 1858 the Rices and Newton reportedly had liquidated their entire holdings, leaving bitterness among the remaining population. For some time Rice had had to defend himself against charges of sacrificing the interests of Superior to those of his own town site of Bayfield to the east on Lake Superior. (He had almost named the place "Corcoran" before being advised not to by Breckinridge.)

Moreover, Rice was associated in the laying out of Duluth, across the river in his own state of Minnesota. Despite disadvantages in natural harbor facilities Duluth was to forge rapidly ahead of Superior, winning later struggles for government and railroad patronage by outbidding the Superior proprietors. Perhaps the latter were hampered by their Democratic ties after the rise of the Republican party. For years Corcoran held his property through Civil War threats of confiscation, high taxes, and accompanying legal difficulties. Only after 1880 was there meaningful progress in railroad connections and town development followed by small profits. See Bright to Hunter, July 19, 1855, R. M. T. Hunter Papers, LC; Rice to Breckinridge, Nov. 23, 25, Dec. 15, 1855, May 23, June 18, July 4, 22, 28, Aug. 2, 1857, Beck to Breckinridge, May 10, 1856, Apr. 27, June 26, 29, July 4, 5, 1857, Rankins to Breckinridge, July 5, 7, 1857, Dawson to Breckinridge, June 21, 1856, Bright to Breckinridge, Aug. 4, 1857, Breckinridge Papers; Deeds, Apr. 20, 1857, tin box number 2, portfolio number 2, Riggs Papers; Bright to C, May 24, 1857, C Papers; Trott to Daly, Feb. 22, 1858, Newton to Daly, Aug. 19, Daly Papers; White to Ramsey, June 21, 1858, Ramsey Papers; Rice to Dousman, Sept. 27, 1860, Dousman Papers; Hyde to Elias Gill, June 23, 1856, C to William F. Roelofson, Feb. 28, Mar. 6, 1857, Hyde to L. Hilliard, Mar. 26, 1864, Hyde to C, Mar. 14, 1864, Mar. 28, Hyde to William Selden, Jan. 11, 1866 (and several dozen other letters as cited in Cohen, "Business and Politics," dissertation version, 499), C Letter Books; St. Paul *Pioneer Democrat,* Oct. 4, 1856; Van Brunt, *Duluth,* 93f; Folwell, *History of Minnesota,* I, 333, n. 12; John L. Harnsberger, "Land, Lobbies, Railroads and the Origins of Duluth," *Minnesota History* 37 (Sept. 1960).

Chapter 12

1. It was deemed inexpedient to have Corcoran's name appear in the transaction. John T. Sullivan furnished the money on his guarantee. See C to Sullivan, Dec. 2, 1851, C Letter Books.

2. The loans to Forney and Jones were $1,500 each. Forney in turn lent to Senator James Mason. See C to ER, Apr. 5, Oct. 5, 1847, C to J. G. Jones, July 7, 1853, C to Forney, Apr. 3, 1854, C to Buchanan, May 26, 1856, C to Magraw, May 26, C to J. E. Thayer & Bro., Feb. 8, 1858, C Letter Books; ER to Buchanan, Jan.

12, 1850, C to Buchanan, Feb. 26, Buchanan Papers, PaHS; Buchanan to C, July 15, 1850, May 3, 1858, C Papers, LC; Forney to Breckinridge July 9, 1854, Breckinridge Papers, LC; Roy F. Nichols, *The Democratic Machine, 1850–1854* (New York, 1923), 67, 70; Nichols, *The Disruption of American Democracy* (New York, 1948), 13, 42, 45, 46; Ulrich B. Phillips, ed., *Correspondence of Robert Toombs, Alexander H. Stephens, and Howell Cobb,* in *Annual Report of the American Historical Association for the Year 1911* (Washington, 1913), II, 330; William Wilson Corcoran, *A Grandfather's Legacy* (Washington, 1879), 81–2; Allan Nevins, *Ordeal of the Union,* 2 vols. (New York and London, 1947), II, 133; Nevins, *The Emergence of Lincoln,* 2 vols. (New York and London, 1950), I, 67–8.

3. Bright, the Indiana Senator who nursed a venomous grudge against President Pierce, warned Douglas and Robert Hunter of Virginia, another candidate, that he would not support either if they went for him "in any way." These last words presumably included acceptance of Pierce's support, without which they had no chance; but the decision to support Buchanan had been taken already and the warning was only a smokescreen. See C to Peabody, Feb. 9, 1856, Peabody Papers; C to Corwin, May 3, 26, C to Punnett, June 2, 4, C to Winslow, Lanier, June 4, C Letter Books; Slidell to Barlow, May 7, 28, June 22, Barlow Papers, HuntL; Bright to Benjamin Fitzpatrick, May 21, NYPL; C to Buchanan, May 27, 31, Martin to Buchanan, June 3, Forney to Buchanan, Nov. 12, Buchanan Papers; Buchanan to Slidell, May 28, copy in Breckinridge Papers; Buchanan to C, May 29, C Papers; Wayne J. Van der Weele, "Jesse David Bright, Master Politician from the Old Northwest" (Ph.D. diss., Indiana University, 1958), 135f, 150; George Fort Milton, *The Eve of Conflict: Stephen A. Douglas and the Needless War* (Boston and New York, 1934), 223–5; Nichols, *Disruption,* ch. 1; Nevins, *Emergence of Lincoln,* I, 81–2, 273–4; Richard C. Bain, *Convention Decisions and Voting Records* (Washington, 1960), 59 and appendix D; ch. 10 and 11, above.

4. Graham Fitch was particularly recalcitrant, finally paying his debt in 1875 after acrimony and litigation. See C to A. J. Harlan, Jan. 12, May 31, Oct. 25, 26, Dec. 24, 27, 1855, Mar. 3, Apr. 21, May 24, 1856, C to Wesley Wilson, Dec. 24, 1855, C&R to Graham N. Fitch, Mar. 12, 27, 1855, Mar. 26, June 6, July 12,

1861, C to Fitch, June 15, 1855, Dec. 21, 1857, Feb. 13, 1866, Hyde to C, Apr. 7, July 16, Aug. 20, 26, 1855, Hyde to C. L. Dunham, Aug. 15, Sept. 21, 1855, C to Dunham, Jan. 21, 1856, C&R to Dunham, Apr. 21, memo, Dec. 20, 1856, Hyde to Bright, Aug. 15, 1855, Nov. 3, 1865, Nov. 25, 1867, Dec. 15, 1869, Apr. 24, 1874, C to Bright, Jan. 3, Nov. 3, 1857, Nov. 27, Dec. 7, 23, 1868, Jan. 6, 1869, May 6, 1870, Hyde to William Henderson, July 16, Aug. 19, 1867, Sept. 30, 1868, Dec. 13, 1869, Henderson to Hyde, copy of Nov. 19, 1868, Nov. 23, C to Henderson, Dec. 10, 14, 21, 28, 1868, Jan. 4, 1869, C to Richard W. Thompson, Jan. 12, 1869, Hyde to Smedberg, Apr. 18, 1870, Hyde to Baldwin, Jan. 13, 1873, C to D. D. Pratt, May 22, 1874, Hyde to Dent & Black, July 17, 1875, C Letter Books; Bright to C, Jan. 15, 16, 30, 1857, R&Co. to C, May 17, 1865, C Papers; C to Bright, Aug. 6, 1866, unbound letterpress copies, C Papers; Bright account, R&Co., ledgers.

5. See Nevins, *Ordeal,* II, 459; Nichols, *Disruption,* 17; Bain, *Convention Decisions,* 59–60, appendix D; ch. 10 and 11, above.

6. Corcoran's loans to Francis Grund helped send that immigrant knight-errant on tour to appeal for the votes of the German-speaking community. Corcoran also tried to recruit at least one Whig leader, Thomas Corwin, taking the opportunity while offering him a loan. Corwin did not convert, however. Bright testified to Corcoran's role: "We had a meeting of Senators and Representatives . . . last evening [July 16], friendly to the election of Buchanan. . . . Mr. Faulkner stated that a Citizen of this District had contributed more than they had received from *all other sources.* The word passed rapidly around the Chamber that *you* must have been that Citizen, though Mr. F. did not mention the name. I heard some remarks then about *your liberality* in such matters, very complimentary to you and which was very gratifying to me as I know them all to be true. . . . Some of our friends here, I mean Douglas, Slidell & etc. think that you have it in your power to do great good in our cause, by traveling through the principal Cities East, representing that a vote from Fremont is a vote for disunion and that his election must ruin all the Commercial and monetary interests of the United States—that your property in this District, you would regard as valueless if the Republican party comes into power &c." Corcoran traveled to New York (several times), Newport, Boston, and Philadelphia between September 1

and October 15, See Corwin to C, June 2, 1856, Bright to C, July 17, Slidell to C, July 24, Sept. 23, C Papers; C to Corwin, June 28, July 21, Hyde to C, July 21, Sept. 3–Oct. 14, Hyde to William Bigler, July 22, C to Elliott, Sept. 23, 25, C to Punnett, Sept. 23, C to Grund, Sept. 29, 1856, Mar. 26, 1857, C to S. H. Kerfoot & Co. (Chicago), Oct. 1, 1856, C to Whelen, Jan. 27, 1857, C Letter Books; Corcoran, *Grandfather's Legacy,* 102–3, 146–7; Nevins, *Ordeal,* II, 415–504; Allan Nevins, *Fremont, Pathmarker of the West* (New York and London, 1939), 452–3.

7. Bright's biographer states that the merger of Know-Nothings and Republicans would *probably* (my emphasis) not have occurred in any case because conservatives preferred Buchanan to Fremont. See memos, Mar. 10, 1855, Mar. 26, 1857, Hyde to Thompson, July 21, 1856, Hyde to C, Aug. 9, C Letter Books; Bright to C, Oct. 12, 25, 1856, C Papers; Thompson account, R&Co. ledgers; Van der Weele, "Bright," 185–8; Roger H. Van Bolt, "The Rise of the Republican Party in Indiana, 1855–1856," *Indiana Magazine of History* 51 (September 1955), 200, 215–6. Elsewhere, too, the Democrats were supporting the Know-Nothings to divide the opposition. See Nevins, *Fremont,* 452–3.

8. Corcoran disliked the violent nativism of the Know-Nothing movement. (But see below, citations in n. 35, for quiet discriminations against Jews.) In 1854, for example, he contributed $1,000 (having offered double that) to the unsuccessful campaign of Whig Joseph R. Chandler, a Protestant running with Catholic support, for reelection to the House. Corcoran later hoped to attract such men to the Democratic party. In 1858 Chandler was appointed Minister to the Kingdom of the Two Sicilies. See C to Jewett, Oct. 13, 1856, C to Fillmore, Oct. 30, C to R&Co., Nov. 6, C Letter Books; John S. Riddle to Sullivan, Sept. 29, 1854, C Papers; Philip G. Auchampaugh, *Robert Tyler* (Duluth, 1934), 182–4; Corcoran, *Grandfather's Legacy,* 147, 152.

9. Corcoran seems to have been disappointed in Buchanan's Cabinet. See C to Fox, Nov. 24, 1856, Hyde to S. L. M. Barlow, Dec. 11, C to Augustus Schell, July 8, 1857, Hyde to Lewis Cass, Oct. 5, 26, 27, C to John B. Palmer, Oct. 26, C to Wetmore, Jan. 4, 1858, C Letter Books; Gov. Henry A. Wise to H. A. Wise, Nov. 27, 1856, Wise to Gov. Wise, Nov. 28 ("Bright, Slidell and Corcoran drive Unicorn in these matters"), Dec. 9, Henry A. Wise Papers, photostats in LC; Bright to C, Jan. 27, 1857, Barlow to

C, Feb. 11, Fay to C, Feb. 26, C Papers; Nevins, *Emergence of Lincoln,* I, 71f; Nichols, *Disruption,* 53; Reinhard H. Luthin, *The First Lincoln Campaign* (Cambridge, 1944), 120.

10. See Hyde to Bright, July 7, 1858, C "To the President of the United States," July 14 (not sent), C Letter Books; C to Peabody, Dec. 29, Peabody Papers; Moore, ed., *Works of James Buchanan* (Philadelphia and London, 1910), XI, 412–3; New York *Tribune,* July 20, 1858; Nevins *Emergence of Lincoln,* I, 124–5. The diplomatic corps boycotted Corcoran for a while but the pleasures of his hospitality soon proved irresistible. He retained some influence through his friends of the original cabal.

11. See C to Louise Corcoran, Aug. n.d., 1835, Aug. 25, 1837, C Papers. Not long after, while his wife was still alive, Corcoran entered the courts in a case with similar overtones. As executor of his father's estate he had sold two girls as life slaves for $666, one-third of their value, on condition that they not be removed or sold south of the Potomac or from the District of Columbia on penalty of receiving their freedom. The defendant promptly sold them down the river. Corcoran sued for their manumission or, their whereabouts being unknown, damages to the extent of the difference between the sale price and actual value. The defendant claimed no damages were due and manumission was the only remedy under the contract, a futile one in the circumstances. The circuit court judge, Cranch, immediately found for the defendant on demurrer without giving an opinion. See *Corcoran* v *Jones,* 6 Federal Cases 544 (no. 3229).

12. He did furnish his good offices to Robert Winthrop to buy the freedom of a slave captured eight years after his escape. The owner, one Ridgely, donated the $400 price received to the African Colonization Society. See C to Winthrop, Oct. 3, 1851, C Letter Books.

13. See C to Newbold, July 9, 1857 (calling the death of Marcy a "national calamity"), May 3, 1858 (with misconceived congratulations on the supposed settlement of the Kansas question in Congress), C Letter Books; Corcoran, *Grandfather's Legacy,* 143, 155, 170–1, 188–9.

14. C to Peabody, Dec. 20, 1859, Sept. 23, 1860, Peabody Papers; C to Belmont, Oct. 22, 1860, C Letter Books; Corcoran, *Grandfather's Legacy,* 193–4.

15. See Winfield Scott memo of Oct. 29, 1860, Scott to Secretary

of War, Oct. 30, copies in C Papers; C to Henry Stevens, Apr. 12, 1861, C to Semmes, Apr. 24, C to Phelps, May 20, C Letter Books; William B. Reed to Thomas Baring, Aug. 6, 1861, BPOC; Corcoran, *Grandfather's Legacy,* 96; Margaret Leech, *Reveille in Washington, 1860–1865* (New York and London, 1941), 25.

16. Wars being what they are, the depredations were probably more a matter of chaos, need, and indiscipline than of persecution. The arrest was another matter, but Corcoran was quickly released. For his part, Corcoran's secretary, Anthony Hyde, having rented quarters to the government for a hospital, tried to repossess in the middle of the war. See Fay to C, Mar. 20, 1861, Fay to Bright, May 17, Scott, pass, July 12, Scott to C, Sept. 9, Appleton to C, Nov. 19, 24, 27, 1861, Jan. 5, 1862, C Papers; C to secretary, Union Club, May 10, 1861, Hyde to Slidell, May 14, C to Thayer & Bro., Nov. 29, Hyde to N. S. Lincoln, Oct. 28, 1861, Feb. 28, 1862, C to Williams, Jan. 6, 9, C Letter Books; Adam Gurowski, *Diary, From March 4, 1861, to November 12, 1862* (Boston, 1862), I, 22; Corcoran, *Grandfather's Legacy,* 197; Gideon Welles, *Diary,* ed. Howard K. Beale, 3 vols. (New York, 1960), I, 99.

17. Corcoran had subscribed $1,000 to help Forney publish the Philadelphia *Press* and Washington *Sunday Chronicle* but, as Grund reminded him, these had become abolitionist. Hyde noted a New York *Times* report that Corcoran had sent $30,000 to help the Democratic campaign. See Blair to Van Buren, Mar. 7, 1861, Van Buren Papers, LC; Hyde to C, Nov. 3, 1862, Hyde to Grund, Feb. 20, 23, 1863, Hyde to B. H. Brewster, July 28, 1864, Hyde to William H. Drayton, Aug. 27, C to Drayton, Jan. 22, 1866, C Letter Books; Grund to C, Apr. 17, Nov. 9, Dec. 27, 1862, Apr. 11, 1863, F. P. Corbin to C, Aug. 26, 1862, C Papers.

18. Hyde told of a number of officers coming to search the residence, having been informed of boxes of such suspicious nature that they "had" to look. After opening one box they declined to go further. When Hyde insisted they stood by while he opened another box, then left, refusing to search further. Nevertheless, late in 1863 both Hyde and Riggs urged Corcoran not to return on grounds that the oath of allegiance might be demanded of him as the precondition of government payment of rents withheld. This might lead to confiscation if he refused; precedents had already occurred in the courts of the District of Columbia. Similar cases leading to banishments were reported elsewhere. (The decline

of his daughter's health was another and more compelling reason for Corcoran's remaining abroad.) Just before the war ended $10,000 of United States bonds were bought as a talking point of loyalty in case of need, although as an investment the purchase seemed unwise. For obvious reasons there had been no such investments during the war. See C to Thayer & Bro., Sept. 18, Oct. 22, 1861, C to Peabody, Oct. 28, Dec. 20, 1861, Mar. 10, 1862, C to R&Co., Mar. 3, 5, 10, May 10, 12, 13, 1862, Hyde to R&Co., May 1, Nov. 3, 1862, Mar. 16, Apr. 4, 1863, Feb. 9, May 1, 3, 1865, memos, Mar. 10, May 13, 20, 26, 1862, Feb. 20, 1869, C to Elliott, June 24, 1862, Hyde to C, Oct. 9, 18, Nov. 3, 1862, Apr. 15, Dec. 3, 1863, Mar. 21, 1864, Feb. 27, Mar. 24, June 5, 1865, Hyde to J. Cooke & Co., Mar. 21, May 5, 6, 1863, Hyde to H. D. Cooke, July 20, Hyde to Bright, Aug. 12, 1863, May 17, 1864, Hyde to David Turpie, July 13, C Letter Books; Hodge to C, Nov. 3, 1862, C Papers. See also n. 21, below.

19. See Hyde to secretary, American Telegraph Co., Aug. 8, 1863, Hyde to C, Aug. 7, 25, 1863, Jan. 12, May 2, June 27, Dec. 6, 1864, May 15, 1865, Hyde to LR, Nov. 30, 1863, C to J. S. Morgan & Co., Apr. 30, June 12, 1866, C Letter Books; C and Louise M. Eustis accounts with Peabody, Erlanger, and Van den Brock Bros., J. S. Morgan to C, Feb. 9, 12, 1864, Peabody & Co. to C, Feb. 15, Van den Brock to C, Feb. 6, 1865, R&Co. to C, Aug. 1, C Papers; tax rolls, Bureau of Internal Revenue Archives, National Archives. A Baring Brothers' correspondent had predicted "The income tax will be evaded in every way." See Reed to Baring, Aug. 6, 1861, BPOC.

20. See Van den Brock to C, Feb. 14, Mar. 14, 1863, Hyde to C, May 26, 1863, Jan. 11, 25, 1864, Belmont to C, Feb. 8, letters on and drafts and proofs of "Question Américaine," article by M.-H. de LaGarde for *Revue des Races Latines,* C Papers; Corcoran, *Grandfather's Legacy,* 202; William Wirt Henry, "Kenner's Mission to Europe," *William and Mary College Quarterly Historical Magazine* 25 (July 1916), 9–12; Ephraim D. Adams, *Great Britain and the American Civil War,* 2 vols. (New York, 1925), 169; J. F. H. Claiborn, *Mississippi as a Province, Territory and State* (Jackson, 1880), 443.

21. The bulk of Corcoran's return of capital occurred from May 3 to June 9, 1869, when almost $700,000 was brought back. Much of the money went into the Gallery of Art, then formally given to

the public. During the war Corcoran had liquidated most of his American securities and invested chiefly in French, Italian, and colonial governments through Rothschild in Paris and J. S. Morgan in London. See Hyde to A. V. Lancaster, Nov. 10, 1865, C to R&Co., Nov. 15, Dec. 23, C to LR, Jan. 26, 29, Mar. 12, 1866, memo, Jan. 14, 1867, C to Rothschild (Paris) and to J. S. Morgan, May 26f, 1869, C to Punnett (Bank of America), May 26, June 11, 12, 14, 17, 26, July 3, statement, June 10–11, C to Jenkins (Bank of America), Aug. 23, 26, 31, Sept. 3, 1869, C to Belmont, Jan. 30, Feb. 1, 2, 4, 1870, Hyde to Quartermaster General, Feb. 27, 1872, Hyde to Boston Courier Publishing Co., May 3, C Letter Books; Hyde to C, Aug. 18, Sept. 22, 1865, Hodge to C, Nov. 6, Slidell to [Eustis, 1865], Hyde to C, Jan. 7, 1868, unbound letterpress copies, C Papers; clipping, *Boston Courier,* May 16, 1869, scrapbook, Corcoran Gallery; Corcoran, *Grandfather's Legacy,* 259.

22. Bright expressed his dislike of the Johnson party of War Democrats and erstwhile Republicans, saying they were not true states-rights Democrats. But, he continued, "acting upon the theory I have heard you and other considerate cautious gentlemen advocate latterly—viz.—'if a man cannot get what he wants, it is *Polocy* [*sic*] to take the nearest to it he can get,' I am inclined to agree with you . . . that it is better to sustain the red republican Tailor of Tennessee than allow such creatures as Stevens Sumner & Co. longer to rule and ruin." Two years later, when Horatio Seymour was the presidential candidate, Corcoran answered the appeals of Montgomery Blair to help raise funds. Moneyed men were peculiar in one respect, Blair noted: they would respond to appeals only from other moneyed men. Corcoran supported August Belmont's conduct of Democratic party affairs and collaborated with him in trying to influence legislation through Senator James B. Eustis, brother of his late son-in-law. See W. F. Carter to C, May 15, 1866, Bright to C, Aug. 2, Ould to C, Aug. 21, 1868, M. Blair to C, Sept. 27, 1868, June 24, 1869, C Papers; C to L. G. Beall, Nov. 28, 1866, Hyde to C, Sept. 6, 7, 1880, unbound letterpress copies, C Papers; C to Schell, Sept. 17, 1872, C to Belmont, Jan. 11, 1878, C to J. B. Eustis, Feb. 24, 1879, Hyde to Sommers, Aug. 27, 1880, Hyde to Belmont, Sept. 7, Hyde to committee, second congressional district, Norfolk, Va., Oct. 7, C to William Pinkney White, Oct. 9, Nov. 24, C to Slaughter, Oct. 12, Hyde to William A. Wallace, Nov. 24, C to Beck, to Thomas F. Bayard, to Thomas F. Randolph,

and to Francis Kernan, Jan. 26, 1881, C to Philip B. Thompson, Jr., Apr. 24, C to H. G. Davis, Dec. 4, C to Bayard, Mar. 13, Apr. 8, 1885, C Letter Books; Stewart Mitchell, *Horatio Seymour of New York* (Cambridge, 1938), 463.

23. It was reported that unnamed California investors were large buyers of Washington real estate. The Forneys were treated with great leniency when they had difficulty repaying their debt, receiving prolonged extensions and a gift of $500 as well "in view of your past sacrifices to principle." The debt was assigned to the Gallery. See Hyde to C, July 17, 1865, C Papers; memo, Nov. 18, 1871, Hyde to Stockton, and to Casserly, Jan. 31, 1873, C to Forney, Nov. 13, 1873, Jan. 20, 1879, Mar. 23, 1881, Hyde to D. C. Forney, Nov. 21, 30, 1873, May 23, 1879, Hyde to J. C. Miller, Mar. 5, Aug. 30, Oct. 12, 1875, Hyde to Mrs. E. M. Forney, Oct. 26, C Letter Books; William H. Whyte, *The Uncivil War: Washington in the Era of Reconstruction* (New York, 1959), 61, 98, 132; Constance McLaughlin Green, *Washington: Village and Capital, 1800–1878* (Princeton, 1962), 334–62 passim.

24. See Hyde to C, July 22, 1871, unbound letterpress copies, C Papers; C to H. D. Cooke, Alexander R. Shepherd, J. W. Thompson and five others, Sept. 11, 1871, C to Commissioners of Sinking Fund, Apr. 23, 1875, copy of certificate, Dec. 16, 1879, C Letter Books; Whyte, *Uncivil War,* 126.

25. See C to Whitelaw Reid, Apr. 21, 1873, C to Shepherd, Sept. 23, 1873, Jan. 5, 9, Feb. 14, 28, Mar. 11, 1878, C to Wilson, Colston & Co., Dec. 20, 1873, C to Joint Committee of Investigation in the Affairs of the District of Columbia, Feb. 28, 1874, C to John W. Garrett, Mar. 25, 1881, C Letter Books; clippings, Washington *Sentinel,* Baltimore *Sun,* New York *Tribune,* and many others, Feb. 7f, 1874, scrapbook, Corcoran Gallery; New York *World* obituary, collection in manuscript division, NYPL.

26. He continued to contribute, although on a somewhat more modest scale. See C to W. S. Rosecrans, Apr. 17, 19, 1882, C Papers; William Ernest Smith, *The Francis Preston Blair Family in Politics,* 2 vols. (New York, 1933), 482–4; C. Vann Woodward, *Reunion and Reaction: The Compromise of 1877 and the End of Reconstruction* (Boston, 1951), 137–40.

27. It is a pity the account is so brief and staccato. It is drawn from George Eustis, undated outline draft, Eustis Papers, LC. Evidently intended for expansion into a pamphlet or book, the

project was apparently cut short by premature death, concern for the feelings of friends in the fallen South, or a shrug of the shoulders.

28. Corcoran was understood to have agreed to buy the James M. Mason papers, apparently for donation to the Southern Archives at Montgomery, Alabama, and to relieve the poverty of the former Senator and his daughter; but for some reason this fell through. He considered buying the Confederate State Department archives for $25,000 but finally declined from fear that the Federal government might claim possession. (Money aside, John T. Pickett, who held the papers, hoped "to keep them from falling into the hands of an Administration hostile to the South and to the Democratic Party.") Corcoran did indulge a patriotic celebrant's interest in history. He gave a few Jefferson manuscripts to the State Department archives and the Virginia Historical Society. Through J. S. Morgan he bought the Dinwiddie papers, which included Washington letters, and presented them to the Virginia Historical Society. The Librarian of Congress, who had been expected to compete, deferred to him. See John T. Pickett, copy of memo, June 2, 1873, Brock Collection, HuntL; C to William Evarts, Aug. 12, 1878, C to H. B. Grigsby, Oct. 12, C to R. A. Brock, Apr. 23, 29, June 21, 1881, C to J. S. Morgan, May 3, June 29, Hyde to Morgan, July 15, C to Frederick Frelinghuysen, Oct. 14, 1882, C to Reid, May 7, 1884, Hyde to Alex. Doyle, Dec. 3, C to William Endicott, Dec. 8, 1887, C to McLane, Dec. 8, 9, C to Hugh Taggart, Jan. 31, 1888, C Letter Books; Dunbar Rowland, ed., *Jefferson Davis, Constitutionalist, His Letters, Papers, and Speeches,* 10 vols. (Jackson, 1923), IX, 209, 379.

29. At first, and as late as the end of 1872, Corcoran declined requests for large contributions for southern education on grounds that economic recovery should have the region's first priority. (Still earlier he had declined to invest in southern securities because of the uncertain political situation.) He had already made exceptions to this rule, however, helping reopen William and Mary College in 1867 with a $1,000 donation and furnishing introductions to wealthy New Yorkers who also gave. An old friend from happier days, Fillmore's Interior Secretary Alexander Stuart, was president at Virginia when those gifts were made. Among the trivia in Corcoran's effects is an envelope from Colonel J. J. White containing a lock of hair from General Lee's war-horse.

In 1872 Corcoran made an interest-free loan of $26,000 to the city of Georgetown to pay overdue salaries of public school teachers during a financial crisis. More modestly, a room of his personal library was made available without charge for the free education of poor children. In 1808 his father had made the first appeal on behalf of public schools, one chronicler has said. See Hyde to C, and to Ironside, July 26, 1859, C to Townsend, Wheeler, & Co., Feb. 15, 1866, C to John B. Palmer, Feb. 17, C to R. H. Maury & Co., Dec. 3, 1866, May 6, 1867, C to Ould, Apr. 3, 1867, C to Brown, Sept. 12, 1871, C to N. Sargent, Nov. 28, Dec. 1, 1873, C to D. H. Maury, Dec. 5, 6, C to O'Sullivan, May 5, 1878 (referring to "Ex-Presdt. Davis"), Hyde to Polkinhorn, Jan. 24, 1879, C to Steward, Aug. 13, 1878, Hyde to Warren, Oct. 10, Hyde to Devens, Nov. 30, C to Venable, Nov. 24, 1880, C Letter Books; Ricketts et al. to C, Aug. 11, 1862, Ewell to C, Apr. 17, May 25, Aug. 2, 1867, A. R. Blakey to C, Dec. 3, 1872, C to Blakey, Dec. 17, copy of Breckinridge to Polkinhorn, Feb. 5, 1877, C Papers; C to Winthrop, Feb. 5, 1870, unbound letterpress copies, C Papers; Corcoran, *Grandfather's Legacy,* 223 (a good example of his South-will-rise-again letters), 282–3, 503–5; Jackson, "People and Places in Old Georgetown," *Records of the Columbia Historical Society,* 1932, 150–1; Green, *Washington,* 378.

30. Of course northerners were less needy than "Southrons." Apart from reflecting his personal loyalties, aid to fallen southerners did have some prewar precedent in his support for defeated nationalist revolutionaries. Corcoran had paid the travel expenses from New York to new homes in the West for 130 Hungarian exiles of 1848. His largest charitable gift before the war was one of $5,000 by Corcoran & Riggs for relief of famine-stricken Irish, in response to Elisha Riggs' challenging assertion that New Yorkers would do their part. There were also some small gifts to churches, including some as far away as Arkansas at the request of Senator Solon Borland of that state. See ER to C&R, Feb. 11, 1847, R Letter Book; Solon Borland to C, Feb. 6, 1849, C Papers; Corcoran scrapbook, Corcoran Gallery; Wise to C, Feb. 27, 1866, Bright to C, Mar. 25, Aiken to C, Nov. 24, 1868, June 15, 1869, P. G. T. Beauregard to C, May 30, June 12, 1875, C Papers; Hyde to C, Dec. 19, 1871, unbound letterpress copies, C Papers; C to Hunter, Nov. 29, Dec. 4, 1865, Dec. 8, 1866, Jan. 8, 17, Mar. 2, 14, 1867, Nov. 28, Dec. 5, 23, 1868, Jan. 4, 12, 19, 1869, C to Anderson, Dec. 11, 17, 1866, Hyde to C, Dec. 15, 1866, memo, Nov. 15,

1871, C to W. H. Trescott, June 21, 1866, Oct. 22, 1875, C to Punnett and Aiken, June 26, 1869, C to Garrett and to Beauregard, Oct. 8, 1872, C to Clemson, Nov. 16, 1875, Nov. 11, 1880, C to H. Gourdin, Nov. 16, 1875, C to James A. Jones, May 26, 1885, C to William A. Courtenay, Apr. 18, 1887, C Letter Books; Corcoran, *Grandfather's Legacy,* 224, 467, 470. Through Corcoran, Hunter and others sold their Superior interests to Pennsylvania Railroad magnate Thomas A. Scott. See Hyde to Scott, Apr. 11, 1867, Hyde to Hayes, Apr. 25, C to Anderson, June 8, statement, Oct. 22, Hyde to Barclay, Oct. 22, Dec. 11, Hyde to Hunter, Nov. 21, Dec. 14, 1867, Jan. 20, June 2, 1868.

31. Corcoran handled the financial affairs of Dolly Madison and joined other Democrats and Virginians such as John Y. Mason in secret and anonymous deposits in her bank account. She evidently learned of the source: there is among Corcoran's papers at the Library of Congress a token of gratitude—a lock of the hair John Quincy Adams had given her. (A lock of James Madison's hair was listed but is not to be found.) A name on a number of pension lists was "Beau" Hickman, "Prince of Bummers," a kind of Beau Brummel deadbeat jester to Washington life.

32. Many of those helped were widows, including Mrs. Robert J. Walker and Mrs. Chubb, widow of the banker who failed in 1857. Individuals received anywhere from two-figure amounts to a maximum of $2,500. The earliest notes date from the fifties. See J. Y. Mason to C, Mar. 11, 1847, J. Madison Cutts to C, July 20, 1849, and envelope with lock of hair, C Papers; lists, Jan. 11–12, 1867, Nov. 15, 1871, Hyde to Mason, June 9, 14, 1880, example of form letter, Apr. 19, 1883, Hyde to Rep. J. R. Neal, Jan. 18, 1888, C Letter Books; New York *World* obituary, Ms. Div., NYPL; Allen C. Clark, "Beau Hickman (Robert S. Hickman)," *Records of the Columbia Historical Society, 1940,* 94.

33. Corcoran's gifts to the Louise Home were estimated to total $500,000, with an added bequest of $50,000. One chronicler refers to the Home as having been intended for the "gentlewomen of the South." See list, Apr. 21–22, 1871, Hyde to M. F. Maury, June 29, 1872, C to Marshall, Nov. 14, C to John J. Hemphill, Feb. 24, 1887, C Letter Books; Corcoran Will, number 3001, probated Feb. 29, 1888, register of wills, District of Columbia; Ward Thoron, ed., *Letters of Mrs. Henry Adams, 1865–1883* (Boston, 1936), to Robert W. Hooper, Jan. 1, 1882; Cordelia Jackson, "People and Places in Old Georgetown," *Records of the Columbia Historical*

Society (1931–1932), 150–1; anecdote told by Roland T. Carr, vice-president, Riggs Bank.

34. His first recorded gift was a lot to St. John's Church, Georgetown in 1839. By 1870 the inpouring of pleas for donations from churches around the country had become so great that he decided to give only to those in the District. The only exceptions were some burdensome absentee land holdings. See C to Eustis, May 10, 1867, Eustis Papers; Eustis to C, Jan. 30, Apr. 25, 1870, C Papers; Hyde to Martin, Aug. 12, 1872, C Letter Books; C to Winthrop, Jan. 22, 1875, Winthrop Papers, MassHS.

35. See C to Burchell, May 6, 1876, C to Vestry of Ascension Church, May 16, memos, Jan. 7, Feb. 21, 1878, Jan. 6–7, 1882, Hyde to Lee, Aug. 10, 12, 1886, Jan. 26, Feb. 2, 1887.

Foreclosing a church was an unpalatable business to creditors. In response to an inquiry about a lot for a church on his St. Louis property Corcoran indicated he would agree to the project, "presumed to be a Christian Church, that would not be a disadvantage to the residue of the property.

"I would be disposed to sell them such a lot (in view of the above remark) on a long credit, at a fixed valuation, provided they will give ample security *other than the Church property.*" See C to Josiah Dent, Apr. 9, 1869, C Letter Books.

36. The formal presentation to the public was made in 1869 although construction had begun a decade earlier. Corcoran also became president of the Washington Art Club, organized in 1877, and donated several thousand dollars to aid in establishing a school of design a year later. See statement, May 17, 1876, Hyde to D. C. Forney, to Roberts, and to Bell, May 20, C to Mann, May 22, C to Trustees, July 4, 1878, Hyde to Forney, Nov. 26, Dec. 2, 1880, C Letter Books; Corcoran Will; Leila Mechlin, "Art Life in Washington," *Records of Columbia Historical Society,* 24 (1922), 173–4.

Corcoran wanted to add a building for a national portrait gallery but was frustrated by the refusal of an adjacent landowner to part with the property. He owned a few good portraits, including one of Washington by Stuart and one of Jackson by Sully. His sectional loyalty was expressed in purchasing or finding buyers for works sold by needy southerners. Corcoran also gave huge canvasses of the battles of New Orleans and Yorktown to the states of Louisiana and Virginia. Mordecai Ezekiel, who had fought under Lee, received sizeable commissions for sculpture and ornamentation for the gallery. Corcoran lobbied to have him commissioned for the Confederate monument at Montgomery, Alabama. (However he refrained from ordering a copy of Ezekiel's statue of Lee for the gallery, fearing sectional hostility would be aroused at a time when it was requesting tax exemption in Congress. The exemption bill passed.) See C to N. N. Barlow, Nov. 27, 1869, Feb. 21, 1870, C to James Chesnut, May 30, 1876, statement, June 17, C to Mordecai Ezekiel, Apr. 10, 1878, Mar. 24, 1884, Dec. 18, 1885, Dec. 11, 1886, C to Albert Bierstadt, July 1, 1878, C to Governors Francis T. Nichols and F. W. M. Holliday, May 22, 1878, C to William Wetmore Story, Dec. 13, C to Mrs. Walden, Dec. 16, C to Mrs. Sophia Page, Dec. 5, 1883, Hyde to Ezekiel, Dec. 26, C to H. Herbert, Feb. 15, 1886, C to John S. Barbour, Jan. 12, 1887, C to Gourdin, Jan. 11, 1888, C Letter Books; Bierstadt to Samuel Ward, Jan. 18, 21, 1878, Ward to C, Jan. 20, C Papers; ch. 6, above.

37. The 107-piece Barye collection was apparently bought from the sculptor en bloc, the only such comprehensive acquisition. See Hyde to Kirby, Apr. 16, 1881, C to Walker Blaine, Apr. 26, C to O'Brien & Bro., Mar. 22, 1882, C to L. P. Morton, Apr. 14, Hyde to Knoedler & Co., Mar. 8, 28, 1883, Hyde to American Art Association, Apr. 8, 1885, Hyde to James C. Welling, Aug. 2, 6, 1886, Hyde to Carl Becker, Dec. 6, 1887, Hyde to Eduard Schulte, Dec. 8, C to Gourdin, Jan. 11, 1888, C Letter Books; W. G. Constable, *Art Collecting in the United States of America: An Outline of a History* (London, 1964), 74, 99, 141–2.

38. The monument to and reinterment of L'Enfant were not brought about until 1909. In the same vein, Corcoran brought the remains of John Howard Payne, writer of "Home Sweet Home," from Tunis for reinterment in the Oak Hill Cemetery. See C to John A. Kasson, Apr. 17, 1884, C Letter Books; C scrapbook, Corcoran Gallery; John William Reps, *The Making of Urban America: A History of City Planning in the United States* (Princeton, 1965), 252, 256, 262, 325f, 505; ch. 6, above.

39. See C to Story, Dec. 13, 1878, C to Capt. George Davis, Dec. 18, C to Joint Commission for Completion of Washington Monument, Dec. 21, C Letter Books; Winthrop to C, Dec. 17, 19, C Papers.

40. See C to Story, Jan. 5, Mar. 23, May 13, July 3, 1880, C to J. S. Morrill, June 22, C Letter Books.

41. See C to G. P. A. Healy, Feb. 4, 1870, Hyde to Walters,

May 20, 1871, Hyde to Childs, May 23, C to H. T. Jones, Nov. 1, C to Slaughter, Dec. 16, 1880, Lanman to C, Apr. 19, 1881, C to Mallory, Mar. 2, 1882, C to Lee, May 21, 1883, C to Duvall, Nov. 19, 1885, C Letter Books; Corcoran, *Grandfather's Legacy,* 358; Charles Richard Williams, ed., *Diary and Letters of Rutherford Birchard Hayes,* 5 vols. (Columbus, 1922–1926), III, 525; Thoron, ed., *Letters of Mrs. Henry Adams,* 170, 227–8, 241.

Hyde was well rewarded for his labors. Reputedly the son of an old and prominent Maryland family, he was a temporary employee of the Treasury Department in 1847 where Corcoran helped him obtain the maximum allowable salary of $4 per day. From there he went to work for the banker. Typical was his promise of assiduous service during his employer's absence on a trip: "I shall hope that, having done this, I shall receive on your return the 'well done, good and faithful servant.' " He seems not to have taken a vacation in decades. He fretted to the point of ulcers over all the minutiae, as well as over the larger matters, of his principal's existence. Between the desires to do nothing that might be disapproved and to relieve Corcoran of the weight of endless concerns, the former almost invariably won out. Hyde's heart overflowed with gratitude when Corcoran, on returning from exile, awarded him a $3,000 bonus and doubled his salary to that amount per year. In addition his son Thomas was taken into Riggs & Co., becoming a partner in 1874 and eventually vice-president of the Riggs National Bank. (Apparently a descendant is on the present board of directors.) Finally, as co-executor of Corcoran's estate Hyde received 2½ percent of its assessed valuation of $1 million.

Corcoran took pleasure in choosing worthy and able young men, preferably of imposing appearance and good local or southern family, for a future with the institution he co-founded. One whom he particularly favored was Charles C. Glover, later a dominant figure in the Riggs Bank, whose aggressive management eventually led to the separation of the Riggs family from the institution bearing its name. See list, May 25, 1847, Hyde to Walker, Feb. 15, June 8, 1848, Hagner to Walker, Feb. 18, AB Letters; Hyde to C, July 10, 1855, C to Hyde, Nov. 16, 1865, C Letter Books; Hyde to C, Oct. 3, 1862, C Papers; C will and auditor's reports.

42. C to Ficklin, Dec. 31, 1877, C to Stuart, Mar. 18, 1878, C Letter Books; New York *World* and *Tribune* obituaries and other

clippings, Mss. Div., NYPL. An amusing mythic touch is visible in Bledsoe's *Southern Review,* wherein the five-foot–six-inch Corcoran was described as almost six feet tall, and his wife as eighteen at her marriage. See "A Romance of Real Life," *Southern Review* (July 1872), 167.

Corcoran's annual income at death was about $125,000, predominantly from Washington property. See C will and auditors' reports.

Chapter 13

1. Suppose statesmanship had succeeded in delaying the crisis for a few years until the presumed inevitable concentrations of economic and accompanying political power had matured. Given the relatively low priority slavery held for so many Americans, would there have been a crisis? Would a more cohesively structured (if still intensely competitive) society with a constantly stronger business motivation, sensitive to southern tenaciousness, and valuing stability and the security of property rights, have accepted the necessity for change? Or would a better-knit society have achieved reform? Questions like these must be asked even if they are empirically, finally unanswerable.

Anarchy and fears of anarchy have ever lurked in the American mind. The ablest and most thorough of the conventional historians dealing with this era, for example Nevins and Nichols, verge upon but never quite grasp the full meaning of the economic processes. Brilliant insights are offered by William A. Williams, *The Contours of American History,* Quadrangle ed. (Chicago 1966); but, without going into the serious ideological obstacles between him and some of his critics, by publishing his conclusions without the necessary inductive demonstrations, he has left himself open to attack. In some ways most intriguing of all is the recurrence of the theme of fear of disintegration, like a dialectical leitmotif, in Perry Miller's tragically unfinished *The Life of the Mind in America: From the Revolution to the Civil War* (New York, 1965). Of course his (dramatic, I am tempted to call it) emphasis was on the cohesive commonalities of thought; how might his counter-theme have reappeared in Book V, "Freedom and Association: Political Economy and Association," and how in Book IX, "The Self"?

I headed my conclusions with a quotation from Alexis de Tocqueville, *Recollections,* ed. J. P. Mayer (New York, 1949), 63–4. It may be appropriate to end by quoting the passage more fully:

> I have come across men of letters, who have written history without taking part in public affairs, and politicians, who have only concerned themselves with producing events without thinking of describing them. I have observed that the first are always inclined to find general causes, whereas the others, living in the midst of disconnected daily facts, are prone to imagine that everything is attributable to particular incidents. . . .
>
> For my part, I detest these absolute systems, which represent all the events of history as depending upon great first causes linked by the chain of fatality, and which, as it were, suppress men from the history of the human race. . . .
>
> I believe . . . that many important historical facts can only be explained by accidental circumstances, and that many others remain totally inexplicable. Moreover, chance, or rather that tangle of secondary causes which we call chance, for want of the knowledge how to unravel it, plays a great part in all that happens on the world's stage; although I firmly believe that chance does nothing that has not been prepared beforehand. Antecedent facts, the nature of institutions, the cast of minds and the state of morals are the materials of which are composed those impromptus which astonish and alarm us.

Bibliography

Primary Sources

MANUSCRIPT

Individuals

BANCROFT, GEORGE. MassHS. NYPL
BARLOW, SAMUEL L. M. HuntL
BAYARD, JAMES A. and RICHARD H. LC
BAYARD, THOMAS F. LC
BEVERLY FAMILY. VHS
BIDDLE, NICHOLAS. LC
BIGELOW, JOHN. NYPL
BIRD, ROBERT M. UPa
BLACK, JEREMIAH. LC
BLAIR–LEE FAMILY. PriU
BRAYMAN, MASON, ChiHS
BRECKINRIDGE, JOHN C. Breckinridge Family Papers, LC
BROCK, R. A. HuntL
BUCHANAN, JAMES. PaHS
BURKE, EDMUND. LC
CARLISLE, JAMES M. UNC
CHASE, SALMON P. LC
CLAYTON, JOHN M. LC
COOKE, C. D. WisHS
CORCORAN, WILLIAM WILSON. LC; scrapbook of clippings, Corcoran Gallery of Art; will, District of Columbia courthouse
CORNING, ERASTUS. Alb. Inst.
CORWIN, THOMAS. LC
CORYELL, LEWIS. PaHS
CRITTENDEN, JOHN J. LC

CURTIS, EDWARD. LC
CUSHING, CALEB. LC
DALLAS, GEORGE MIFFLIN. Diary, 1849–1850, PaHS (photostat)
DALY, CHARLES P. NYPL
DIX, DOROTHEA. HU
DIX, JOHN A. ColU
DODGE, HENRY. IowaSt
DONELSON, ANDREW J. LC
DOUGLAS, STEPHEN A. UChi
DOUSMAN, HERCULES L. WisHS
EUSTIS, GEORGE. LC
EWING, THOMAS. LC
FARNAM, HENRY. YU
FELCH, ALPHEUS. DetPL
FILLMORE, MILLARD. BuffHS
FLAGG, A. C. ColU
FRENCH, B. B. LC
GERE, WILLIAM B. and THOMAS P. MinnHS
GOMEZ FARIAS, VALENTIN. UTex
GORMAN, WILLIS A. MinnHS
GREEN, DUFF. SoHC, UNC
GWIN, WILLIAM M. Memoirs on the history of the United States, Mexico, and California, 1850–1861 (manuscript). LC (photostat)
HOYT, OTIS. WisHS
JACKSON, ANDREW. LC
JONES, GEORGE WALLACE. IowaSt
JOY, JAMES F. UMich
MARCY, WILLIAM L. LC
MEREDITH, WILLIAM M. PaHS
NEWBOLD, GEORGE. NYHS
OGDEN, WILLIAM B. ChiHS
OLCOTT, THOMAS W. ColU
PAUL, GEORGE H. WisHS
PEABODY, GEORGE. EI, Salem, Mass.; Letter Book, LC
PICKETT, JOHN C. HuntL
PIERCE, FRANKLIN. LC
POLK, JAMES K. LC
PRUYN, JOHN V. L. Alb. Inst.
RAMSEY, ALEXANDER. MinnHS
RIGGS FAMILY PAPERS. LC
ROBERTSON, DANIEL A. MinnHS
RUGGLES, CHARLES H. NYPL
RUSK, THOMAS J. UTex
SEWARD, WILLIAM H. URoch
SIBLEY, HENRY H. MinnHS
SMITH, CALEB B. LC
SMITH, GEORGE B. WisHS
STEELE, FRANKLIN. MinnHS
STEVENS, JOHN A. NYHS
STEVENS, JOHN H. MinnHS
STRONG, MOSES M. WisHS
TENNEY, HORACE A. WisHS
TILDEN, SAMUEL J. NYPL
TYLER, JOHN. LC
U.S. v. *Estate of W. W. Corcoran.* VHS (photostats)
VAN BUREN, MARTIN. LC
WALKER, ROBERT J. NYHS; LC; UPitts
WARD, THOMAS W. MassHS
WASHBURNE, ELIHU B. LC
WEBB, JAMES WATSON. YU
WEBSTER, DANIEL. LC; NHHS
WEED, THURLOW. URoch
WINTHROP, ROBERT C. MassHS
WISE, HENRY A. LC
WOODBURY, LEVI. LC
WOODMAN, CYRUS. WisHS

Government

NATIONAL ARCHIVES

Interior Department: letters to and from the Secretary; General Land Office, abstracts of sales.

State Department: instructions, dispatches, notes, Mexico; Domestic and miscellaneous letters.

Treasury Department: letters and reports to Congress (E Letters); letters to banks; letters to the Secretary; letters from executive officer (AB Letters); cabinet and bureaus (B Letters); Richard Ela, agent (YA Letters); Treasurer's office, bank and sub-Treasury accounts; issues and abstracts of Treasury notes; relative to issue of Treasury notes (K Letters); loan letters, bids, Ledgers, Registers; expenditures on account of public debt, 1837–1873; letters and receipts, Mexican indemnity 5 percent stock; Texas debt claims, registers, audited certificates, etc.; California debt papers

LIBRARY OF CONGRESS

U.S. miscellaneous manuscripts, 1840–1860; United States Treasury miscellany, 1789–1858

DOUGLAS COUNTY COURTHOUSE, SUPERIOR, WISCONSIN

Deed Records

Business

Bank of Commerce, Morgan Guaranty Trust Co., New York

Bank of the United States. President's Letter Books. LC

Bank of the United States of Pennsylvania (in liquidation). PaHS

Baring Brothers and Company. Official Correspondence (BPOC); Letter Books (BPLB); etc.; Archives of Canada, Ottawa

August Belmont letters. de Rothschild Frères, Paris.

Alex. Brown & Sons. LC

Chicago, St. Paul & Fond du Lac records. Chicago & North Western Railway offices, Chicago

Corcoran & Riggs ledgers and letters. Riggs National Bank

Illinois Central Archives. Newberry Library

La Crosse & Milwaukee minute books. Chicago, Milwaukee, St. Paul & Pacific Railway offices, Chicago

Manning & Mackintosh Papers. University of Texas

Riggs & Co. ledgers. Riggs National Bank
See also under ("Individuals")

PUBLISHED GOVERNMENT DOCUMENTS

Great Britain

Parliamentary Papers; British and Foreign State Papers

Mexico

Esteva, Jose Ignacio. *Exposicion . . . Ministerio de Hacienda.* Mexico City, 1851
Hacienda, Secretaria de [M. Romero]. *Memoria de Hacienda y Credito Publico. . . .* Mexico City, 1870
Junta del Credito Publico. *Inventario de los Titulos de la Deuda Interior.* Mexico City, 1852
Olasagarre, M. *Cuenta . . . de los Diez Millones de Pesos que Produjo et Tratado de la Mesilla. . . .* Mexico City, 1855

United States

CONGRESS

Congressional Globe
House Journals
Senate Journals
House Documents: 29th Cong., 1st sess., 174 (series 485), secretary of the Treasury on changes in depositories
House Executive Documents: 26th Cong., 1st sess., 172, condition of the state banks; 32d Cong., 1st sess., 32 (series 640), report on remaining installments of Mexican indemnity; 32d Cong., 1st sess., 42 (series 640), correspondence in reference to payment of Mexican indemnity; 33d Cong., 2d sess., 35 (series 783), suit against Minnesota & North Western Railroad; 142 (series 808), case of Thomas H. Bayly
House Miscellaneous Documents: 34th Cong., 3d sess. (unnumbered; series 911.2), list of private claims before Senate, 14th through 33d Congress
House Reports: 28th Cong., 2d sess., 182 (series 468), Banks of District of Columbia; 31st Cong., 1st sess., 489 (series 585),

Ewing investigation (Indian claims); 32d Cong., 2d sess., 1, Gardiner investigation; 33d Cong., 1st sess., 352 (series 744), alteration of text of House Bill No. 342; 33 Cong., 1 sess., 353 (series 744), Colt patent, etc.: illegal and improper lobbying in Congress; 354 (series 744), Thomas H. Bayly; 369 (series 744), Gardiner and Mears (Mexican claims); 33 Cong., 2 sess., 132, Colt arms lobby; 34 Cong., 3 sess., 243 (series 914), alleged corrupt combinations of members of Congress; 35th Cong., 1st sess., 179, lobbying

Senate Documents: 21st Cong., 1st sess., 72 (series 356), message from the President on banks recently suspended; 26 Cong., 1 sess., 595 (series 361), memorial of Patriotic Bank of Washington for extension of charter

Senate Executive Documents: 30th Cong., 1st sess., 52 (series 509), correspondence relating to, and proceedings of U.S. Senate in regard to Treaty of Guadalupe Hidalgo; 32 Cong., 1 sess., 15 (series 637), message in regard to last installment of indemnity due Mexico, President Fillmore; 51st Cong., 1st sess., 122, payment of old California war bonds

Senate Reports: 33 Cong., 1 sess., 50, Domercq claims; 182, report of Select Committee on Mexican claims; 334, bill to pay Texas creditors; 33 Cong., 2 sess., 547 (series 775), report on joint resolutions H.R. 48 and 49; 34 Cong., 3 sess., 440 (series 891), report on memorial of M. O. Roberts in regard to mail contracts of A. G. Sloo

STATE DEPARTMENT

Manning, William R., ed. *Diplomatic Correspondence of the United States: Inter-American Affairs, 1831–1860.* Vols. VIII, IX, *Mexico*. Washington, 1937

Miller, D. Hunter, ed. *Treaties and other International Acts of the United States of America.* Vol. V. Washington, 1937

TREASURY DEPARTMENT

Reports of the Secretary

COURTS

Corcoran v. *Jones*. 6 Federal Cases 544

Dirst v. *Morris*. 81 U.S. 484

Riggs v. *Boyland*. 20 Federal Cases 774, 776

Riggs v. *Collins.* 20 Federal Cases 824, 81 U.S. 491
Wright v. *Mattison.* 18 Howard 50

State

MISSISSIPPI

Senate *Journal*

NEW YORK

Assembly *Journal*
Senate *Journal*
Banking Department. *Annual Reports of the Superintendent*
Comptroller. *Annual Reports*

TEXAS

House Journal, 6th legislature, adjourned session, 1856

WISCONSIN

Legislature, 1858. *Report of Joint Select Committee . . . Alleged Frauds and Corruption in the Disposition of the Land Grant by the Legislature of 1856. . . .*

OTHER PUBLISHED PRIMARY SOURCES

Letters of Mrs. Henry Adams. Ed. Ward Thoron. Boston, 1936.
Works of James Buchanan. Ed. John Bassett Moore. Philadelphia and London, 1910.
Mackenzie, William L. *The Lives and Opinions of Benj'n Franklin Butler. . . . Jesse Hoyt. . . .* Boston, 1845.
Chesnut, Mary Boykin. *Diary from Dixie.* Ed. Ben Ames Williams. Boston, 1949.
Corcoran, William Wilson. *A Grandfather's Legacy.* Washington, 1879.
Life of John J. Crittenden, with Selections from his Correspondence and Speeches. Ed. Mrs. Chapman Coleman. 2 vols. Philadelphia, 1871.
Jefferson Davis, Constitutionalist: His Letters, Papers and Speeches. Ed. Dunbar Rowland. Jackson, 1923.
Douglas, Stephen A. *A Brief Treatise upon Constitutional and Party Questions. . . .* Ed. J. Madison Cutts. New York, 1866.

The Letters of Stephen A. Douglas. Ed. Robert W. Johannsen. Urbana, 1961.

"Diary of Thomas Ewing, August and September, 1841." *American Historical Review.* Oct. 1912.

Foote, Henry S. *A Casket of Reminiscences.* Washington, 1874.

Forney, John W. *Anecdotes of Public Men.* New York, 1873.

Gurowski, Adam. *Diary, from March 4, 1861 to November 12, 1862.* Boston, 1862.

Diary and Letters of Rutherford Birchard Hayes, 1865–1881. III. Ed. Charles Richard Williams. Columbus, 1924.

Diary of Philip Hone. Ed. Bayard Tuckerman. 2 vols. New York, 1889.

Diary of Philip Hone, 1828–1851. Ed. Allan Nevins, 2 vols. New York, 1927.

Correspondence of Robert M. T. Hunter. Ed. Charles H. Ambler. American Historical Association, *Annual Report* . . . 1916. II. Washington, 1918.

Autobiography of Amos Kendall. Ed. William Stickney. Boston, 1872.

Kilbourn, Byron. *Review of the Report Made by the Committee of Investigation . . . Relating to the Land Grant.* Milwaukee, 1858.

Payno, Manuel. *Memoria en que Manuel Payno da Cuenta al Publico de su Manejo en el Desempeno del Ministerio de Hacienda. . . .* Mexico City, 1852.

Payno, Manuel; Olarte, Ramon; and Pesado, Jose Joaquin. *Cuestion de Tehuantepec.* Mexico City, 1852.

Diary of James K. Polk During His Presidency, 1845–1849. Ed. Milo M. Quaife. 4 vols. Chicago, 1910.

Ramirez, José F. *Memorias, Negociaciones y Documentos para Servir a la Historia de las Diferencias que Han Suscitado entre Mexico y los Estados-Unidos.* Mexico City, 1853.

Ramirez, José F. *Statement of Rights and Just Reasons (Question of Tehuantepec). . . .* Mexico City, 1852.

Richardson, James D., ed. *Compilation of the Messages and Papers of the Presidents, 1789–1879.* Washington, D. C., 1900.

Strong, George Templeton. *Diary.* Ed. Allan Nevins and Milton Halsey Thomas. 4 vols. New York, 1952.

"Letters to and from Jacob Thompson." Ed. P. L. Rainwater. *Journal of Southern History.* Feb. 1940.

Correspondence of Robert Toombs, Alexander H. Stephens, and Howell Cobb. Ed. Ulrich B. Phillips. American Historical Association, *Annual Report* . . . 1911. II. Washington, 1913.

Autobiography of Martin Van Buren. Ed. John C. Fitzpatrick. Washington, 1920.

Mackenzie, William L. *The Life and Times of Martin Van Buren: The Correspondence of his Friends, Family and Pupils.* Boston, 1846.

Welles, Gideon. *Diary.* Ed. Howard K. Beale. 3 vols. New York, 1960.

Wentworth, John. *Congressional Reminiscences.* Chicago, 1882.

Whittlesey, Charles. *Railway Connections with Lake Superior: Letter to the Hon. Truman Smith.* Cleveland, 1853.

NEWSPAPERS

Great Britain
London *Times*

Mexico
Mexico City *Monitor Republicano; Siglo Diez y Nueve*

United States
DISTRICT OF COLUMBIA
Washington *National Era; National Intelligencer; Union*

ILLINOIS
Chicago *Democratic Press*
Springfield *Illinois State Register*

IOWA
Dubuque *Daily* and *Weekly Express and Herald; Daily Times*

LOUISIANA
New Orleans *Daily Picayune*

MINNESOTA
Minneapolis *North Western Democrat;* Weekly *Minnesota Democrat*
St. Anthony *Express*
St. Paul Weekly *Minnesota Democrat; Pioneer and Democrat*

MISSISSIPPI

Houston *Southern Argus*
Jackson *Flag of the Union*
Monticello *Southern Journal*
Natchez *Courier*

NEW YORK

New York *Courier and Enquirer; Evening Post; Express; Herald; Journal of Commerce; Times; Tribune*

PENNSYLVANIA

Philadelphia *North American*

TEXAS

Austin *Texas State Gazette*

WISCONSIN

Madison *Argus and Democrat; Wisconsin Patriot*
Milwaukee *News; Daily Sentinel; Wisconsin*

PERIODICALS

American Railroad Journal (New York)
Bankers Magazine (Baltimore to 1849, Boston to 1851, thereafter New York)
Bankers Magazine (London)
Railroad Record (Cincinnati)

Secondary Sources

GENERAL REFERENCE WORKS CONSULTED EXTENSIVELY WITHOUT EXPLICIT CITATION

AGNEW, DWIGHT L. et al., eds. *Dictionary of Wisconsin Biography.* Madison, 1960

JOHNSON, ALLEN, and DUMAS MALONE, eds. *Dictionary of American Biography,* 20 vols. New York, 1928–1936

U.S., 81st Cong., 2d sess., *House Document 607, Biographical Directory of the American Congress, 1774–1949*. Washington, 1949

BOOKS

ACKERMAN, WILLIAM K. *Historical Sketch of the Illinois Central Railroad*. Chicago, 1890.

AGUILAR, GUSTAVO F. *Presupuestos Mexicanos*. Mexico City, 1940.

ALBION, ROBERT GREENHALGH. *The Rise of New York Port, 1815–1860*. New York and London, 1939.

AUCHAMPAUGH, PHILIP GERALD. *Robert Tyler, Southern Rights Champion, 1847–1866: A Documentary Study, Chiefly of Antebellum Politics*. Duluth, 1934.

BAIN, RICHARD C. *Convention Decisions and Voting Records*. Washington, 1960.

BANCROFT, HUBERT HOWE. *History of the Pacific States of North America*. Texas, 1801–1889. XI. San Francisco, 1889.

BAYLEY, RAFAEL A. *National Loans of the United States from July 4, 1776 to June 30, 1880*. Washington, 1882.

BLOOMFIELD, ARTHUR I. *Monetary Policy under the International Gold Standard: 1880–1914*. New York, 1959.

BOGART, ERNEST LUDLOW. *Financial History of Ohio*. Urbana-Champaign, 1912.

BORCHARD, EDWIN M. *Diplomatic Protection of Citizens Abroad*. New York, 1925.

BREVARD, CAROLINE MAYS. *History of Florida*. Florida as a State. II. Ed. James Alexander Robertson. Deland, Fla., 1925.

BROOKS, NOAH. *Washington in Lincoln's Time*. New York and Toronto, 1958.

BROWN, WILLIAM ADAMS. *Morris Ketchum Jesup: A Character Sketch*. New York, 1910.

BROWNSON, HOWARD GRAY. *History of the Illinois Central Railroad to 1870*. Urbana, 1915.

BRYAN, WILHELMUS B. *A History of the National Capital*. 2 vols. New York, 1914–1916.

CALLAHAN, JAMES M. *American Foreign Policy in Mexican Relations*. New York, 1932.

CALLCOTT, WILFRID HARDY. *Church and State in Mexico, 1822–1857*. Durham, 1926.

CAPERS, GERALD M. *Stephen A. Douglas, Defender of the Union.* Boston, 1959.

CARLSON, THEODORE LEONARD. *The Illinois Military Tract: A Study of Land Occupation, Utilization, and Tenure.* Urbana, 1951.

CASASUS, JOAQUIN D. *Historia de la Deuda Contraida en Londres. . . .* Mexico City, 1885.

CATTERALL, RALPH C. H. *Second Bank of the United States.* Chicago, 1903.

CHADDOCK, ROBERT E. *Safety Fund Banking System in New York State, 1829–1866.* U.S., 61st Cong., 2d sess. *Senate Document 581.* Washington, 1910.

CHANDLER, ALFRED D., JR. *Henry Varnum Poor, Business Editor, Analyst, and Reformer.* Cambridge, 1956.

CLAIBORNE, J. F. H. *Mississippi as Province, Territory and State.* Jackson, 1880.

CLAPHAM, SIR JOHN. *The Bank of England: A History.* 2 vols. Cambridge, Eng., 1958.

CLARK, IRA G. *Then Came the Railroads: The Century from Steam to Diesel in the Southwest.* Norman, 1958.

CLIFFORD, DEREK. *A History of Garden Design.* New York, 1963.

CLOUGH, SHEPARD B. *A Century of American Life Insurance: A History of the Mutual Life Insurance Company of New York, 1843–1943.* New York, 1946.

COCHRAN, THOMAS C. *Railroad Leaders, 1845–1890: The Business Mind in Action.* Cambridge, 1953.

COLE, DAVID. *Development of Banking in the District of Columbia.* New York, 1959.

CONSTABLE, W. G. *Art Collecting in the United States of America: An Outline of a History.* London, 1964.

CORLISS, CARLTON J. *Main Line of Mid-America: Story of the Illinois Central.* Austin, 1949.

COTNER, THOMAS EWING. *Military and Political Career of José Joaquin de Herrera, 1792–1854.* New York, 1950.

CURRENT, RICHARD N. *Daniel Webster and the Rise of National Conservatism.* Boston and Toronto, 1955.

DAVIS, LANCE EDWIN, and PAYNE, PETER LESTER. *Savings Bank of Baltimore, 1818–1866.* Baltimore, 1956.

DAVIS, WILLIAM WATSON. *Civil War and Reconstruction in Florida.* New York, 1913.

DEKNIGHT, WILLIAM F. *History of the Currency of the Country and of the United States . . . to June 30, 1896.* Washington, 1897.

DERLETH, AUGUST W. *The Milwaukee Road: Its First Hundred Years.* New York, 1948.

DESTLER, CHESTER MCARTHUR. *American Radicalism, 1865–1901: Essays and Documents.* New London, 1946.

DILLISTIN, WILLIAM H. *Historical Directory of the Banks of the State of New York.* New York, 1946–1956.

DONALD, DAVID. *Lincoln Reconsidered: Essay on the Civil War Era.* 2d ed. New York: Random House, Vintage Books, n.d.

DUCKETT, KENNETH W. *Frontiersman of Fortune: Moses M. Strong of Mineral Point.* Madison, 1955.

ELAZAR, DANIEL J. *American Partnership: Intergovernmental Cooperation in the Nineteenth Century United States.* Chicago, 1962.

ELLIOTT, JONATHAN. *Funding System of the United States and Great Britain.* U. S., 28th Cong., 1st sess., *House Executive Document 15.* Washington, 1845.

ELLIS, DAVID M., ed. *The Frontier in Western Development: Essays in Honor of Paul Wallace Gates.* Ithaca, 1969.

FANKHAUSER, WILLIAM C. *Financial History of California.* Berkeley, 1913.

FARNAM, HENRY W. *Henry Farnam.* New Haven, 1889.

FLOWER, FRANK A. *The Eye of the North-West.* Superior, 1890.

FOLWELL, WILLIAM WATTS. *A History of Minnesota.* 4 vols. St. Paul, 1956.

FRASER, HUGH RUSSELL. *Democracy in the Making: The Jackson-Tyler Era.* Indianapolis and New York, 1938.

GATES, PAUL WALLACE. *Fifty Million Acres: Conflicts over Kansas Land Policy, 1854–1890.* Ithaca, 1954.

GIBBONS, J. S. *The Banks of New York, Their Dealers, the Clearing-House, and the Panic of 1857.* New York, 1858.

GILLET, R[ANSOM] H. *Life and Times of Silas Wright.* 2 vols. Albany, 1874.

GOODRICH, CARTER. *Government Promotion of American Canals and Railroads, 1800–1890.* New York, 1960.

GOUGE, WILLIAM M. *The Fiscal History of Texas.* Philadelphia, 1852.

GOUVERNEUR, MARIAN. *As I Remember.* New York, 1911.

GOVAN, THOMAS PAYNE. *Nicholas Biddle, Nationalist and Public Banker, 1786–1844.* Chicago, 1959.

GREEN, CONSTANCE MCLAUGHLIN. *Washington: Village and Capital, 1800–1878.* Princeton, 1962.

HAMILTON, HOLMAN. *Zachary Taylor, Soldier in the White House.* Indianapolis, 1951.

———. *Prologue to Conflict: The Crisis and Compromise of 1850.* New York, 1966.

HAMMOND, BRAY. *Banks and Politics in America: From the Revolution to the Civil War.* Princeton, 1957.

HANEY, LEWIS H. *Congressional History of Railways in United States.* 2 vols. Madison, 1908–1910.

HASSE, ADELAIDE R. *Index of Economic Material in Documents of the States . . . New York, 1789–1904.* Washington, 1907.

HAWTREY, R. G. *A Century of Bank Rate.* London, New York, and Toronto, 1938.

HEARON, CLEO. *Mississippi and the Compromise of 1850.* Vol. 14. Publications of the Mississippi Historical Society.

HEDGES, JOSEPH EDWARD. *Commercial Banking and the Stock Market before 1863.* Baltimore, 1938.

HEPBURN, A. BARTON. *History of Currency in the United States.* New York, 1915.

HERNDON, DALLAS T., ed. *Centennial History of Arkansas.* Chicago and Little Rock, 1922.

HIBBARD, BENJAMIN H. *A History of the Public Land Policies.* New York, 1939.

HIDY, RALPH W. *The House of Baring in American Trade and Finance: English Merchant Bankers at Work, 1763–1861.* Cambridge, 1949.

HITTELL, THEODORE H. *History of California.* III. San Francisco, 1897.

HOLMES, FRED L., ed. *Wisconsin: Stability, Progress, Beauty.* I. Chicago, 1946.

HUBERT, PHILIP G., JR. *The Merchants National Bank of the City of New York . . . 1803–1903.* New York, 1903.

HUNGERFORD, EDWARD. *Story of the Baltimore & Ohio Railroad, 1827–1927.* 2 vols. New York and London, 1928.

HUTCHINS, JOHN G. B. *American Maritime Industries and Public Policy, 1789–1914.* Cambridge, 1941.

JACKSON, RICHARD P. *Chronicles of Georgetown, D.C., from 1751 to 1878.* Washington, 1878.

JOHNS, JOHN E. *Florida during the Civil War.* Gainesville, 1963.

JOHNSON, ALLEN. *Stephen A. Douglas: A Study in American Politics.* New York, 1908.

JOHNSON, ARTHUR M., and SUPPLE, BARRY E. *Boston Capitalists and Western Railroads: A Study in the Nineteenth Century Investment Process.* Cambridge, 1967.

JOHNSON, JACK T. *Peter Anthony Dey.* Iowa City, 1939.

KINLEY, DAVID. *The History, Organization and Influence of the Independent Treasury of the United States.* New York and Boston, 1893.

KNAPP, FRANK AVERILL, JR. *Life of Sebastian Lerdo de Tejada, 1823–1889.* Austin, 1951.

LARSON, HENRIETTA M. *Jay Cooke, Private Banker.* Cambridge, 1936.

LEECH, MARGARET. *Reveille in Washington, 1860–1865.* New York and London, 1941.

LEMLY, JAMES HUTTON. *The Gulf, Mobile and Ohio.* Homewood, Ill., 1953.

LILL, THOMAS R. *National Debt of Mexico: History and Present Status.* New York, 1919.

LODGE, HENRY CABOT. *Daniel Webster.* Boston, 1883.

LOKKEN, ROSCOE L. *Iowa Public Land Disposal.* Iowa City, 1942.

LUTHIN, REINHARD H. *The First Lincoln Campaign.* Cambridge, 1944.

MCCALEB, WALTER F. *The Public Finances of Mexico.* New York and London, 1921.

MACGILL, CAROLINE E., et al. *History of Transportation in the United States before 1860.* Washington, 1917.

MCGRANE, REGINALD C. *Foreign Bondholders and American State Debts.* New York, 1935.

MALIN, JAMES M. *The Nebraska Question, 1852–1854.* Kansas, 1953.

MILES, EDWIN ARTHUR. *Jacksonian Democracy in Mississippi.* Chapel Hill, N. C., 1960.

MILLER, EDMUND THORNTON. *A Financial History of Texas.* Austin, 1916.

MILLER, NATHAN. *The Enterprise of a Free People.* Ithaca, 1962.

MILTON, GEORGE FORT. *Eve of Conflict: Stephen A. Douglas and the Needless War.* Boston and New York, 1934.

MITCHEL, STEWART. *Horatio Seymour of New York.* Cambridge, 1938.

MOORE, JOHN BASSETT. *History and Digest of the International Arbitrations to Which the United States Has Been a Party.* 6 vols. Washington, 1898.

MYERS, MARGARET G. *The New York Money Market: Origins and Development.* New York, 1931.

NEU, IRENE D. *Erastus Corning, Merchant and Financier, 1794–1872.* Ithaca, 1960.

NEVINS, ALLAN. *Abram S. Hewitt, With Some Account of Peter Cooper.* New York and London, 1935.

———. *Grover Cleveland: A Study in Courage.* New York, 1932.

———. *The Emergence of Lincoln.* 2 vols. New York and London, 1950.

———. *Fremont, Pathmarker of the West.* New York and London, 1939.

———. *The Ordeal of the Union.* 2 vols. New York and London, 1947.

NICHOLS, ROY F. *American Leviathan.* New York, 1966.

———. *The Democratic Machine, 1850–1854.* New York, 1923.

———. *The Disruption of American Democracy.* New York, 1948.

———. *Franklin Pierce, Young Hickory of the Granite Hills.* Philadelphia, 1958.

OBERHOLTZER, ELLIS PAXSON. *Jay Cooke, Financier of the Civil War.* 2 vols. Philadelphia, 1907.

OLDT, FRANKLIN T., ed. *History of Dubuque County.* Chicago, n.d.

OVERTON, RICHARD C. *Burlington Route: A History of the Burlington Lines.* New York, 1965.

PARRISH, WILLIAM E. *David Rice Atchison of Missouri, Border Politician.* Columbia, Mo., 1961.

PEARSON, HENRY GREENLEAF. *An American Railroad Builder: John Murray Forbes.* Boston and New York, 1911.

PERKINS, JACOB R. *Trails, Rails and War: The Life of General Grenville M. Dodge.* Indianapolis, 1929.

PIERCE, BESSIE LOUISE. *A History of Chicago.* 3 vols. New York, 1937–1957.

POAGE, GEORGE RAWLINGS. *Henry Clay and the Whig Party.* Chapel Hill, N. C., 1936.

PORTER, KENNETH WIGGINS. *John Jacob Astor, Business Man.* 2 vols. Cambridge, 1931.

PRESSLY, THOMAS J. *Americans Interpret Their Civil War*. Princeton, 1954.

RAINWATER, PERCY LEE. *Mississippi Storm Center of Secession, 1856–1861*. Baton Rouge, 1938.

RANEY, WILLIAM FRANCIS. *Wisconsin: A Study of Progress*. New York, 1940.

RATCHFORD, B. U. *American State Debts*. Durham, 1941.

REDLICH, FRITZ. *The Molding of American Banking: Men and Ideas*. 2 vols. History of American Business Leaders. II. New York, 1946–1951.

RIGGS, JOHN BEVERLY. *The Riggs Family of Maryland*. Baltimore, 1939.

RIPPY, L. FRED. *The United States and Mexico*. New York, 1931.

ROLL, CHARLES. *Colonel Dick Thompson, the Persistent Whig*. Indianapolis, 1948.

ROWLAND, DUNBAR. *History of Mississippi, the Heart of the South*. 2 vols. Chicago and Jackson, 1925.

SANBORN, JOHN BELL. *Congressional Grants of Land in Aid of Railways*. Madison, 1899.

SCHOLES, WALTER V. *Mexican Politics During the Juarez Regime, 1855–1872*. Columbia, Mo., 1957.

SCOTT, WILLIAM AMASA. *Repudiation of State Debts*. New York and Boston, 1893.

SELLERS, CHARLES GRIER, JR. *James K. Polk, Jacksonian, 1795–1843*. Princeton, 1957.

SHENTON, JAMES P. *Robert John Walker, A Politician from Jackson to Lincoln*. New York and London, 1961.

SHORTRIDGE, WILSON PORTER. *The Transition of a Typical Frontier . . . The Life of Henry Hastings Sibley. . . .* Menasha, Wis., 1919.

SLAUSON, ALLAN B., ed. *History of the City of Washington: Its Men and Institutions*. Washington, 1903.

SMITH, ALICE E. *James Duane Doty, Frontier Promoter*. Madison, 1954.

SMITH, WALTER BUCKINGHAM. *Economic Aspects of the Second Bank of the United States*. Cambridge, 1953.

——— and COLE, ARTHUR HARRISON. *Fluctuations in American Business, 1790–1860*. Cambridge, 1935.

SMITH, WILLIAM ERNEST. *The Francis Preston Blair Family in Politics*. 2 vols. New York, 1933.

STEINER, BERNARD C. *The Life of Reverdy Johnson.* Baltimore, 1914.

[STENNETT, W. H.] *Yesterday and Today: A History of the Chicago and North Western Railway System.* Chicago, 1910.

STILL, BAYRD. *Milwaukee: The History of a City.* Madison, 1948.

TAFT, ROBERT. *Artists and Illustrators of the Old West, 1850–1900.* New York, 1953.

TAUS, ESTHER ROGOFF. *Central Banking Functions of the United States Treasury, 1789–1941.* New York, 1943.

TAYLOR, GEORGE ROGERS. *Transportation Revolution, 1815–1860.* New York and Toronto, 1951.

——— and IRENE NEU. *The American Railroad Network, 1861–1890.* Cambridge, 1956.

THOMSON, A[LEXANDER] M. *Political History of Wisconsin.* Milwaukee, 1902.

TREAT, PAYSON JACKSON. *The National Land System, 1785–1820.* New York, 1910.

TURLINGTON, EDGAR. *Mexico and Her Foreign Creditors.* New York, 1930.

U.S. BUREAU OF THE CENSUS. *Historical Statistics of the United States, Colonial Times to 1957.* Washington, 1960.

VAN BRUNT, WALTER, ed. *Duluth and St. Louis County, Minnesota: Their Story and People.* 3 vols. Chicago and New York, 1931.

VAN DEUSEN, GLYNDON G. *Thurlow Weed, Wizard of the Lobby.* Boston, 1947.

WARREN, CHARLES. *The Supreme Court in United States History.* 2 vols. Boston, 1937.

WHYTE, JAMES H. *The Uncivil War: Washington during the Reconstruction.* New York, 1958.

WILLIAMS, DAVID A. *David C. Broderick: A Political Portrait.* San Marino, 1970.

WILLIAMS, ELGIN. *The Animating Pursuits of Speculation: Land Traffic in the Annexation of Texas.* New York, 1949.

WILLSON, BECKLES. *John Slidell and the Confederates in Paris (1862–1865).* New York, 1932.

WILTSE, CHARLES N. *John C. Calhoun, Sectionalist, 1840–1850.* Indianapolis and New York, 1951.

WOOD, ELMER. *English Theories of Central Banking Control, 1819–1858, with Some Account of Contemporary Procedure.* Cambridge, 1939.

WOODBRIDGE, DWIGHT E. and JOHN S. PARDEE, eds. *History of Duluth and St. Louis County, Past and Present.* 2 vols. Chicago, 1910.

WOODWARD, C. VANN. *Reunion and Reaction: The Compromise of 1877 and the End of Reconstruction.* Boston, 1951.

WYNNE, WILLIAM H. *State Insolvency and Foreign Bondholders, 2: Selected Case Histories. . . .* New Haven, 1951.

YOUNG, MARY ELIZABETH. *Redskins, Ruffleshirts and Rednecks: Indian Allotments in Alabama and Mississippi, 1830–1860.* Norman, 1961.

ARTICLES

BERND, JOHN M. "The La Crosse and Milwaukee Railroad Land Grant, 1856." *Wisconsin Magazine of History,* Dec. 1946.

[BLEDSOE, A. T.]. "Romance of Real Life." *Southern Review,* July 1872.

CLARK, ALLEN C. "Beau Hickman (Robert S. Hickman)." *Records of the Columbia Historical Society,* 1938–1939.

COZZENS, ARTHUR B. "The Iron Industry of Missouri." *Missouri Historical Review,* July–Oct. 1941.

DORFMAN, JOSEPH. "A Note on the Interpenetration of Anglo-American Finance, 1837–1841." *Journal of Economic History* 11 (1951).

ERBE, CARL H. "Constitutional Limitations on Indebtedness in Iowa." *Iowa Journal of History and Politics,* July 1924.

EVANS, RICHARD X. "The Ladies Union Benevolent and Employment Society." *Records of the Columbia Historical Society* 39.

FELT, THOMAS E. "The Stephen A. Douglas Letters in the State Historical Library." *Journal of the Illinois State Historical Society,* Winter 1963.

FERRIN, A. W. "The Great Banks of New York." *Moody's Magazine,* July 1914.

FITZSIMMONS, MARGARET LOUISE. "Missouri Railroads during the Civil War and Reconstruction." *Missouri Historical Review* 35 (Jan. 1941).

GATELL, FRANK OTTO. "Spoils of the Bank War: Political Bias in the Selection of Pet Banks." *American Historical Review,* Oct. 1964.

GATES, PAUL WALLACE. "Disposal of the Public Domain in Illinois, 1848–1856." *Journal of Economic and Business History* 3 (Feb. 1931).

———. *Frontier Landlords and Pioneer Tenants.* Ithaca, 1945. Reproduced from article in *Journal of Illinois State Historical Society,* June 1945.

———. "Land Policy and Tenancy in the Prairie States." *Journal of Economic History* 1 (May 1941).

———. "The Railroads of Missouri, 1850–1870." *Missouri Historical Review* 36 (Jan. 1932).

GLICK, EDWARD B. "The Tehuantepec Railroad: Mexico's White Elephant." *Pacific Historical Review* 22 (1953).

GREEN, CONSTANCE MCLAUGHLIN. "The Jacksonian 'Revolution' in the District of Columbia." *Mississippi Valley Historical Review,* Mar. 1959.

HALE, CHARLES A. "The War with the United States and the Crisis in Mexican Thought." *Americas* 14 (Oct. 1957).

HAMILTON, HOLMAN. "Texas Bonds and Northern Profits: A Study in Compromise, Investment, and Lobby Influence." *Mississippi Valley Historical Review* 43 (Mar. 1957).

HAMMOND, BRAY. "The Chestnut Street Raid on Wall Street, 1839." *Quarterly Journal of Economics* 61 (Aug. 1947).

———. "Jackson, Biddle, and the Bank of the United States." *Journal of Economic History* 7 (May 1947).

———. "Long and Short Term Credit in Early American Banking." *Quarterly Journal of Economics* 49 (Nov. 1934).

HARNSBERGER, JOHN L. "Land, Lobbies, Railroads and the Origins of Duluth." *Minnesota History* 37 (Sept. 1960).

HENRY, WILLIAM WIRT. "Kenner's Mission to Europe." *William and Mary College Quarterly Historical Magazine,* July 1916.

HERSHKOWITZ, LEO. " 'The Land of Promise': Samuel Swartwout and Land Speculation in Texas, 1830–1838." *New York Historical Society Quarterly,* Oct. 1964.

HIDY, RALPH W. "A Leaf from Investment History." *Harvard Business Review,* Autumn 1941.

HODDER, FRANK HEYWOOD. "The Genesis of the Kansas-Nebraska Act." *Proceedings of the State Historical Society of Wisconsin,* Madison, 1913.

———. "The Railroad Background of the Kansas-Nebraska Act." *Mississippi Valley Historical Review* 12 (June 1925).

JACKSON, CORDELIA. "People and Places in Old Georgetown." *Records of the Columbia Historical Society,* 1931–1932.

JOHANSSEN, ROBERT W. "Reporting a Pacific Railroad Survey: Isaac Stevens' Letters to Stephen A. Douglas." *Pacific Northwest Quarterly,* Oct. 1956.

JORSTAD, ERLING. "Minnesota's Role in the Democratic Rift of 1860." *Minnesota History,* June 1960.

KELLOGG, LOUISE PHELPS. "The Rise and Fall of Old Superior." *Wisconsin Magazine of History,* Sept. 1940.

MECHLIN, LEILA. "Art Life in Washington." *Records of the Columbia Historical Society* 24.

NICHOLS, ROY F. "The Kansas-Nebraska Act: A Century of Historiography." *Mississippi Valley Historical Review* 43 (Sept. 1956).

PAXSON, FREDERIC L. "Railways of the Old Northwest before the Civil War." *Transactions of Wisconsin Academy of Sciences, Arts, and Letters* 17.

PLATT, D. C. N. "British Bondholders in Nineteenth Century Latin America—Injury and Remedy." *Inter-American Economic Affairs* 14 (Winter 1960).

PRIMMER, GEORGE H. "Railways at the Head of Lake Superior." *Economic Geography,* July 1937.

RADER, BENJAMIN G. "William M. Gouge, Jacksonian Economic Theorist." *Pennsylvania History,* Oct. 1963.

ROSENBERG, MORTON M. "The First Republican Election Victory in Iowa." *Annals of Iowa,* Summer 1962.

———. "The Kansas-Nebraska Act in Iowa: A Case Study." *Annals of Iowa,* Fall 1964.

RUSSEL, ROBERT R. "The Issues in the Congressional Struggle over the Kansas-Nebraska Bill, 1854." *Journal of Southern History* 29 (May 1963).

———. "The Pacific Railway Issue in Politics prior to the Civil War." *Mississippi Valley Historical Review,* Sept. 1925.

SARRO, ENRIQUE. "La Deuda Exterior de Mexico." *Revista de Hacienda* (Mexico) 4 (Aug. 1939).

SHERIDAN, PHILIP J. "The Committee of Mexican Bondholders and European Intervention in 1861." *Mid-America,* Jan. 1960.

SHIPPEE, LESTER BURRELL. "The First Railroad between the Mississippi and Lake Superior." *Mississippi Valley Historical Review,* Sept. 1918.

SMITH, THEODORE CLARKE. "The Free Soil Party in Wisconsin." *Proceedings of the State Historical Society of Wisconsin* 42.

TRESCOTT, PAUL B. "Federal-State Financial Relations, 1790–1860." *Journal of Economic History*, Sept. 1955.

VAN BOLT, ROGER H. "The Rise of the Republican Party in Indiana, 1855–1856." *Indiana Magazine of History*, Sept. 1955.

WILLETT, THOMAS D. "International Specie Flows and American Monetary Stability, 1834–1860." *Journal of Economic History*, Mar. 1968.

WORLEY, TED R. "The Arkansas State Bank: Ante-Bellum Period." *Arkansas Historical Quarterly*, Spring 1964.

UNPUBLISHED

Doctoral dissertations

BLOOM, ROBERT L. "The Philadelphia *North American:* A History, 1839–1925." Columbia University, 1952.

BROWN, WALTER LEE. "Albert Pike, 1809–1891." University of Texas, 1955.

DAVIS, LANCE EDWIN. "United States Financial Intermediaries in the Early Nineteenth Century: Four Case Studies." Johns Hopkins, 1957.

HIDY, MURIEL EMMIE. "George Peabody, Merchant and Financier, 1829–1845." Radcliffe College, 1939.

JORSTAD, ERLING THEODORE. "The Life of Henry Hastings Sibley." University of Wisconsin, 1957.

LICHTERMAN, MARTIN. "John Adams Dix, 1798–1879." Columbia University, 1952.

MCFAUL, JOHN M. "The Politics of Jacksonian Finance." University of California, 1963.

MULLER, ERNEST PAUL. "Preston King: a Political Biography." Columbia University, 1957.

RALSTON, LEONARD FLOYD. "Railroads and the Government of Iowa, 1850–1872." State University of Iowa, 1960.

RICE, HERBERT W. "The Early History of the Chicago, Milwaukee and St. Paul Railway Company." State University of Iowa, 1938.

ROSENBERG, MORTON MERVIN. "The Democratic Party of Iowa, 1850–1860." State University of Iowa, 1957.

SHAW, REGINALD MATHISON. "Historical Geography of Superior, Wisconsin." University of Wisconsin, 1938.

THOMPSON, ARTHUR W. "David Yulee: A Study of Nineteenth Century American Thought and Enterprise." Columbia University, 1954.

TIMBERLAKE, RICHARD HENRY, JR. "Treasury Monetary Policies from Jackson to Lincoln." University of Chicago, 1959.

TRESCOTT, PAUL B. "Federal Finance and the American Economy, 1790–1860." Princeton University, 1954.

VAN DER WEELE, WAYNE J. "Jesse David Bright, Master Politician from the Old Northwest." University of Indiana, 1958.

YOUNG, MARY ELIZABETH. "Redskins, Ruffleshirts and Rednecks: Indian Allotments in Alabama and Mississippi, 1830–1860." Cornell University, 1955.

Other

DOW, JOHN G. "The Collins Line." Master's thesis, Columbia University, 1937.

MCCONKEY, M. C. "James F. Joy." Ms in Michigan Historical Collections, University of Michigan Library, n.d.

Index

Business and Politics in America from the Age of Jackson to the Civil War was composed in Linotype Times Roman, with Times Roman display type, by The Book Press, Brattleboro, Vermont. The entire book was printed by offset lithography.